THE CHURCH IN SEARCH OF ITS SELF

THE CHURCH IN SEARCH OF ITS SELF

by

ROBERT S. PAUL

WILLIAM B. EERDMANS PUBLISHING COMPANY
Grand Rapids, Michigan

Library of Congress Catalog Card Number: 72-77573
ISBN 0-8028-3422-1
Printed in the United States of America

In Memory of

EVAN THOMAS DONALD JAMES
1921-1971

A true friend and a faithful minister of Jesus Christ

MORE AN APOLOGY THAN A PREFACE

Looking back it appears that this book on the Church was destined from the first. It represents a confluence of interests that come to a focus in the apparent absurdity of the Church's presence in the modern world.

It began with a historical problem, with the Puritans who on the one hand protested their separation from this world, but who on the other hand became so involved in that world that they fought and won a civil war, seized political power, and established a cultural ascendancy in America that gave a new basis for nationalism. The paradox was intensified as I became more deeply engaged pastorally and ecumenically, for if almost a decade within a pastorate strengthened my denominational loyalty, the years spent with the World Council of Churches deepened my ecumenical convictions. The absurdity and the seeming contradictions embraced the total dimension of the Church, confessional and ecumenical.

In 1960 I unwittingly launched myself into more than a decade of preoccupation with the central paradoxes in ecclesiology. *The Atonement and the Sacraments* tried to show how the Protestant understanding of the sacraments is related to what is believed about man's salvation, but one could hardly raise these issues without at once raising the question of the ministry. Then Vatican II and the questions theological students were beginning to have about ordination in the mid-1960s raised the issue even more pertinently, and *Ministry* appeared in 1965.

It was very soon clear that the subject would have to be pursued to its central paradox in the doctrine of the Church. Many aspects of the twentieth-century world clamored for consideration in our understanding of the Church—the sociological critique of religious pluralism among Protestants, the interest in basic ecclesiology among Catholics, and the theology of the 'secular' to name but a few. Even the credibility gap between the churches and the younger generation was simply an aspect of the Church's basic paradox of being *simul iustus et peccator.* The old clear-cut distinctions between churches were no longer appropriate or even possible, for it was clear that if the Church had something to say to the world in the name of Jesus Christ, it would have to face up to what the world had learned from Jesus Christ about truth and honesty. These values were forcing the churches to question the very authorities on which their exclusive doctrines of the Church had been based; and if this meant that Christians were becoming excited or scared by the ecumenical possibilities, it also meant that they were left uncertain and groping at the very point where they had previously been most sure of themselves—why they belonged to one church rather than another.

Are the apparent contradictions in the Church's paradoxical situation due to a central fallacy or a central miracle? This book is the third part of an unintended trilogy, and such unity as it presents with its predecessors is due less to a common authorship than to the unified answer that is given to that question.

In one of his most scathing reviews, Macaulay remarked that the tome he was reviewing might have been considered light reading by the patriarchs before the Deluge, but it demanded for the modern reader "too large a portion of too short an existence." That would have been even more true of this book if we had dealt with the subject as comprehensively as it deserves.

The systematic theologian might be prompted to complain that in the present work the major theologians of our time seem to have been slighted. They have been deliberately omitted from detailed consideration for two reasons—first, because we are primarily concerned with those who affected the churches' contemporary self-understanding; and although Barth, Bultmann, Tillich, and the rest may have had great influence on the climate in which the ecclesiological issue has been discussed, I question whether their systematic treatment of the Church had any direct influence upon the way the churches thought of themselves or on the way they organized their life to meet the challenge of this age. To see the influence of Karl Barth at this point, for example, we have to trace his influence on other theologians, Protestant and Catholic, who addressed themselves more directly to the problem of the Church's self-identity. Secondly, I suspect that the real impact of what the major theologians said about the Church may be appreciated more logically after we have faced the issue raised in Part Four of this book. That is where the debate has to be taken up anew. For if the earlier bases of ecclesiology are no longer reliable, and if the doctrine of the Church is established in the nature of God and his self-revelation to man, then we will begin to understand the significance of what men believe about God for the eventual shape of the community of faith that professes to be his people.

To whom, then, is the book addressed—theologians, pastors, theological students, laymen, Catholics, Protestants, Orthodox, Liberals, Conservatives? I should like to think that I am addressing the Church itself, in its variety, and that anyone concerned about the Church would be able to find sufficient in it to understand his or her own place in the Church's mission. I hope this is true whatever the state of the reader's theological preparation, the brand of ecclesiastical affiliation, or the quirks of historical prejudice. And I hope this understanding may be gained even if all the footnotes are ignored.

My thanks to others who helped to make this book can never be dismissed as a formality. Many insights I have made my own have had their genesis in others—in books half-forgotten, in chance remarks of my colleagues, in conversations with students or friends within the ecumenical dialogue. I have acknowledged the debt where it is conscious, but I hope the book itself may be received as acknowledgment of my debt to the whole community of faith.

I am deeply grateful to Mrs. Elizabeth Eakin, my secretary at the Pittsburgh Theological Seminary, for typing the final copy, and for interpreting my eccentric handwriting and mid-Atlantic spelling with such cheerful competence; also to the

Reverend Dean Tapley, my son-in-law, who in undertaking the thankless task of preparing the index must now appreciate Jacob's labors for Laban. Finally to Eunice, my wife, and to the other members of the family, who day by day show me what ministry means within the gathered community of the home. In a sense too deep for me to describe or for them to comprehend their contribution is at the heart of this book on the Church.

Robert S. Paul

Pittsburgh
Advent 1971

CONTENTS

PART ONE

CLEARING THE GROUND

Chapter I

CLASSIFYING THE ECCLESIOLOGIES

1

WHERE DO WE START? THE PROBLEM OF CLASSIFICATION

From my window I can see the churches of Pittsburgh. It is true that they share common characteristics, such as a vague tendency to point upwards, but the overall impression is of almost chaotic diversity.

Yet as one looks more closely the architecture does fall into recognizable categories: there are towers that remind us of the Norman, spires that reflect the influence of European Gothic or English Colonial, and the gables and turrets of Victorian eccentric. If ecclesiastical architecture ought to reflect a church's theology, it certainly reflects historical periods that the churches have regarded as classic: it is not an accident that Roman Catholic churches reproduce Gothic, that Episcopal churches turn to the church architecture of rural England, that Orthodox churches are recognizably Byzantine, or that other denominations reflect the periods of their greatest influence. Nor is it any accident that in their recent building churches have moved away from the styles of their historic past and searched for a form that would proclaim involvement in the thought of this century. Perhaps it is to be expected that often modern church buildings reflect considerable uncertainty as to how a style that is uncompromisingly up-to-the-minute can also relate both to an authentic history and to an ever changing future: it is not easy to achieve continuing contemporaneity without giving the impression of restlessness, or to ensure that the 'courageous experiment' of 1972 will not be a horrible monstrosity in the year 2000 or even 1980.

Of course there would be little problem in remaining up to date if we could use free-form plastic bubbles. Such temporary structures would always be in fashion, because as soon as they became démodé they could be removed, revised, or recycled; and let it be admitted that there is a vitally important aspect of the doctrine of the Church that calls for flexibility in all its structures, for if the Church is characteristically the *pilgrim* people of God, it had better travel light.

However, that image does not present the whole picture. To use an Old Testament figure, the pilgrim people not only is called to move from the tabernacles of the present to the tents of the future, but it has to carry with it the Ark of the Covenant—it has to bear the imperishable inheritance that it has received from the past, through which the true nature of its mission is revealed and which alone makes it a significant people. All the other furniture of the pilgrimage may be readily disposable, but the people of God cannot throw out the Ark of the Covenant without losing its *raison d'être* as the people of *God.*[1]

We have to transpose our illustrations from ecclesiastical architecture or the history of Israel into the field of ecclesiology. In the Church's understanding of itself, the problem is evident: how are we to define and protect the inalienable inheritance that the Church has received, and how is this to be held within ecclesiastical forms that neither permit the treasure to be lost nor bring the pilgrimage to a stop by the sheer weight of antique packaging?[2]

The questions are not unique to our age, although the rapidity of change that we face may be unique and may put

1 Cf. Exodus 25:1-22; 37:1-10; 40:20; Numbers 10:33ff.

2 Here we see that even the figure of the Ark of the Covenant can be pushed too far, for in certain respects the essential gospel is also like manna, on which the Israelites fed in the desert—something to be received anew day by day, but which turns rancid when we try to preserve it for future use. Cf. Exodus 16:13-21.

intolerable strain upon the traditional forms that the Church has taken. There were certainly centuries when the Church thought it had the problem neatly solved and the answer permanently organized, but repeatedly through history the tension between essential freedom and essential tradition has arisen to test the Church's unity and its charity. Sometimes the solution was sought by trying to relate a measure of freedom to the corpus of tradition, and at others by retaining a modicum of tradition within unstructured freedom; but the history of the Christian denominations is largely composed of variations on this theme.

The problem is paralleled in the relationship between freedom and order within secular society; and if the Church, like society at large, has tended to place its primary accent on the tradition, its present uncertainty is due at least in part to the rapidity with which public opinion in the 1960s veered towards the primacy of freedom. This suggests that the relationship between theological opinion and the spirit of any age may be much more intimate and much more complex than we are usually prepared to recognize.[3]

However, it should be clear that if the polar emphases we have mentioned represent radically different approaches to ecclesiology, they may represent equally honest desires to ensure that the Church expresses its own essential nature. It may be premature to assert that each is equally valid, since we have not yet determined the bases on which validity can be judged; but we can affirm that there is a historical inheritance (tradition) that is essential, and there is also an essential freedom in interpretation and form that the Church dare not ignore—indeed, if it rejects either it runs the risk of ceasing to be the Church. This is an irreducible paradox, centering in the

[3] Cf. Donald A. Schon, *Beyond the Stable State* (London: Temple Smith, 1971). Schon's book shows that the Church is only one institution in our society that is having to review its traditional structures in the face of changes that have been imposed by the whole of society. The relationship between church polity and the structure of society has always been clear, especially for churches that had a close relationship to the state. James I of England recognized this when in 1603 he affirmed the relation of episcopacy to his own monarchy in the terse statement, "No bishop, no king!" There is obvious significance in that in the sixteenth and seventeenth centuries Catholic countries were absolute monarchies while Reformed countries tended to take a more oligarchical or democratic form.

paradox of the gospel which affirms that God gave up his divine freedom to take the limitations of a mortal form so that mortal men might be free to become the sons of God.

The results of this paradox are reflected in the historical ecclesiologies, and hence in our attempt to classify them we are looking for guidelines that will help us understand the Church's nature and discern the relationship between that essential nature and the forms that the Church should take to fulfil its purpose. To classify any ecclesiology is an attempt to see it in relationship to others, and this at least may help us see how and why this particular church reached this view of its own nature, and more specifically what it has regarded as priorities in that self-understanding: it may help us distinguish between things that are peripheral and the things that must be regarded as belonging to the *esse* of the Church. This is our focus, for if we can determine what the churches have been saying to each other about the *essential* nature of the Church, we shall be in a position to ask how this relates to the form and the mission of the Church today.

Throughout the remainder of this chapter we will be looking at two different ways of classifying the churches—first, through the categories employed by the great German historian and sociologist Ernst Troeltsch, and secondly, through the churches' own definition of themselves in terms of distinctive polities. Both methods lead us to important insights about the Church, and there is value in using them together—the one fundamentally phenomenological and descriptive, and the other fundamentally theological and prescriptive—because they illustrate two aspects of the Church that we cannot ignore in any serious study of the churches—what they have become and what they had intended to be.

2

A DESCRIPTIVE TYPOLOGY

In 1911 Ernst Troeltsch published 'his greatest book,' *Die Soziallehren der Christlichen Kirchen und Gruppen,*[4] which is

[4] Translated by Olive Wyon as *The Social Teaching of the Christian Churches* (New York: Macmillan, 1931).

perhaps the most comprehensive attempt to understand the Church as a social phenomenon that has yet appeared. Troeltsch's theology may be open to the serious criticisms leveled at him by Karl Barth.[5] He has also been criticized for using the idea of 'ideal types' employed by his friend Max Weber, although for his examination of the Church I find this method extremely significant.[6]

He distinguished three forms in which Christianity had manifested itself,[7] each of which he suggested has had reasonable grounds within the New Testament records and the tradition of early Christianity for justifying its form.

A. The church-type[8]

This is the structure that the church assumes whenever men have attempted to identify the church closely with the society

[5] Cf. Karl Barth, *Protestant Thought from Rousseau to Ritschl* (New York: Harper, 1959). However, Benjamin Reist has put up a spirited defense of Troeltsch's basic theological concern in *Toward a Theology of Involvement* (Philadelphia: Westminster, 1966). Cf. n. 20, below.

[6] It has been argued that churches are never as 'ideal' as the typology suggests, and that must be conceded. On the other hand critics have failed to see that it is precisely Troeltsch's focus on 'ideal' types that is significant in his treatment of the churches, for that is what their theology says they intend to be. They may never reach the ideal form because they are still human; but presumably if they did reach their ideal form, what Troeltsch describes indicates what it would be like. The relationship of Troeltsch's typology to the divine channels of spiritual authority discussed in our next chapter is extremely significant.

[7] *The Social Teaching of the Christian Churches,* I, 379-381. Those who use Troeltsch's categories often concentrate almost exclusively on the first two, the church-type and the sect-type; and this leads to some curious anomalies. For example, in *How the Church Can Minister to the World Without Losing Itself* (New York: Harper, 1964), Langdon Gilkey makes good use of Troeltsch, but ignores the 'third type.' This has some unfortunate effects—first, I think he misses the true significance of the Radical Reformation and the Quakers; secondly, he does not recognize that 'reason' has always been operative as an 'authority' and does not simply enter at the enlightenment; and thirdly, he does not know quite what to do with Methodism (cf. pp. 7f., notes). On the other hand, I have a very high opinion of Langdon Gilkey's main thrust, as I have tried to show below, pp. 179ff.

[8] I have elsewhere expressed my dissatisfaction with the terms 'church-type' and 'sect-type.' Cf. Thomas Goodwin, *An Apologeticall Narration,* ed. Robert S. Paul (Boston: United Church, 1963), p. 68, n. 1. Although Troeltsch intended them to be purely descriptive—he was not very concerned about terminology since it did not affect his main argument (*op. cit.,* I, 340f.)—the word 'sect' has a pejorative meaning. Moreover, since the word 'sect' implies an inferior type of churchmanship, it tacitly works against his thesis that all three types of churchmanship can justify their form in terms of the Scriptures and church tradition. The protest of the

in which it is set. Its classic form is to be seen in the Constantinian settlement and in the church of the medieval papacy. But, although the sixteenth-century Reformers may have been motivated by a different theology when they broke from Rome, they readily adopted church-type characteristics as soon as they began to enter into alliance with the state. The unification of church and state had been in operation for over a thousand years before the Reformation, and this relationship was, after all, the only one known to them.

The pastoral organization of such a church is fundamentally geographical—often diocesan and parochial—since each priest or minister is responsible for the spiritual welfare of all the inhabitants in the area to which he is assigned, and each native is automatically received into membership of the church by infant baptism. Ideally in this system church and state are identical in their membership.

The concern of such a church thereafter is not primarily evangelism, for there is little left to evangelize, but the spiritual education and nurture of the members and their safe conduct through life and, it is hoped, beyond via the spiritual nurture that Mother Church provides. Often this will be based on a sacramental system that remains in the hands of the church's professional hierarchy, and in earlier centuries these hierarchies in Europe paralleled the monarchical form of the state. In countries where Protestant churches were established by the government the sacramental route to salvation was exchanged for a system of piety based on regular attendance at the preaching services.

But whatever its basic theology, Catholic or Protestant, the church-type tends to be governed clerically, its services and leadership tend to be formal and professional rather than charismatic, and it tends to support the political and social status quo and hence to be conservative. As long as the instruments of education are under its own control, it will emphasize education and progress in bringing in the Kingdom of God; but this will be understood as a gradual process that is not consummated until the end of history.

sect-type cannot be understood unless it is recognized that it offers an alternative to the existing form of the Church: it regards itself not as a sect, but as *the Church.*

Such churches have positive emphases that must not be ignored. First, as any Roman Catholic will remind us, the church-type takes the organic and visible unity of the Church with deep if not ultimate seriousness. Furthermore, it asserts that the Kingdom of God *can* come on earth, and through its generally optimistic view of human society and culture it recognizes that Christ came to offer salvation to *this* world. To that extent it is 'world-affirming' rather than 'world-denying.' Because it accepts responsibility to the total society within which it is set, it offers pastoral care to all men; despite all the temptations to social prestige, established churches have often been able to exercise a ministry in slums or in experimental situations where churches of a different order have either written off the constituency as irredeemable or assumed that every mission project should be economically self-supporting.

On the other hand, when a church of this type exercises exclusive control, it is open to some damning criticisms. Even the national form in which its unity was often cast has obscured the actual dividedness suffered by the Church, for the divisions themselves were preserved by states that had a vested interest in the prestige of a particular church. Furthermore, through its alliance with the state and through its emphasis on visible unity, this kind of church has exercised the most bitter intolerance and persecution against others. The history of established churches shows that the dominance of the clergy often entails the formalization of religion, takes from the individual believer his proper responsibility before God, and drives a wedge between the minister and the people to whom he ministers. But perhaps the most obvious danger comes from the status of being 'established,' for there is always the temptation to allow its ethical standards to be compromised by those of society, to allow (in the worst sense) the invasion of the Church by the lowered morality and cynicism of this world.

Although the classic examples of this type are provided by the medieval papacy, the union of the church and the czars in Orthodox Russia, and the Elizabethan settlement in England, it is by no means limited to the catholic and episcopal form. It is to be found in the Lutheran state churches, in Calvin's Geneva, Knox's Scotland, and John Cotton's New England theocracy. It can even be found among 'free churches' through the alliance of the churches with the controlling economic forces in a capitalistic society.[9] The basic element is not formal state establishment as such (although that may be the quickest way to it), but the readiness of the church to identify itself with society to the point where the church (or churches) and society are mutually supportive and the church is tempted to compromise its prophetic role.

It is worth noting that if the union proposed by the Consultation on Church Union (COCU) is successful, the U.S.A. will be nearer than at any period since colonial times to a unified Protestant church, and a vast majority of American Christians will be represented by a unified Protestantism and a unified Catholicism. This is certainly desirable insofar as it would present a more visible unity and a more unified Christian witness, but only if these churches can develop the structures that will enable them to exercise a prophetic and critical role towards American society. If they fail in that, the dangers of the church-type will be very real.

B. The sect-type

The sect-type is diametrically opposed to the church-type, because it is constitutionally prophetic. Where the church-type stresses the identity of church and society in the name of some common civilization or culture,[10] the sect-type proclaims that the true Church is always in a state of war with the world, its culture, and all forms of civil status. Where the former is naturally in alliance with the ruling and educated classes, the latter initially becomes the spiritual refuge of those at odds

9 Writing of Nonconformity in England during the nineteenth century, F. H. Lovell Cocks observes, "The evangelists who set out to convert the middle classes were themselves converted into good bourgeois Liberals. It is no accident that the career of political Nonconformity exactly coincides with the duration of the 'Liberal Experiment' in European history . . . . As a substitute for a truly Christian politics Liberalism was by no means worthless; but it was certainly not 'just as good.' And these nonconformist politicians laboured under the delusion that Liberalism and Christian politics are the same thing. When all is said, Nonconformity was the established Church of the middle classes." *The Nonconformist Conscience* (London: Independent Press, 1943), p. 81.

10 E.g., 'Christendom,' 'Western Culture,' 'the American Way of Life.'

with society—the disenfranchised, the poor, and the ignorant.

> Whereas the Church assumes the objective concrete holiness of the sacerdotal office, of Apostolic Succession, of the *Depositum fidei* and of the sacraments, and appeals to the extension of the Incarnation which takes place permanently through the priesthood, the sect, on the other hand, appeals to the ever new common performance of the moral demands, which, at bottom, are founded only upon the Law and the Example of Christ. In this, it must be admitted that they are in direct contact with the Teaching of Jesus . . . . Scripture history and the history of the Primitive Church are permanent ideals, to be accepted in their literal sense, not the starting-point, historically limited and defined, for the development of the Church.[11]

The foundation texts for the sect-type's rejection of the world and its establishments are "Be ye not conformed to this world," and "come ye out from among them and touch no unclean thing," as they were for the English Separatists when they were arraigned before the bishops in 1570.[12]

If the church-type is geographical, the sect-type presents itself as a spiritual fellowship, a 'gathered church' of covenanted Christians;[13] and instead of emphasizing the comprehensiveness of the parish with its mixture of saints and sinners, it emphasizes the exclusiveness of the Church as a company of 'visible saints.' The ethical standards of the New Testament are required of every member; the ethics of the New Testament, often interpreted literally and universally applied, represent the only standard of conduct tolerated with the church community. Moreover, through congregational discipline each member is expected to accept responsibility for the spiritual

[11] Troeltsch, *op. cit.,* I, 336. In this passage Troeltsch is obviously using Catholicism for his example of the church-type.

[12] Romans 12:2; II Corinthians 6:17. Cf. Champlin Burrage, *The Early English Dissenters* (Cambridge: C.U.P., 1912), II, 17.

[13] It may be noted that I have avoided describing the sect-type as a 'voluntary society,' although within the pressures of a modern pluralistic society, and particularly when the 'sects' have lost their sense of divine call, this is what they become; but the early pioneers of the concept insisted that the Church comes into existence not by the will of its members but by the call of God. "The Church planted or gathered," wrote Robert Browne in 1583, "is a company or number of Christians or believers, which *by a willing covenant made with their God,* are under the government of God and Christ, and keep his laws in one holy communion." *A Booke which sheweth the life and manners of all true Christians,* sect. 35, *The Writings of Robert Harrison and Robert Browne,* ed. Albert Peel and Leland Carlson (London: Allen & Unwin, 1953), p. 252. Italics mine.

nurture of his fellow members. It is therefore lay-oriented and 'democratic' rather than clergy-oriented and hierarchical.

Towards the world the sect-type's emphasis is upon evangelism rather than upon education, for hope is centered not in the gradual christianization of society, but in the apocalyptic advent of God's Kingdom. In this world the Church can only declare God's judgment, and—like the voices that came to Bunyan's Pilgrim—urge men to 'flee from the wrath to come!' for salvation is not universal, but individual, 'even as many as the Lord our God shall call': it is not a guaranteed process conducted by priests within a sacramental system, but it is a personal response to the gospel—an individual decision that in some sect-type congregations is symbolized in believers' baptism—and the Church is centered in the local community of the elect. This local company of believers is, as the Independents of the Westminster Assembly repeatedly urged, *ecclesia prima.* The center of church life is not the rhythm of the Church's Year and its sacraments, but the proclamation of the gospel to a doomed world and the preparation of the few for salvation, while the Elect await the apocalyptic advent of God's eschatological Kingdom.

The positive and negative sides of the sect-type churchmanship are obviously at opposite poles to those of the church-type. Positively, it tries to be absolutely faithful to the will of Christ and the ethical standards of the New Testament, although its interpretation of Christ's will can be narrow, literalistic and individualistic. But it does not sell its spiritual birthright for any political or social 'mess of pottage.' Furthermore, since churches of the sect-type have generally refused relationship with the state, they have rarely been tempted to persecute others or had the power to do so. What this position lacks in the universalism of the catholic forms, it makes up in terms of its intense fellowship at the local level, insisting on a community in which there is mutual ministry and virtually no separation between clergy and laity.

On the other hand, churches of the sect-type have almost always been ready to give up the visible unity of the Church too easily, and if they have not been noticeably guilty of persecution, they have often fallen into the spiritual pride of exclusivism. Although they have recalled the Church to the ethics of the New Testament, the literal way in which the scriptural standards have been interpreted often reveals the characteristics of law rather than the freedom of grace. Because it takes a fundamentally pessimistic view of human nature, this type is often unnecessarily antagonistic to human culture and discounts too readily the contribution that scientific progress can make to human happiness. By its emphasis on the narrowness of the gate and the small number of the Elect it can forget that the great theme of redemption was initiated because "God so loved *the world,*" and its gloomy assumption of the world's future doom often reveals ugly lack of concern for other people's fate. As a result, the church of this type may retreat within itself, insulating itself within a pietistic shell from all contamination, and letting the rest of the world go to hell.

Stephen Leacock's humorous description of the mythical church of St. Osoph's, which was "too presbyterian to be any longer connected with any other body whatsoever," hits very close to the mark.[14] Of course, there is no such church as St. Osoph's; but in another sense the history of the sect-type provides us with many St. Osophs—the rigorism, the exclusivism with its implied spiritual superiority, the Olympian unconcern with the unity of the Church or with the fate of others, they are all represented here, and this is where the sect-type leads when it is regarded as the absolute form of the Church.

C. *The 'third type'*

Troeltsch really didn't know what to call this type, but he recognized that there is another form of churchmanship distinct from both the church-type and the sect-type, which reaches its focus in the type of Christian liberalism he saw

14 After describing the last secession in which St. Osoph's had been involved, Leacock observed, "The dispute ended in a secession which left the church of St. Osoph's practically isolated in a world of sin whose approaching fate it neither denied nor deplored." *Arcadian Adventures with the Idle Rich,* p. 125.

developing in the twentieth century. Karl Barth accused Troeltsch of having a romantic attitude to modern man as the climax of Christian civilization,[15] and it may have been because of this romanticism that Troeltsch regarded his 'third type' of liberal mystics as the inevitable expression of Christianity to which both church-type and sect-type had pointed in their time.

On the other hand, Troeltsch recognized that it is hard to specify what this type of Christianity represents because it is extremely vague about its programs and theological bases.[16] He saw that sometimes it manifested itself as a mystical approach to religious truth, that it was more a movement of the spirit than an organized form of churchmanship, and that alongside the mysticism it also had an integral relation to rationalism. As a movement it may claim to "represent the highest ethical ideals of humanity," and yet "it is still unable easily to formulate for itself the unwritten programme which the gospel contains, nor apply it clearly to the conditions which oppose it."[17]

So far we might be tempted to wonder whether Troeltsch was simply guilty of a rare lapse into vagueness or whether what he is describing deserves to be recognized as a distinct 'type' of the Church. But I believe he had discerned something distinctive and, for reasons that may be clearer in our next chapter, I suggest that his own inability to be specific about the 'third type' is not to be dismissed as imprecision but is rather evidence of the breadth and complexity of all those forms of Christianity which have made their fundamental appeal to the immediacy of the Spirit.[18]

Troeltsch recognized that the religious individualism and inward experience which are the chief characteristics of such

[15] *Op. cit.*, pp. 225ff.

[16] *Op. cit.*, I, 445. Cf. his criticism of the theological dilemma of the *Evangelisch-Soziale Kongress.* If it were not an anachronistic use of the term, we might suggest that 'Christian secularism' well describes the position Troeltsch was trying to describe.

[17] *Ibid.*, p. 381.

[18] Compare the difficulty George H. Williams had in classifying the complex movements of the radical Reformers. *The Radical Reformation* (Philadelphia: Westminster, 1962).

movements lead only to the loosest kind of association, "the formation of groups on a purely personal basis, with no permanent form, which also tend to weaken the significance of forms of worship, doctrine, and the historical element."[19] Perhaps his own interest in modernity prevented him from noting that the temptation of this movement, with its emphasis upon the 'cultured' and the 'modern,' is its gnostic bias towards intellectual snobbery: the 'Church' is regarded as a fellowship of 'right-minded' people.

This type of Christian social expression does represent a persistent movement in the history of the Church,[20] a climate of secular-religious experience that has been particularly noticeable in our own century; but it is almost too diffuse to be analyzed in detail. Indeed, because of its essential subjectivity, its adherents are always reluctant to think of the Church as in any sense institutional, and prefer to think of themselves as the leaven working in society.

Troeltsch noted that this distinctive witness can arise from within either a 'church' or a 'sect,' and he may have regarded it as the eschatological form of Christianity for this reason; but there is also plenty of evidence for the opposite trend–i.e., when such a group arises it will either develop a structured

19 *Op. cit.*, II, 993.

20 A major thrust in Benjamin Reist's *Toward a Theology of Involvement* is that Troeltsch was preparing the way for a theological understanding of the Church in relation to the modern world. For me, his point is well taken. Often Troeltsch sounds like Bonhoeffer's 'world come-of-age' and the 'secular theology' of the 1960s. However, he was too good a historian not to notice that the humanistic groups at the time of the Reformation were "to be swept away by a new wave of ecclesiastical life in the sixteenth and the seventeenth century, to return once more with the modern world." *Op. cit.*, I, 378.

Troeltsch's expectation that the earlier twentieth-century expression of the liberal spirit was this time here to stay was to be disappointed: the humanism of 1911 soon suffered eclipse under the impact of world war and the theological reaction of Crisis Theology. This reaction lasted from the appearance of Karl Barth's *Römerbrief* in 1922 until the publication of J. A. T. Robinson's *Honest to God* in the 1960s; but the humanist thrust appears again, fully fledged, in the 'secular theology' of that decade and in Harvey Cox's *The Secular City*.

This history, however, suggests that far from disappearing, the polar trends return, and that the time between the point of apogee is becoming rapidly reduced. It further suggests that theologians, instead of looking for the next bandwagon, might begin to ask what both these trends validly contribute to the gospel, and what would be the shape of a theology that recognized that paradox.

form and become sect-type or church-type,[21] or it will disappear among the general movements of culture.[22] This cautionary tale may carry within it a warning for moderns.[23]

In the summary at the end of his book Troeltsch observed that from the beginning "these three forms were foreshadowed, and all down the centuries to the present day, wherever religion is dominant, they still appear alongside of one another, while among themselves they are strangely and variously interwoven and interconnected."[24] Whether Troeltsch's three-part typology is adequate for a sociology of 'religion' is immaterial at this point. His significance for our purpose is that he applied it historically to the Christian Church and indicates the essential relation that forms of the churches bear to the churches' theology. For he had put his finger on a phenomenon that is of great importance to our understanding of the doctrine of the Church when he showed that each of these three major types of church organization can find justification within the Christian gospel. By implication, the evidence for his typology in the history of the Church suggests that each becomes a virtual denial of that gospel when it excludes the others—a temptation that is particularly real for the first two, the church-type and the sect-type,[25] because

21 The Quakers are a good example. Many of the sects that Troeltsch discusses under the heading "The Sect-type and Mysticism within Protestantism" either started with 'third type' characteristics or developed branches that rapidly moved in that direction; but there is obviously a significant interplay between all three types, for even the medieval papacy produced the religious orders and the monastic movement, which were essentially a sect-type response to the demands of the gospel.

22 Troeltsch recognized this, *op. cit.*, I, 378. It was also seen very clearly by Claude Welch in *The Reality of the Church* (New York: Scribner, 1958). He pointed out that 'spiritual' churches have to come to terms with institutional forms: "None of these have in fact been able to dispense altogether with such fundamental signs, but to the extent to which they have approximated such an end, they have either rapidly vanished or so fundamentally altered as to be no longer recognizably the same community" (p. 59, n. 7).

23 If modern 'Christian secularists' are defining the Church of the immediate future wholly in terms of Troeltsch's 'third type,' the onus is on them to prove that their movement can be built into anything more stable, or more pervasive and persistent, than such movements have been in the past.

24 *Op. cit.*, II, 993f.

25 It is not so obvious with regard to the 'third type' because its aversion to organization and the subjective individualism of its members cause its exclusive claims to be lost in the secular.

they always exist in tension and often have stood in violent opposition to each other.

The examination of Troeltsch's types of churchmanship therefore leads us to certain propositions which underlie much of our thinking throughout the rest of this book.

(1) Behind these three types of church organization there are three different approaches to ecclesiology. If there are valid theological reasons for their appearance as the embodiment of distinctive ecclesiologies, then we cannot afford to ignore any of them, especially if we are ecumenically serious when we look for a church that expresses the *fulness* of the gospel. We need to understand how these different ecclesiologies witness to each other, and, even in their apparent opposition, support each other, for if they each contain vital truth, it is only by the testimony of all three that the Church will reach its goal.

(2) The testimony of both the church-type and the sect-type points to the Kingdom of God—to the time when Christian values become totally infused into the whole of society: the Church by its very nature points to the Kingdom, and the appearance of the 'third type' may be testimony to this ultimate goal. However, this does not mean that at any given moment we can assume that the Kingdom has now arrived in its fulness. History has always dealt very unkindly with such presumption, because in our history spiritual truth *needs* to be made incarnate. Troeltsch recognized that when his 'third type' claims success too prematurely, it simply fades into obscurity and is without any further visible effect.[26]

(3) This last point is simply an illustration that each of the three types can easily become too caught up with a particular period of history (in the case of the 'third type' it is the immediate present) to be the Church in its true sense. The truth is even more evident in the institutional forms of the church-type and the sect-type.

However, if all these types of churchmanship are authentic responses to the gospel, then the theological values they represent must be incorporated into any form of the Church that lays claim to ecumenicity. The questions this proposition

26 *Ibid.*, I, 378.

poses for us (and, for example, for COCU) can be stated only in a series of paradoxes—How can the Church be at one and the same time world-affirming and world-denying? How can we identify the Church positively with the progress of human culture without its becoming bemused or besmirched by the values of that culture? How can the Church promote the coming of the Kingdom by means of education and social service without losing the evangelical imperative that brings every individual to the point of personal decision and commitment? There are many others.

Perhaps the most fundamental question is to ask how we can act as priests mediating God's love and forgiveness of sin, while serving as faithful prophets declaring God's judgment on sin. A paradoxical impossibility? Paradoxical it is, but it is impossible only in the sense that the gospel itself is 'impossible': for this paradox centers in the action of God himself, and this gospel paradox constitutes the basic problem with which we wrestle in ecclesiology.

3

PARITY OF POLITIES

Behind the organization of denominations into episcopal, presbyterian, or congregational communities there was originally a very clear relationship between the polity and the basic theology of the denomination—the distinct form that their church assumed expressed something which Episcopalians, Presbyterians, and Congregationalists believed to be of the *esse* of the Church.

This essential relationship of theology to polity is no longer recognized by any but a comparatively few historically inclined antiquarians, and one may be grateful that this fact probably reduces the amount of heat generated between the major confessions. At the same time, there is another aspect of the general church apathy to ecclesiology and denominational origins that should awaken concern, for it may indicate that we have lost our grip on our forefathers' conviction that the Church does have an essential character and that there is a basic relationship between the gospel it proclaims and the form the Church takes in this world. This would be more serious than something we could simply dismiss as 'a pity,' not because we wish to revive old prejudices, but because our ecumenicity needs to be supported by something more solid than a sentimental desire for togetherness or a shrewd eye to the economics of union. We are concerned with the *Church,* and that is no more to be reduced to the casual sentiment of a love-in or the horse-trading of a corporation merger, than the Sermon on the Mount is to be confused with the Gettysburg Address.

Unless Christians have been deceiving everyone including themselves for the last two thousand years, there must be a spark of divinity in the Church—it must be based on an authority that comes from beyond itself and its own members, or else it has no more significance today than a museum or a social club. Our forefathers, despite their partial insights and wrong inferences, had the right concern: they were determined to safeguard what they believed to be the Church's essential character, because this witnessed to its vital connection with Jesus Christ. They may have looked in the wrong places for answers, they often interpreted Christ's will too narrowly and transmitted dreadful mistakes to later generations, but at least they persistently asked the right basic question: what form of the Church expresses the will of Jesus Christ?

The classic way in which the churches have answered this question is in terms of polity—and it provides a means of classification that ranges from Roman Catholicism, with a hierarchical structure headed by the Pope as the 'Bishop of bishops,' to atomistic congregational independency. The three simple patterns that emerged paralleled the three basic systems of civil government known to the ancient world[27] —episcopal (monarchical), presbyterian (oligarchic or aristocratic), and congregational (democratic).

27 Cf. Aristotle's *Politics.* It would be tempting to trace a parallel between these polities and Troeltsch's three types of the Church. There are relationships as we shall see, but not in terms of a simple equation. There is a much closer relation between Troeltsch's three types and the channels of spiritual authority to which they appeal.

However, it should be clear that probably no church today is an 'ideal type' of its original polity, for we are able to recognize oligarchical and democratic elements in denominations that are basically episcopal, just as we are able to admit that presbyterianism and congregationalism have influenced each other and have been influenced by episcopacy.

The century 1560-1660 is one of the most interesting since the Reformation in English church history, because the three systems arose and struggled for power in the English Church, and each had a measure of success.[28] They had arisen at the end of the medieval period when the analogy between forms of government in church and state was unquestioned. "For a thinker of the Middle Ages," Etienne Gilson observes, "the state is to the church as philosophy is to theology and as nature is to grace."[29] By inheriting this framework of thought each polity could not help producing a comprehensive view of life that would affect all aspects of society. Each regarded its position as *de jure divino,* the true Church established by Christ himself, and all other forms were excluded. It is also an interesting commentary on their claims that each sought to win power by essentially political and secular means.

Because of the political situation in England, Presbyterians and Congregationalists were forced to modify their exclusive claims with regard to each other—a concession that is somewhat quaintly expressed by the Congregational authors of the 1658 *Savoy Declaration* when they declared that "Churches gathered and walking according to the minde of Christ, judging other Churches (though less pure) to be true Churches, may receive unto occasional communion with them, such Members of those Churches as are credibly testified to be godly, and to

28 Episcopacy was established during the time of the Tudor and Stuart monarchies up to the outbreak of civil war in 1642 and then again after the Restoration in 1660. In 1643 the Westminster Assembly was called to decide on the new form of the church, and Presbyterianism was in power from 1645 through the Commonwealth (1648-53), but it was never very effective outside London and a few urban areas. By the time Oliver Cromwell became Lord Protector in 1653, Congregationalism had been forced by the war out of its earlier exclusive position and therefore the Protector's religious settlement was established on a broader base, but the lesson had not been learned by the Congregationalists who had emigrated to America before the war and who established their system in New England.

29 *La Philosophie au Moyen Age* (Paris: Payot, 1947), p. 254.

live without offence."[30] It is clear from a study of their practice that by this date they had stretched the boundaries to include Separatists, Baptists, and churches of the Reformed position, but it is equally clear that behind such a statement as the above there was still a 'high church' position which assumed our Lord had laid down specific requirements for the form of his Church on earth, and they still claimed that this was the system they practiced. Although representatives of the three polities differed about the form of the Church, they were entirely agreed that there was a divinely authorized form.

This is where our modern situation differs so radically from the seventeenth century with its clear-cut definitions. Today most Protestants do not claim to know precisely the true form of the Christian Church, or that the form they adhere to excludes all others. Certainly the 'high church' position in its traditional sense lives on in conservative branches of the churches, which inevitably have a reserved if not skeptical view of the ecumenical movement, but in the rest of Protestantism the situation is extremely ambiguous.

Protestants are increasingly conscious that their basic reasons for belonging to a particular church are not so much theological as nontheological; we are more likely to attend a certain church for reasons of birth (we were born into it), or reasons of sociology (it is nearer where we live, or we find the membership congenial), or for aesthetic reasons (we appreciate its architecture or its worship), than because we have thought long and deeply and decided that this is the truest form of the Church. Furthermore, despite all the drumming up of ancient loyalties for denominational purposes, we have a shrewd suspicion that our leaders are no more theological than we are on this score. There is obviously a clear distinction to be drawn between the defense of a polity as the one form of the true Church, and the defense of the same polity for practical reasons.

The latter is strikingly illustrated in Methodism, which is clearly episcopal in form. But Methodism neither originated in

30 Article XXX on Polity. Cf. Williston Walker, *The Creeds and Platforms of Congregationalism* (1893; Boston: Pilgrim, 1960), p. 408.

a distinct doctrine of the Church nor has it ever held episcopacy to be of divine right. The oldest (British) Methodist Church has never had bishops, and it is clear that in American Methodism episcopacy is regarded simply as a practical method of organization: it may be defended (and defended tenaciously) on these grounds, but Methodists would oppose just as rigorously any attempt to represent episcopacy as the Church's *esse* or to raise episcopal consecration to a higher level than the ordination of other ministers. As the Methodist historian Elmer T. Clark has said, "Methodist episcopacy is an office, and not an order, and its functions, even to the extent of consecrating bishops themselves, may be and have been exercised by elders in the absence of a bishop. Methodism everywhere shares the conviction of John Wesley that elders and bishops are one and the same order."[31]

Obviously no *de jure divino* ecclesiology is implied here. The real issue on episcopacy therefore is not only between those churches that hold an episcopal system and the rest, but also between those who maintain an episcopal *doctrine* of the Church and the rest. There is a division within the churches that cuts through all polities and can best be described as between the 'high church' and the 'low church' attitudes to ecclesiology.[32] There are Episcopalians, Presbyterians, and Congregationalists who believe their particular polity was determined by the will of God; there are Episcopalians, Presbyterians, and Congregationalists who adhere to their view of church government not because they believe God laid down

[31] Cf. Vergilius Ferm (ed.), *The American Church* (New York: Philosophical Library, 1953), p. 320. The former Evangelical and United Brethren Church, which united with Methodism in 1968, made this position even more explicit. The bishops in the E.U.B. were described in these terms: "There are bishops in the E.U.B. Church, but the episcopacy has been so modified that the government of the church is more presbyterian than episcopal. Bishops are simply elders of the church who have been elected by general conference for a term of four years to supervise and administer the church. They are agents of supervision, entrusted with administrative power, not priestly, and only for a given period of time. They act for and by the authority of general conference implementing the program which has been determined by that body." Paul Eller, in *ibid.,* p. 364.

[32] These terms are used not to denote any liturgical bent, but to describe relative positions regarding the doctrine of the Church—those who believe the form of the Church should carry the authority of Jesus Christ, and those who think it can be decided on a practical basis.

any specific rules on the matter, but because the polity of their church represents what in their view is the most practical way of administering the Church.

If the situation were faced honestly, we might look theologically at the positive and negative aspects of both positions, and seek a theological base that would do justice to the insights of both. As it is, the traditional bases of our historic doctrines of the Church remain unchallenged, while the churches actually act on pragmatic principles that start from very different premises. This leads the churches not only into bad faith, but also into an impossible situation with regard to their own church membership, for when they are asked to provide theological reasons for actions that are basically pragmatic they try to squeeze theological reasons out of their traditional ecclesiology. Parish ministers and church members recognize that the leaders of their denomination cannot ignore practical issues, but are rightly skeptical when they see what they have been taught as the historic position of the Church being turned to serve practical ends that are not compatible.

Therefore I suggest that failure to work out an adequate doctrine of the Church to meet the ecumenical situation has led denominational leaders into a kind of ecclesiastical double-talk, and has caused many church members and ministers to revert to ecclesiological conservatism whenever they sense they are being maneuvered into a union for which they are theologically and emotionally unprepared. Theological leadership has failed the churches at this point, for, if unions like the one proposed by COCU are ultimately thwarted by local conservatism, it will largely be because the churches' leaders did not take the trouble to establish the theological groundwork for a truly ecumenical doctrine of the Church, or the time to draw the membership into their confidence. Failing such a restatement of ecclesiology it is hardly to be wondered at if the rank and file in the churches turn back to the things they were taught in seminary and Sunday School, for although the venerable ecclesiologies may be inadequate, at least they assert that the Church, just because it is the Church of Jesus Christ, traces its existence and its form to the will of God.

In other words, we have to get beyond the specific polities

of former ages to the concern that was common to high churchmen of all kinds, the conviction that the Church is called into being by God, and that its form should bear a recognizable relationship to Jesus Christ and his gospel. If the ecumenical movement in Protestantism has lost something of its former drive, it may be because it lost its grip on this fundamental insight from its own earlier history.

It will be argued in these pages that any doctrine of the Church that concentrates exclusively on a particular form of church government—whether based on a legalistic theory of apostolic succession or on a literalistic appeal to New Testament polity—is obsolete. But we must be careful that we understand what makes it obsolete. It will be inadequate not because the doctrine of the Church *per se* has become obsolete, but because neither historical legalism nor biblical literalism is a sufficient guarantor of the gospel. It will further be argued that far from being obsolete, a genuinely ecumenical doctrine of the Church is the only sound basis for seeking to change the existing form of the churches, for we are concerned not with change for its own sake, but with the changes that are necessary to make the Church a more authentic and a more effective instrument of Christ's will in this world.

However, the fundamental issue lies much deeper than the shape of the Church: it is the problem of establishing the basic authority on which any Christian proclamation can be made whether in word or form. Until that issue has been faced and resolved, not only the shape of the Church but even the essential content of the gospel will remain unclear.

Chapter II

AUTHORITY AND THE DOCTRINE OF THE CHURCH

1

CHANNELS OF AUTHORITY

If Jesus Christ had not spoken with his own distinctive authority, there would be no problem of Christian dividedness, for there would be no Christian Church. Ecclesiastical divisions themselves may have arisen from our misunderstanding of the message, but their persistence centers in the claim by all Christians that the message is unique. There would be no contest if we had not all been convinced that we have been defending God's truth.

The authority of Jesus Christ is not in question, but the problem of dividedness arises from the way the churches claim his authority has been transmitted to them, and from their conflicting interpretations of the message they have received by those means. How does the will of Jesus Christ become contemporary for the Church? This is the point at which denominations start to make claims against each other, and where we begin to see the shape of different doctrines of the Church.

The ecumenical uncertainty of our time exists because the churches no longer accept the exclusivity and infallibility of those channels by which in the past they claimed to have received the authority of Jesus Christ and which authenticated their claim to be 'the Church.' A recent writer quotes a church official as saying that "the crisis confronting the churches today has arisen because we have not faced up to the consequences and implications of the fact that we have been too long deceiving the polity"; and if those words mean what they seem to imply, what is being criticized is the unwillingness or inability of the churches to take their own polity (ecclesiology) seriously.[1]

If this is so, why has it happened? Can it be dismissed simply as faithlessness, or has it a deeper reason? We agree with Langdon Gilkey when he commented that the denominations have "long since dispensed with their earlier religious or theological foundations," and that there has been a consequent "general drift of the life of the church away from its theological foundations."[2] But with regard to the exclusive claims based on these channels of spiritual authority, which loyal churchmen were taught to accept as the very foundation of their own denomination's title against those of other churches, it is not simply a case of no longer believing—which might be faithlessness—but that many churchmen find they *can* no longer believe—which is a question of honesty.

Let there be no misunderstanding. It is not suggested that Christians doubt the authority of Jesus Christ. On the contrary, I believe there is a great yearning for "a new stance of authority" in the Church, of the quality that Peter Berger called for;[3] but the problem is to see how Christ's will is made contemporary, credible, and authoritative to the churches when they no longer wholeheartedly believe in institutional forms, by which, certainly, valid insights came to them in the past, but which now seem to be vessels too partial and too pretentious to contain all that they claimed.

This presents us with a unique dilemma. On the one hand, the churches' ecclesiologies can be increasingly questioned for the best of all possible reasons, that they do not appear to be wholly faithful to the spirit of Jesus Christ; but on the other

[1] Quoted in Jeffrey K. Hadden, *The Gathering Storm in the Churches* (Garden City, N.Y.: Doubleday, 1969), p. 5.

[2] *How the Church Can Minister to the World Without Losing Itself,* p. 145.

[3] At Denver, September 27, 1971. See the report by Eleanor Blau, *The New York Times,* September 28, 1971.

hand each church could point to valid insights from the gospel that it has received, and *faute de mieux,* still do formal homage to its traditional ecclesiology. This means that the ecumenical debate is more often than not conducted as if "as it was in the beginning, is now, and ever shall be" referred specifically to ecclesiologies that are more and more disregarded by the churches themselves. However, it indicates why we cannot afford to ignore the inherited channels of authority, because they represent the official basis for a denomination's doctrine of the Church, particularly in the eyes of its conservative members.

If we can find the foundation principle, the chain of command, the documentary proof to which a church appeals for its spiritual authority, or the distinctive 'gift' that links this denomination to our Lord and his message, we shall uncover the foundation of its claim to be 'the Church.' This involves not only a basic authenticating 'authority' that is the source of appeal—unbroken tradition, scriptural record, the promise of the Spirit—but also the channels of grace by which the authority of Christ has been preserved and transmitted—e.g., apostolic succession, New Testament patterns of churchmanship, the possession of special charisma—and to which the church points as 'proof' of its authentic call. For many denominations these channels of spiritual authority focus in a sacramental Ministry, and it is my contention that the exercise of 'ministry' in word, deed, and presence is at the heart of all ecclesiology.[4]

Three fundamentally different approaches to the doctrine of the Church have developed from the three distinct answers given to the problem of spiritual authority, how and by what means it is transmitted and received by the Church. These different concepts of the Church and its authority may not be identical with Troeltsch's descriptive typology, but they are close enough to be extremely significant, and to suggest the theological basis for the types of churchmanship that Troeltsch described.[5]

[4] This was the thesis of my *Ministry* (Grand Rapids: Eerdmans, 1965). For the following discussion see especially pp. 165-190. As in that book, we here capitalize Ministry and Minister when they are used of ordained officers of the Church.

[5] These channels of the Holy Spirit's grace also have a very close relationship to

A. Appeal to the Church

The Catholic form of churchmanship comprises churches that base their appeal on the authority of the Church itself as the living custodian of the gospel, and trace their own claim *as* the Church to unbroken historical continuity with the church of the apostles. Within these churches the ministers are specifically related to the sacramental 'mysteries' that enshrine the Faith, and among ministers bishops have special primacy as custodians of the Faith and its mysteries. Therefore this historical transmission of authority is seen essentially in terms of an authentic episcopal consecration from the time of the apostles until now—the Apostolic Succession. When this logic is carried one stage further to affirm Peter and his successors in Rome as the supreme guardians on earth of the *depositum fidei,* the hierarchical structure is complete and authority is vested in the papacy.

As we have seen, there were sociological and political reasons that made such a hierarchical structure extremely congenial to earlier monarchies, and even today in some countries an episcopal form of the Church remains the classic exemplar of Troeltsch's church-type. How far this form of church was originally chosen by political establishments because of its similarity to their own structure, or how far its structure was conditioned by establishment, is a nice point for historians to discuss; but it is clear that the comprehensiveness of Catholicism in all its forms gives it a natural affinity to geographical organization (national, diocesan, parochial), and hence to the theological and sociological premises of Troeltsch's church-type.

B. Appeal to the Bible

Sharply distinguished from this approach is the main line of Protestantism, which traces the authority in the written record of the gospel. The older branches of Protestantism arose in

the three routes by which Max Weber suggested authority is actually exercised in the Church—control of tradition, the rational-legal processes, and the charismatic leadership. Cf. Max Weber, *The Theory of Social and Economic Organization* (New York: Oxford, 1947).

criticism of churches that based their authority on historical continuity, and therefore rejected this argument as any guarantee that the 'church' is the Church. In their view, historical development had led to serious regression, and therefore in advancing their own doctrine of the Church they bypassed the intervening history, and set themselves the task of restoring the Apostolic Church of the New Testament as it had existed before being 'corrupted.' The fundamental authority was *sola scriptura.*

We are reminded of what Troeltsch said about the sect-type, with its insistence on the universal application of New Testament standards and its fundamental appeal to the simple meaning of Scripture. Adherents of the sect-type, he said, "are in direct contact with the Teaching of Jesus . . . . Scripture history and the history of the Primitive Church *are permanent ideals,* to be accepted in their literal sense, not the starting-point, historically limited and defined, for the development of the Church. Christ is not the God-Man, eternally at work within the Church, leading it into all Truth, but He is the direct Head of the Church, binding the Church to Himself through his Law in Scriptures."[6]

This is where Protestantism started, but in the major churches of the Reformation the New Testament standard for the Church was neither reached nor sustained.

In the first place, it is clear that although some of the Protestant Reformers began with *sola scriptura* as their basic theological principle of authority, their approach was modified by the exigencies of their social and political situation. The principle of authority was in fact changed from appeal to the Scriptures themselves to an appeal to those aspects of scriptural ecclesiology acceptable to the civil authorities.[7]

This was the real point at issue between the Anabaptists and Reformers such as Luther and Zwingli. That which separated Zwingli, for example, from the Swiss Brethren was his refusal to apply the same strict biblical principle to the sacrament of baptism that he had applied to his understanding of the

6 *Social Teaching of the Christian Churches,* I, 336f. Italics mine.

7 I hold that Luther's initial approach to ecclesiology pointed in a decidedly restorationist direction. Cf. below, pp. 130ff.

Eucharist and to other aspects of ecclesiology. It may also partially explain the violence of the Reformers' reaction to the Anabaptists—the former were very sensitive to the charge that they were not prepared to follow the logic of their own scriptural principle; but they recognized that if they did follow that line to its absolute conclusion, the churches they represented would become sect-type, gathered churches, whereas the success of the Reformation seemed to depend on their maintaining a national footing with the support of the civil rulers.

The unwillingness of the Reformers to follow biblical literalism to its logical conclusion in respect to ecclesiology is significant. We may grant that political expediency, medieval prejudices, and mixed motives were at work, but we should see that there were *theological* concerns that would cause some men to shy away from the rigorous application of biblical restorationism: the Reformers may have allowed an element of political pragmatism to affect their understanding of the Church, but their position was not necessarily devoid of theological insight.[8] It was also an admission that the principle of *sola scriptura* needed to be exegeted, and that the scriptural forms of the Church must be applied with reference to time and place.

This need for a less literal principle of hermeneutics soon became a problem. Although the Bible appeared to be the focal point around which all Christians *should* be able to agree, in practice they did not. Its interpretation was open to many serious but honestly held differences of opinion regarding both the form of the New Testament Church and many other crucial aspects of church belief and practice. These differences not only produced the divisions of Protestantism, but also eventually made the old exclusivism untenable: the churches were sooner or later forced into the present-day pluralism.

[8] It was raised in its sharpest form on the issue of baptism. In an age that believed that valid baptism was the prerequisite for salvation, the Anabaptists raised a radical question about the salvation of all the previous ages of the Church back to the time of the Apostolic Church, and they did not seem unduly concerned about consigning the previous generations to damnation. But is the God of the biblical revelation this kind of God? A further question of theological import was the Anabaptists' readiness to exchange catholicity for the sectarianism implied by the absolute autonomy of their gathered congregations.

Nevertheless, there is a primary element of restorationism, and hence of the sect-type, in any church of the Reformation, both by reason of its fundamental appeal to Scripture and more specifically in its turning initially to the New Testament for its own form.[9] Some of them (the Baptists particularly, but to a lesser extent Reformed churches) went a considerable distance with Troeltsch's sect-type before the political opportunities of the moment or gradual assimilation into the prevailing culture led to withdrawal from the restorationist ideal, while others drew back very soon when they discovered they could no longer follow the restorationist literalism or logic.

I submit that this illustrates two features of Protestant churchmanship that need to be more clearly understood: first, that the Reformation itself was fundamentally sect-type and restorationist in its appeal to the Scriptures, and secondly that this was very soon modified by the Reformers themselves. The first step in this latter direction was taken when the authority of the civil ruler was virtually put alongside the Bible in determining the practical organization of the Church, but the same effect can be noticed when later churches of a restorationist stamp come to terms with society and begin to recognize the existence of 'churches' other than themselves. Again we may concede the less worthy features of this trend which have stimulated the continual protest of new sects against the worldliness and flaccidity of settled denominations and calling for a return to the New Testament norm; but beyond this I suggest that the modification of restorationism, despite its obvious dangers, may hide a theological insight that focusses on the need to measure our literalist logic by the God of the Scriptures—for the God revealed in Jesus Christ is a Living God whose will for the Church must be interpreted anew in every age and place.[10]

[9] Cf. the first major apologia of the Church of England against the Church of Rome, *Apologia Ecclesiae Anglicanae,* by John Jewell, Bishop of Salisbury, which appeared in 1562. A translation of this work by Lady Anne Bacon was published in 1564 as *An Apologie or answere in defence of the Churche of Englande.* Jewell argued that the charge of novelty was more properly leveled against the papacy than against the Church of England; *The Works of John Jewell,* Parker Society, ed. John Ayre (Cambridge: C.U.P., 1848), III, 100; cf. pp. 86-93; Latin text, pp. 41f. Cf. below, pp. 89f.

[10] If I am right in tracing the distinction between the three types to the channel

C. Appeal to 'the Spirit'

However vague Troeltsch's 'third type' may have been in terms of ecclesiastical organization, ever since historians discovered the wide variety and vitality of the forms taken in the 'radical reformation' we have recognized that this type of religious expression has been a recurrent and persistent influence on Christian history. Spiritual authority for the radical mystics was to be traced to the promptings of the Spirit in the heart of the individual, and this was the only form in which any ultimate spiritual authority could be recognized: holy book and holy church must give way before that. The militant radicals of Cromwell's army were just as prepared to get rid of the Bible as they were to attack the ecclesiastical hierarchy.[11]

At the same time we cannot simply categorize this insight as 'mystical.' When all objective standards are rejected, it becomes practically impossible to distinguish between the authority of the Spirit and decisions that have a much more mundane and rational origin. The pragmatism that slips into even ecclesiastical and biblical doctrines of the Church, always has a much more obvious influence on those who rely wholly on the immediate promptings of the Holy Spirit: if such movements are charismatic and mystical at their origin, they often drift into very thinly disguised rationalism.

But whether rational or mystical in orientation, those who look to the authority of the Spirit seek 'the Church' in the fellowship of Christian individuals who hold loose to all forms of orthodoxy, and who recognize an ultimate authority in that which speaks to their own heart. In a sense this form of churchmanship de-emphasizes 'the Church' and anticipates 'the Kingdom.' The theological wheel has turned full circle, for whereas in the church-type the church is identified with soci-

of spiritual authority to which they ultimately appeal, then the line between Troeltsch's sect-type and his 'third type' does *not* run between the mainline reformers and the radicals, as has so often been assumed, but it goes through the center of the radical movement, separating biblicist Anabaptists from Anabaptist mystics and rationalists further to their left. I see the major reformers as, in principle, exponents of the sect-type, who were not able or ready to follow the absolute logic of the literalist position.

11 Cf. Baxter's visit to Cromwell's troops and his description of those who were "against the tying of our selves to any Duty before the Spirit move us," *Reliquiae Baxterianae,* ed. Matthew Sylvester (London, 1691), I, 53.

ety in order gradually to bring in the Kingdom, in the kind of churchmanship we are describing the church is identified more and more with society as an earnest or sign of the realization of the Kingdom of God; whereas the church-type and the sect-type look for the Kingdom in some future time, the mystics proclaim it here and now. The reality of the Church is revealed and authenticated by the eschatological evidence of Christ's immediate presence.[12]

This claim is made against the counterclaims to possess either an impeccable historical succession or an infallible scripture. So a modern Quaker describes Quakerism as "an explicit and developed manifestation of one of the three main forms of Christianity; the other two being Catholicism and Protestantism,"[13] and goes on to describe its distinctiveness by pointing out that "Whenever and wherever religion becomes too formal, too dependent upon external expression, the mystic rises up in protest and points the way to a religion which is internal, independent of outward forms of organization and centered in the direct apprehension of God. This experience requires no intermediary of church, priest or book." According to the writer, however, Quakerism is to be distinguished from Eastern mysticism precisely because it is communal rather than individual, "a group mysticism, grounded in Christian concepts."[14]

The history of the Quaker movement provides an illustration of what Troeltsch describes as the mystical-type of churchmanship with its tendency to humanism and distrust of institutional forms, except we would suggest that insofar as Quakerism formalized its protest against ecclesiastical and

[12] Perhaps this accent inevitably appears when there is a strong expectation of the End. Cf. Joachim of Fiore's belief that the End was to be ushered in by the 'Age of the Spirit,' or the eschatological frenzy of Thomas Müntzer, Melchior Hofmann, and many others at the time of the Reformation, or the militant hopes of the Fifth Monarchists and even many sober Puritans during the English Civil War. This suggests that the sect-type always causes the 'third type' to appear with it; for the sect-type tends to biblical literalism, and since biblical literalism stimulates apocalyptic hopes and Pentecost as an eschatological sign, one sure sign of the End is the pouring out of the Spirit on all flesh (Joel 2:28; cf. Acts 2:17). Once the authority of immediate revelation is claimed, the 'third type' inevitably follows.

[13] Howard Brinton, *Friends for Three Hundred Years* (London: Allen & Unwin, 1953), p. x.

[14] *Ibid.*, p. xiii.

scriptural authority, it moved in a sect-type direction: in order to maintain a community, even a community of mystics needs tacit recognition of 'discipline' within the group. Without this, Troeltsch's mystical-type becomes a loose association of individualists and finally disappears among the general liberalizing influences of society or into churches of the other two types. It would, however, be unrealistic not to recognize, even in its constant tendency to become submerged in other forms, the leaven that this form of spirituality has provided for the rest of Christianity.

It must be clear, however, that we cannot make a complete identification between the three approaches to the theological question of ultimate spiritual authority and Troeltsch's three forms of the Church. Nontheological factors have to be taken into account: the support of a prince like William the Silent in Holland, or the sudden success of the nobility in Scotland, or the unexpected ease with which a colonial expedition to Massachusetts was undertaken, could very soon stimulate a sect-type community to become a church-type community, just as a change in intellectual opinion towards scientific humanism could send it in the opposite direction. Naturally, such changes in ecclesiological stance could not be allowed to pass without some theological justification, and this resulted in some incredible intellectual gymnastics as the exponents of a 'gathered church' ecclesiology tried to expound a 'parish church' practice.

But when all due allowance is made for the modifications, the parallels are still striking: in tracing the broad differences of attitude that churches have taken to the problem of spiritual authority, we can discern corresponding differences in the structures they have adopted and in their relationship to contemporary society; and although probably no denomination today can be regarded as wholly in one camp or the other, we can still see in their traditional theologies and forms the basic shapes that we have outlined above. Roman Catholics, Eastern Orthodox, and Anglicans *have* emphasized historical continuity, and it still remains at the heart of their traditional positions. Presbyterians, Congregationalists, Baptists, and Disciples *have* all claimed, at one time or another, to restore the

Church on the New Testament pattern; and even though this may now be an embarrassment to their leaders, it remains deeply embedded in the prejudices of their conservative laity. Though the Quakers may look like simply another denomination in the general pluralism of our time, the original claim of that movement and its founder *was* to the 'inner light' of the Holy Spirit. The pattern may not be absolute, but it is certainly discernible.

2

AUTHORITY IN THE CHURCH: A REVISION

In *Ministry* I suggested that Christians discover their ultimate spiritual authority in the authority of the Church itself, in the authority of the Scriptures, or in the immediate sense of the Spirit's presence, and that these different ways of resolving the problem of authority concentrate on what the particular denomination believes are the essential means by which it receives the authority of our Lord. So churches have arisen that find the *esse* of the Church in the historical succession maintained by their own hierarchy, or in particular patterns of order and worship derived from the New Testament, or in the experience of the Holy Spirit's presence.

Furthermore, I suggested that although Christians claim different channels of grace, each channel has been used by the same Holy Spirit and testifies to the same Living Christ. As one writer put it a few years ago, "For though neither Church, Scripture, nor Conscience is in itself infallible, we have *in Christ himself an infallible authority,* and can trust him to use the fallible, mediated authorities of Church, Scripture, and conscience, to keep us from error. We do not need to try to erect infallible authorities of our own: the infallible Church, the infallible Scripture, and the infallible conscience are nothing more than idols."[15] But if it is the *same* Christ who speaks to us through all these vehicles of his grace, then surely the recognition of this means something for our unity as Christians. The ecumenical imperative is written into our ap-

[15] The late Joseph Newbold Sanders in "The Meaning and Authority of the New Testament," in *Soundings: Essays concerning Christian Understanding,* ed. A. R. Vidler (Cambridge: C.U.P., 1963), p. 138.

parent differences. "It is not a different Spirit or a different Christ that speaks to us through these witnesses, but the same Word of God that we see manifested in the gospel story; and the answer to our problem of authority is therefore not to set off Bible against Church, or Church against a Christian's conscience, but to discover their proper relationship."[16]

If this insight is correct, there is little theological justification for doctrines of the Church that are mutually exclusive.[17] But we are led to reflect that the basic sin of the churches towards each other, indeed the place where they have often become diabolic, has been at the point where they have pushed the logic of their own view of spiritual authority to the extreme of denying the Spirit of Christ in other churches: overzealous loyalty to a part of Christ's truth that denies the law of *agape,* contradicts the very claim we make about the Holy Spirit's presence in our midst and is close to the unforgivable sin.

These insights are, I believe, still valid. But we must amend what was written in that chapter, not so much for what was said but for what was omitted.[18] The problem of the purely theological approach is that one can unwittingly ignore nontheological factors that still have theological significance, and I suggest there is one such factor that can no longer be ignored in our consideration of authority because it has particular significance when the issues are translated into terms of church order and practice. This is the gift of human Reason.

How can we find a place for Reason, and for the ecclesiastical pragmatism that follows from it, in a schema that is by definition theological? Yet we cannot deny that it does represent a kind of God-given independent 'authority' by which, in practice, we judge the theological systems of our own and other churches. Further, it is clear that we cannot disregard this 'authority' without denying our own human responsibility, and it cannot be overtly theological without losing the very character of independence that makes man what he is as man:

16 *Ministry,* p. 172.

17 Especially if one accepts what was said later in that chapter about the *character* of the Spirit's authority in the Church. Cf. *ibid.,* pp. 180-190.

18 *Ibid.,* chapter 6, pp. 165-190.

Reason must be granted the independence and respect that God himself seems to grant to our humanity.

In all apprehension of truth, theological or not, we are forced to employ this essentially nontheological faculty. We cannot evaluate the significance of the Church's historical development, we cannot discern the true meaning of Scripture, we cannot accept the Christian imperative for our own conscience without reviewing each through the eye of Reason. Certainly faith has ultimate primacy, but although it may see beyond the boundaries of Reason, it cannot ignore what Reason sees.

I am therefore suggesting that the recognition of Reason is a necessary part of our theological framework because of a fundamentally theological principle—because God treats us as responsible (and hence, rational) persons; we could not be truly human if our reason were placed under any outside control or constraint. And in considering the Holy Spirit's authority in the institutional forms of the Church, this implies that we must also take into account the influence of rational pragmatism on the forms and structures of the Church. This presents us with a problem of description, for we cannot introduce Reason into our theological scheme without seeming to do violence to either the one or the other.

In describing the question of spiritual authority I used the following diagram:

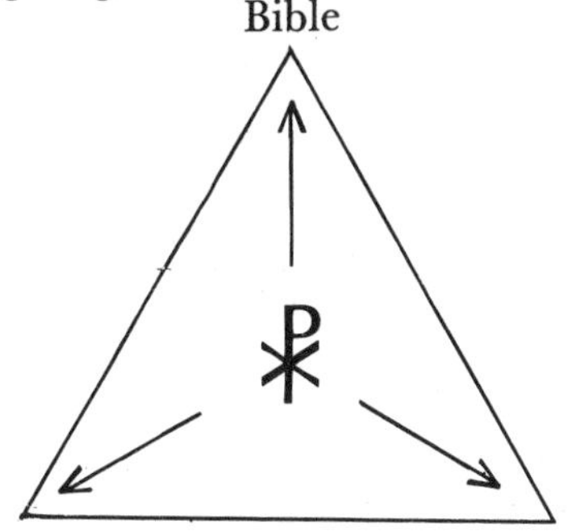

In this diagram the three points of the triangle represent the three distinctive positions on authority, centering in the Church, the Bible, and Individual Revelation. It was intended to show that the Holy Spirit mediates the will of Christ through all these channels. As a statement of the purely theological issue it may be true enough, but where are you to insert Reason without making either some dangerous assumptions, or claims that would seem more than presumptuous to those outside the Church?

The problem arises because Reason belongs to an entirely different dimension. It belongs to the sphere of nature rather than revelation. We need a new diagram, one that recognizes a wholly different perspective that does not see the issues simply in the theological plane. The case would not be met by simply adding a new point to the triangle, by turning it into a triangular prism or tetrahedron. That would suggest that Reason is a channel of the Holy Spirit's grace similar to the others, and it is not.[19] It *must* be essentially independent of the Holy Spirit, and on two counts it is of a totally different order from the vehicles of grace; first, because it carries only human authority, and secondly, because although it stands apart from the other channels of authority, it exercises that independent human judgment on them all.

A more appropriate figure for us to use would be that of an eye which sees the whole triangle. The human eye can see the relationship of the triangle as a whole; it can place it in its own particular perspective even as it stands in relationship to it; and as it interprets the meaning of what it sees, it can also distort the image. We need a revised diagram to illustrate the point.

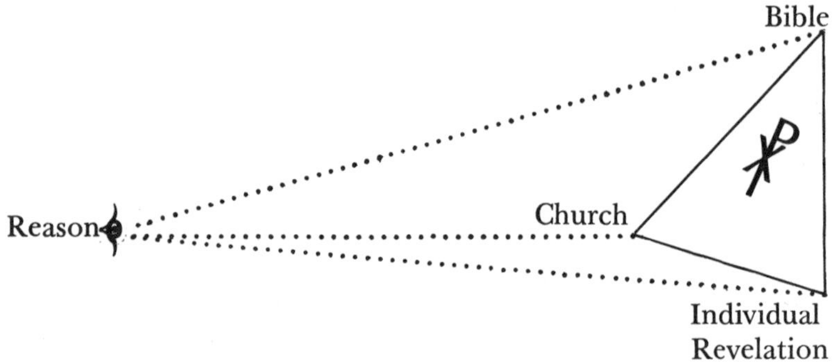

19 Does the Holy Spirit influence human reason? Can we know? The medieval theologians, probably under the influence of Aristotelian thought, related Reason to

The point I am making is that Reason is a nontheological authority that enters into our understanding of the Holy Spirit's authority and of the means whereby the will of Christ has come down to us. It does so not as a foreign intrusion into our theological system, but because God wills us to be responsible and human.

On the other hand, because we are human, our reason is subject to all the same imperfections, prejudices, and plain human cussedness that fallen nature is heir to. It is certainly not infallible in its judgments about the divine revelation or impeccable in its attempts to express the will of God in institutional forms. Yet it stands apart from all our theological formulations and ecclesiological theories and 'judges' them by God's own permission.

Therefore if human rationality occupies the position of an independent authority in relation to our theological constructions, God must be prepared for distinctively human imperfections to enter into our understanding of the Church. Perhaps we are not intended to have infallible absolutes, any absolute authority through divine institution, sacred book, or inspired prophet to which we are expected to give the obedience due to God alone. That we have to recognize our own pragmatism at many points in the organization and operation of the institutional church *ought* to keep us from the danger of deifying one particular form of the Church. As A. R. Vidler observes, "No definitions made by the Church *in via* are in themselves final or irreformable, however faithfully they serve to mediate to mankind the final authority of God for practical pur-

the soul; and many of the *Spiritualisten* of the Reformation confused the immediate revelation of the Spirit with Reason, moving from one to the other without distinguishing clearly between them. We note that secular rationalists have often been better witnesses to Christ's Spirit in their day than representatives of the Church—to which the bitter history of religious intolerance bears witness: the history of social progress represents many triumphs of reason over the unchristian dogmatism of ecclesiastical orthodoxies.

But one point we must safeguard is that the Holy Spirit cannot *govern* human reason, for God does not coerce men's intellect. If rational man follows the will of Christ, he does so because he recognizes it as 'good' and from his own volition. One must defend this essential freedom in man before God; and although this does rule out the 'persuasion' of the Holy Spirit in ways beyond our consciousness, it suggests that we must be very careful in speaking of his influence upon Reason or of implying that man is not truly free.

poses."[20] Which seems to be another way of saying that a pilgrim people is called to walk by faith.

3

THE 'AUTHORITY' OF REASON

Although we can trace the effects of reason with its pragmatic forms in all branches of the Church, it has had a special influence upon those who look for spiritual authority primarily through individual revelation, the exponents of Troeltsch's 'third-type.' It may be hard enough to distinguish between the Holy Spirit's guidance of the clerical hierarchy and the practical decision to wear certain garments (later adopted as liturgical) because of the temperature in the medieval cathedrals, or between the Protestant appeal to Scripture and Cromwell's practical employment of Psalm 117 before giving chase to the enemy,[21] but it is particularly difficult to distinguish between the promptings of the Holy Spirit and our own human reasoning.

It has been pointed out that Puritanism stood as an inheritor to the Renaissance as well as to the Reformation, and this would inevitably raise questions about the authority of reason.[22] Although the influence of pragmatic rationalism on Protestantism may be traced much further back than the Enlightenment, Langdon Gilkey is entirely right to stress the devastating effects of Enlightenment thought on Protestantism in general and on the ecclesiology of American Protestantism in particular: the erosion of the older forms of church discipline had already started, and the Enlightenment simply accelerated the tendency to swing between an individualist

20 A. R. Vidler, in *Soundings,* p. 145. On reading Vidler's note on 'Authority' (pp. 142ff.) I became aware how closely my own thoughts in this chapter seem to parallel his, particularly in the recognition of Reason as an 'authority' in the Church. However, my view was reached independently and from a very different ecclesiological base, which may reinforce the argument.

21 It is the shortest Psalm, and Cromwell used it for a Thanksgiving before chasing the Scots from the field of Dunbar in 1650.

22 Cf. Geoffrey Nuttall, *The Holy Spirit in Puritan Faith and Experience* (Oxford: Blackwell, 1947), p. 35. The whole of chapter 2 in Nuttall's book is germane to this issue.

religion of the heart and an individualist religion of the head.[23] Reason had always been a factor, but now it became a much more open factor in the debate.

Yet those who arose on the left wing of Protestantism were very conscious of the distinction between the Holy Spirit and the workings of the human mind, and Geoffrey Nuttall observes that "it is remarkable how regularly the Puritans in general distinguish the Holy Spirit in man from man's reason and conscience, and insist that, though associated with both, the Spirit's working cannot satisfactorily be defined in terms of either."[24] He quotes from a well-known sermon, 'The Spirits Conviction of Sinne,' which Peter Sterry preached before the English Parliament in 1645, in which the preacher was at pains to show the difference between 'reason' and 'the spirit' and insisted on the superiority of the latter because "Reason makes man. The Spirit is the principle of a Saint."[25] Or, we might quote from another of his sermons when he describes human reason as "an inferior, imperfect, dependent Principle; unsuitable at best to Divine things; unsure at first, apt to be deceived; deceived; now depraved in all men."[26] Sterry's concern is the more interesting, and even the more significant, because he was one of the Cambridge Platonists, and might have been expected to magnify reason.

As far as George Fox is concerned, Nuttall shows that Thomas Goodwin was incorrect in believing that the Quakers

23 Langdon Gilkey, *How the Church Can Minister to the World Without Losing Itself,* chapter 2, and especially pp. 29ff., 47ff. The swing between pietism and rationalism in American Protestantism is brilliantly indicated by Richard Hofstadter in *Anti-Intellectualism in American Life* (New York: Knopf, 1963). Cf. the following: "Puritanism had always required a delicate balance between intellect, which was esteemed as essential to true religion in New England, and emotion, which was necessary to the strength and durability of Puritan Piety" (p. 64). This was probably true for all Protestant forms in the seventeenth century, and the polar tendencies could be held together either by the authority of the state or by a strong doctrine of the Church with a firm ecclesiastical discipline. Once these constraints were removed, however, the individualist pressures into pietism or rationalism would come into play. Protestantism would become divided and subdivided still further, and would begin swinging between the theological extremes.

24 Nuttall, *op. cit.,* p. 37.

25 As quoted, *ibid.*

26 "The Teachings of Christ in the Soule," 1648, preached before the House of Peers.

equated the Holy Spirit with conscience.[27] If Fox's understanding of the Spirit was essentially experimental, it was also essentially christocentric. When he challenged people with the question, "Art thou a child of Light, and hast thou walked in the Light, and what thou speakest is it inwardly from God?" the 'Light' was Jesus Christ; and if he was speaking of an inner testimony of the Holy Spirit, it was testimony to the same Spirit which had inspired the Scriptures, and which Christ and the apostles had enjoyed and possessed.[28]

These spiritual insights were not to be confused with reason, for Fox testified, "I did not see by the help of man, nor by the letter, though they are written in the letter, but I saw them in the Light of the Lord Jesus Christ, and by His immediate spirit and power, as did the holy men of God by whom the Scriptures were written." In breaking free from the biblical literalism of his contemporaries, and in emphasizing the ultimate authority of a revelation that is immediate and personal, Fox clearly had no intention of breaking from the Christ to whom the Scriptures testified. His intention was rather to set the living reality of Christ in the heart at liberty from the false bondage of 'the letter.' For he went on to declare, "I had no slight esteem of the Holy Scriptures, but they were very precious to me, for I was in the spirit *by which they were given forth:* and what the Lord opened in me, I afterwards found agreeable to them."[29]

Certainly George Fox gave priority to the experienced testimony to God's will within the heart; but it is clear that for him this testimony was the authentic voice of the Holy Spirit because he found that his experience agreed with the spirit of Christ revealed in Scripture, just as later in the history of his work the same spirit was witnessed in the community of believers through the 'sense of the meeting.' For this reason Fox provides us with a classic example of an essentially Chris-

[27] Nuttall, *op. cit.,* p. 38. The reference to Goodwin is to "A Discourse of the Glory of the Gospel," *The Works of Thomas Goodwin, D.D.* (Edinburgh: James Nichol, 1862), IV, 344.

[28] Cf. Margaret Fell's account of her conversion in Brinton, *Friends for Three Hundred Years,* pp. 15f.; also Fox's own account, *The Journal of George Fox,* ed. Norman Penney (London: J. M. Dent, 1924), p. 67.

[29] *The Journal of George Fox,* p. 20. Italics mine.

tian and theological approach to the problem of authority.[30]

On the other hand, his appeal was primarily to 'the Light within,' and for those whose grasp on the scriptural revelation was not as sure as Fox's own, it could become individualistic and confused with personal 'notions,' or 'imaginations,' such as those which afflicted poor James Naylor.[31] Because the Light to which Fox appealed was that which "lighted every man that cometh into the world,"[32] it could be confused with reason or conscience; and although Thomas Goodwin may have been wrong in reference to Fox himself, he may not have been too short of the mark for many of Fox's followers.

Even in Fox himself it is not altogether clear, when, for example, he becomes convinced that the 'hireling priests' were all 'miserable comforters,'[33] whether he arrived at his conviction by direct revelation of the Holy Spirit or by the simple exercise of his rational faculties. One suspects that both were involved; and later Quakers, once the movement had lost its original evangelistic and pentecostal qualities, had far more difficulty in maintaining the distinction between the Inner Light and the Platonists' 'candle of the Lord.'

The problem may be just as clearly illustrated from the period of the sixteenth-century Reformation. When historians began to turn their attention to the vast wealth of nonconforming opinion to the left of the major reformers, their interest was focussed first of all upon the Anabaptists; but it very soon became evident that the movement covered a far greater variety of religious experience than those who technically qualified for that name. Perhaps the movement could be

[30] Cf. also Nuttall's quotations from Fox, *op. cit.*, pp. 41f., 45f.

[31] James Naylor (1618-1660), one of Fox's associates, failed to distinguish adequately between the 'Inner Light' within himself and the Third Person of the Trinity. Under the persuasion of some of his women followers he seems to have thought of himself as a new Incarnation, and entered Bristol in 1656 in a manner that paralleled Christ's entry into Jerusalem. Parliament punished him for blasphemy.

[32] Margaret Fell's account in Brinton, *op. cit.*, p. 15. Fox was clearly following the thought in John 1:6-13. Is 'general revelation' suggested in this passage? What is the relationship between the Holy Spirit and the special gifts to the Church on the one hand, and 'the light that lighted every man' on the other? We are back to the mystery to which we alluded earlier; above, n. 19.

[33] *Journal of George Fox*, p. 5.

called 'The Anabaptist and Spiritual Writers,' but even that was seen to be not broad enough, for it must include revolutionaries like Thomas Müntzer, humanists like Sebastian Franck, and ethical and theological rationalists like Castellio and Servetus. Clearly, the definition of a 'spiritual writer' would have to be stretched somewhat. George H. Williams, who has given us the definitive work on the movement, has called it 'The Radical Reformation'—a blanket term that must cover everything from the mystical spirituality of Schwenckfeld, through the wide range of the Anabaptist movement, to pure rationalists.

The problem the historians had in searching for an adequate term to define the movement[34] underlines the point at issue. It indicates that we are dealing with a religious phenomenon in which revelation, 'the Spirit,' and reason are intimately related and often inextricably confused. Furthermore, although a small group of spiritual mystics may begin with a very sincere belief in immediate revelation, and be able to distinguish clearly in their own religious experience between the immediate revelation of the spirit and the rationalizations of the mind, the same is not true for those who have touched only the edges of the group, or for the second and third generations who claim 'birthright' privileges. And a religion based on the final authority of immediate revelation is in an embarrassing position when it has to judge the authenticity of those who, on the same basis, confess a very different experience.

As we have seen, Troeltsch himself had difficulty in finding an adequate term to describe this religious expression. Sometimes he describes its adherents as 'spiritual mystics,' but this does not fit very well the humanists and rationalists among them. The one characteristic that he is quite sure remained common to the religious radicals was their thoroughgoing individualism—"religious individualism which has no external organization." They represent a 'third type,' neither church-type nor sect-type in thought or structure, and they are the

[34] E.g., Rufus Jones, *Spiritual Reformers in the Sixteenth and Seventeenth Centuries* (1914); George H. Williams and Angel M. Mergal (ed.), *The Spiritual and Anabaptist Writers* (Library of Christian Classics [Philadelphia: Westminster], XXV, 1957); George H. Williams, *The Radical Reformation* (1962).

exponents of a 'spiritual religion' whose spirituality "finally (as usually happens) changed into rationalistic and philosophical reason."[35]

There, the cat is out of the bag!—for that is the point. Once the external authorities of Church or Scriptures are discarded and final authority becomes entirely internalized, the 'promptings of the Spirit' and Fox's Inner Light begin, almost inevitably, to shade into the operations of an ethical rationalism and the standards of an enlightened conscience. If this is recognized we can begin to understand why this form has tended to rationalism,[36] and has often disappeared into the general humanism of liberal thought.

4

PRAGMATISM AND THE CHURCH

When reason is authoritative in matters of organization, the result is pragmatism; but because religious individualism tends to rationalize itself into the surrounding culture it has not left us a developed ecclesiology. Those groups from this wing of Christianity which have survived in a distinctive form, have had to develop qualities out of their own 'tradition' that could resist the individualistic tendencies.[37] Therefore, to examine

35 *The Social Teaching,* II, 776. Langdon Gilkey also noted this, which makes his disregard of Troeltsch's 'third type' all the more surprising. What he describes in one of his footnotes is obviously what Troeltsch had in mind. Gilkey, *op. cit.,* p. 110, n. 9.

36 It should be noted that this is not the only route that rationalism takes in Protestant thought. Rationalism has also arisen directly out of extreme biblical orthodoxy. For example, the Protestant scholasticism that produced some of the most clear-cut statements of Protestant orthodoxy in the seventeenth century (e.g., The Westminster Confession of Faith) continued its intellectual logic during the next few decades in an Arian direction, and thence into Deism and Socinianism. The history of the English Presbyterians, the church that produced the Westminster Standards, is instructive at this point. (Cf. Robert S. Paul, *The Atonement and the Sacraments* [Nashville: Abingdon, 1960], p. 130 and note.) Another example is to be seen in the Christadelphian sect, which is both unitarian in doctrine and literalist in its approach to Scripture. It is ironical that spiritual individualism and biblical literalistic orthodoxy finally meet in rationalism whenever their logic is pushed to its limit.

37 I.e., sect-type or even church-type tendencies. The forms taken by the Quaker societies, for example, are intriguing and baffling. They have obviously

the ecclesiological significance of pragmatism we must look in another direction.

Church history provides us with two important denominations that did not take their starting-point from a dogmatic view of the Church, and which have therefore followed a different route in their approach to the nature of the Church than that taken by most other Protestant churches. Both Lutheranism and Methodism took their original point of departure from the evangelical principle governing individual salvation, and although this was to have tremendous implications both for the question of authority and for ecclesiology, they did not separate from their mother churches because of a different doctrine of the Church *per se.* So, although Lutheranism may have taken its stand on *sola scriptura,* the starting-point of Luther's theology was Justification by Faith, and the ordering of the church was left largely to the practicalities in the local situation; and similarly, although Methodism accepted the common Protestant appeal to the Bible, Wesley regarded this of little value without the personal assurance of salvation.

These denominations did not have their *raison d'être* in a distinct theory of the Holy Spirit's transmission to the Church and they were therefore not tied to a carefully articulated ecclesiology. It left them comparatively free to deal with the ecclesiastical situation in response to the needs of their time; and although this has not prevented the development of denominational traditions and loyalties just as tenaciously held among their followers as among Presbyterians or Anglicans, it left them without a binding theory of the Church. It was not

withstood successfully any tendency to disappear in atomistic individualism, but only by strengthening the sense of corporate discipline that is typical of the 'sect.' There also seems to have been an implicit restorationism, which found in the forms of Quaker simplicity and worship a return to 'the spirit' of New Testament Christianity. This can become almost legalistic in its refusal to accept any more liturgical structure. When these community sanctions were established, Quaker 'tradition' was a potent force in keeping them alive in the societies. Similar tendencies in the sect-type direction seem to have been stimulated in the Schwenckfelder communities by Pietism. On the other hand, at the point in history when the sect-type and the 'mystical-type' come together, as in George Rapp's Harmony societies, church-type tendencies appear as soon as the group reaches the comparative freedom of Pennsylvania and can develop its own community structure without outside interference.

an accident that John Wesley could be called "a practical administrator, one of the greatest executive minds of his century," or that his "constant criticism of the British bishops was that their superintendency was not effective for *practical* godliness."[38]

There is some evidence that both Luther and Wesley originally considered moving in a restorationist direction,[39] but then for essentially practical (Luther) and reasonable (Wesley) considerations allowed their followers to be organized so that the needs of the time would be met. In point of ecclesiology both Luther and Wesley were ready to employ a kind of evangelical pragmatism, i.e., a pragmatism that was intended to serve the immediate objectives of the gospel.

Obviously we must be extremely careful to distinguish between this and the pragmatism that ultimately serves itself rather than the gospel, for the exponents of even the most enlightened forms of ecclesiastical pragmatism never seem to steer completely free of this danger. The pragmatic approach we are speaking about has a wholly evangelical goal—to proclaim the gospel in the service of God's world.

We have suggested that the doctrines of the Church may be classified theologically according to three basic approaches to the ecclesiological problem—the appeal to historical continuity through apostolic succession, to restoration of the New Testament ecclesia, and to evangelical pragmatism.

In the next part of this book we shall review them—first, because each has genuine insights that make an indispensable contribution to our understanding of the Church; secondly, because we need to understand the issues that stimulated the different forms of ecclesiology; and thirdly, because we must distinguish between the genuine insights contained within each doctrine of the Church, and the actual forms that the churches have taken.

Beyond this, and more fundamental than the disparity between churches as they are and churches as they conceive

38 Umphrey Lee, *John Wesley and Modern Religion* (Nashville: Cokesbury, 1936), p. 263. Italics mine.

39 Cf. below, pp. 130ff., 148ff.

themselves to be, there is the fact that the traditional channels of authority have been undermined if not discredited. It forces us to ask whether any ecclesiology is tenable today on its traditional basis, and to suggest that this makes our present situation full of danger, excitement, and promise.

This is why we cannot allow the ecumenical movement to get lost in sideshows, and why we need to become involved with full knowledge of the ecclesiological inheritance and of the task in which we are currently engaged. For perhaps the most exciting element in our situation is that Catholics and Protestants seem to be thrown into the same boat together, although not all churchmen recognize that with enthusiasm. It takes a lot of getting used to; but perhaps this is the opportunity God has granted to this eschatological time—the opportunity of seeking the new forms together, the willingness to be made one, "so that the *world* may believe."[40] From a human perspective, it appears to be our last chance.

[40] Cf. John 17:20-23.

PART TWO

HISTORICAL PERSPECTIVE

Chapter III

HISTORICAL CONTINUITY

Bertrand Russell's obituary in *Newsweek* observed that at the age of ninety-seven impatience is utterly rational. If the present reader feels that life is traveling too fast to spend part of it surveying the historical roots of the ecclesiological problem, he had better proceed directly to Part Four. For the sake of intelligent ecumenical involvement, however, we hope he will stay with us at least through the next three chapters.

The churches' crisis of authority is much deeper than the failure to impose obedience or to hold their members' allegiance. It has arisen from basic doubts about the 'infallible' channels of authority through which they have received the gospel and defined their own meaning and character. The crisis of Authority, as we define it, includes all that Jeffrey Hadden included under separate headings as the 'Crisis of Meaning and Purpose,' the 'Crisis of Belief,' and the 'Crisis of Authority'—all of which, he rightly showed, has issued in a fundamental identity crisis for the churches and their ministers.[1] The churches have reached an ecumenical impasse because their doctrines of the Church were traditionally represented as mutually exclusive rather than as mutually corrective, and ecumenical understanding centers in recognizing the historical dimensions of this ecclesiological dilemma.

[1] Jeffrey K. Hadden, *The Gathering Storm in the Churches.*

1

APOSTOLIC SUCCESSION

The most venerable ecclesiologies are those held by Catholics.[2] Their basis of spiritual authority is in the Church's historical continuity from the apostles, and their *esse* is found in the apostolic succession of the clerical hierarchy: i.e., the fundamental authority and structure of the Church is centered in the succession of episcopally consecrated bishops from the time of the apostles until now.

Traditional Roman Catholic doctrine carries this a stage further and relates the apostolic succession of bishops to the primacy and jurisdiction of Peter and the Roman pontiffs as his plenary successors. So Fr. Tanquerey's *Manual of Dogmatic Theology* moves from our Lord's foundation of the Church as a *society*, through the institution of the Church as a *hierarchical* society (by the calling of the apostles, the appointment of bishops as their successors, and the continuation of apostolic authority in the college of bishops), to the establishment of the Church as a *monarchical* society in the primacy of Peter, the recognition of the bishops of Rome as Peter's successors, and their consequent infallibility.[3] The various theses in this line of argument are regarded as 'historically certain and theologically *de fide.*'

The ordering of the argument—from apostolic (and episcopal) authority to Petrine (and papal) authority[4]—raises some

[2] The word 'Catholic' in this chapter is not limited to Roman Catholic, but includes all those churches that base their claim to universality on continuous tradition, whether Roman Catholic, Orthodox, or Anglican.

[3] A. Tanquerey (and J. B. Bord), *Manual of Dogmatic Theology,* trans. Msgr. John J. Byrnes (New York, etc.: Desclee, 1959), especially Vol. I, Part I, Tract III on "The Church of Christ." Within this tractate, chapter 2, "The Divine Institution of the Church is Proved from History," contains the main focus of the argument, although Tract IV, chapter 2, "The Authority of the Church," is also germane; pp. 95-140, 143ff.

[4] Tanquerey's *Manual* originated in French Catholicism, but a similar progression of thought may be traced elsewhere. Cf. *Sacrae Theologiae Summa* by Michaele Nicolau, S.J. and P. Ioachim Salaverri, S.J. (Madrid: Biblioteca de Autores Cristianos, 1952), Vol. I, Book II, chapters 1 and 2 (pp. 648-705). Theses 12-14 are particularly to the point: "12. Christ the Lord instituted authentic magistracy [magisterium] in the Apostles, to be perpetual and infallible. 13. The

nice points for future debate about the relationship of the Pope to the college of bishops and about the *real* center of infallibility in Roman Catholic tradition, and it at least poses the question of what will happen if the collegial 'infallibility' of the apostles' successors and of Peter's successors meet on collision course—issues that are no longer abstractions since Vatican II. Whatever the answers to these questions, the basis of the Roman Catholic Church's claim rests on its historical continuity with the Church of the apostles. One Roman Catholic writer, Msgr. Journet, put the issue frankly only a few years before the pontificate of John XXIII and Vatican II:

> If it has been revealed that the Church is to rest actually, structurally, and vertically, until the consummation of the world on the foundation of Peter and on the chain of his successors . . . it is implicitly revealed at the same time, by virtue of the exceptional privilege which was destined to cease with his death, that Peter could determine the conditions which would enable the chain of his successors to be recognized. By uniting in an indissoluble manner the office of bishop of Rome and the universal transapostolic office Peter made clear to the future Church in a precise way where the chain of his successors was to be found. This fusion of the two pontifical offices, this absorption of the first in the second, appears as a dogmatic fact.[5]

Msgr. Journet had no doubts about where the primacy lay, and he was simply stating what he held to be the traditional Roman Catholic position, although we recognize that today all Roman Catholics might not interpret the primacy of Peter or his successors in precisely that way. For our purpose, however, the principle is the same whether episcopal succession is regarded as dependent upon papal succession, whether the Pope is understood as *primus inter pares,* or whether episcopal

Bishops, as successors of the Apostles, are infallible, because both inside the Council and outside the Council, united under the Roman Pontiff they prescribe [imponunt] the doctrine to be definitively held by the faithful. 14. The Roman Pontiff, when he speaks *ex cathedra,* prevails because of that infallibility by which the divine Redeemer wills his Church to be instructed."

[5] Charles Journet, *The Primacy of Peter,* trans. John Chapin (Westminster, Md.: Newman, 1954), p. 104. Msgr. Journet, however, based his fundamental appeal not upon historical proof but on dogmatically conditioned faith: "But the indissoluble union of the office of the bishop of Rome and the universal transapostolic pontifical office and authority is a dogmatic fact for us, which history of course can never contradict, but which at the same time it can never establish, and which depends on a certitude higher than that of history" (p. 106).

succession is independent of Rome: the principle traces the *esse* of the Church to its historical and apostolic continuity.

This is illustrated in Eastern Orthodoxy. The position taken by the Eastern Orthodox churches must be distinguished from that of the churches in the West. That they maintain the three orders of hierarchy and apostolic succession through duly consecrated bishops is not in doubt, but the Orthodox do not appear to emphasize this succession *per se* as that which constitutes the Church: "the Orthodox Church is hierarchical, but in no wise a hierocratic Church, at least not in the sense in which this word is commonly understood in the West."[6]

The divine constitution of the Church is revealed in the principle of continuity itself—the Holy Tradition, which is to be understood as a unity of faith, order, worship, and ongoing life. "The unity which Orthodoxy represents," insisted the Orthodox spokesmen at Oberlin in 1957, "rests on identity of faith, order, and worship. All three aspects of the life of the Church are outwardly safeguarded by the reality of the unbroken succession of bishops which is the assurance of the Church's uninterrupted continuity with apostolic origins. This means that the uncompromised fulness of the Church requires the preservation of both its episcopal structure and sacramental life."[7]

This goes further in a Western 'validating' direction than most earlier Orthodox statements on the subject, possibly in reaction to ecumenical debate in a decidedly Western, Free-Church context. Most of the earlier statements were more concerned to show the wholeness of Orthodoxy's concept of unity than to put any undue emphasis upon the episcopal succession as such. Sergius Bulgakov declared that "to prove that in the first century there existed a hierarchy with three

[6] Stefan Zankov, *The Eastern Orthodox Church,* trans. and ed. Donald A. Lowrie (Milwaukee: Morehouse, 1929), p. 88.

[7] "Christian Unity as Viewed by the Eastern Orthodox Church"—a statement by the Representatives of the Eastern Orthodox Churches in the U.S.A. at the North American Faith and Order Study Conference; in *The Nature of the Unity We Seek,* ed. Paul Minear [The Official Report of the North American Conference on Faith and Order, September 3-10, 1957, Oberlin, Ohio] (St. Louis: Bethany, 1958), p. 161.

orders, in the sense accepted to-day, is hardly possible, and scarcely necessary,"[8] because it is the totality of the tradition (which includes episcopal succession, but is not necessarily constituted by it) that is basic. "It is," writes Paul Evdokimov, "the witness to the identity of the same faith, the same dogma, the same worship, the *same eucharist.* The 'apostolic succession' reveals the Church as the *permanent Sacrament of the Truth.*"[9]

When Professor Alivisatos presented his statement in the preparatory volume for the Lund Faith and Order Conference, he did not mention apostolic succession, although it is certainly implied when he says "an order in the visible Church through specially delegated men, to maintain the continuity of the governing body, is of vital importance for the very existence of the Church."[10] The actual evolution of administrative forms is of 'secondary importance' because once the Church had been constituted by Christ, it is what it is, and "there can be no substitute."[11] His claim is that the Church of our Lord is preserved within Orthodoxy, and that it "exists even now intact and is *preserved undivided and whole, unchanged and uncorrupt.*"[12] Historical continuity is therefore the evidence that the claims of the Church are those of the gospel.

On the other hand, for all its difference of emphasis from the churches of Western Catholicism, the Orthodox doctrine

[8] Sergius Bulgakov, *The Orthodox Church,* trans. Elizabeth S. Cram and ed. Donald A. Lowrie (London: Centenary, 1935), p. 52.

[9] Paul Evdokimov, *Orthodoxie* (Neuchâtel and Paris: Delachaux et Niestlé, 1959), p. 161: "c'est le témoinage de l'identité de la même foi, du même dogme, du même culte, de la *même eucharistie.* 'La Succession apostolique' démontre l'Eglise comme *Sacrement permanent de la Vérité.*" See also Alexander Schmemann's protest against juridical Western categories of thought in which most of the ecumenical debate is cast. "Orthodoxy," he states, "cannot be simply reduced to the 'Orthodox doctrine' of apostolic succession, seven sacraments, three degrees of hierarchy, and it is even doubtful whether such 'doctrines' exist in a clearly defined form." "Moment of Truth for Orthodoxy," in *Unity in Mid-Career,* ed. Keith Bridston and Walter D. Wagoner (New York: Macmillan, 1963), p. 55.

[10] Hamilcar Alivisatos, "The Holy Greek Orthodox Church," in *The Nature of the Church,* ed. R. Newton Flew (London: S.C.M., 1952), p. 46.

[11] *Ibid.*

[12] *Ibid.,* p. 44. My italics.

of the Church is just as—perhaps even more—rigorously exclusive:

> The Orthodox Church teaches that she has no need to search for a "lost unity," because her historic consciousness dictates that she is the *Una Sancta* and that all Christian groups outside the Orthodox Church can recover their unity only by entering into the bosom of that Church which preserved its identity with early Christianity.
>
> These are claims that arise not from presumptuousness, but from an inner historical awareness of the Orthodox Church. Indeed, this is the special message of Eastern Orthodoxy to a divided Western Christendom.
>
> The Orthodox Church, true to her historical consciousness, declares that she has maintained an unbroken continuity with the church of Pentecost by preserving the apostolic faith and polity unadulterated.[13]

This Oberlin document produced perhaps the most explicit statement regarding apostolic succession to be found in Orthodox writing:

> We regret that the most vital problem of ministry and that of the apostolic succession without which to our mind there is neither unity, nor Church, were not included in the program of the conference. All problems of order seem to be missing in the program. These, in our opinion, are basic for any study of unity.
>
> Visible unity expressed in organizational union does not destroy the centrality of the Spirit. Where there is the fulness of the Spirit, there too will outward unity be found. From apostolic times the unity of Christian believers was manifested by a visible, organizational structure. It is the unity in the Holy Spirit that is expressed in a unified visible organization.[14]

Both in the passage quoted earlier, in which the writers spoke of the "unbroken succession of bishops" as the "assurance of the Church's uninterrupted continuity with apostolic origins," and in this passage where Apostolic Succession is regarded as a witness to the reality of the Spirit, Orthodoxy seems to be expressing itself in more 'Western' categories.[15] In the twen-

[13] *The Nature of the Unity We Seek,* pp. 160f.

[14] *Ibid.,* p. 162.

[15] Cf. the following explicit statement on Apostolic Succession in George H. Demetrakopoulos' *Dictionary of Orthodox Theology* (New York: Philosophical Library, 1964), p. 17. This book is an introductory work for Western readers. Its precision, however, has lost something of the Orthodox emphasis on the wholeness

tieth-century ecumenical debate this was perhaps inevitable: or possibly that which was implicit was now made explicit.

Western Catholicism has not fully resolved the relation of the Pope to the collegiality of the Bishops. Some churches separated from Rome on this issue—old Catholic and Polish National Catholic—and enjoy intercommunion with the Anglican churches. The International League for Apostolic Faith and Order was supported mainly by this wing of Catholicism and by Anglo-Catholics, and although it would be unfair to suggest that valid episcopal succession is the only consideration,[16] it is certainly regarded as the prime consideration in guaranteeing the transmission of the apostolic faith. So in declaring its intention "to work for the unity of all Christians according to the Apostolic Faith and Order," the International League went on to define its terms:

> By "Apostolic Faith" is meant "the faith once delivered to the saints" (Jude 3), the living doctrine revealed by our Lord Jesus Christ, handed down to us from the Apostles through the Bible and preserved in purity by the Creeds and the fulness of the Holy Tradition of the undivided Church.
>
> By "Apostolic Order" is meant the priestly threefold ministry of bishops, priests and deacons duly consecrated or ordained by bishops in the Apostolic Succession and in the Communion of the Catholic Church.[17]

Apostolic succession through episcopal consecration is of the *esse* of the Church. Archbishop Andreas Rinkel of the Old Catholic Church pointed out the implications of this when he said, "We may never proceed to a recognition of it [presbyterian ordination] as equal with our own Ministry, and we shall

of its unity: "Apostolic Succession is the transmittal in a direct, continuous and unbroken line, of the powers given by Christ to the Apostles and to the successors of the Apostles, the bishops. Before the Apostles died, they passed on their powers by ordination to the bishops and priests. The bishops, in turn, transmitted them to their successors, and so on to the present day. Every bishop of the Orthodox Church can trace his line of succession back to the Apostles. The Apostolic Succession is one of the characteristics of the true church in contrast to those that have broken or completely rejected it."

16 Apostolic Order is always linked to Apostolic Faith. It guarantees the transmission of the Faith preserved in the apostolic kerygma, the creeds, and the undivided Church.

17 Michael Bruce (ed.), *Barriers to Unity* (London: Faith, 1959), p. 11.

never be allowed to regard the sacraments performed in the execution of such Ministry as valid sacraments as meant by the Mind of Christ and His apostles." Even if it is true that the New Testament leaves the question of Church Order unclear,

> . . . the faith-perception of the Church has given a definite answer, for the earliest Church completely adopted the episcopal system. Therefore a Church of Catholic origin will never be able to co-ordinate her Ministry with that of a presbyterian Church, and she must always consider the Ministry of the latter as imperfect and irregular; the more so because of old the Church declared herself, with full conviction, as bound from apostolic times to the regular and legitimate, and therefore holy, transmission of office by the laying-on of hands in the direct "ordination by the Holy Ghost" of which Acts 20:28 speaks.[18]

The Anglo-Catholic position that developed out of the Oxford Tractarian movement is identical with this position. "The apostolate which is first will also be last; it is permanent," declared Canon T. A. Lacey, and he went on to ask, "Then where do we find it now? We answer without hesitation that it is identical with the Episcopate. I think there is no other serious claimant."[19]

These quotations illustrate three basic questions that are raised by the Catholic position. In the first place, unless one is prepared to appeal to dogmatic faith (as Journet does), historical proof of a *continuous* succession in history is essential to this ecclesiology, and hence the argument seems to be centered in legality rather than in the things the gospel has at its center. So Bishop Gore brushed aside Lord Macaulay's doubts about the historical evidence for the theory, and argued that

> even if we take the absurd supposition of one consecrator in twenty at any particular moment of history having been, through some accident, himself not validly consecrated, the chances would be 8000:1 against all three consecrators in any given case being in like position, and the chances against a bishop consecrated under such circumstances, who would thus be no bishop, being combined with

18 *Ibid.*, p. 26.

19 *The Anglo-Catholic Faith* (London: Methuen; New York: Doran, n.d. [*circa* 1926]), p. 82.

> coadjutors similarly incapacitated to continue the succession, are "as 512,000,000,000 to unity."[20]

The impression we get is that this really mattered to Charles Gore. Any accidental break in the chain of valid episcopal consecrations really *would* have incapacitated the innocent victim and invalidated all his episcopal actions: the ecclesiology depends upon historical legality.

Secondly, for all churches, with the exception of the Roman Catholic Church, the theory of development presents problems, because one has to justify accepting the episcopal form that had been adopted by the time of Ignatius without being prepared to accept the Roman primacy that was commonly accepted by the fourth century.[21] Nikolai Grundtvig, the Danish Lutheran theologian, had a good deal of sympathy with the Tractarians and visited England several times between 1829 and 1843, but he discerned the dangers in Newman's Development Theory. After the reception of Newman into the Roman Catholic Church, Grundtvig's correspondent Nugent Wade observed, "two years ago you foresaw that all this might come any day in the case of Newman and those who with him adopted the Development Theory."[22]

Thirdly, for Anglicans the emphasis upon historical continuity raised a very acute ecumenical problem, for this effectively separated the Anglican Church from the Protestant churches which were its nearest neighbors. For all Grundtvig's sympathy with the desire to make the Church of England more catholic, he had to protest when the Tractarians insisted on the absolute necessity of the episcopal succession. "I am certainly afraid we

20 Charles Gore, *The Church and the Ministry* (London: Green, 1888; 1913), p. 99. Gore obtained the figures from W. E. Gladstone's *Church Principles*, pp. 235f.

21 The problem is one of consistency, and it leaves ecclesiologies based on episcopal succession squeezed between biblical restorationists on the one hand and the papacy on the other. Return to apostolic simplicity may be justified logically, and also a theory of development that accepts the eventual primacy that the Church accepted; but it is difficult to justify the selection of the brief period of monarchical episcopacy as normative for the Church in all ages.

22 P. G. Lindhardt, *Grundtvig: An Introduction* (London: S.P.C.K., 1951), p. 68, n. 5; see also Wade's letter of January 22, 1846, "How true a prophet you have proved about the issue of the New Theory of Development–it has landed there where you said it would." *Ibid.* Cf. also pp. 67f.

do not agree," he wrote to E. B. Pusey in 1843, "as you seem to exclude us and all congregations without a genuine bishop from the Catholic Church, and on the contrary from long standing and strong experience I am fully satisfied that not only my baptism but also my ordination as presbyter has been valid."[23] The issue was not whether bishops are desirable, but whether indisputable succession is essential for the Church.

This episcopal logic was expressed by the Anglican bishop Charles Gore, when he declared that "the various presbyterian and congregational organizations, however venerable on many and different grounds, have, in dispensing with the episcopal successions, violated a fundamental law of the Church's life"; and he went on to raise the issue of 'validity' that has haunted ecumenical discussions ever since:

> It follows then—not that God's grace has not worked, and worked largely, through many an irregular ministry where it is exercised or used in good faith—but that a ministry not episcopally received is invalid, that is to say, falls outside the conditions of covenanted security and cannot justify its existence in terms of the covenant.[24]

Here is the point of separation. The problem in this position is not so much that one group of Christians excludes other groups that claim to be churches—that may be painful but necessary in defense of truth—but because the reasons given for that exclusion are based on very questionable theology, and God is represented as normally judging those who confess him in terms of strict legality.

The year 1910, with the great missionary conference at Edinburgh, is usually regarded as the watershed of the modern ecumenical movement. Possibly under the influence of that new climate in ecclesiastical relationships, Canon J. M. Wilson stated the ecumenical issue to his fellow Anglicans:

> The real point seems to some of us to be to ascertain whether history shows that the Episcopal Churches, Greek, Roman, Anglican, and others, are so exclusively the branches of the Catholic Church that we are debarred by fundamental principles from recognizing the non-Episcopal bodies as true branches of the one Catholic Church; whether men are right in saying, what is sometimes stated, that we alone have a divinely commissioned fellowship, and that others have their ministry and their sacraments from below, that is, from human

[23] *Ibid.*, p. 66.

[24] Gore, *op. cit.*, p. 313.

> appointment. Are we justified in claiming exclusive privileges?—that sacramental grace is only given through Episcopal orders?[25]

J. M. Wilson seems to have recognized that by making historical succession the *sine qua non,* the Catholic branches of the Church had worked themselves into a theological box, from which if there was no means of entry there was equally no means of escape.[26] Maybe the box was the best of all possible boxes, and for Charles Schulz's Linus a box is the essence of security; but is security what the Church should be looking for? Was the concern of the Church simply to prevent those on the outside from being admitted? Furthermore, the very institution of episcopacy that was offered as evidence of the Church's unity actually manifested itself as evidence of schism, with Roman Catholics and Eastern Orthodox recognizing each other's bishops but refusing to have any dealings with each other, and neither church, at that stage, being prepared to recognize the Anglican bishops or the minor Orthodox churches in the Near East.[27]

One may hazard the guess that Wilson felt uneasy about the lack of solid theological base for the ecclesiologies based on succession, for he himself had gone a considerable distance towards providing one in his book, *The Gospel of the Atonement.* In this Wilson had argued that the Incarnation *is* the Atonement, and that all Christ's redemptive work should be subsumed under his willingness to become incarnate and to be made in the likeness of man. If the Church is regarded as a continuation of that incarnation its visibility and form are not irrelevant.

In an earlier work I suggested that it makes a significant

[25] Quoted in the Preface of *Essays on the Early History of the Church and the Ministry,* ed. H. B. Swete (London: Macmillan, 1918), p. ix.

[26] Wilson's concern seems to have stimulated the Archbishop of Canterbury to initiate a fresh study, which issued in H. B. Swete's *Essays (ibid.).* However, the book did not say much that was new and the authors simply repeated—albeit in a less angular tone—the positions previously expressed by Charles Gore. Very soon after this, however, under the influence of the burgeoning Faith and Order Movement, Anglicans were to review their doctrines of Church and Ministry with more care than any time since that of Newman and Pusey. I have discussed this in some measure in *Ministry,* pp. 45ff., 191ff.

[27] Cf. *Ministry,* p. 200; and *Catholicity of Protestantism,* ed. R. Newton Flew and Rupert E. Davies (London: Lutterworth, 1950), pp. 30f.

difference to our understanding of the Church and its sacraments whether the Incarnation or the Atonement is taken as the starting-point of theology—i.e., whether we take the divine *presence* among us or the divine *action* for our salvation as the fundamental revelation of God's nature.[28] Obviously there ought to be no fundamental opposition between the two approaches, but it is clear that one has been essentially Catholic while the other is just as essentially Protestant. J. M. Wilson rightly discerned that the theological basis of the ecclesiology represented in his own church was essentially incarnational, and the implications for the doctrine of the Church may be illustrated in the following quotation from W. N. Pittenger's *His Body the Church:*

> If it be true that the Church is the Body of Christ, it is also true that the development of that Body through the centuries must have some bearing upon its essential nature. Its development cannot have been a haphazard development if the Church is informed by the Holy Spirit. Now it is clear that within a very short time after the initial historical impulse which gave rise to the Christian movement, that movement had articulated its ministry into such form that the episcopate had been accepted as the ordaining agent for the Church. And once it had been so articulated, it was preserved with a surprising tenacity. It would therefore seem to be in some genuine sense integral to the Church as the Body of Christ.[29]

Beyond their historical exclusivism the Catholic branches of the Church have taken the Incarnation with complete seriousness, and this forces Protestants to be attentive to their witness. It brings us naturally to the positive contributions they offer to the Church.

2

THE CASE FOR

Truth is not governed by majority votes. That Catholics of all kinds outnumber Protestants by about four to one does not ultimately prove anything, but honest recognition of the sheer numerical weight of Catholics should induce the Protestant to look seriously at the theological principles which his Catholic

[28] *The Atonement and the Sacraments,* pp. 225-27, 282-86, 371-74.

[29] *His Body the Church* (New York: Morehouse-Gorham, 1945), pp. 80f.

brethren so tenaciously defend.[30] A Protestant who is concerned to be a Christian first and a Protestant only secondarily should not rest content until he understands why the Catholic feels that the Christian Faith itself is called into question when certain Catholic positions are challenged.

It is difficult and often misleading for one outside a particular ecclesiastical ethos to evaluate it, for there are many aspects of faith that cannot be understood until they have been experienced. But we must make the attempt, with apologies in advance to Catholic friends if through ignorance, unconscious prejudice, or plain dim-wittedness their position is misrepresented.

The most important theological aspect of the Catholic position is the central place it gives to the Incarnation, and the seriousness with which it translates into the concrete terms of human community the fact that in Christ God became incarnate: in its doctrines of the Church and the Sacraments it affirms that "*God* was *in* Christ reconciling the world *to himself*" (II Corinthians 5:19). This means that in their understanding of the Church, Catholic Christians are affirming that we must take with equal seriousness, first God's divine call and presence among us, and secondly, the fact that he uses the stuff of human existence, receiving it into himself, and enabling the human institutions of the Church to share in Christ's divinity as agents of salvation. Catholicism does not spiritualize the Church or deny its institutional character, nor does it disregard the divine initiative by turning the Church into a human voluntary society: fundamentally the Church reflects the incarnate nature of Jesus Christ.

We can summarize this in terms of the following three major emphases that are supremely important in our ecumenical endeavor:

(1) The Church is the result of God's initiative rather than the initiative of men. It is the community of those who have

30 In 1959 the authors of *Barriers to Unity* considered themselves to be a very small minority opposed "to the majority of the ecumenical movement" (p. 9). They found themselves "always on the defensive." In view of the great influx of Orthodox churches into the World Council of Churches since and the phenomenally rapid growth of Roman Catholic involvement since Vatican II, I doubt whether they feel so isolated today.

been "born not of blood nor of the will of the flesh, but of God" (John 1:13), and therefore the Church is 'given' and the form of the Church is not to be left to accident.

Despite its reliance on historical proofs Catholicism points to the fact that the nature of the Church is theological, i.e., that at its deepest level the Church reflects the nature of the God whom we worship, and that it does so in its organization, its inner life, and in its claims upon men. Just as the divine nature of God was integrated into a relationship with human nature in the person of Jesus Christ, so too the community instituted to fulfil that mission must manifest the divine presence in the form of a human society. The Church's unity is essential because God is a unity.

We have often been conscious of the structural parallels between the Roman Empire and the medieval papacy, but we have failed to see that beyond this, men thought of both civil and ecclesiastical society in this way because this was the way they thought of God's essential relationship to his Creation: the all-powerful, omniscient paternalism of both Church and Empire were no more than the reflection of God's supreme rulership of the cosmos. Whether we accept this today as an adequate view of the divine order or of God's essential nature is not the point at issue. We are simply pointing out that the *essentially* hierarchical form of the Church also mirrored within its structure what the people of that time regarded as God's essential relationship to the world. So the Church taught men and served men through its officers and brought Christ's sacrifice to them in the sacraments, but—reflecting its divine origin—it demanded obedience and stood supreme in honor, power, and visible glory. All forms of Catholicism from Episcopacy, through the Patriarchates to Papacy, were in this fundamental sense theological.[31]

(2) The Catholic branches of the Church emphasize that

[31] This should indicate why a radical revision in our understanding of God is intimately related to a radical review of the Church's visible structure, because what the Church *is* in society is an inevitable commentary upon what it is proclaiming about God. If this is true, then it also indicates why the Catholic branches of the Church, in order to have any viability, have been forced to re-examine the nature of hierarchical authority and the relationship of these structures to the essential concept of service.

the Church is called to operate *in this world.* They are committed to forms that are concrete, visible, and having structures that are also an essential part of the Church's nature. At this point they are more honest than certain kinds of Protestantism which often seem to suggest that there is something rather embarrassing about 'the Body' and imply that ecclesiastical institutions are really an unfortunate part of the heritage that we would discard if we were truly spiritual beings! Doubtless when we have arrived at the point in history where "the kingdoms of this world are become the kingdoms of our Lord, and of his Christ," there will be no need of a distinct and visible form of the Church, but one has never been very impressed by the Olympian dogmatism—whether of the 'right' or of the 'left'—of those who seem to know the date of the Kingdom's arrival. The Catholic churches emphasize that the human material out of which the Church is built is an essential part of its nature.

(3) This means that history is taken seriously. The Church is based upon events and is committed to a historical existence. From this stance Catholicism should never fall into the error of trying to reduce the Christian Faith to a set of principles or of confusing theology with philosophy. Beyond the fact that the Incarnation is a historical event and that God uses historical form to achieve his purpose, the significance of the Catholic churches' historicity is that God is concerned with what happens in history and respects the rules of the historical process. The eruption of God into history through the Incarnation is certainly a miracle, but it is not a miracle that destroys the historical context or sets aside the rules of time: our Lord was a man with a real birth, a real life, and a real death, and the Church on earth is subject to temporal rules as is any other society.

These considerations may help us see the emphasis upon historical continuity in a positive light. It should be noted that the Church grew up in a period when legal proof of natural origin was the fundamental claim to inheritance and legitimacy. Just as proof of human generation tells something about the legality of a person's claims to the family estate, and may even say a good deal about the characteristics he has inherited through the family's genes, so apostolic succession should tell us something about the Church's inheritance and may incidentally say something about the spiritual characteristics of the household of faith. Not that these emphases can be regarded as absolute, since strange things can happen even in families with an impeccable heredity; but neither are they totally irrelevant. Something of the form and features of apostolic Christianity has been preserved in the various forms of Catholicism, or there would have been no Augustine, no history of medieval devotion, no Bernard of Clairvaux or Francis of Assisi, no Sisters of Mercy, no Mount Athos or record of Orthodox devotion through the bitter years of Ottoman power, no Lancelot Andrewes or Thomas Ken. Furthermore, for all the charisma exercised by such witnesses, the gift of the gospel in Catholicism is essentially possessed and transmitted by a sacramental community: as far as possible the transmission of the faith and its mysteries is removed from the whims and vagaries of individuals and set within concrete, essentially corporate and tangible institutions that have their existence in history.

These, I suggest, are positive theological aspects of the Catholic position that cannot be ignored if the ecumenical plea for the 'fulness' of the Church is to be taken seriously.

3

THE CASE AGAINST

There is, of course, another side. When Sydney Smith, the nineteenth-century English wit, was asked if he believed in apostolic succession, he is reputed to have said that he had to believe in it, for how otherwise could he explain the succession of the Bishop of Exeter from Judas Iscariot![32] In expressing his distaste for Dr. Philpotts, Smith was simply using an argument that had been more seriously, if more ponderously, employed by sixteenth-century Separatists against the Elizabethan bishops.[33] Behind it was the claim that there is an integral relationship between our theology and the way we act,

32 Sydney Smith was a Whig and Dr. Philpotts was a convinced Tory.

33 See Robert Harrison's *A Little Treatise on the firste Verse of the 122. Psalm,* quoted in *Ministry,* pp. 204f. For Harrison and his Separatist contemporaries it was

between doctrine and ethics: although we may allow that an individual theologian may have an impeccable theology but be a bad man morally, a *doctrine* of the Church that produces unchristian actions says something very important about the claims of that church to be *the* Church. Therefore, when the actions of the Elizabethan bishops, considered not only as individuals but as a corporate episcopate, appeared to be contrary to the ethics of the New Testament, the argument from historical continuity boomeranged onto the heads of those who used it.

These arguments, however, are not valid against historical continuity, historical concreteness, or apostolic succession as such. They have validity only when the logic of historical continuity drives Catholics to the point of claiming that it is the one indispensable guarantee of the gospel, the *sine qua non,* for the end-result of that claim is to make historical legality more important than the supreme Christian law of love. It is against this background that the following criticisms should be seen.

(1) The Catholic position theoretically holds a balance between the human framework and the divine calling of the Church, but in practice the emphasis upon the Church as a continuation of the Incarnation often leads to a deification of the institution and its hierarchy. As I have said in another place, Catholic teaching believes, with a good deal of biblical justification, that if the Church is the Body of Christ, then it is also by implication the extension of his incarnation in Time. The visible Church itself is an indispensable and integral part of God's act of Redemption. But the problem becomes acute for Protestant and Catholic when, arguing from this link between the Incarnation and the Church, the further step is taken to identify the institutional Church with our Lord's sinlessness, and by that means to claim sinlessness and infallibility for a particular institutional Church as his Body. Many of those who argue from the Catholic position boldly make this claim, maintaining that although Christians may sin, the

obvious that Rome was antichrist—the persecutions of Mary I's reign were only a generation away—and since the Anglican bishops traced their consecration to this source, the implication was self-evident; for how could a bad tree bring forth good fruit?

Church cannot sin precisely because it is his Body in the world.[34]

The corrective of this is to understand the Church as an extension of the Incarnation *only for the purpose of redemption:* it gives evidence of 'perfection' only as it fulfils and exemplifies the redemptive purposes of its Lord. Indeed, this 'perfection' of the Church is not something it can claim but only something it can be awarded: we cannot claim by right that which God grants us by grace.

The danger is that of being tempted to drive the logic of God's divine call to the point where the institution becomes obsessed with its own special character and privileges. When that happens the sin of Lucifer is not far away, and it is not surprising that the institution begins to deny by its actions the *agape* that should be the chief evidence of the Holy Spirit's presence, the basic proof of its claims. It then produces a doctrine of the Church in which the Church appears to have no further need of penitence, and in which the means of grace are so automatically bestowed and so legally written into the structure that 'grace' itself becomes a denial of its own true nature.[35]

(2) Emphasis upon the Visible Church, to the point of virtually denying the possibility of salvation beyond it, reinforces this exclusivity. Catholic writers who point out that the New Testament knows nothing of the 'Invisible Church' that the Reformers seem to have picked up from Augustine are correct, but perhaps the Reformers' use of the idea should be

[34] *The Atonement and the Sacraments,* pp. 282f.; cf. pp. 225-27, 283-87, 371-74. This book was published in 1960, before the present trend in Roman Catholic theology was evident. Cf. also *Ministry,* pp. 95-100, 122-25.

[35] The danger of deification was pointed out by J. B. Sumner, the Evangelical Bishop of Chester in the early nineteenth century. In a charge issued against the Tractarians in 1842, he declared, "We may personify the body for the convenience of discourse, and by degrees forget that the community is not a person. And it is worse still if the body which was first personified comes afterwards to be deified. Yet a process of this kind has gone on with regard to the Christian Church. The Church has been made an abstraction, and then a person, and then a Saviour. The Church thus invested with divinity, has the minister as her visible representative; and he . . . has assumed the place of God." As quoted by B. D. Till in *The Historic Episcopate,* ed. Kenneth M. Carey (Westminster: Dacre, 1954, 2nd ed. 1960), p. 88. Dean Till added the comment that "No doubt the Evangelicals undervalued Church order but their protest against an undue exaltation has a permanent place in Christian thought."

seen in relation to the pastoral situation they faced. By employing the idea of the 'Invisible Church' they held that the Church, known to God, is not limited to the empirical Church that we know; and this concession might mean that they were trying to find room for the charity of the gospel—i.e., they were trying to avoid the dogmatic exclusivism that they saw in the Roman Catholic Church (which limited salvation to those in communion with the see of Rome), and in the Anabaptists (who limited salvation to those who obeyed literally the New Testament injunction to 'repent and be baptized'). One cannot defend the Reformers when they were as unchristian as their opponents, nor does one necessarily wish to keep the idea of the Invisible Church; but the warning that comes through the use of the term is that in stating our view of the Church we must leave room for a charity that goes beyond our sight and knowledge.

(3) A distinction must be drawn between a doctrine of the Church that respects the historical context and human institutions, and one that virtually binds God's actions to them. Does the Incarnation so limit the Holy Spirit to historical agents that these can always claim to act in his name, always claim his authority for their effective decisions, always fix the boundaries to grace? Certainly our Lord gave the 'power of the keys' to the Church,[36] but what happens when the institutional 'Church' claims this privilege while negating the Spirit of our Lord in exercising it? Does this power extend to the point where representatives of the Church can claim they act in Christ's name when they are obviously acting in private interests, in pique or prejudice, or when they enforce their will by means that are in flat contradiction of the gospel? This is a crucial area for future definition in ecumenical discussion, but from our present standpoint we must, like the Latin particle *num,* imply the answer 'No!'

(4) In sum, the critics argue that to base the doctrine of the Church *essentially* on the Church's historical continuity with the Church of the Apostles is to reduce the action of the Holy Spirit in the Church to legality. Their criticism is a protest against pushing logic to the point where it negates the gospel

[36] Matthew 16:18-20; 18:15-20.

and disregards the fruits of the Spirit that are essentially spiritual and ethical. Lineal descent, such as the tactual consecration of bishops from the apostles, may prove the historical foundation and succession of the episcopal office, but it proves nothing about the essential transmission of the Holy Spirit, or the essential relationship of the ecclesiastical institution with the Living Christ: "by their fruits ye shall know them." The basic criticism of Catholic theory is that you cannot use law to prove the possession of grace. The appeal to historical legitimacy is fundamentally an appeal to law, but the essential quality of the Church belongs to grace.[37]

On the other hand, there are substantial signs that the force of this criticism is not unrecognized even within those churches that have been the most rigorous champions of apostolic succession. In discussing Luther's strictures against Rome, for example, Hans Küng freely admits that the Catholic Church "will have to acknowledge culpability," and says "in this connection we must, however, take note that the apostolic character of the Church must be credibly present 'not in the persuasive words of wisdom, but in the demonstration of the Spirit and of power, that your faith may rest, not in this wisdom of men, but on the power of God' (I Cor. 2:4 f.)" [38] This seems to be another way of saying that any ecclesiology that claims to be based on that which constitutes the *esse* of the Church must manifest the Spirit of Christ. For, to quote Küng again, "neither do appeals to Catholic tradition nor to the Protestant Reformation release them [Catholics and Protestants] from the obligation to *embody* the constantly new, which is the crucial factor, if one desires the designation 'apostolic': namely, *essential agreement with the apostolic message.*"[39]

The change among Roman Catholics has been even more pronounced since Hans Küng's book appeared, and the authors of the theological study on the priestly life and ministry sponsored by the U.S. bishops appear to have put the issue to their own bishops about as bluntly as it could be put:

37 Cf. the illustration in *Ministry*, pp. 85f.

38 *Structures of the Church* (New York: Nelson, 1963), p. 107.

39 *Ibid.*, p. 110. My italics.

> As scholars reflect on the data of scripture and the earliest tradition of the church, they realize that the older popular understanding of apostolic succession has been too mechanical and oversimplified. It has perhaps been too quickly assumed that the 12 apostles appointed immediate successors, from whom in turn further successors were commissioned in an unbroken historical chain down to the present day . . . .
>
> The episcopal college does not derive its union with the apostolic college from any sort of formalistic or ritual continuity. Rather it appears more in consonance with historical and theological evidence to say that the prerogatives of apostolicity derive from the basic apostolic character of contemporary church doctrine, which is in essential accord with the faith of the apostolic church. For this reason, the authenticity and effectiveness of ministry in other Christian churches may be evaluated along lines different from our previous norms.[40]

The genesis of this revision in Rome's traditional stance towards the doctrine of the Church is to be found in Vatican II and its documents—not only in that *Lumen gentium* begins with the biblical concept of the Church as the pilgrim People of God rather than with the primacy of its hierarchy, but in the spirit that is made explicit in the *Decree on Ecumenism*. These documents indicate that however revered historic continuity and apostolic succession may have been as the bases of Rome's claims, they cannot be allowed to proscribe recognition of the Holy Spirit's work in others.

Of course, the fact that a theological report is officially sponsored does not mean that it is necessarily going to be accepted; and the doubts raised by theologians do not mean that modern Catholics, Roman or otherwise, are forthwith prepared to relinquish all their traditional positions. Furthermore, if Protestants are serious about looking for the Church of Jesus Christ in its fulness, they should probably not wish them to do so; but it does suggest that as we look towards the Christ of the scriptural revelation we find ourselves closer together. It also offers the hope that the churches will become less exclusive and more truly catholic.

[40] From the extracts in *The National Catholic Reporter*, 7/42 (October 8, 1971), 14. Cf. also Carl J. Armbruster and John J. Begley, "Ministry, Office, and Ordination," in *Worship*, 45/8 (October 1971), 450-464.

Chapter IV

BIBLICAL RESTORATIONISM

The founder of Howard University told of a Congregational gentleman taking an Episcopal lady to his church. As they walked she tried to show him how far his church fell short of being the true Church. "The gentleman replied as they entered the vestibule: 'All right; perhaps yours is better than mine as you claim, but this one, dear madam, is mine! Your home may be nicer than ours, yet ours is ours!' "[1]

The story well illustrates the individualism of nineteenth-century Protestantism. The reply of a seventeenth-century Congregationalist would have varied in only one particular, but it would have implied a universe of difference: 'All right; perhaps yours is better than mine as you claim, but this one, dear madam, is God's! Your home may be nicer than ours, yet ours is God's!'

However much psychological, aesthetic, and other factors may have contributed to the pluralism of the Church, the original differences in ecclesiology were justified only by an appeal to higher authority than that of individual preference. If the Catholic appealed to the historical continuity of his church with the apostles, the Protestant claimed that he was restoring to the Church the apostolic character that had been lost or smothered.

The confrontation of these two standpoints was illustrated

[1] Major-General Oliver Otis Howard in his introduction to Albert E. Dunning's *Congregationalists in America* (New York: J. A. Hill, 1894), p. xvii.

by the late Douglas Horton when he compared the position taken by the Counter-Reformation Cardinal Bellarmine (1542-1621) with that of the Puritan theologian, William Ames (1582-1637). "The thinking of these two men," Horton observed, "met and clashed. The meeting was unambiguous, head-on . . . ."[2] Both believed in a view of the Church that was *de jure divino.* Bellarmine believed that the Church was composed of those, and only those, who were in communion with the historic see of Rome (i.e., historical continuity); Ames believed that the Church was composed of those who were gathered in the strict New Testament pattern (i.e., biblical restorationism), and equally for him there could be no other church. The issue was a simple 'either . . . or'—the *esse* of the Church resided *either* in its apostolic continuity with the Church of the past, *or* in its apostolic fidelity to the form of the New Testament community. There was no room for compromise.

1

REFORMATION RESTORATIONISM

Any reform movement is almost necessarily a movement of restoration, an attempt to return to a purer, simpler, and more authentic form. As John T. McNeill says, "with a considerable degree of insight, though not with logical consistency, the early Protestants attempted, in thought and organization, the recovery and promotion of catholicity in Christianity."[3] The key-word for our purpose is 'recovery': it was a conscious attempt to go back to the earlier, more simple and, from their point of view, more apostolic form of the Church.

The biblical restorationism in many Protestant doctrines of the Church springs from the Reformation principle of *sola scriptura.* The Reformers appealed to a spiritual authority that they held was a purer, more authentic repository of God's will for the Church than the Petrine succession. Both Catholic and Protestant made absolute claims for the principle of authority

[2] *Toward an Undivided Church* (New York: Association and Notre Dame, 1967), p. 14.

[3] *Unitive Protestantism* (Richmond: John Knox, 1964), p. 87.

recognized by their churches, but the former had the medieval legacy. In comparison with that legacy, the Scriptures seemed far less subject to adulteration by the wickedness of men or the whims of history: In the sixteenth century the Bible could be represented as the infallible 'Word of God' in an absolute and very concrete sense.

It is true that political circumstances, particularly the support of civil authorities, often caused Protestants to modify this principle; but, in order to maintain their position, it was essential that such modifications should often remain hidden to the Reformers themselves. Zwingli could not obey the full logic of his scriptural position on the question of baptism, and he thereby laid himself open to the charge of inconsistency by the Anabaptists; but by specious use of Old Testament references to circumcision he was able to justify his position to his *own* satisfaction;[4] face to face with the political realities of the 1520s, Luther had to modify his early suggestions for a more scriptural form of the Church, but by stretching a few biblical passages[5] he was able to hand over the organization of the Church to the princes with a clear conscience.[6]

The Anabaptists, in contrast, were entirely logical. For example, the Swiss Brethren took their stand uncompromisingly on the authority of the simple biblical evidence both for their doctrine of the Church and more specifically for their view of baptism.[7] It is recognized that although "Anabaptists such as Grebel were familiar with the classical ideal, the prevalence of religious primitivism in Anabaptism is due more to the fact that Christianity is a historical religion with a

[4] Cf. his treatise *On Baptism* in *Zwingli and Bullinger,* trans. and ed. G. W. Bromiley (Library of Christian Classics, XXIV, 1963), pp. 129ff.

[5] E.g., Romans 13:1-7; I Timothy 2:2; I Peter 2:17.

[6] This is intended to sound ironical, because the Reformers were not only unable to accept the logic of their exclusive scriptural foundation, but were unwilling to admit that they had shifted their ground. There were sound enough *theological* reasons for changing their position; the criticism is not that they modified the absolute rule they had set up, but that they hid this fact from themselves and continued to speak as if their position was unchanged.

[7] Cf. the implicit literalism on this point in Conrad Grebel's "Letters to Thomas Müntzer" in *The Anabaptist and Spiritual Writers* (Library of Christian Classics, XXV), pp. 73ff.

sacred book in which all reforms seek their inspiration and confirmation."[8] They were biblical restorationists.

This represents the historic position of the churches that trace their history directly to sixteenth-century Anabaptism,[9] and to later churches that have sought inspiration in that movement.[10] The appeal was essentially to Scripture, and to the plain meaning of Scripture. Balthasar Hübmaier, in propounding his *Eighteen Dissertations* (1524)—clearly a very preliminary document in the direction of reform—admonishes his readers "by the bonds of brotherly love, by the holiness of Christian peace, and by the name of our Lord Jesus Christ, that in these dissertations, you may perceive a Scriptural foundation,"[11] and he charges them when they come together to "bring your Bibles, or in case you have none, your mass-books with you,[12] so that we may share one with another, and thoroughly, the God-given words of Christian instruction."

One has to remember the newness of the Bible to these people, the immense release of being able for the first time to read 'God's word' in one's own native tongue, and, in reaction to scholastic theology, the incentive to give the words of Scripture a simple and literal meaning. The Schleitheim Confession of 1527 is noteworthy because it was occasioned by the activities of "certain false brethren" which had caused some to turn aside "in the way they intend to practice and

[8] Franklin Littell, *The Anabaptist View of the Church* (later published in paperback by Macmillan as *The Origins of Sectarian Protestantism,* 1964) (Boston: Starr King Press, 2nd ed. 1958), pp. 54f. Cf. especially chapter 3, "The Restitution of the True Church."

[9] Mennonites and Hutterites.

[10] E.g., the Baptists, and various forms of the Brethren movement.

[11] "Eighteen Dissertations concerning the entire Christian life and of what it consists, Propositions upheld at Waldshut by Dr. Balthasar Friedberger, and others," printed in *Baptist Confessions of Faith* by William L. Lumpkin (Chicago, etc.: Judson, 1959), p. 20. Lumpkin points out that Hübmaier often used the pseudonym 'Friedberger,' since he was born in Friedberg.

[12] They were asked to bring their mass books for perhaps two reasons—to provide a point of comparison with the Bible's pattern of churchmanship, but also because of the biblical material they contained. For many this would be the only book they possessed.

observe the freedom of the Spirit and of Christ."[13] The issue seems to have been between those who claimed the immediacy of the Spirit as final authority and those who held to the plain meaning of Scripture, and for the Anabaptist leaders at Schleitheim "the command of the Lord is clear."[14] In reply to all those who questioned the tenets of their position, they simply say, "Hear what the Scripture says," "Observe the meaning of this Scripture," or "Hear the Scripture."[15] That was sufficient: in all matters connected with the ordering of the Church and the discipline of the Christian life these Anabaptists had one concluding and conclusive rule, "Christ is simply Yea and Nay, and all those who seek him simply will understand His word."[16]

By the time Calvin came on the scene, the Reformation was far more stable than it had been in the time of Zwingli or Luther. Although Calvin is not to be confused with the Anabaptists or with their simplistic literalism, the relative stability of his situation allowed a much more clearly articulated doctrine of the Church than had been possible for his predecessors.[17] His approach to this as to all other aspects of doctrine was fundamentally scriptural, and to that extent it was implicitly restorationist—quite clearly an alternative to the Roman system. Moreover, there were factors in the situation, particularly as it developed in Britain, that would push Calvinists into a much more literal approach to the Scriptures and hence further into a restorationist doctrine of the Church.[18]

13 *Ibid.*, p. 24. The Schleitheim Confession is printed in *Baptist Confessions of Faith*, pp. 23-31.

14 *Ibid.*, p. 26.

15 *Ibid.*, p. 29.

16 *Ibid.*, p. 30. Note, too, the emphasis upon 'the perfection of Christ' in which the disciple is expected to walk (p. 27). It occurs again in the insistence of English Separatists and Puritans that the members of the Church are to be 'visible saints.' This, and other similarities in their doctrines of the Church, does not prove that the English were influenced by Continental Anabaptism, but suggests rather that they approached the Bible in the same way.

17 *Institutes of the Christian Religion*, Book IV, chapters i-xix. This becomes more clear in chapter ii, in comparing 'the False and the True Church,' and in chapter iii, when Calvin begins to discuss the church officers. His point of reference is always the biblical pattern.

18 Here we must insert a note about the way in which literalism seems to have developed. It is often assumed that it was a necessary consequence from the *sola*

The practical result of this was that the churches that followed Calvin and those influenced by Anabaptism both tried to justify their forms of the Church by a direct appeal to the Church of the New Testament. They might argue long and acrimoniously among themselves about the forms of baptism, or in favor of presbyterian or congregational polity; but they appealed to the same authority—the New Testament Church. Even the early episcopal Calvinists did not hesitate to appeal to the New Testament Church in justifying the Church of England against the Church of Rome. At the beginning of his *Apology* Bishop John Jewell says that "if we do show it plain, that God's holy gospel, the ancient bishops, and the primitive church do make on our side, and that we have not without just cause left these men, and have rather turned to the apostles and the old catholic fathers . . . we then hope and trust, that none of them will be so negligent and careless of his own salvation, but he will at length study and bethink himself, to whether [i.e., which] part he were best to join him."[19] Later in the same work he made the claim, "we have called again to the original and first foundation of that religion which hath been so foully foreslowed [neglected] and utterly corrupted by these men. For we thought it meet thence to take the pattern of reforming religion, from whence the ground of religion was first taken; because this one reason, as saith the most ancient father Tertullian, hath great force against all heresies: 'Look, whatsoever was first, that is true; and whatso-

scriptura principle of the Reformers, and this certainly headed Protestants in that direction. But the Reformers were not literalists and each employed his own hermeneutical principle. Similarly the early Puritans were not the literalists and restorationists they became later.

The reasons for the change may be sought in the events of Elizabeth's reign. Henry Jacob was to point out that in their struggle with the Puritans the Episcopalians would have to shift their ground (below, p. 101) and in the writings of John Whitgift, Richard Hooker, and Richard Bancroft this shift was made. The episcopal writers argued, in effect, that where Scripture was silent, rules could be made for the Church (and must be obeyed) simply by royal will. In opposition to this, the Puritans had to claim a higher law than that of the Queen, and the Bible became the book of God's law to which they inevitably appealed. To do the Puritans justice, we have to recognize that the episcopal legalism they opposed was a major factor in driving them into biblical literalism.

19 *An Apologie or answere in defence of the Churche of Englande,* III, 56. Cf. *Library of Christian Classics,* XXVI.

ever is latter, that is corrupt.' "[20] That is implicit restorationism.

On the other hand, in their arguments with Puritans the Episcopalians very soon took their stand on other grounds. Cotton Mather put it very succinctly when he said, "In short, the first Age was a golden Age: to return to that, will make a man a Protestant, and, I may add, a Puritan."[21] All Puritans stood for the restoration of the primitive Church, and similarly all kinds of restorationism, from seventeenth-century Presbyterians, Congregationalists and Baptists, to nineteenth-century Disciples or twentieth-century Pentecostalists, are in a measure puritan. However, despite their agreement about the basic scriptural authority for the doctrine of the Church, the intermural argument about polity has been bitter—does the New Testament evidence 'prove' presbyterianism, or were the New Testament churches congregational?[22]

2

THE GRAND DEBATE

The classic form of this particular debate took place in the Westminster Assembly during the English Civil War of the seventeenth century. In 1643 the English Parliament sought the help of the Scots in the war against Charles I, and one of the prices they had to pay was to sign the Solemn League and

[20] *Ibid.,* p. 100. Perry Miller quotes Bishop John Hooper of Worcester (and Gloucester) as saying, "Leave not until the matter be brought unto the first, original, and most perfect church of the Apostles. If thou find by their writings, that their church used the thing that the preacher would prove, then accept it; or else, not . . . . " Quoted from Hooper's *Early Writings,* p. 83, in Miller, *Orthodoxy in Massachusetts 1630-1650* (1933; Boston: Beacon, 1959), p. 17.

[21] *Magnalia Christi Americana; or Ecclesiastical History of New England* (London, 1702; Hartford, Conn.: Silus Andrus, 1853), I, 27.

[22] Note the plural form—'churches.' The 'congregational' interpretation of the New Testament held that each congregation was independent, and therefore these denominations have regarded themselves as 'churches' in association or union rather than as 'a Church.' The virtual change from a restorationist ecclesiology was illustrated when the former Congregational Christian Churches become a part of the United *Church* of Christ in 1957, or when the Congregational *Union* of England and Wales became the Congregational *Church* in England and Wales in 1967.

Covenant. It should be noted that the Scots had endured at least three attempts during the preceding forty years to impose the English form of episcopacy on the Scottish Kirk, and one can hardly blame them for using their military advantage to nail this threat once and for all. The English commissioners, who were certainly not Episcopalians, found themselves promising:

> That we shall sincerely, really and constantly, through the grace of God, endeavour in our several places and callings, the *preservation* of the reformed religion in the Church of Scotland . . . ; the *reformation* of religion in the kingdoms of England and Ireland . . . *according to the Word of God,* and the example of the best reformed Churches; and we shall endeavour to bring the Churches of God in the three kingdoms to the *nearest conjunction and uniformity* in religion, confession of faith, form of Church government, directory for worship and catechising, that we, and our posterity after us, may, as brethren, live in faith and love, and the Lord may delight to dwell in the midst of us.[23]

The English Parliament was certainly not averse to ecclesiastical change in the Reformed direction. The calling of the Westminster Assembly in 1643, with its overwhelming preponderance of members who favored the presbyterian system, is a clear indication of that; but the Scots apparently thought the main task of the Assembly was to ratify a form of the Church that had been already determined by the Solemn League and Covenant, namely, that it would sanction and encourage the imposition of the Scottish ecclesiastical system throughout the British Isles.[24]

23 Italics mine. Article I, in S. R. Gardiner, *Constitutional Documents of the Puritan Revolution* (Oxford: Clarendon, 1913), p. 268. See also the nineteenth-century reissue of the complete work of the Assembly, *The Confession of Faith, the Larger and Shorter Catechisms. . . . Covenants, National and Solemn League . . . . Directories for Public and Family Worship; Form of Church Government, etc.* (Pittsburgh: United Presbyterian Board of Publication, 1871), p. 465.

24 The italics in the passage quoted above accent the points that are significant. Note the distinction that the reformed religion is to be *preserved* in Scotland, but introduced to England and Ireland by a *reformation* of the churches there. For the Scots, the engagement of the English Parliament to bring the Church of England 'to the nearest conjunction and uniformity in religion' (i.e., identity with the Scottish form) was no idle promise, and the emphasis on uniformity is carefully maintained. For example, when *The Form of Church Government and of Ordination of Ministers, agreed upon by the Assembly of Divines at Westminster* was published by the Scots in 1645 its title-page announced it as "part of the covenanted uniformity in religion betwixt the Churches of Christ in the Kingdoms of Scotland, England,

Perhaps it was not accident that among the negotiators sent to Scotland by the English Parliament were two convinced Congregationalists—Sir Henry Vane, who had briefly been governor of Massachusetts during the Anne Hutchinson dispute, and the Reverend Philip Nye, one of the most adroit political ecclesiastics of the seventeenth century, who had been converted to the 'Congregational Way' through the writings of John Cotton.

It was due to the insistence of these men that the passage quoted above included the provision that the intended 'reformation' should be 'according to the Word of God.' For all their emphasis upon uniformity and deference to 'the example of the best reformed Churches,' even the Scottish presbyterians could not disagree with that clause without implying that their system would not stand up to the scriptural test. It was on the basis of this very little caveat that the important debates on polity took place in the Westminster Assembly, and the small band of half a dozen or so Independents (Congregationalists)[25] initiated a filibuster that lasted almost fifteen months!

Almost the only parts of the Assembly's work that are remembered are the Westminster Confession of Faith and the Catechisms; and since these are all concerned with credal doctrine and not specifically with justifying the presbyterian order of the Church,[26] this has meant that the scriptural basis

and Ireland"; and the Act of General Assembly which authorized publication and was printed with the Order made it quite clear that this uniformity—"now more straitly and strongly united by the late Solemn League and Covenant"—was seen fundamentally as a bastion against any future invasion of the Scottish Kirk by the Church of England (p. 504).

25 The English Congregationalists in the Civil War were called 'Independents' by their opponents. Cf. the protest of the Dissenting Brethren: "*That* proud and insolent title of *Independencie* as affixed unto us, as our claime; the very sound of which conveys to all mens apprehensions the challenge of all Churches from all subjection and dependence, or rather a trumpet of defiance against whatever *Power, Spirituall* or *Civill;* which we doe abhor and detest: Or else the odious name of *Brownisme* . . . must needs be owned by us: Although . . . it hath been acknowledged we differ much from them." *An Apologeticall Narration,* pp. 23f.

26 There was no need to deal with the doctrine of the Church in detail in the Westminster Confession or in the Catechisms, since the Form of Presbyterial Church-Government had already been issued as a separate authoritative document of the Assembly. So chapter XXV "Of the Church" in the Confession deals with the visible Church in general terms, but does not say anything about polity,

claimed by the fathers of modern presbyterianism has been obscured. Reference to the brief extract from the Solemn League and Covenant quoted above will indicate that the Scots projected a comprehensive system that would include a "Confession of faith, form of Church government, directory for worship and catechising."

This program was precisely carried out. The publication of the Westminster Confession and of the Larger and Shorter Catechisms was preceded by the appearance of the Form of the Presbyterial Church-Government and of the Ordination of Ministers, and of the Directory for the Public Worship of God, both of which dealt with matters that were much more urgent for the situation in Britain at that time than the restatement of doctrine by a unanimously Calvinist Assembly. These earlier documents virtually contained the only matters of real dissension among the members of the Assembly.

The Form of Presbyterial Church-Government[27] begins with the statement that "There is one general church visible, held forth in the New Testament," and that "the ministry, oracles and ordinances of the Church are given by Jesus Christ." Furthermore it insists equally with Congregationalists that "Particular churches in the primitive times were made up of visible saints, viz. of such as, being of age, professed faith in

although the presbyterian system put forward by the Assembly was implicit in chapters XXX and XXXI, which treat "Of Church Censures" and "Of Synods and Councils." For example, it is stated that the decrees of synods and councils, "if consonant to the word of God, are to be received with reverence and submission, not only for their agreement with the word, but also for the power whereby they are made, as being an ordinance of God, appointed thereunto in his word" (XXXI.iii). Even so, this was stated in a form that would permit the Independent members of the Assembly to accept the Confession. We should expect, therefore, the Confession and Catechisms to be rather less precise on these debated points than the Form of Government.

The Larger Catechism includes a few questions relating to the visible (Questions 61-63) but concentrates upon the Invisible Church (Questions 64-66, 82, 83, 86), but the Shorter Catechism includes virtually nothing on the Church. This is clearly because the Form of Government had already appeared and was the authoritative pronouncement on church polity.

27 The quotations are from the 1871 Pittsburgh edition of the documents of the Westminster Assembly, *The Confession of Faith, the Larger and Shorter Catechisms, with the Scripture-Proofs at Large . . . . Directories for Public and Family Worship, Form of Church Government, etc.,* issued by the United Presbyterian Board of Publication. The Form of Presbyterial Church Government is on pp. 503-534.

Christ, and obedience unto Christ, according to the rules of faith and life taught by Christ and his apostles; and of their children."

On the church officers, pastors, teachers, elders and deacons, the two branches of the Reformed faith could reach general agreement, as also on the principle that the government of the Church is *de jure divino:*

> Christ hath instituted a government, and governors ecclesiastical in the church: to that purpose, the apostles did immediately receive the keys from the hand of Jesus Christ, and did use and exercise them in all the Churches of the world upon all occasions.
>
> And Christ hath since continually furnished some in his church with gifts of government, and with commission to execute the same, when called thereunto.
>
> It is lawful, and agreeable to the word of God, that the church be governed by several sorts of assemblies, which are congregational, classical,[28] and synodical.[29]

So far, so good. It was only when the Form of Government went on to assert that "The scripture doth hold forth, that many congregations may be under one presbyterial government," and to 'prove' this by asserting that the 'churches' in Jerusalem and Ephesus consisted of many congregations and were therefore under a unified presbytery, that the Independents objected. And similarly, they objected when it was asserted that "It is lawful, and agreeable to the word of God, that there be a subordination of congregational, classical, provincial, and national assemblies, for the government of the church"; or when the new order argued that the New Testament placed the power of ordination exclusively in the hands of the presbytery.

One has to look behind the Form of Presbyterial Church-Government, however, and even beyond its array of scriptural

[28] I.e., organized in 'classes' or presbyteries. Cf. John Cotton's distinction, "Wherefore if there must needs be some note of difference to decypher our estate, and to distinguish our way from a National Church-way, I know none fitter, then to denominate theirs Classicall, and ours Congregationall." *The Way of the Congregational Churches Cleared* (1648), p. 11.

[29] "Of Church-Government, and the several sorts of Assemblies for the same." It is interesting that no biblical proofs are adduced for this *de jure divino* position, possibly because the divines were conscious of the opposition to this concept among the Erastians in both the Assembly and Parliament.

proofs, to discover the real toughness of the debate and the firmness with which both parties maintained biblical justification for their own forms of church government. In 1647 the House of Lords ordered that all the documents relating to the debate about the presbyterian Order should be printed, and these appeared as *The Grand Debate Concerning Presbytery and Independency* in 1652.[30] A survey of this material reveals that the arguments were based upon literal exegesis of the New Testament texts dealing with the nature and form of the Church, and rigorously debated according to the principle set down in the Westminster Confession that "the infallible rule of interpretation of scripture is the scripture itself, and therefore, when there is a question about the true and full sense of any scripture, (which is not manifold, but one) it must be searched and known by other places that speak more clearly."[31]

This fundamental appeal to Scripture and the restorationist claim was made explicit by an influential group of London ministers in 1646. They published an apologia for the presbyterian system, *Jus Divinum Regiminis Ecclesiastici: or, The Divine Right of Church-Government, asserted and evidenced by the Holy Scriptures, etc.*[32] More significantly, this book was republished in 1844, not as an antiquarian curiosity but as a sound statement of what Presbyterians believed then about the doctrine of the Church.[33] The 1844 title-page makes the restorationist claim even more explicit, if that is possible, than it was in 1646, viz., *The Divine Right of Church-Government:*

30 The contents of *The Grand Debate* read like an ecclesiastical 'house that Jack built.' This tedious method of charge, detailed answer, counter-charge, etc. was simply the normal way in which ecclesiastical debate was conducted in the sixteenth and seventeenth centuries. Most of these papers had been published during the course of the Assembly's work, 1643-45, and the Order of the House of Lords simply meant that this material was brought together in a convenient form.

Its significance for our purpose is that it represents almost 400 pages of detailed biblical proof-text reasoning.

31 Westminster Confession, I, ix. Cf. the parallel statement from William Perkins, below, p. 102.

32 Cf. Robert Baillie's comment about the appearance of this book, in his letter to William Spang, January 26, 1646/7. *The Letters and Journals of Robert Baillie, A.M.*, ed. David Laing (Edinburgh, 1861-2), III, 2, and n. 1.

33 The book was edited by 'T. H.' of Paisley, Scotland in 1799, and published in a "New Edition, Corrected and Amended" by R. Martin, New York, in 1844. It is significant that the middle of the nineteenth century saw the republication of a

wherein it is proved that the Presbyterian Government, by Preaching and Ruling Elders, in Sessional, Presbyterial, and Synodical Assemblies, may lay the only lawful claim to a Divine Right, according to the Holy Scriptures. This claim was put forward by means of the following logical steps:

> The rule or standard of church government is only the holy Scriptures. Thus in the description, church government is styled a power or authority revealed in the holy Scriptures. For clearing hereof, take this proposition, viz.: Jesus Christ our Mediator hath laid down in his word a perfect and sufficient rule for the government of his visible Church under the New Testament, *which all the members of his Church ought to observe and submit unto until the end of the world.*[34]

This is clear and unambiguous biblical restorationism.

The authors argued that since Jesus was certainly an even more faithful servant of God than Moses, who had laid down very specific rules for Israel, "can we imagine that he hath not as carefully laid a pattern of church government to his apostles, and the Church officers of the New Testament, the Church being now come to full age and maturity?" They asserted that "the holy Scriptures are now completely and unalterably perfect, containing such exact rules for the churches of God in all states and ages, both under the Old and New Testaments, that not only the people of God, of all sorts and ages, but also the men of God, and officers of the Church, may be made perfect, thoroughly furnished unto all good works." And, "if the Scriptures be thus accurately perfect and complete, they must needs contain a sufficient pattern, and rules of church government now under the New Testament." They went on to affirm that "all the substantials of church government under the New Testament are laid down in the word in particular rules, whether they be touching officers, ordinances, censures, assemblies, and the compass of

great deal of orthodox Calvinist doctrine, e.g., William Beveridge's translation of Calvin's *Institutes,* 1845; the complete *Works* of John Owen, 1850-1855; and the complete *Works* of Thomas Goodwin, 1861-1864. This was clearly a vigorous response to the attacks that were coming from the German biblical critics, the High Anglican Tractarians, and the scientists.

34 Italics mine. The quotations are from the 1844 edition (New York: Martin), pp. 53ff.

their power . . . and all the circumstantials are laid down in the word, under the general rules of order, decency, and edification . . . . Consequently," they declare, "there is a perfect and sufficient rule for church government laid down in the Scriptures, which is obligatory upon all."

One could hardly find biblical restorationism stated any more explicitly than this. That this was basically the official position of Presbyterian churches until well into the nineteenth century is also indicated by the wide distribution of Samuel Miller's *Manual of Presbytery,* which held that presbyterianism was "the only truly primitive and apostolic constitution of the Church of Christ."[35]

The classical forms of Congregationalism were similarly restorationist. This is amply demonstrated in the *Reasons* given by the Dissenting Brethren in *The Grand Debate,* but it is equally true whether one thinks of Congregationalism as a development of sixteenth-century Separatism, or, as modern scholars tend to do, as a Puritan movement that arose alongside the Presbyterian and Separatist views in the early seventeenth century.[36]

From the Separatist side it is not so much explicitly stated as clearly assumed. Robert Browne indicates his exegetical method in the preface to *A Booke which sheweth the life and manners of all true Christians,*[37]

> first we take heed to the words of the text that we understand the meaning. If some words be doubtful or the manner of speaking, we search out that. . . . This pain I took, to search out of the Scrip-

35 Philadelphia: Presbyterian Board of Publication, 2nd ed. 1847. This volume also contained a work by the Rev. John G. Lorimer on "The Character and Advantages of Presbyterianism ascertained by Facts." Earlier printings of Miller's work had appeared in 1835, 1836, and 1840. I am indebted to M. Eugene Osterhaven for showing that the *de jure divino* position also appears in Charles Hodge's *Discussions in Church Polity* (New York: Scribner, 1878), p. 123, in Robert Ellis Thompson's *The Historic Episcopate* (Philadelphia: Westminster, 1910), and in the nineteenth-century work by Thomas Witherow, *The Apostolic Church: Which Is It?,* which was reprinted (Glasgow: Adshead) as late as 1954.

36 Following the researches of Champlin Burrage in his *The Early English Dissenters,* and Perry Miller's *Orthodoxy in Massachusetts* (Cambridge, Mass.: Harvard, 1933).

37 Published at Middleburg, Holland, in 1582. *The Writings of Robert Harrison and Robert Browne,* ed. Peel and Carlson, pp. 221-395.

> tures, all the points of Divinity, and to set them in order as is shewed in the book, and then also to apply the whole Scriptures unto them, not only in meditation and writing, but also in speech and mutual edifying.[38]

The scriptural and restorationist basis of the Separatist doctrine of the Church is also seen in the biblical texts used at every point of Henry Barrow's *A True Description out of the Worde of God, of the Visible Church;*[39] but more particularly it is the implicit assumption behind all the Separatists' writings.

The Congregational Puritans came to a very similar ecclesiastical position through their own independent study of the Scriptures. The Dissenting Brethren of the Westminster Assembly, having considered the 'dark part' of church government, i.e., the negative aspects of administration and worship in the Church of England, declared:

> we were cast upon a farther necessity of enquiring and viewing the *light part,* the positive part of *Church-worship* and Government; And to that end to search out what were the first Apostolique directions, pattern and examples of those Primitive Churches recorded in the New Testament, as that sacred pillar of fire to guide us. And in this enquirie, we lookt upon the word of Christ as impartially, and unprejudicedly, as men of flesh and blood are like to doe in any juncture of time that may fall out.[40]

In the course of this enquiry they applied certain basic principles, the first of which puts them firmly within the restora-

38 *Ibid.,* pp. 224f. I have somewhat modernized the spelling for the sake of clarity.

39 Which appeared probably in 1589. It is printed in *The Writings of Henry Barrow, 1587-1590,* ed. Leland H. Carlson (London: Allen & Unwin, 1962). Cf. *The Writings of Henry Barrow, 1590-1591* (1966) and *The Writings of John Greenwood, 1587-1590* (1962). In a joint writing by Barrow and Greenwood, *The True Church and the False Church,* the authors say, "Before we can judge the false church, it is expedient that we discerne the true church, which is described in the Scriptures. The true planted and rightlie established church of Christ is a companie of faithfull people; seperated from the unbeleevers and heathen of the land; gathered in the name of Christ, whome they trulie worship, and redily obey as thier only king, priest, and prophet; joyned together as members of one bodie; ordered and governed by such officers and lawes as Christ in his last will and testament hath thereunto ordeyned; all and each one of them standing in and for thier christian libertie to practice whatsoever God hath commanded and revealed unto them in his holie word . . ." (p. 98).

40 *An Apologeticall Narration,* p. 3.

tionist camp, for they declare, "First, the supreame rule *without us*, was the Primitive patterne and example of the churches erected by the Apostles. Our Consciences were possessed with that reverence and adoration of the fulnesse of the Scriptures, as to make the *man of God perfect*, so also to make the Churches of God perfect . . . if the directions and examples therein delivered were fully known and followed."[41] They admitted that they did not have a perfect answer for all possible contingencies, but they had enough to go on, "and the observation of so many of those particulars to be laid forth in the Word, became to us a more certaine evidence and cleare confirmation that there were the like rules and ruled cases for all occasions whatsoever, if we were able to discerne them." Where they could not find clear scriptural evidence they suspended judgment "untill God should give us further light."[42]

The restorationism is explicit in Henry Jacob, who is an earlier and somewhat neglected figure in the history of seventeenth-century Congregationalism. Champlin Burrage, indeed, thought that the beginnings of Independency (Congregational Puritanism) could be traced to Jacob, and there is some evidence for that view.[43] Even more significantly, it has been shown recently that Jacob seems to personify the point where the Puritan and Separatist wings of the movement met.[44] In 1604 he appealed to the new king, James I, that the Church of England should be reformed in accordance with scriptural principles. *Reasons taken out of God's Word and the best humane testimonies proving a necessitie of reforming our Churches in England* was written while Jacob was still a

41 *Ibid.*, p. 9.

42 *Ibid.*, p. 10.

43 See Champlin Burrage, *op. cit.*, I, 33f.; also Robert S. Paul, "Henry Jacob and Seventeenth-Century Puritanism," *Hartford Quarterly*, 7/3 (Spring 1967), 92ff., and especially pp. 107-113.

44 The older argument about whether Jacob influenced John Robinson or vice versa is sterile: the influence appears to have been mutual. Cf. Paul, *op. cit.*; and J. von Rohr's "*Extra Ecclesiam Nulla Salus:* An Early Congregational Version," *Church History*, 36/2 (June 1967), 107ff. For other recent material on Jacob, see von Rohr's "The Congregationalism of Henry Jacob," *Transactions of the Congregational Historical Society* (London), 19/3 (October 1962), 107ff.; and Walter R. Goehring, "The Life and Death of Henry Jacob," *Hartford Quarterly*, 7/1 (Fall 1966), 35ff.

minister in the Church of England, but it immediately got him into trouble with the authorities. More important for our purpose, it shows clearly the direction in which his thinking about the Church was taking him, for at the very beginning of the book Jacob laid down four basic theses:

> 1. It is necessarie to reforme the Churches of England, their Ministries and ceremonies.
>
> 2. For the space of 200 years after Christ the Visible Churches using government were not Diocesan Churches, but particular ordinary Congregations only; and the Bishops (as they were peculiarly called after the Apostles) were only Parishionall not Diocesan Bishops, differing from other Pastors only in prioritie of order not in Majoritie of rule.
>
> 3. The Scriptures of the New Testaments do containe & set forth unto us (besides the government by Extraordinary Offices, Apostles, Prophetes, Evangelistes) an ordinary form of Church-government used then.
>
> 4. The ordinary form of Church-government set forth unto us in the New Testament, ought necessarily to be kept still by us; it is not changeable by men, and therefore it only is lawful.[45]

Restorationism could not be any more explicit than that. "Who is it," he asks, "that may presume to ordaine any forme of a Church save Christ only?"[46] Jacob takes the highest of Puritan 'high church' positions, because to him the Church is an indispensable part of the plan of salvation: "To want any maine part of the ordinary appointed meanes of salvation," he argues, "is 'contrary to God's word' and necessarie to be reformed. But the right and true Discipline Ecclesiasticall in *each* proper *Visible Church,* is one maine part of the ordinary meanes of salvation appointed by God for every soule: and this we in England do utterly want."[47] Therefore reform of the Church for Jacob sprang from his concern *for* the Church, and at this point the seventeenth-century English Puritan and the tridentine Roman Catholic spoke the same language. Indeed, against the Anglicans in general and Thomas Bilson,

45 The *Reasons,* A.1.verso.

46 *Ibid.,* p. 25.

47 *Ibid.,* p. 51. The 'high church' character of Jacob's ecclesiology is brought out more fully in von Rohr's articles, cited above.

Bishop of Winchester, in particular, Henry Jacob pointed out that "the very Papistes do see and acknowledge this that I say; viz. both that these grounds of the Scriptures absolute perfection in all Ecclesiasticall matters (whereon we exactly do stand) are the true and right principles of the *Protestants* Religion & also that the Diocesan L[ord] Bishops, do, and must needes turne away from these principles, & deny them when they deale with us . . . ."[48] Bellarmine might not agree with Ames, but at least he could appreciate the basis of the position.

The scriptural basis, with its implicit restorationism concerning the Church, was the supreme authority for Puritans of almost all kinds. Thomas Cartwright, the most important figure in the attempt to reform the Elizabethan church,[49] gave Scripture an absolute primacy in the study of theology,[50] and William Perkins,[51] who probably had a more profound influence on the next generation of Puritans than any other, declared that "The soveraigne or supreame judgment concerning matters of faith belongeth to the holy Ghost speaking in the Scriptures. The ministerie of judgement (or a ministeriall judgement) is onely given unto the Church because she must judge according to the Scriptures; and because she does not this alwaies she sometimes faileth."[52] More specifically in matters of ecclesiastical dispute he said that "the supreame &

48 *Reasons,* p. 71.

49 Cartwright (1535-1603) had been briefly Lady Margaret Professor of Divinity at Cambridge in 1569, but had raised a storm by the Puritan reforms and church structure that he advocated in his lectures. He was deprived of his chair and his fellowship, but wrote the Second Admonition to Parliament in 1571 and conducted a vigorous literary war with John Whitgift. Whitgift, who became Archbishop of Canterbury in 1583, prevented him from any suitable preferment in the Church of England; but Cartwright remained the most prominent figure among Elizabethan Puritans.

50 Cf. Cartwright's letter, "For Direction in the Study of Divinity" in *Cartwrightiana,* ed. Albert Peel and Leland H. Carlson (London: Allen & Unwin, 1951), pp. 109-115.

51 William Perkins (1558-1602) was a Fellow of Christ's College, Cambridge, 1584-1592, and was the most influential Calvinist at the university in his time. Although he died as a comparatively young man, his influence extended far beyond his own country, and he "was esteemed in the seventeenth century little inferior to Hooker or Calvin."

52 *The Art of Prophesying,* in Perkins' *Works* (1609 ed.), II, 735.

absolute determination & judgement of the controversies of the Church" ought to be given to the Bible.[53]

Perkins is also significant because he was the leading exponent of the effective Puritan 'plain style' of preaching.[54] It was not only the centrality of the Bible that was important, but also the way in which it was interpreted. In his influential treatise, *The Art of Prophesying,* Perkins declared that the fourfold approach to scriptural exegesis allowed by the mediaeval theologians—the literal, allegorical, tropological, and anagogical interpretations—"must be exploded and rejected. *There is one onely sense, and the same is the literall.* An allegorie is onely a certaine manner of uttering the same sense. The Anagoge and the Tropologie are waies, whereby the sense may be applied."[55] His limitation of interpretation to the literal meaning is not quite as absolute as at first he implied, but he certainly gives priority to the obvious sense of the text,[56] for "the supreame and absolute meane of interpretation is the Scripture it selfe."[57] He warns ministers against reliance on their own erudition or cleverness.[58] In his preaching the minister is so to "behave himself, that al, even ignorant persons &

53 *Ibid.,* p. 732.

54 For more on the Puritan 'plain style' see William Haller, *The Rise of Puritanism* (1938; New York: Harper Torchbook, 1957), pp. 128ff.; and John F. Wilson, *Pulpit in Parliament* (Princeton, N.J.: Princeton U.P., 1969), pp. 173ff.

55 *Works,* II, 737.

56 Paradoxically, in this expository method we see the beginnings of a critical approach to the biblical text. Cf. the following: *"If a word given in the Bible, whether it be an Hebrew word or a Greeke, if first it doe agree with Grammatical construction, and with other approoved copies: if also it doe agree in respect of the sense with the circumstances and drift of the place, and with the analogie of faith, it is proper and natural.*

I lay downe this rule, not because I thinke that the Hebrew and Greeke text is in all copies corrupted through the malice of the Jewes, as *Lindanus* doth wickedly calumniate, and after him all Papists; but that the divers readings, which in some places have crept in, either by reason of the unskilfulness, or negligence and oversight of the Notaries, might be skanned and determined." *Ibid.,* p. 749.

57 *Ibid.,* p. 737.

58 "*Humane wisdome* must be concealed, whether it be in the matter of the sermon, or in the setting forth of the words: because the preaching of the word is the *Testimonie of God, and the profession of the knowledge of Christ,* and not of humane skill . . . .

If any man thinke that by this meanes barbarisme should be brought into pulpits; he must understand that the Minister may, yea & must privately use at his unbeleevers may judge that it is not so much he that speaketh, as the Spirit of God in him and by him."[59]

So as the debate on the nature of the Church came to its climax in the struggle between King and Parliament, the Puritan went to his primary source and looked for its plain meaning. Henry Burton, for example, in a sermon before Parliament in 1641, urged that

> if any Minister shall doe any thing in the Church of God, which he is not able to prove out of the Scripture; if he preach otherwise, If he use any manner of Ceremony, administer the Sacrament, which he cannot prove, make a law, that they may be punished . . . .[60]

This was the basic position from which the doctrine of the Church was thrashed out during the interminable sessions of the Westminster Assembly, and in the voluminous pages of Presbyterian and Congregational ecclesiology. It produced the argumentative spirit of the soldiers in Major Bethel's troop who, Richard Baxter complained, "allowed of no Argument from Scripture but what was brought in its express words,"[61] for fundamentally it was an appeal to an authority that everyone could read and understand, to the plain sense that was in Scripture before theology had become a university monopoly, and to the simple Church before My Lord Prelate had identified it with the hierarchy.

libertie the artes, philosophy, and varietie of reading, whilest he is in framing his sermon: but he ought in publike to conceale all these from the people, and not to make the least ostentation. Artis etiam est celare in artem; it is also a point of Art to conceale Art." *Ibid.*, p. 759.

59 *Ibid.* See also the place where Perkins emphasizes the way in which a preacher should appeal to his hearers—in hatred of sin and love for the sinner: "But alwaies, in the very hatred of sinne, let the love of the person appeare in the speeches: and let the Minister include himselfe (if he may) in his reprehension, that it may be more milde and gentle" (p. 757).

60 *Englands Bondage and Hope of Deliverance*, preached before Parliament, June 20, 1641 (1641), p. 32. Cf. the sermon preached before the House of Lords for a Fast Day, Feb. 24, 1646/7 by Nathaniel Hardy, in which he said, "as Law is the bound of a Commonwealth, so right Reason is the limit of Law; and as Religion is the bound of a Church, so Scriptures are the limit of Religion, beyond which nothing ought to be required as essential and necessary." *The Arrainment of Licentious Libertie and Oppressing Tyrranie*, February 24, 1646/7 (1647), p. 9.

61 *Reliquiae Baxterianae*, ed. Matthew Sylvester, Part I, p. 54. It should be pointed out, however, that among the same troops Baxter found some who were "against the tying of our selves to any Duty before the Spirit move us" (p. 53). The religious ferment of the time included everything from rigid literalists to those who rejected all authority but immediate revelation.

3

THE CONTINUING THEME

For every early Presbyterian or Congregational writer who took this stand we could cite others from the ranks of the Baptists, the Disciples, the Brethren, or from later groups such as the Assemblies of God. Biblical restorationism is a recurring theme in the history of the Church, and particularly in the history of Protestant ecclesiology.[62] It has been the natural response of those who have been forced to appeal to the simple meaning of Scripture and the simple form of New Testament Christianity against the various kinds of legalism by which ecclesiastical establishments supported their position and prestige.

Restorationism is at the heart of the original Baptist movement. Historically the Baptist churches arose out of the Separatist-Puritan movement in England, and must be seen as a part of that movement. The General (Arminian) Baptists originated from the Scrooby-Gainsborough Separatists who emigrated to Holland in 1608 under John Smyth and John Robinson. Smyth's group settled in Amsterdam, and under his leadership the members accepted believers' baptism but returned to England in 1612 under Thomas Helwys when their pastor decided to join the Mennonites.[63] Similarly the Particular (Calvinistic) Baptists arose from a split in 1641 within the Puritan congregation that Jacob had established at Southwark in 1616. They produced the first Baptist Calvinistic confession in 1644.

As Dale Moody observed, after the appearance of the West-

[62] Perhaps the most thorough recent study of doctrines of the Church among Protestant 'Free churches' is Donald F. Durnbaugh's *The Believers' Church* (New York: Macmillan, 1968). Durnbaugh includes some good treatments of restorationism (pp. 146-172, 216-220). The main point at which we differ is that I see restorationism as normative for *all* reforming movements: the attempt to realize 'the Believers' Church' is, in some sense, always an attempt to return to an earlier and more authentic form of Christianity. This I suggest is true even when biblical authority gives way to a more charismatic principle, or when one aspect of New Testament Christianity (e.g., primitive communism, or eschatology) appears to take precedence over the rest.

[63] Cf. Champlin Burrage, *op. cit.*

minster Confession, "almost all Particular Baptist confessions followed it except in regard to believers' baptism and congregational government."[64] Their differences with the confession were not due to any quarrel with its basic doctrines, but were simply another example of the intramural argument among restorationists represented in the Grand Debate. This can be seen from the form and content of the articles on the Church in Baptist confessions of the period.[65]

Baptists represent an extension of the Separatist-Puritan movement. By their insistence on the scriptural basis for believers' baptism and their repudiation of infant baptism, the Baptists carried restorationism further than either Presbyterians or Congregationalists were prepared to go. In origin, Baptists are of all Protestants perhaps most essentially restorationist; as a Baptist scholar commented, "Popularly they have expressed their historical premise by the simple formula: Whatever can be learned about the beliefs and practices of the first generation of disciples must be followed conscientiously."[66]

This position was forcefully reasserted, for example, as late as 1944 in H. E. Dana's *A Manual of Ecclesiology.*[67] Dana reviewed the various forms of polity adopted by confessional families, and he very significantly made a distinction between the government of the Congregational Church and what he regards as the true congregational polity.[68] The restorationism of his denominational position is explicit:

64 In *What Is the Church? A Symposium of Baptist Thought,* ed. Duke K. McCall (Nashville: Broadman, 1958), p. 16.

65 Cf., for example, the articles together with their biblical proofs in the English Declaration at Amsterdam (§§9-13), The Propositions and Conclusions of 1612 (§§ 64, 65, 69), The London Confession of 1644 (§§ XXIX, XXXIII-XXXVI), and the Second London Confession of 1677 (chapter XXVI), Lumpkin, *Baptist Confessions of Faith,* pp. 116ff., 124ff., 154ff., 241ff. These are simply illustrative; any of the early confessions would bear out the same point.

66 S. A. Newman in McCall's *What Is the Church?,* p. 46. For other Baptist views of the Church, see Winthrop S. Hudson (ed.), *Baptist Concepts of the Church* (Chicago: Judson, 1959).

67 Kansas City, Kansas: Central Seminary Press, 1944.

68 *Ibid.,* pp. 148f. "The *Congregational* Church government lies between what we have described as congregational and connectional polity. The Congregational churches regulate their own affairs, but the Church at large acts in local matters in

> The Congregational type of church government is represented among the Baptists, Disciples, Seventh Day Adventists, and others. *It is the modern reproduction of apostolic church polity.* The center of organization is the local church which is a sovereign and independent body, with no organic relation to any other church or governing assembly of representatives from local churches. This type of church government has all that is essential to effective organization: *it is the most faithful reproduction of the real New Testament idea of the Church;* and very forcefully commends itself to common reason by its simplicity and democracy. Since it possesses these superior qualities, and, through nineteen centuries of history, has proven itself adequate to all the needs of the kingdom, it has established beyond question its right to prevail.[69]

Despite its obvious restorationism, this actually represents a step away from the older and stricter Baptist tradition, for the claims of evangelism have exerted a relentless pressure on Baptist polity towards pragmatism.[70] However, Dana clearly

an advisory capacity. They believe in what they call 'the fellowship of the churches,' and seek to maintain an organic relation between the local churches, and hence are really of the connectional type. Their church organization is quite similar to Presbyterians" (p. 148). The distinction Dana hints at is really that which we observe between the atomistic independency of Separatism and the Puritan Apologists of the Westminster Assembly. Cf. *Apologeticall Narration,* p. 23; cf. also pp. 5, 21, and John Cotton's *The Way of Congregational Churches Cleared* (1648), p. 11.

69 *A Manual of Ecclesiology,* p. 149. My italics. This is not the only view represented among Baptists. Some Baptists trace their heritage to the Congregational Puritan tradition, and are no less insistent than Congregationalists on 'the fellowship of the churches.' Cf. *Review and Expositor,* 52/4 (October 1955), and also Hudson, *op. cit.*

70 There is also a strong pragmatic emphasis in his polity (cf. *op. cit.,* pp. 199f.). I am indebted to one of my graduate students, the Rev. Walter Ellis, for the following note on this pragmatic trend in the Baptist churches:

During the eighteenth century revivalism produced a loose evangelicalism which was reflected among Baptists in a drift towards a more pragmatic ecclesiology; this is evidenced by the experimentation of the New Connexion General Baptists and the formation in Great Britain and America of special interest societies which rivaled the associations. Andrew Fuller (1754-1815), who also served as secretary of the Baptist Mission Society, asserted that the Bible provided no fixed pattern of government or worship, and he advocated the use of reason in developing church order, while others such as Isaac Backus (1724-1806) and John Leland (1754-1841) advocated radical congregational independency. Finally, the democratic individualism of Francis Wayland (1796-1865) produced a view of the church as but another voluntary society whose polity should be determined by its function—the conversion of souls. By 1825 strict biblical reconstruction had been all but abandoned as the foundation of Baptist polity and practice. Cf. Winthrop Still Hudson, "The Association Principle Among Baptists," *Foundations,* 1/1 (January 1958), 10-23; also *Baptist Concepts of the Church;* Robert G. Torbet, *A History of the Baptists*

indicates the dependence of ecclesiology on one's basic authority. "As we seek criteria for the definition of the fundamental principles and practices of church activity, to what source shall we look?" asks Dana; "nothing is more important to the study of ecclesiology than to be clear on this point."[71] He then reviews the doctrines of the Church based on Tradition, Expediency, and Scripture, which run parallel to our own classification of Historical Continuity, Evangelical Pragmatism and New Testament Restorationism. The significance of his position is that although he does not believe that the scriptural pattern imposes "detailed and mechanical rules,"[72] as the earlier restorationists often did, he still believed that

> this scriptural church polity is not only feasible, but it is the most effective that can be devised for successfully promoting the interests of God's kingdom on earth. If truly scriptural, then it may be regarded as having the approval of Christ and as the authoritative norm that should determine the life of his churches in all ages. *This view frankly and positively accepts the New Testament as the authoritative source of church polity.* It is believed that it was the Savior's purpose to leave a general pattern for the church in his written record of revelation, and that any radical departure from this apostolic pattern is a perversion of his divine plan.[73]

Whether that runs true to the spirit of the first century may be a matter for argument; but few could doubt that it stays reasonably close to the spirit of the seventeenth!

The Disciples are of particular interest because, despite the Scots-Irish background of Thomas and Alexander Campbell, the movement belongs to the nineteenth-century American frontier. Yet the emphasis on the simple interpretation of the New Testament and restorationist ecclesiology is as pronounced in the early history of the Disciples as in sixteenth-century

(Philadelphia: Judson, 1950); and his article "In What Sense Is the American Baptist Convention a Manifestation of the Church?", *Foundations,* 8/2 (April 1965), 117-131. Of particular interest in this regard is an English pamphlet to be found in the American Baptist Historical Association Archives at Rochester, N.Y., "On the Utility of Associations," *The Circular Letter From the Ministers and Messengers of the Buckinghamshire Association of Baptist Churches, Statedly Meeting at Chesham, Assembled at Risborough, May 27, 1818.*

71 *Op. cit.,* p. 196.

72 *Ibid.,* p. 201.

73 *Ibid.,* pp. 200f. My italics.

Separatism.[74] The Disciples, said Alexander Campbell, "regard all the sects and parties of the Christian world as having, in greater or less degrees, departed from the simplicity of faith and manners of the first Christians, and as forming what the apostle Paul calls 'the apostacy.' "[75]

Their restorationism was given classic expression in the "Declaration and Address" of his father, Thomas Campbell:

> Dearly beloved brethren, why should we deem it a thing incredible that the Church of Christ, in this highly favored country, should resume that original unity, peace, and purity which belong to its constitution, and constitute its glory? Or, is there anything that can be justly deemed necessary for this desirable purpose, both to conform to the model and adopt the practice of the primitive Church, expressly exhibited in the New Testament? . . .
>
> Were we, then, in our Church constitution and managements, to exhibit a complete conformity to the apostolic Church, would we not be, in that respect, as perfect as Christ intended we should be? And should not this suffice us?
>
> It is, to us a pleasing consideration that all the Churches of Christ which mutually acknowledge each other as such, are not only agreed in the great doctrines of faith and holiness, but are also materially agreed as to the positive ordinances of the Gospel institution . . . .[76]

For Disciples, Christ's will, "published in the New Testament, is the sole law of the Church."[77]

The movement is important for another reason. More clearly than any other restorationist group the Disciples reveal that restorationism has often been motivated by a fundamentally ecumenical intention. Many of these churches have been estab-

[74] For a full discussion of the tension between Christian unity and restorationist exclusivity among Disciples, see George Hugh Wilson, *Unity and Restoration in the Ecumenical Thought of the Disciples of Christ,* Ph.D. Thesis, Hartford Seminary Foundation, 1962.

[75] Alexander Campbell, *The Disciples of Christ* (1833; Lexington, Kentucky: Bosworth Memorial Library, 1951), p. 7.

[76] Thomas Campbell, "Declaration and Address," in Smith, Handy, and Loetscher, *American Christianity* (New York: Scribner, 1960), I, 580. See also Proposition 2 at the end of the document: "yet what directly and properly belongs to their immediate object, the New Testament is as perfect a constitution for the worship, discipline, and government of the New Testament Church, and as perfect a rule for the particular duties of its members, as the Old Testament was for . . . the Old Testament Church, and . . . its members" (pp. 583f.).

[77] Alexander Campbell in the *Christian Baptist,* quoted in Royal Humbert (ed.), *A Compend of Alexander Campbell's Theology* (St. Louis: Bethany, 1961), p. 157.

lished in the belief that the wounds of divided Christianity could be healed by calling all true believers into an apostolically patterned church. This was clearly the belief behind Thomas Campbell's "Declaration and Address,"[78] but the relation between the ecumenical intention and the restorationist result has been a point of tension rather than of unity.[79] Furthermore, when the offer of unity on restoration terms is refused, it is almost too easy to conclude that this refusal is simply evidence of 'the apostacy,' and to descend into sectarian exclusivism. This tension, which appears endemic to restorationism, may perhaps explain why churches that began in this way count among their numbers some of the ecumenical movement's most persistent advocates and some of its most determined opponents.

The restorationist theme has been repeated in many different periods and in a variety of national contexts. The Dunkers, German Baptists, or Brethren of the early eighteenth century were founded by Alexander Mack in 1708. They arose as a pietist reaction to the sterile religion in the established churches, but their distinctive ecclesiological emphases arose from their study of the Scriptures. We read that

> the society thus organized was a strictly legalistic sect, seeking to reproduce in faithful detail the exact conditions pertaining in the primitive church. They waived apostolic succession, refused subscription to all written creeds, and sought to derive all their principles direct from the New Testament. Central in worship was the agape, or love feast; it was held in the evening, preceded by foot washing, and consisted of a full meal followed by wine and unleavened bread. In further conformity to the New Testament pattern the Dunkers greeted each other with a kiss, anointed their sick with oil, covered the heads of their women during services, wore the plainest clothing, refrained from all amusements, and refused to take oaths, bear arms, or engage in lawsuits.[80]

78 Cf. the opening words of the "Declaration and Address": "That it is the grand design and native tendency of our holy religion to reconcile and unite men to God, and to each other, in truth and love . . . will not, we presume, be denied . . . ." See also Propositions 1 and 10 at the end of the document. Smith, Handy, and Loetscher, *op. cit.,* I, 579, 583, 585.

79 Cf. Hugh Wilson's thesis cited above for a fuller treatment of this.

80 Elmer T. Clark, *The Small Sects in America* (New York and Nashville: Abingdon-Cokesbury, 1937, 1949), pp. 208f.

Similarly we witness the rise of the Plymouth Brethren about a century later in Ireland. The movement started first through the Bible study of Anthony Norris Groves and Edward Cronin, and it was later extended to Britain and the continent of Europe by the missionary work of a former Anglican priest, John Nelson Darby. In each case biblical authority and its inevitable restorationist pattern repeat themselves. Cronin was a former Roman Catholic, but when pressed to join the Protestants we read that "he was perplexed and uneasy about the divisions within the Church. Finally he decided that they were not ordered according to biblical teaching and kept himself aloof, studying the Bible on his own."[81] Darby too had been converted from his previous high-church Anglican position through independent Bible study. He discovered that "Ministry was given by the Spirit and not by a church organization," and in 1829 "he published a booklet giving these views, called *Considerations of the Nature and Unity of the Church of Christ,* which was the first of what was to become an avalanche of Brethren pamphlets."[82]

The emphasis on the relationship between ministry and the Holy Spirit that we find in Darby links the literalistic Plymouth Brethren to the charismatic wing of restorationism, just as the choice of the nonconfessional term, 'Brethren,' and the accent upon the Church's true unity bring them close to the Disciples of Christ. For restorationism does carry within it significant charismatic overtones—a reflection of the Spirit-filled Church of Pentecost—that often modify the rigidity and literalism of its appeal to Scripture. Whether a Bible-centered movement reacts to the established forms of the Church in terms of New Testament legalism or New Testament pentecostalism will depend very largely upon the prophetic needs of the time and the particular abuses against which it is protesting.

The charismatic emphasis is seen in the work of Richard Spurling, the Pentecostalist preacher who brought revival to

81 Donald F. Durnbaugh, *The Believers' Church,* p. 163.

82 *Ibid.,* p. 165.

Monroe County, Tennessee, in the 1880s. Spurling, however, also emphasized the need "to restore primitive Christianity and bring about the unity of all denominations,"[83] and in this he was just as much a restorationist as Conrad Grebel, the divines of the Westminster Assembly, Alexander Mack, or the early Disciples on the frontier. Yet the differences between Spurling's movement, the sixteenth-century Anabaptists, or nineteenth-century Disciples and Plymouth Brethren appear to be very wide. It is only when we discern their common source in the Christianity of the New Testament that we can understand that which makes them kin. Spurling, the Campbells, and Darby might have disagreed on interpreting the New Testament emphasis, but they have agreed upon the essential goal—to recapture the unity of the Church by restoring the primitive, apostolic, and authentic Christianity. What Franklin Littell says of the Anabaptists is true of all restorationist churches at their genesis:

> The norm is the past, the hope of the future is the Restitution of the Early Church. There is on the one hand an attitude that is conservative, even reactionary; on the other there is a revolutionary spirit which can burst the most secure of ecclesiastical or social forms. The idea of Restitution represents a studied effort to reverse the verdict of history, to shed the accumulated power and intellectual sophistication which seem to corrode and obscure the pure and inspired faith of the founders of the church.[84]

4

PROS AND CONS

Restorationists aimed at recapitulating the form of the New Testament Church, but this is often no longer true in denominations that began as distinctly restorationist. This shift has inevitably produced a tension between 'liberals' who seem to have broken with the biblical foundation and 'conservatives' who try to maintain the New Testament pattern intact—

[83] Charles W. Conn, *Like a Mighty Army, Moves the Church of God* (Cleveland, Tennessee: Church of God Publishing House, 1955), p. 8.

[84] *The Anabaptist View of the Church,* p. 53. This is a major theme of Littell's book (cf. especially chapter 3, "The Restitution of the Church").

although one has the impression that out of loyalty to denominational 'principles' many who are liberals in every other respect remain virtual fundamentalists in matters of church polity.[85] Sooner or later, however, when biblical faith rests on no firmer foundation than denominational tradition, the erosion of the doctrine of the Church sets in.

Admittedly, the basic concern of conservatives, that the Church should be able to document its essential relation to Jesus Christ, has been too lightly passed over by liberals; but equally, conservatives have been too ready to brush aside the liberal claim that a church can have little to do with Jesus Christ if it is unwilling to confront and reject its earlier pretensions. If we are to understand the present dilemma in ecclesiology, and the practical polarization in our churches, we must recognize the reasons why many contemporary Christians can no longer hold the view of the Church that was revered by their forefathers—reasons that raise fundamental questions about the basic authority on which the traditional doctrine of the Church was founded, about the suitability of the institutional forms the churches have taken, and about the effectiveness of church discipline.

A. The authority for ecclesiology

The most fundamental attack on the restorationist position comes from a century of scientific biblical studies, in light of which many Christians can no longer sustain a literal approach to the Scriptures. Honesty forces them to admit that there are areas in which they cannot be as dogmatic as their forefathers. "The claim of the authority of the Bible for one form of Church order over another can no longer be sustained," declared the Congregationalist, the late Leslie E. Cooke. "All forms of Church order may find authority in Scripture."[86] He might have been echoing the thought of the Baptist, W. O. Carver, who admitted that the New Testament "nowhere has

[85] E.g., liberal Baptists or Congregationalists who oppose union with other churches.

[86] *Bread and Laughter* (Geneva: World Council of Churches, 1968), p. 146.

an explicit definition or description of the Church,"[87] while Ronald Osborn bluntly draws the conclusion for the Disciples when he says, "in the realm of apostolicity, Disciples find in their heritage a mistaken emphasis on restoration which must be abandoned."[88] All these churchmen are simply reflecting the results of a century of honest, critical study of the biblical sources. We can no longer be as sure as were the Anabaptists of the sixteenth century, the Westminster divines of the seventeenth century, or the frontier evangelists of the nineteenth century that the Bible speaks with a single unequivocal voice on the form of the Church, or that our own preferred polity has 'divine right' granted by apostolic sanction. In the New Testament we seem to find traces of all three major forms of polity, congregational, presbyterian, and episcopal, and even—let it be whispered—occasionally some hints of Petrine leadership!

B. The form of the Church

The sheer complexity of this revolutionary age has thrown us into a radically different world from that of the first century.[89] We are beginning to realize that to meet the contemporary challenge by applying the literal form of the New Testament Church may be like using an abacus when we need a computer. Certainly the underlying spiritual issues presented to us in the New Testament are real enough still, but the Palestinian setting and first-century customs and thought

87 In *What Is the Church?,* p. 3.

88 In *The Reformation of Tradition,* ed. Ronald E. Osborn (St. Louis: Bethany, 1963), p. 146.

89 This seems to be particularly true since 1960. Geoffrey Barraclough's thesis is that 1880-1959 represents an interim period between earlier history and contemporary history, and that the 1960s ushered in a new period of human history. One could point to the incredible scientific changes that symbolize this—cybernetics, the moon landing, heart transplants, the isolation of the gene, *et al.*—but to me the most symbolic events occurred in the realm of ecclesiastical affairs and theology. The Second Vatican Council began to break down the comfortable prejudices of centuries, and the debate on the nature of 'God' revealed the extent to which the new view of the cosmos caused traditional ideas to be reexamined. Cf. Geoffrey Barraclough, *Introduction to Contemporary History* (1964; Baltimore: Penguin Books, 1967).

forms were just as bound up with that land and age as the culture of any other place and time in history.

That which is of permanent value in the New Testament understanding of the Church has less to do with the forms the Church adopted then than with its purpose, its message, and the extent to which its forms were a true expression of the gospel *for* that age and place. There may be no more sense in trying to maintain the exact form of the Church in Jerusalem, in Corinth, or even in the Rome of the Apostle Paul, than there would be in continuing to dress in a seamless robe like our Lord, or in regarding Paul's preference for celibacy as binding on all Christians.

C. Discipline in the Church

Modern pluralism has shown that when a church loses the exclusive view of its own ecclesiology, discipline cannot be maintained on the earlier basis. The individual who is excommunicated by one denomination has no difficulty in transferring allegiance to another, and in this setting discipline becomes meaningless.

In large measure the erosion of ecclesiastical discipline is due to a pluralistic society, and to the movement from a predominantly rural and static culture to one that is urban and constantly changing. Restorationist churches, however, as restitutions of the Church of the New Testament, were very firmly centered in a society that was rural and static, in which relatively small, closely knit fellowships could live in covenant relationship, and could maintain that relationship with members throughout their whole life span. Church discipline could be maintained because every member knew every other member, and often in an English market town or New England village generations of the same families had lived together in the covenant. Hence if a case came up for discipline, there were those in the congregation or the presbytery who could really tell if 'young Bradford' was sincere in his profession of penitence, because they had known him and his family since he was 'knee high to a grasshopper.' Even the autonomy of the local congregation made some sense when young Bradford and his family lived in the same town or village for decades, or in the scattered rural communities of the frontier, when it was none too easy to take counsel with other congregations. It may make very little sense, however, even as discipline is virtually ineffective, in an anonymous urban megapolis, or dormitory suburb, where young Mr. Bradford's family is one among thousands, and where they will stay for only a few months until the head of the family takes his next step up the corporation ladder.

Side by side with these three negative aspects of restorationism I would set three positive insights, of which the Church must continue to take note if it is to be the Church of Jesus Christ.

(1) By their constant reappearance in church history, the restorationist churches remind us that there is a constant temptation for established churches to drift away from the gospel and to put their faith in other things such as the State, the American Way of Life, or even their own ecclesiastical institutions. When that happens it is never far from self-idolatry. We need the prophetic corrective that is to be found in the Gospel accounts, to review again the history of the Church's origins, and to measure our churches by the Christ they worship.

"As for Histories to prove Bishops," wrote John Milton, the Puritan poet, "the Bible—if we mean not to run into errors, vanities and uncertainties—must be our onely History."[90] Although many twentieth-century Christians are not able to read the Bible in the simplistic way it was accepted by earlier generations, this book still contains God's Word. To regard it as irrelevant is ultimately to declare that Christianity itself is irrelevant. To discover the essential contribution that restorationist movements have made to our common Christian history, we must look beyond the biblicism to which they have been prone, beyond their pharasaic striving for a demonstrable purity in the visible church, to their insistence that Christians

90 *Eikonoklastes: In answer to a Book Intitl'd Eikon Basilike, The Portrature of his Sacred Majesty in his Solitudes and Sufferings,* in *The Works of John Milton* (London: William Pickering, 1851), III, 463. Milton was answering the argument, put forward for episcopacy by the royal author in the *Eikon Basilike,* based upon Christian history and tradition.

must return constantly to their Source, and to their claim that the Church of the gospel should reflect the nature of that gospel.

Perhaps this is what Paul Tillich had in mind when he wrote:

> The end of the Protestant era is not a return to the Catholic era and not even, although much more so, the return to early Christianity; nor is it a step to a new form of secularism. It is something beyond all these forms, a new form of Christianity to be expected and prepared for, but not yet to be named. Elements of it can be described but not the new structure that must and will grow: *for Christianity is final only in so far as it has the power of criticizing and transforming each of its historical manifestations: and just this power is the Protestant principle.*[91]

If the Protestant principle is the power in Christianity "of criticizing and transforming each of its historical manifestations," the only kind of criticism that means anything to the Church is that which is 'according to the mind of Christ,' and to discover that mind we must go back to its historical source. In that sense, reform must always mean return.

(2) When it has freed itself from its own temptation to bibliolatry, the Bible-centered theology of Protestantism has understood that the essential 'apostolic succession' is that of the gospel itself and of the witnessing Church. As Peter Taylor Forsyth said, "the strict successor to the Apostles is the New Testament, as containing the precipitate of their standard preaching,"[92] or as the authors of *The Catholicity of Protestantism* said when they pointed out that Irenaeus' view of episcopacy "has its authority in virtue of its proclamation of the Word; the office is contingent on the Word, not the Word on the office."[93]

Here again we must insist that to speak of the New Testament or of 'the Word' in this way as successor to the apostles is not to conceive the Bible as a dogmatic legacy but as living

91 *The Protestant Era* (Chicago: University of Chicago Press, 1948), p. xxii. The italics are mine.

92 *The Church and the Sacraments* (1917; London: Independent, 1947), p. 137.

93 *The Catholicity of Protestantism,* ed. R. Newton Flew and Rupert E. Davies, p. 26. Cf. also the extract from *The National Catholic Reporter,* above, p. 90.

testimony within the Church. For me, this has been best expressed by Daniel Jenkins:

> We are as ready, therefore, as traditional Catholicism is, to assert that apostolicity is the essential mark of catholicity, but our position is distinguished from theirs by the fact that we are compelled to insist that it is their *testimony* which constitutes the Apostles as Apostles .... It is not their faith or their religious genius or any special charismata they possessed, like the gift of the spirit by the laying on of hands, and certainly not any accident of historical association, but their testimony which constitutes them Apostles....the test of a Church's catholicity is always whether its testimony to Jesus Christ is the same as that of the Apostles, 'the eye-witnesses of His majesty.'[94]

Jenkins goes on to speak of the Scriptures as 'the indispensable token of the revelation,' but emphasizes that they can be understood as testimony "only to those who have heard Jesus Christ speaking through them and have obeyed his voice."[95] That is, they are understood as testimony to Jesus Christ within the living context of the Church.

(3) But we must push these emphases further. This constant reference to the biblical record, this insistence on the primacy of the apostolic witness and the context within which it was first proclaimed, holds within itself the means of correcting the sterility of literalism; for it is impossible to take the restoration of the New Testament Church seriously without also recognizing that this was a church that lived in the power of the Holy Spirit. Insistence on the New Testament Church should mean insistence on the living and correcting presence of the Holy Spirit in the Church.

We admit that churches which began to restore the New Testament pattern often stopped before they reached that point. Their efforts sometimes seemed to be more like attempts to reconstruct a *status quo ante* than to allow resurrection life to take hold of a living organism, but this is when they have not taken their own attempts at restoration seriously enough. Taken with proper seriousness, restoration of the New Testament pattern of the Church must point from the

94 *The Nature of Catholicity* (London: Faber and Faber, 1942), pp. 24f. The whole of Jenkins' book is germane to this theme. See also *Ministry,* pp. 195ff.

95 *Ibid.,* pp. 24f., 28.

letter to the Spirit, must, in fact, lead the Church from obedience to a written document to the living Spirit to which the document testifies.

We see evidence of this in the history of the churches. Sometimes, as among the radicals of the Reformation and during the English Civil War, this charismatic reaction led to the rejection of Scripture in favor of the 'Inner Light'; but there were times when the testimony of the written Word and the testimony of the Spirit united to bring new light into dark places, as in the experiences of George Fox himself. The Apologists who dissented from the majority in the Westminster Assembly had a glimmering of it. Their first principle in ecclesiology was obedience to the scriptural rule, but they went on to say:

> A second Principle we carryed along with us in all our resolutions, was, Not to make our present judgement and practice a binding law unto ourselves for the future, which we in like manner made continuall profession of upon all occasions. We had too great an instance of our own frailty in the former way of our conformity; and therefore in a jealousie of our selves, we kept this reserve, (which we made open and constant professions of) to alter and retract (though not lightly) what ever should be discovered to be taken up out of a mis-understanding of the rule . . . .[96]

It is true that for them the 'rule' was still the letter of Scripture, but at least they did not close themselves from such future insights in its interpretation as the Holy Spirit might grant. John Robinson, the pastor of the Pilgrims, made much the same point in his farewell sermon to the emigrants. Edward Winslow said that "he charged us, before God and his blessed angels, to follow him no further than he followed Christ: and if God should reveal anything to us by any other instrument of his, to be as ready to receive it, as ever we were to receive any truth by his Ministry. For he was very confident the Lord had more light and truth to break forth from his holy Word."[97]

96 *An Apologeticall Narration,* pp. 10f.

97 From Edward Winslow's account in Walter H. Burgess, *John Robinson* (London: Williams and Norgate, 1920), pp. 239f.

Robinson went on to deplore the situation of the Protestant churches, which "were come to a period [i.e., a stop] in religion," because the Lutherans "could not be drawn to go beyond what Luther saw," and the Calvinists "stick where he left them"; and he concluded that "it is not possible the Christian World should come so lately out of such thick darkness; and that full perfection of knowledge should break forth at once."[98] Robinson's words show us something that was implicit in true restorationism; it may have been limited in its understanding of the Church and literal in its application of the biblical rule, but insofar as it sought to set up the Church of the New Testament, it had Pentecost at its center: it contained something that would be too big for literalism.

Gilbert Keith Chesterton once made an acid comment about the English sects of the seventeenth century. The trouble with them, he said, is that "they really died young, and what has infected our culture since has not been their life, nor even their death, but their decay."[99] One is tempted to say the same about all forms of restorationism that stop at the letter without ever risking exposure to the Spirit that gives it life; for return to the New Testament is viable only if we are prepared to learn of the Spirit that gave it forth; and if we do that seriously enough, more light and truth are apt to break forth in all sorts of unexpected ways.

98 *Ibid.*, p. 240.

99 "On the Fossil of a Fanatic," in *Avowals and Denials* (London: Methuen, 1934), p. 124.

Chapter V

"THE SPIRIT" AND EVANGELICAL PRAGMATISM

1

THE PROBLEM OF THE 'THIRD TYPE'

An interesting meeting took place in the middle of the English Puritan Revolution between Oliver Cromwell, his General Council of Officers, and the Leveller 'Agitators' (Agents) of the troops.[1] They came together to discuss civil policy—more particularly, a new constitution for England in the Levellers' Agreement of the People.[2] What makes this incident fascinating is that they met not so much as soldiers or revolutionaries, or even as concerned citizens, but as Christians. The debate was manifestly theological, and the participants saw no incongruity in trying to resolve their differences by calling a prayer meeting.[3]

[1] October 28, 1647. The full text of the Putney Debates appears in A. S. P. Woodhouse (ed.), *Puritanism and Liberty* (London: J. M. Dent, 1938), pp. 1-124.

[2] The text of this document is to be found in S. R. Gardiner (ed.), *The Constitutional Documents of the Puritan Revolution 1625-1660* (Oxford: Clarendon, 3rd rev. ed. 1906), pp. 333-35. It should not be confused with the more expanded, but politically more moderate version that was published in 1649 (pp. 359-371).

The Levellers were a politically republican and socially radical party that arose in England in 1645/6 under the leadership of John Lilburne and others. They were extremely influential among the troops of the parliamentary army, and have been regarded as the first political party to arise in modern Europe.

[3] The proposal for a prayer meeting was made by Lt.-Col. William Goffe, one of

More to our purpose, the occasion illustrates the problem that arises when two groups, each claiming the Holy Spirit, differ in their interpretation of the Spirit's guidance. Cromwell unconsciously represented the pragmatic element when he admitted that although there were many plausible ideas in the Agitators' proposal, they ought to consider the practical question whether "the spirits and temper of the people are prepared to receive and go along with it." But he went on to reveal his awareness of the deeper issue:

> I know a man may answer all difficulties with faith, and faith will answer all difficulties where it is, but we are very apt, all of us, to call that faith, that perhaps may be but carnal imagination, and carnal reasonings .... It is not enough to propose things that are good in the end, but suppose this model were an excellent model, and fit for England and the kingdom to receive, it is our duties as Christians and men to consider consequences, and to consider the way.[4]

Although the issues debated in 1647 were secular politics, Cromwell's tortuous phrases illustrate the problems we face when we try to define the ecclesiology of Troeltsch's 'third type.' What is the relationship between our human reason and the guidance of the Holy Spirit? Reason has certainly influenced every ecclesiology because churches have had practical problems to solve, but when churches that claim 'divine right' solve ecclesiological problems by practical means, they usually prefer to keep the fact hidden, even from themselves.

On the other hand, where the gospel is justified by a frank appeal to religious experience, the situation is different. The way is open to subjective intuitions and reasonable solutions, and one cannot distinguish too precisely between solutions that arise from the one or the other. The channel of authority may express itself through the whole range of personal cognition from immediate revelation to rational pragmatism, but an honest man might be unable to say where the influence of the

the most 'spiritual' of the officers. He urged those at the meeting to "show the spirit of Christians, and let us not be ashamed to declare to all the world that our counsels and our wisdom and our ways, they are not altogether such as the world hath walked in; but we have had a dependency upon God, and that our desires are to follow God, though never so much to our disadvantage in the world if God might have the glory by it" (*Puritanism and Liberty*, p. 20).

4 *Ibid.*, p. 8.

Holy Spirit ended and his own human reason had taken over.

Cromwell understood that even a man of genuine faith may confuse the two; but he hints that the dilemma can be even more complicated, for reason brings its own *authentic* judgment to bear on our ideal theological solutions. He recognized that the solution to a political dilemma may not necessarily be the ideal 'christian' solution, and yet be the *best* solution—that we should ask of any action whether it is practical and 'consider consequences.' In other words, when we seek to discover God's will in our society, pragmatism has a legitimate place.

We have remarked that once church discipline ceased to function effectively (particularly after the Enlightenment), Protestantism veered between two apparently polar but actually closely related forms of individualism—the individualism of the heart and the individualism of the head.[5] They meet in Troeltsch's 'third type' where the closeness of their relationship becomes evident, for the individual's apprehension of 'the Spirit' shifts ultimate theological authority from objective dogma to subjective experience. The seventeenth-century Quaker who followed the 'Inner Light' and a Cambridge Platonist who described Reason as 'the candle of the Lord' might disagree radically about their interpretation of the Holy Spirit, but their spiritual sons and daughters would probably arrive at perfect agreement. That agreement centers in the ultimate subjectivism of the authority they recognize, an area in which it is virtually impossible to distinguish precisely between emotion, religious intuition, and rationalization. Therefore the 'third type' includes movements that cover the distance between the purest spiritualism and the purest rationalism, and occasionally this radical change can occur in the history of a single group.[6] Such a broad spectrum of Christian experience brings together groups that merge into restorationism on the

[5] Above, p. 53, n. 23.

[6] The most obvious example of this is the Quaker movement. In the seventeenth century the Quakers were essentially charismatic and evangelistic, but after a generation or so the movement had become formal and was largely under the influence of the prevailing Deism.

one hand and those that disappear into humanism on the other.

Our concern is not with their differences, nor yet with the wide variety of forms presented, but with the common element that makes this variety possible. Despite its strong internal pressure towards religious individualism, the significance of the 'third type' in its voluntary associations is this insistence that the Church must be free to meet the spiritual needs of every age. It recognizes that the Church can become bound by *a priori* assumptions about its own structure, so that it is not free to fulfil its essential task. It represents the claim that in the light of the Church's essential task all ecclesiastical institutions are secondary, if not irrelevant, and that if institutional structures are to be used from time to time, they should be set up to meet the needs of the moment and should be modified or discarded as soon as the immediate task of the Church has been fulfilled. When that task is clearly understood as the proclamation of "the faith which was once for all delivered to the saints" (Jude 3), we are speaking about a kind of 'evangelical pragmatism'—a pragmatism that is brought into the service of the gospel. This is the direction in which the ecclesiology of the 'third type' points.

Charismatic movements such as the seventeenth-century Quakers or nineteenth-century Pentecostalists stand on the edge of the sect-type, and as they develop ongoing corporate structures almost inevitably move further into restorationism;[7] but they reveal their basic affinity to the 'third type' by standing loose to ecclesiastical forms and by insisting that methods, organization, and institutions must be judged in relation to the evangelical goals of the group. Within the 'third type' as a whole there may be little agreement as to what those goals are, but there will be a great deal of agreement that the 'church' (however interpreted) should proclaim its message and fulfil its task without too much concern about 'pure

[7] Pentecostalists tend to follow patterns of New Testament congregationalism, and there is an obvious bias towards restorationism in the literal appeal to the Pentecost experience. Until recently, Pentecostalism has had very close relations with biblical fundamentalism. Cf. Elmer T. Clark, *The Small Sects of America,* p. 107.

forms' or 'traditional order.'[8] A Quaker Social Service Committee and a Pentecostalist Missionary Society may differ radically on what they regard as the gospel, but they will both accept the guidance of the Holy Spirit in their meetings as final, and they will judge particular programs by their effectiveness. In the planning sessions to fulfil their chosen ends, practical concern is just as likely to govern their discussions as on the Board of General Motors.[9] A 1963 British Quaker statement on the controversial subject of sex declared, "If Christianity is a true faith, there can be no ultimate contradiction between what it demands of us and what in practice works . . . . We have no hesitation in taking now and then an empirical approach."[10]

On the other hand, the groups that belong to the 'third type' have revealed problems within their history that intrigue and perplex all who have tried to classify them. First, the very subjectivity by which mystical-rational religion arrives at its understanding of theological truth makes it impossible to examine 'typical' structures of churchmanship and belief as we may review the typical structures of the church-type or sect-type.[11] Even more seriously for the fate of such groups in history, this subjectivity can reduce religion to an individualism that ceases to have any recognizable religious or social

[8] Cf. *Ministry,* pp. 115f., where a similar emphasis is noted in a frontier missionary situation. Even Restorationist churches cannot allow church order to take precedence over mission in such conditions without ignoring the central place that Pentecost occupies within the New Testament.

[9] Of course, something similar will be true of a Roman Catholic college of cardinals, an Episcopal bench of bishops, a Baptist convention, or a Presbyterian synod; but the point of ultimate appeal will be different. In the first two cases the measures under discussion will be brought into line with ecclesiastical precedents, i.e., with tradition; in the latter two cases the ultimate appeal will be to the Scriptures—or at least what one eloquent or erudite brother is able to represent as the true interpretation of the Scriptures. Even in Congregational associations exponents of pure pragmatism feel they should occasionally doff their caps to 'theology'!

[10] Quoted by Pierre Berton, from *Towards a Quaker View of Sex,* ed. Alistair Heron (London: Friends Home Service Committee, 1963) in *The Comfortable Pew* (Philadelphia and New York: Lippincott, 1965), p. 49.

[11] The 'third type' was vague in Troeltsch because the only thing that could be regarded as typical about it was its atypicality. The appeal to 'the Spirit' as ultimate authority is the clue that helps us understand this.

impact. Christianity must certainly free itself from obsolete formulations and insensitive literalism; it may also demand from time to time a radical break with the formal structures of its past inheritance;[12] but if it 'liberates' itself *wholly* from the content of this inheritance we should give up speaking about the Christian Church or claiming any distinctive Christian gospel.

If one could share the apocalyptic view of Joachim of Fiore, one might regard the destruction of all church forms as the advent of the Kingdom of God and the universal Reign of the Spirit; but whenever this prospect has arisen in the past, the exemplars of the New Age have fallen woefully short of the New Testament. Modern exponents are no more impressive. Flexibility and structurelessness as new dogmatic requirements do not appear to be any answer to the Church's contemporary problem, for the issue is not simply that of adapting the Church's forms to the temper of the time, but of doing this in such a way that the uniqueness of the inherited gospel may be proclaimed and exemplified with both relevance and fidelity: Redemptive incarnation needs a form, a presence, in order to act, and so that its actions may be acknowledged.[13] We need to see pragmatism of the kind we have described brought into faithful relationship with the content of the historic Faith.

2

LUTHER AND THE WESLEYS: THE EVANGELICAL EXPERIENCE

Martin Luther and John Wesley assume significance in the ecclesiological debate for the paradoxical reason that they did not start with a 'new' doctrine of the Church. Both men were concerned with something far more primary—the salvation offered to the individual by faith in Jesus Christ.

[12] As Rosemary Radford Ruether convincingly argues in her book, *The Church Against Itself* (New York: Herder & Herder, 1967).

[13] Rosemary Ruether naturally wishes to rid ecclesiology of any connection with an incarnational theology with its danger of deifying church structure. (Cf. *The Church Against Itself*, especially chapters 2 and 5.)

If the Church as a 'continuation of the incarnation' is thus to be turned into a *metaphysical* truth, I agree with her; but if it is to be a *metaphorical* truth about

Luther rediscovered within the teachings of Paul the principle—it seems almost too narrowly academic to call it a doctrine—of Justification by Faith. His insight came as the climax of a religious experience in which he had already been engaged for many years: he was a monk, dedicated to the service of God and committed to his Christian pilgrimage; but the insight came with all the reality of a new birth.

> At last, God being merciful, as I thought about it day and night, I noticed the context of the words, namely, "The justice of God is revealed in it; as it is written, the just shall live by faith." Then and there, I began to understand the justice of God as that by which the righteous man lives by the gift of God, namely, by faith . . . .
>
> This straightforward made me feel as though reborn and as though I had entered through open gates into Paradise itself. From then on, the whole face of Scripture appeared different . . . .[14]

Yet Luther would have denied vehemently that this insight was due to any cleverness of his own, or that his own religious experience constituted a new infallible authority; rather he would have claimed that "when we cry, 'Abba! Father!' it is the Spirit himself bearing witness with our spirit that we are the children of God" (Romans 8:15f.). The Spirit who speaks to the individual is the same Spirit that speaks through the Scriptures and through the historic witness of the Church.

The Wesleys entered into this evangelical inheritance. The events of Whitsuntide 1738 came as the climax of a long religious quest,[15] but when the moment came for Charles and

the Church I doubt whether we can dissociate the Church from the incarnation, or even whether the idea of the Church as 'avant-garde' permits us to. Avant-garde of what, or of whom?

In *The Atonement and the Sacraments* (1960) I suggested that the objection is not to the idea of incarnation itself—which belongs centrally to the Good News—but to the false separation of incarnation from its *purpose*—reconciliation and redemption; i.e., the danger arises when the presence of God is claimed without the saving *action* that in fact reveals the presence for what it is. If we are to speak biblically, we cannot speak of incarnation without always understanding it as *redemptive* incarnation. Cf. pp. 226f., 282-87, and 371-74.

14 From Luther's preface to the Wittenberg Edition of his *Collected Latin Works* (1545). The translation is that of Wilhelm Pauck in his introduction to *Luther: Lectures on Romans* (Library of Christian Classics, XV, 1961), p. xxxvii; cf. *D. Martin Luthers Werke* (Kritische Gesamtausgabe, Weimar, 1888, etc.), LIV, 186. (This edition is abbreviated hereafter as *WA*.)

15 The point is particularly well made by Albert C. Outler (ed.) in his Introduction to *John Wesley* (New York: Oxford, 1964), pp. 1-33, also pp. 51-3; cf. also Philip S. Watson, *The Message of the Wesleys* (London: Epworth, 1965), pp. 1-26.

John Wesley the effect was the same as it had been for Luther. Charles Wesley's conversion, on Whitsunday 1738, came after his reading Luther's *Commentary on Paul's Epistles to the Galatians;* and John Wesley was listening to Luther's *Preface to the Epistle to the Romans* at the meeting in Aldersgate Street when he felt his heart "strangely warmed."[16] The Apostle Paul and Luther were an unbeatable evangelical team.

John Wesley later spoke as if he had not been a Christian before that time, yet both he and his brother Charles had been actively pursuing the goal of Christian perfection for many years. In 1725 he had read Jeremy Taylor's *Holy Living and Holy Dying* and had followed this with some of the great classics of Christian devotion. Two years after reading Taylor, on reading William Law's *Christian Perfection* and his *Serious Call,* Wesley records "I determined, through his [God's] grace (the absolute necessity of which I was deeply sensible of) to be *all-devoted* to God: to give him *all* my soul, my body and my substance"; perhaps Albert Outler is justified in saying that was "a conversion if ever there was one."[17] One feels that the later experience, with its strong sense of assurance and the outpouring of the Spirit in the Evangelical revival that followed, has as much to do with Pentecost as it does with the Damascus road.

Be that as it may, Lutheranism and Methodism began in the personal acceptance of faith in Jesus Christ. Their criticism of the established churches of their own times did not begin as a criticism of the Church *per se,* nor yet as a protest against the belief that the Church should have tangible form, but with the fact that the forms seemed to have taken priority over the gospel itself: ecclesiastical structures seemed to hide the New Testament insight that personal response in faith is essential to salvation.[18] Of course, this implied a devastating critique of

[16] It is probably no accident that Methodist scholars such as Rupert E. Davies, Gordon Rupp, and Philip Watson have contributed so much to the study of Luther, or that scholars of Lutheran background, e.g., Franz Hildebrandt and Martin Schmidt, have been attracted to Wesley.

[17] *John Wesley,* p. 7. Outler also points to some of the curious anomalies connected with Wesley's Aldersgate experience, pp. 51ff.

[18] One interesting parallel between the two movements in their concern for personal religion is their emphasis on the use of hymns. The influence of Charles Wesley's hymns on the course of Methodism is too obvious to need further

the existing ecclesiastical structures; but the significant point is that neither Luther nor Wesley set out initially to re-form the Church, but sought to recall it to its essential life and witness. Given their insight into the nature of the gospel and given the churches with which they had to deal, the restructuring of the Church may have been inevitable; but it was incidental to their primary purpose. Because they began with the Spirit's testimony in faith, they did not start with an alternative 'doctrine of the church,' and they therefore share potentially with Troeltsch's 'third type' its characteristic flexibility to polity and structure.[19]

On the other hand, one has only to think of Luther storming back from the Wartburg to stamp out the literalism of Andrew Karlstadt and the spiritualism of the Zwickau prophets,[20] or of Wesley's strictures against the Antinomians and his loyalty to Anglican order, to know that they cannot be placed

comment, but it should be noted that the use of hymns in the vernacular was an early development in Lutheranism. Luther's *Eight Hymns* appeared in 1524, the first Danish hymnal appeared in 1528, a Swedish hymnal in 1530, and Michael Agricola introduced a hymnbook into Finland in the 1550s.

[19] It is interesting to notice that although Langdon Gilkey concentrated exclusively on the church-type/sect-type dichotomy, he perceptively places Quakers and Methodists in the same category because of their inward and subjective appreciation of the Spirit. So, emphasizing that sectarian and evangelical religion are not without their own sense of the holy, he comments: "In an old Quaker meeting or in a Methodist revival, the holy was present and worship had tremendous power. But the media, though definite and understood, were inward and subjective rather than outward and objective. That is to say, the holy was experienced inwardly, in the inner consciousness—as in the Inner Light of Quakerism or the moving of the Spirit in Methodism—not through the objective media such as a sacramental element, an icon, a cross, or even a doctrine or sermon." *How the Church Can Minister to the World Without Losing Itself,* pp. 109f.

It is more difficult to see the connection between Lutherans and Quakers, both because of what Lutheranism became under the influence of the German state and later Lutheran theology, and also because Quakerism changed its character in the eighteenth century. But it is perhaps not so difficult to see similarities between the experience of Martin Luther and George Fox. Also it should be remembered that Lutheranism has always had its pietist wing.

[20] There is an excellent treatment of the incident in Gordon Rupp's article, "Andrew Karlstadt and Reformation Puritanism," *Journal of Theological Studies,* N.S. 10 (October 1959). Karlstadt seems to have been enigmatically unstable, and his career illustrates the crisis of authority in the sixteenth century. He veered from reliance on immediate revelation of the Spirit (as in his friendship with the prophets of Zwickau) and literal application of the Scriptures (as in his reforms at Wittenberg at Christmas 1521). Sometimes he seems to forecast Quakerism (in his reversion to

unequivocally in that box. There are times when they speak as traditionalists, while at other times they seem to be restorationists.

However unconsciously, Luther and Wesley illustrate the complexity of the problem of spiritual authority. The groups that fit fully into Troeltsch's 'third type,' whether they interpret the 'Spirit' in rational or pietistic terms, make the same exclusive appeal to its authority as any restorationist does to the Scriptures or as the traditionalist does to the apostolic succession. This is not true for Luther or for Wesley, since their appeal to the authority of the Spirit in justifying faith and the evangelical experience was not exclusive. It had primacy for them in their own religious experience and because personal faith had been neglected in the churches of their own times, but beyond this both Luther and Wesley recognized that Scripture and the tradition of the Church claim a similar authority in defining the gospel and the life of witness into which the man of faith is born. When we read Luther we recognize that alongside justification by faith we have to place the principle of *sola scriptura,* and the inheritance of Word and Sacrament: no reformer was less ready to break with the traditional forms of the Church for the sake of iconoclasm.

Wesley was equally unready to move recklessly from the established tradition of his mother church. Indeed, he accepted the doctrine of justification by faith only when he had convinced himself that it was consistent with the doctrine of the Church of England,[21] and in his defense of the principle

lay title and status), but at other times he foreshadows the Separatists (cf. the title of his book, *Ob man gemach faren soll?* [Must one always go slowly?], which forecasts Robert Browne's protest in *A Treatise of Reformation without Tarrying for Anie*).

Although I cannot accept Rupp's strictures on Puritanism (in its most precise historical sense), what he describes certainly characterized later Separatism, and he is right in seeing that Karlstadt represented this sectarian emphasis in the Wittenberg reformation. Karlstadt could not understand the practical *balance* of Luther's approach to the question of spiritual authority: for Karlstadt it was a simple and exclusive 'either . . . or,' as it was for the later Separatists; but he could never quite make up his mind which it should be.

21 Cf. Outler's Introduction in *John Wesley,* p. 16. Wesley demonstrated the doctrine's consistency with the doctrine of the Church of England in the Homilies; cf. *ibid.,* pp. 123-133.

of *sola scriptura* he sounds like a biblical restorationist: "If by catholic principles you mean any other than scriptural, they weigh nothing with me. I allow no other rule, whether in faith or practice, than the holy Scriptures."[22]

The importance of this is that both Luther and Wesley unconsciously bring the authority of the Holy Spirit mediated through individual experience into relationship with the authority of the Spirit through the received tradition and in Scripture. They were conservatives forced simply by their fidelity to the historic gospel into a reforming position. Whatever psychological leanings they may have had to the evangelical experience, their theological training and social prejudices were against it. The reality of their own spiritual experience enabled them to be flexible regarding church forms, but always with insistence that its testimony could never be divorced from the testimony of Church and Scripture. For this reason they were unwilling to see the Church disintegrate into structurelessness.

Of course, their conservatism could lead them astray. One cannot feel happy about Luther's diatribe against the Peasants in 1525 or his dogmatic literalism at the Marburg Colloquy in 1529, any more than we wish to follow Wesley in his acceptance of ghosts or in his views about the American War of Independence; but the significance of both men is that in spite of the quirks that show them to be fallible men of their own centuries, they tried to bring their own immediate experience into living relationship to the gospel that the Church had inherited. The Spirit immediately apprehended was a channel of ultimate authority, but only as it helped them sift the authentic gospel in Scripture and tradition from the things that had obscured that gospel from men's view.

3

LUTHER AND THE ECCLESIOLOGICAL PROBLEM

The sixteenth-century reformers were on their own. Even if Luther had the intention of being a 'reformer' in the sense we

22 Quoted from a letter to Thomas Adams, in Watson, *The Message of the Wesleys,* p. 31.

understand the term, which he did not, there were no ready-made patterns of what a Reformation should be or how a reformer should proceed. Starting with an insight into the nature of the gospel that was essentially religious, as experiential as it was theological, he set in motion the series of events in which the Reformation took place and in the course of which he became a 'reformer.'

This means that Luther did not suddenly become a 'modern'—he remained a man of the sixteenth century, and, with regard to some of his deepest prejudices, a man of the fifteenth century.[23] He trusted tradition more than he trusted innovation; and we are reminded that when he returned to Wittenberg in 1522 to oppose the radicals, he preached in his parish church deliberately attired in his Augustinian habit. As Gordon Rupp observes, "the whole of his reformation was in that touch."[24] It also means that Luther had no *a priori* ideas on what the Church should be like or how it should be organized. He was concerned in the first instance with the essentially religious nature of the Church as the community of faith, and his primary concern was that the visible church should be free to belong more recognizably to the Christ who redeemed it.

Luther did not immediately see that by taking this evangelical stand he was bound to bring a crisis of authority into the Church. In making his judgment on the ecclesiastical situation of his time he appealed both to the Scriptures and also to that echo within his own heart that confirmed the Scriptures; but as the break with Rome became more obvious and the appeal of his opponents to the authority of the papacy more insistent, Luther had to appeal more and more to the objective authority for his faith, the Scriptures themselves. In his 1520 treatise *On the Papacy at Rome,* described as "the earliest of his writings to present a full outline of his teachings on the nature of the Christian Church,"[25] his reliance on Scripture is explicit.

23 E.g., his support of the feudal structure of society, or his antipathy to usury. Cf. *An Open Letter to the Christian Nobility.*

24 *Op. cit.,* p. 316.

25 This was written in reply to the attacks made by Augustine von Alveld, the Franciscan of Leipzig. *The Papacy at Rome,* in the Philadelphia Edition of *Works of*

However, the treatise is primarily concerned with the claims made for the papacy, and the positive statements about the Church are in general evangelical terms. The Church is a community of faith consisting of "all who live in true faith, hope and love; so that the essence of the Church is not a bodily assembly, but an assembly of hearts in one faith, as St. Paul says, 'one baptism, one faith, one Lord.' "[26] Throughout the work this evangelical note is struck, and as far as the visible church is concerned, he declares that "The external marks, whereby one can perceive where this Church is on earth, are baptism, the Sacrament, and the Gospel; and not Rome, or this place, or that."[27]

The significance of this particular work for Luther's ecclesiology was that he very carefully established the scriptural base, and the method he would employ in interpreting Scripture. It indicates how initially Luther would inevitably turn in a restorationist direction. The Scriptures were the base. He noted—and it would be significant for his future approach to ecclesiology—that "the Scriptures speak of the Church quite simply."[28] Indeed, he shared with restorationist Protestants of all kinds their insistence that the plain sense of Scripture should not be allegorized away. Luther put very strict limitations on the use of typology in expounding the Bible, and maintained that if biblical texts are to be used in theological argument they should be clearly speaking to that point. In a sarcastic comment on his opponent's eclectic use of biblical texts he said:

> Heretofore I have held that where something was to be proved by the Scriptures, the Scriptures quoted must really refer to the point at issue. I now learn that it is enough to throw many passages together helter-skelter, whether they are fit or not. If this is to be

Martin Luther (Philadelphia: Muhlenberg, 1943), I, 330, from the Introduction by Theodore E. Schmauk. (This edition is cited as *PE* in later footnotes.)

26 *Ibid.*, p. 249; *WA*, VI, 293.

27 *PE*, I, 361; *WA*, VI, 301. Cf. also the strong evangelical note in Luther's statement, "he is the better Christian who is the greater in faith, hope and love; so that it is plain that the Church is a spiritual community, which can be classed with a temporal community as little as spirits with bodies, or faith with temporal possessions." *PE*, I, 353; *WA*, VI, 295.

28 *PE*, I, 349; *WA*, VI, 292.

> the way, then I can easily prove from the Scriptures that beer is better than wine.[29]

So again, in arguing against the bizarre use of typology he lays down a basic principle that "where faith is concerned, one must contend not with uncertain Scripture texts, but with those that refer to the issue in a way that is certain, clear, and simple."[30] He declared flatly that he contended for two basic things in respect to the papacy, first, he could not tolerate a pope who propagated new articles of faith and declared everyone a heretic who refused to accept them, and secondly, "All that the pope receives and does I will receive, on this condition, that I first test it by the Holy Scriptures. He must remain under Christ and submit to be judged by the Holy Scriptures." If these two things were granted, he went on to say, then he would "help to exalt him as high as they please; if not, he shall be to me neither pope nor Christian."[31] It is clear that for Luther in ecclesiology, as in all things else, the Scriptures would be basic.

The years 1523-25 appear to have been the crucial 'restorationist' period in Luther's approach to the doctrine of the Church. In the instructions he sent out for the organization of the parish of Leisnig[32] and in his letter written to the Bohemians[33] it is clear that Luther was turning to the New Testament to find explicit directions regarding the form that the Church should take.[34] Indeed, it has been admitted that in the latter

29 *PE*, I, 361f.; *WA*, VI, 301.

30 *PE*, I, 369; *WA*, VI, 306. It has perhaps not been sufficiently realized that the Protestant emphasis upon the 'plain sense' of Scripture—together with the literalism that this sometimes invoked—was a clear step towards the scientific study of the biblical text on critical historical principles. Luther's words make it very clear that this could not happen while the Scriptures were under the allegorizing exegesis of the medieval Church.

31 *PE*, I, 391f.; *WA*, VI, 322.

32 *WA*, XII, 1-37.

33 *Luther's Works*, ed. Jaroslav Pelikan and Helmut T. Lehmann (Philadelphia: Muhlenberg, 1955-), XL, 4-44 (this edition is referred to hereafter as *LW*); *WA*, XII, 160-196.

34 The evidence for this is provided by Manfred K. Bahmann in *The Development of Luther's Principle of Ecclesiastical Authority (1512-1530) in the German Reformation.* Unpublished Ph.D. dissertation of the Hartford Seminary Foundation, 1967.

"supporters of the most advanced type of congregationalism can find confirmation of their views."[35] The same may be said of his provisions for the parish of Leisnig, for they would have ensured the ecclesiastical independence of the parish in perpetuity. We must perhaps not argue too much from Leisnig, for the 'independence' may have been dictated in part by social and political considerations;[36] on the other hand we can hardly imagine Luther at this stage of his career making such far-reaching proposals without reference to fundamental biblical theology.

Indeed, the two most significant features of Luther's proposals to Leisnig were, first, that they were prompted by a practical issue, the setting up of a 'common chest,' and secondly, that they were put forward when Luther was most clearly under the influence of radical biblical theology.

The significance is brought out even more clearly in what he wrote to Bohemia. The main part of the letter to the Bohemians[37] reviews the seven distinct functions claimed by the Roman priesthood—the preaching of the Word, baptism, the consecration of the eucharistic elements, the binding and loosing of sins, the sacrifice of the Mass, Intercession, and the ability to judge between true and false doctrine. In opposition, Luther claimed that the only valid Christian priesthood is the royal priesthood that belongs to every Christian:

35 Conrad Bergendoff in his Introduction to *Church and Ministry, LW,* XL, x. Bergendoff minimizes the ecclesiological significance of this letter by pointing out "that the situation in Bohemia was highly abnormal and that Luther's suggestion is confined to an emergency. He advocated no such solution for Germany." If Bahmann is correct in what he shows with regard to the Leisnig parish, this is questionable. Bahmann, *op. cit.,* pp. 227-241 and appendices.

36 Cf. § 14, which provided that the chest should have four locks, the keys of which should be in the charge respectively of the nobility, the city council, the town citizens, and the rural peasantry. It is clear that Luther is very conscious of the need for a balance of interests within the social structure.

37 The Bohemians—spiritual descendants of John Hus—were not in communion with the Church of Rome, but were struggling to maintain a priesthood based on apostolic succession. They had been reduced to intriguing for their ordinations from Italian bishops. A Bohemian priest, Gallus Cahera, persuaded Luther in 1523 that his countrymen were moving towards a reformation on Lutheran lines. This was premature, and Luther's overture to the Bohemian church was abortive. (Cf. Bergendoff's Introduction, *LW,* XL, 4f.)

> Here we take our stand: There is no other Word of God than that which is given to all Christians to proclaim. There is no other baptism than the one which any Christian can bestow. There is no other remembrance of the Lord's Supper than that which any Christian can observe and which Christ has instituted. There is no other kind of sin than that which any Christian can bind or loose. There is no other sacrifice than of the body of every Christian. No one but a Christian can pray. No one but a Christian may judge of doctrine. These make the priestly and royal office.[38]

This does not mean that Luther was ready to jettison ordination. "Ordination indeed," he declared, "was first instituted on the authority of Scripture, and according to the example and decrees of the Apostle, in order to provide the people with ministers of the Word. The public ministry of the Word, I hold, by which the mysteries of God are made known, ought to be established by holy ordination as the highest and greatest of the functions of the church, on which the whole power of the church depends, since the church is nothing without the Word and everything in it exists by virtue of the Word alone."[39] Again, we would need a good deal of care to exegete what Luther meant by 'the Word,' for it was Christ *in* Scripture rather than the letter of Scripture itself; but where the Bible gives explicit directions or advice, Luther stands with it, and it is on this basis that he offers his recommendations, for "I am not an authority on something new," he declared; "I can only give counsel and encouragement."[40]

At the same time, the full force of that counsel and encouragement was used to dissuade them from continuing the degrading practice of obtaining ordination by subterfuge from Roman bishops. Conrad Bergendoff says that "the statement does clearly prove that apostolic succession in the Roman sense, or the doctrine of an indelible character in ordination, meant nothing to Luther, and that there may be times when a small band of Christians must establish a ministry based on nothing but the right of a congregation to elect those who shall preach the Word to it."[41] Luther suggested a more

38 *LW,* XL, 34f.; *WA,* XII, 189f.

39 *LW,* XL, 11; *WA,* XII, 172f.

40 *LW,* XL, 7; *WA,* XII, 169.

41 Conrad Bergendoff in *LW,* XL, x.

apostolic procedure, pointing out that in the time of Paul "the authority and dignity of priesthood resided in the community of believers," and that this community's rights

> demand that one, or as many as the community chooses, shall be chosen or approved who, in the name of all with these rights, shall perform these functions publicly. Otherwise there might be shameful confusion among the people of God, and a kind of Babylon in the church, where everything should be done in order, as the Apostle teaches [I Corinthians 14:40]. For it is one thing to exercise a right publicly; another to use it in time of emergency. Publicly one may not exercise a right without consent of the whole body of the church. In time of emergency each may use it as he deems best.[42]

Note that the basis is scriptural *and* pragmatic, but the pragmatism serves and is governed by the gospel—the New Testament requires that the church should normally have a duly recognized public Minister for the sake of good order, even though in times of emergency any Christian may exercise any of the functions of ministry. In both instances the gospel itself is of primary importance, but the method is practical—in the one case the election of a public Minister is a practical step by which the Church prevents 'shameful confusion,' while in an emergency every Christian has the practical responsibility of seeing that the gospel is proclaimed.[43]

To implement this order Luther suggested that those Bohemians who wanted a more reformed church should come together for prayer, petitioning Christ for his help and in full confidence:

> Bring your supplications and prayers that he may send his Spirit into your hearts. For he works in you, or rather, works in you both to will and to do [Philippians 2:13]. For if this thing is to be done auspiciously and to continue successfully, it is necessary that there

[42] Cf. *LW*, XL, 34f.; *WA*, XII, 189f.

[43] This runs somewhat counter to Conrad Bergendoff, who discounts Luther's ecclesiology in this letter on the grounds that the Bohemian situation was abnormal and Luther's suggestions were confined to an emergency situation. [Cf. above, p. 134, n. 35.] Certainly the Bohemian situation was not normal and Luther describes what might be done in an emergency; but if one looks at his specific suggestions within their context, it will be seen that they represent what Luther felt should be the *normal* practice. In an emergency, any baptized Christian could fulfil the functions of priesthood; but for the sake of good order it was better that the church should usually follow the apostolic, and presumably normal, practice of electing ministers to fulfil these functions as the public ministry of the Church.

> be in you the divine strength which, as Peter testifies, God supplies [I Peter 4:11].

Both the spiritual pulse of evangelical Christianity and its New Testament basis are shown here. Luther then suggests that, having prayed to God that their venture should be motivated not by their own desires but by God's will, they should

> Then call or come together freely, as many as have been touched in heart by God to think and judge as you do. Proceed in the name of the Lord to elect one or more whom you desire, and who appear worthy and able. Then let those who are leaders among you lay hands upon them, and certify and commend them to the people and the church or community. In this way let them become your bishops, ministers, or pastors. Amen. The qualifications of those to be elected are fully described by Paul, in Tit. 1 [:6 ff.], and I Tim. 3 [:2 ff.].[44]

Although this sounds like practical common sense, there is no doubt that Luther believed this 'common sense' method to reflect the simplicity of the New Testament. He regards his suggestions to Bohemia as no novelty but as the apostolic pattern of the Church: "They object and say, 'A new thing and unprecedented, so to elect and create bishops.' I answer, it is the most ancient custom, following the example of the Apostles and their disciples, but abolished and destroyed by the contrary examples and pestilential teachings of the papists."[45] This has been the claim of every New Testament restorationist.

On the other hand, this is only part of Luther's approach to ecclesiology. Immediately after he laid down what he obviously believed was the ideal, apostolic pattern of church government, he went on to make this qualification:

> It is not necessary, I think, to put this form of election immediately into practice in the Diet of Bohemia as a whole. But if individual

[44] *LW,* XL, 40; *WA,* XII, 193.

[45] *LW,* XL, 39; *WA,* XII, 192. Cf. the instructions given to those appointed to visit parishes in Saxony (*LW,* XL, 265-324), when the political situation in Germany caused Luther to request action by the state. He justified this action by appeal to Scripture. His argument seems to have been that whereas authority in the church was still uncertain, the authority of princes was certain. Implicitly he assumes that the prince's power was established in Scripture. Cf. *LW,* XL, 271, 273.

> cities adopt it for themselves the example of one will soon be followed by another. The Diet might well consider whether this form should be adopted by all of Bohemia, or if one part might accept, and another part postpone decision or even reject it altogether. For none should be forced to believe. We must give freedom and honor to the Holy Spirit that he may move wherever he will. We cannot hope that these things will be acceptable to all, especially right away . . . . As the venture succeeds, with the help of the Lord, and many cities adopt this method of electing their bishops, then these bishops may wish to come together and elect one or more from their number to be their superiors, who would serve them and hold visitations among them, as Peter visited the churches, according to the account in the Book of Acts [Acts 8:14ff.; 9:32ff.]. Then Bohemia would return again to its rightful and evangelical archbishopric, which would be rich, not in large income and much authority, but in many ministers and visitations of the churches.[46]

This is a passage in which both New Testament simplicity and practicality are balanced, and we should note that in deference to the freedom of the Holy Spirit even the biblical ideal of elective bishops was not to be enforced where the situation did not make it practical. Luther clearly felt that New Testament simplicity and the apostolic example were the best pattern for the Church, but he did not hold this 'restoration' view of the Church in a doctrinaire way. Practical considerations might prevent the establishment of the ideal, even one that seemed to have scriptural and apostolic warrant; but these practical considerations should be respected for the overriding evangelical reason that the Spirit must be free to lead God's people in the way that best serves the gospel. Instead of Karlstadt's impatient protest, *Ob man gemach faren soll?*—the distinctive cry of every revolutionary restorationist—Luther urged the Bohemians to do what was practical, for obedience to the Spirit's will was the prime consideration.

However, Luther was a man of his time, and this influenced his understanding of what the Spirit was saying to the churches, and hence the later development of Lutheran ecclesiology.

One of the practical facts of life in the sixteenth century was the autocratic power of territorial princes, and to Luther

[46] *LW,* XL, 40f.; *WA,* XII, 194.

this power seemed to be ordained by God to stand between the tyranny of the ecclesiastical right and the anarchy of the ecclesiastical left. In the years that immediately followed the 1520 treatises a problem of enormous proportions developed in the German Church. It was not only the problem of organizing something to take the place of the papal administration, or of preventing local magnates and petty bullies from robbing the Church of its property,[47] but it was also the question of how the evangelical faith was to survive in the face of Imperial pressure. Then came the Peasants' Revolt, which threatened political and social anarchy on top of the disruption of the Church. Clearly, something practical had to be done within the Church, and done quickly.

Luther turned to the princes. Visitation of the churches was to be undertaken (following apostolic practice); but because ecclesiastical authority was then unclear, Luther asked the prince to take the initiative,[48] for "while His Electoral grace is not obligated to teach and to rule in spiritual affairs, he is obligated as temporal sovereign to so order things that strife, rioting, and rebellion do not arise among his subjects."[49] Luther may have held to the New Testament pattern as the most desirable method of procedure, but the concrete situation was too pressing to allow for the gradual growth of the episcopal office from local congregations which Luther had advocated in 1523. Moreover, because he had a horror of innovation, he therefore looked to the one established authority that seemed to have clear scriptural warrant, the civil magistrate.[50]

47 Cf. Bahmann, *op. cit.*, p. 259.

48 Cf. Luther's Preface to his "Instructions for the Visitors of Parish Pastors in Electoral Saxony," *LW*, XL, 269-273; *WA*, XXVI, 195-240.

49 *LW*, XL, 273; *WA*, XXVI, 200. Others did the same, although not always for the same motives: "Under the pressure of this emerging situation, many churches therefore followed the same course of action which the Abbott of Buch [the Cistercian abbott who had claims on Leisnig parish] had pursued in 1524. Without being specifically told so, they simply dropped their problems in the lap of the elector since he was the only one who seemed to be able to offer any help." Bahmann, *op. cit.*, p. 259.

50 This change has been duly noted by Hans Küng, *Structures of the Church*, pp. 125f. (cf. 98f.). In chapter 5 and the first part of chapter 6 Küng provides an extremely fair analysis of Luther's basic approach to ecclesiology. With respect to

Practicality had to be seen in relation to the gospel. This was the issue that faced Luther in 1525 and made him ask the Elector to intervene. As Manfred Bahmann observes, "The transfer of episcopal responsibilities for the administration of the church to the prince as 'a bishop in emergency' did not originate with Luther himself but was born out of the disorder which followed the peasants' uprising."[51] A detailed study of how this pragmatic element in Lutheran ecclesiology was worked out in sixteenth-century Europe would demand treatment not only of Luther, but also of the brilliant administrators such as Johann Bugenhagen and Johann Benz who were sent out to set up evangelical systems of church government that would work.[52] It would also need to take notice of the forms Lutheran church government took in the countries where it was established, and to recognize that the civil ruler was a dominant reality in the situation with which the reformers had to deal. The temptation of the Lutheran churches in later years, however, was to assume that the support of the state—admittedly an inescapable factor in the sixteenth century—was a permanent or necessary element in ecclesiastical structure.

It was not, and there was nothing in Luther's essential ecclesiology that demanded it. His theological principles went beyond ancient tradition, doctrinaire restorationism, and materialistic pragmatism: we have to give full weight to the doctrine of the Holy Spirit within his concept of justifying

the episcopal structure of the Church, he shows convincingly that Luther's concern was not to attack episcopacy as such but to insist that it should be reformed in accordance with the gospel (pp. 128ff.). However, in partial response to Küng's criticism of later Lutheran ecclesiology, I would submit that 'historical considerations' (e.g., the danger from the left-wing radicals) could be just as much responsible for the episcopal form in later Lutheranism, as the intransigence of the prelates had been for Luther's earlier more biblically literal views. The key to both is what Luther regarded as an 'emergency'—one emergency led to emphasis on the New Testament pattern, and the other to reliance on traditional forms. Through it all we see Luther wrestling with the complex nature of spiritual authority in (and for) the Church.

51 Bahmann, *op. cit.,* p. 259. Cf. also pp. 272-283 for the discussion of the prince as 'emergency bishop'; Küng, *op. cit.,* pp. 140ff.

52 For a brief account of the work of these men, cf. Conrad Bergendoff, *The Church of the Lutheran Reformation; A Historical Survey of Lutheranism* (St. Louis: Concordia, 1957), pp. 78ff., 80f.

faith. Specific New Testament practices, however desirable, were to be brought into relationship to what the Spirit was saying to the churches in their contemporary situation. Appeal to the letter of Scripture is not enough, for the Word is more than the words, and the gospel is more than literalism; so Luther was not afraid to pass on to others what he had learned "under the Spirit's guidance,"[53] and to safeguard the Christian's fundamental liberty and freedom of conscience.[54] Where the meaning of Scripture was plain, it should prevail; but it is always brought to life by the faith that justifies and is interpreted by the Spirit whose characteristic is love.[55]

In actual situations that the Church faced, practical considerations would be important, but they would be important not because they were practical but because they were intended to serve the gospel and the proclamation of the Word in word and action. In this way Luther recognized the authority of the Spirit that witnessed to the Word of God in Scripture and which was genuinely responsive to the Word in every age. Once we see Luther's understanding of *sola scriptura* in relation to this evangelical and spiritual principle, the characteristics of Luther's ecclesiology become more clear. Indeed, instead of becoming so tied to the state, Lutheran churches should have been most free to relinquish all forms of secular control and to seek new forms of churchmanship more responsive to the Living Christ.

4

WESLEY AND THE ECCLESIOLOGICAL PROBLEM

When George Whitefield introduced John Wesley to open-air preaching in the Spring of 1739, Wesley confessed, "I could scarce reconcile myself at first to this strange way of preaching in the fields, of which he set me an example on Sunday; having

[53] E.g., in his treatise on "The Babylonian Captivity of the Church," *PE,* II, 240; *WA,* VI, 540.

[54] *PE,* II, 235; *WA,* VI, 537.

[55] Manfred Bahmann recognizes that Luther was no literalist (*op. cit.,* p. 119). Conrad Bergendoff also recognizes that Luther qualified the literal authority of

been all my life (till very lately) so tenacious of every point relating to decency and order, that I should have thought the saving of souls almost a sin if it had not been done in a church."[56] In matters of church procedure and organization Wesley began as a traditionalist priest of the Church of England.

A few days after this incident, however, he said that he "submitted to be more vile, and proclaimed in the highways the glad tidings of salvation,"[57] which shows that once he was convinced that new methods were demanded by the needs of the gospel, he was ready to move away from his own prejudices. The occasion provides us with the clue to understanding Wesley's approach to the doctrine of the Church.

We must first give due weight to the Anglicanism into which he was born. For all the Puritan heritage that he received from both sides of his family,[58] both his father Samuel and his mother Susannah exhibited the zeal of converts in their loyalty to their adopted church and in the care with which their children were raised in its faith and practice. John Wesley

Scripture when he remarks, "*In general* he held to his scriptural authority. He opposed the Anabaptists, who thought there was guidance of the Spirit apart from the Word." (*LW*, XL, 55, my italics.) On the other hand, is Bergendoff fair to the Anabaptists? It was certainly true of the *Schwaermer*, some of whom held Anabaptist opinions, but it is not true for the Anabaptist movement as a whole. Many Anabaptists were much more literal in their appeal to Scripture than Luther, and their major quarrel (e.g., the Swiss Brethren) with the leading Reformers was that the latter were not prepared to follow the principle of *sola scriptura* to its literal conclusion, particularly with respect to baptism.

56 *The Journal of the Rev. John Wesley, A.M.* (Standard Edition), ed. Nehemiah Curnock (New York: Eaton & Mans, 1909), II, 167.

57 *Ibid.*, p. 172.

58 On his father's side, both John Wesley's great-grandfather, Bartholomew Wesley, and his grandfather, John Wesley, were Puritan ministers. Bartholomew had been ejected from his living in 1662, and the elder John eventually became minister of a dissenting congregation in London. His son Samuel, the father of the founder of Methodism, had been first educated in the Dissenting Academy at Stoke Newington, but was converted to Anglicanism and ordained into the Church of England after studying at Exeter College, Oxford.

Susannah Wesley, whom he married, was the daughter of Dr. Annesley, a notable Puritan divine of Presbyterian views. She was converted to the Anglican position while in her teens.

For the general influence of Puritanism on John Wesley, cf. Robert C. Monk, *John Wesley, His Puritan Heritage* (Nashville: Abingdon, 1966).

began his ministry as a convinced if not bigoted believer in the superiority of Anglican polity, in the divine right of episcopacy, and in the scriptural warrant for the order of bishops, priests, and deacons. During his years in Oxford he showed a deep interest in liturgical reform, and the most decisive influences on him appear to have been the classics of Anglican and Catholic devotion, and his association with other members of the 'Holy Club.' The influence of John Clayton and contact with the nonjurors is particularly significant, for the nonjurors represented the most High Church wing of the Church in England at that time. The strict and semi-monastic discipline adopted by the Holy Club, its interest in the discipline and order of the early Church and in the devotion of the Eastern Church,[59] shows that at this stage of their religious experience the members were following a course that came naturally to Anglicans—discovering the sources of Anglican faith and practice in a historical period when the Church's structure had been unmistakably episcopal without yet having become decisively papal.

It was after reading the devotional works of his contemporary, the nonjuror William Law,[60] that John Wesley became convinced "of the absolute impossibility of being *half a Christian,*" and that he determined to be "*all-devoted* to God."[61] What the monastery had meant to Luther, this decision represented to Wesley. The little group of Oxford Methodists sought for an answer to the question what it means to be a Christian, and for assurance that the individual is indeed accepted by God.

59 The evidence for the influence of eastern Christianity on Wesley is set out in Albert Outler's excellent introduction to the Library of Protestant Thought volume, *John Wesley,* pp. 8-10, and especially pp. 9f., n. 26. Outler's book is the fullest compendium of John Wesley's life and thought.

60 William Law (1686-1761) had entered Emmanuel College, Cambridge, in 1705, and had been elected a Fellow in 1711 and ordained. On the accession of George I (1715) he had refused the oath of loyalty and was ejected as a nonjuror. His *Practical Treatise on Christian Perfection* appeared in 1726, and the *Serious Call to a Devout and Holy Life* in 1728; and Wesley must have read these very soon after they were published. Later Law attempted to form a religious community based on his own spiritual principles.

61 Cf. above, p. 127; also Outler, *op. cit.,* p. 7.

It was natural for the members to look for their answers first in an Anglican and Catholic direction. The year 1732 has been noted as "the beginning of John's ritualistic High Churchmanship," a period when Clayton joined the group, and through him Wesley met the Manchester nonjurors including Thomas Deacon, the founder of the 'True British Catholic Church.' Under these influences, the members undertook weekly fasts and intensified their study of the early Church. Writing of this period later, Wesley confessed:

> For many years I have been tossed by various winds of doctrine. I asked long ago, "What must I do to be saved?" The Scripture answered, Keep the commandments, believe, hope, love; follow after these tempers till thou hast fully attained, that is till death; by those outward works and means which God hath appointed, by walking as Christ walked.[62]

Wesley then described the opposing dangers that seemed to present themselves to him. He claims that he never fell into the Catholic error of stressing good works too much, but he had been influenced by those Protestant writers who "magnified faith to such an amazing size that it hid all the rest of the commandments,"[63] and he had been rescued only by the common sense of the English divines. However, they did not always agree, and seemed too little concerned about the essential unity of the Church.

> But it was not long before Providence brought me to those who showed me a sure rule of interpreting Scripture, viz., "Consensus veterum: quod ab omnibus, quod ubique, quod semper creditum."[64] At the same time they sufficiently insisted upon a due regard to the one Church at all times and in all places.[65]

He then immediately went on to admit,

> Nor was it long before I bent the bow too far the other way: 1. By making antiquity a co-ordinate rather than a subordinate rule with Scripture. 2. By admitting several doubtful writings as un-

62 *The Journal,* I, 418f.

63 This comment was written at the beginning of his return from Georgia (Jan. 1738), i.e., before faith had become a personal experience for Wesley.

64 'The consensus of the fathers: what is by everyone, everywhere, and at all times believed.'

65 *The Journal,* I, 419.

> doubted evidence of antiquity. 3. By extending antiquity too far, even to the middle or end of the fourth century. 4. By believing more practices to have been universal in the ancient Church than ever were so. 5. By not considering that the decrees of one Provincial Synod could bind only those provinces whose representatives met therein. 6. By not considering that the most of those decrees were adapted to particular times and occasions; and consequently, when those occasions ceased, must cease to bind even those provinces.[66]

In this passage Wesley shows us reason being used in the service of good theology. Few could better the critical honesty with which John Wesley faced the historical problems related to early church tradition. At the same time, he indicates the High Church tendencies of the Holy Club during this period, and gives us clear evidence of the legalism with which the members sought their authority in the tradition of the early Church. One feels that the search for salvation and personal assurance had been conducted just as legalistically and literally as any biblical restorationist might approach the doctrine of the Church. Even the good works that characterized their common life in Oxford seem to have been undertaken less from gratitude to God and love for fellow men than from the intention of fulfilling the conditions of the Great Assize.[67]

This was the religious situation of John and Charles Wesley when the mission to Georgia was undertaken. As John Wesley described it later:

66 *Ibid.*, pp. 419f.

67 Cf. Matthew 25:31-46. In recording the steps leading up to his conversion, Wesley later wrote: "In 1730, I began visiting the prisons; assisting the poor and the sick in town; and doing what other good I could by my presence or my little fortune, to the bodies and souls of all men. To this end I abridged myself of all superfluities, and many that are called necessaries of life. I soon became a by-word for so doing, and I rejoiced that my name was cast out as evil. The next spring I began observing the Wednesday and Friday Fasts, commonly observed in the ancient Church; tasting no food till three in the afternoon. And now I knew not how to go any further, I diligently strove against all sin. I omitted no sort of self-denial which I thought lawful.... Yet when, after continuing some years in this course, I apprehended myself to be near death, I could not find that all this gave me any comfort or any assurance of acceptance with God....

Soon after, a contemplative man... instructed me how to pursue inward holiness, or a union of the soul with God. But even of his instructions (though I then received them as the words of God)... were, in truth, as much my own works as visiting the sick or clothing the naked; and the union with God thus pursued was

> From a child I was taught to love and reverence the Scripture, the oracles of God; and, next to these, to esteem the primitive Fathers, the writers of the three first centuries. Next after the primitive church, I esteemed our own, the Church of England, as the most scriptural national Church in the world. I therefore not only assented to all the doctrines, but observed all the rubric in the Liturgy; and with all possible exactness, even at the peril of my life.
>
> In this judgment, and with this spirit, I went to America, strongly attached to the Bible, the primitive church, and the Church of England, from which I would not vary in one jot or tittle on any account whatever. In this spirit I returned, as regular a Churchman as any in the three kingdoms; till, after not being permitted to preach in the churches, I was constrained to preach in the open air.[68]

The invitation to Georgia seemed to be a providential opportunity to keep a nucleus of the Holy Club together and to maintain the experiment in spirituality. The Wesley brothers, together with Benjamin Ingham, Charles Delamotte, and others studied the Apostolic Constitutions and tried to put the discipline of the early Church into practice in America. So John enforced his belief that infants should be baptized by trine immersion, and refused the Lord's Supper to any who had not been baptized by an episcopally ordained clergyman. America seemed to provide an opportunity to bring into being a pure church, obedient in every particular to the faith and practice of the primitive Church; and it was "a fiasco."[69]

This early experience of John Wesley deserves our attention because it indicates that he had gone almost the whole distance down the traditionalist cul-de-sac.[70] Within the context of his eighteenth-century Anglicanism it represents the equiva-

as really my own righteousness as any I had before pursued under another name." *The Journal,* I, 467-469; Outler, *op. cit.,* pp. 62f. Who was the 'contemplative man'? Outler, following Henry Moore's *Life of the Rev. J. Wesley,* suggested that it was Joseph Hoole, the rector of Haxley near Epworth (cf. *ibid.,* p. 63, n. 17); but one is tempted to speculate whether it could have been William Law, for we know that he corresponded with Law. Cf. *The Works of John Wesley,* ed. Thomas Jackson, 1829-31 (3rd ed., repr. Grand Rapids: Zondervan, 1958-59), XII, 49-53.

68 "Farther Thoughts on Separation from the Church" (1789) in *The Works of John Wesley,* XIII, 272.

69 Outler, *op. cit.,* p. 11.

70 One can make a good case for either 'Catholic' or 'Protestant' intentions in Wesley; the former can be traced through this earlier period. The historians' battle on this issue is presented in A. B. Lawson's *John Wesley and the Christian Ministry* (London: S.P.C.K., 1963), which is perhaps the best modern treatment of his ecclesiology.

lent of Luther's experience when he had confessed "I was a good monk, and I kept the rules of my order so strictly that I may say if ever a monk got to heaven by monkery it was I." [71] It was the experience of men who were desperately concerned about salvation, and who had done all that the formal established religion of their day demanded of them, but who discovered that this fell short of what the New Testament seemed to possess and to expect. The Aldersgate experience [72] was a 'conversion' for Wesley, not in the sense that he now served Christ whereas before he had been profligate, but in the sense that now he accepted grace as a free gift, whereas before he had tried to earn it.

Aldersgate did not immediately change John Wesley's view of the Church and ministry. From the point of view of its immediate effects, we must agree that "his conversion effected little or no change in his churchmanship or ideas of ecclesiastical polity."[73] That process, however, had already been begun by the doubts cast upon the authenticity of the Apostolic Canons while he was still in Georgia,[74] and it was to take a decisive turn through his later reading. But it never caused him to break with the church tradition into which he had been born: even at the end of his life he would affirm, "I live and die a member of the Church of England."[75]

On the other hand, although Wesley's further study did not cause him to deny his ecclesiastical heritage, it did cause him to deny the claims it made to exclusive divine right.[76] The

[71] As quoted in Roland Bainton's *Here I Stand* (Nashville: Abingdon, 1950), p. 45.

[72] For the Aldersgate experience, cf. *The Journal,* I, 465-478; Outler, *op. cit.,* pp. 51-69; above, p. 127.

[73] Lawson, *op. cit.,* p. 71.

[74] Cf. the entries for Monday, 13th and 20th September, 1736, *The Journal,* I, 274-78.

[75] *The Works of John Wesley,* XIII, 274.

[76] "It is not to be thought that Wesley did not believe that church order was of God. He did believe it could be, but he also knew that there was much of man's making in it. Therefore, if the choice between ecclesiastical order and the direct revelation of the Divine Will has to be made, the latter must take precedence. He believed that he had a special Divine commission and that necessitated special methods, which often had to cut across tradition." Lawson, *op. cit.,* p. 171.

struggle may have been a long one. We have already noted Wesley's inner struggle on the issue of open-air preaching and his struggle on the divine right of episcopacy extended over a long period. As late as December 1745, in answer to Westley Hall's attempt to persuade him to leave the Established Church, John Wesley declared his conviction that "it would not be right for us to administer Baptism or the Lord's Supper unless we had a commission from those whom we apprehend to be in succession from the apostles," and reaffirmed his belief that "the threefold order of ministers (which you seem to mean by Papal hierarchy and prelacy), is not only authorized by its apostolic institutions, but also by the written Word."[77]

By this date John Wesley had apparently not moved far from his High Anglican ecclesiology, yet within a few months his views were radically challenged by reading Lord King's *An Enquiry into the Constitution, Discipline, Unity, and Worship of the Primitive Church.*[78] This book convinced him that bishops and presbyters were essentially one order in the New Testament,[79] but it may well have led to a much more thoroughgoing revision of the doctrine of the Church.

The more radical recasting of his view came through reading Bishop Stillingfleet's *Irenicum.*[80] In 1756 we find Wesley writing:

77 *The Journal,* III, 229f.

78 Peter King (1669-1734) had published his book in 1691 anonymously, but later acknowledged it as his own work and recanted sufficiently to be received into the Establishment. He eventually was raised to the peerage and became Lord Chancellor.

79 See Wesley's entry in *The Journal* for January 20, 1746(III, 232): "I sent out for Bristol. On the road I read over Lord King's *Account of the Primitive Church.* In spite of the vehement prejudice of my education, I was ready to believe that this was a fair and impartial draught; but, if so, it would follow that bishops and presbyters are (essentially) of one order, and that originally every Christian congregation was a church independent on all others!"

80 Edward Stillingfleet (1635-1699), a Fellow of St. John's College, Cambridge, during Cromwell's Protectorate, found no difficulty in conforming at the Restoration in 1660. His *Irenicum* appeared in 1659 when there was some hope of establishing a comprehensive Church of England to include Presbyterians. It was a hope that proved false. Having conformed, Stillingfleet did not maintain the views he expressed in the Irenicum, although he always belonged to the Broad Church (Whig) wing of the Church of England. He became Bishop of Worcester in 1689. A. B. Lawson has an excellent treatment of both Stillingfleet and Lord King in relation to Wesley; *op. cit.,* chapter 3.

> As to my own judgment, I still believe "the Episcopal form of church government to be scriptural and apostolical." I mean, well agreeing with the practice and writings of the Apostles. But that it is prescribed in Scripture, I do not believe. This opinion, which I once zealously espoused, I have been heartily ashamed of ever since I read Bishop Stillingfleet's "Irenicon." I think he has unanswerably proved, that "neither Christ nor his Apostles prescribe any particular form of church government; and that the plea of divine right for diocesan Episcopacy was never heard of in the primitive church."[81]

Once he had reached this conclusion, it became basic to his view of the Church. "Read Bishop Stillingfleet's Irenicon, or any impartial history of the ancient church," he wrote to Charles in 1780, "and I believe you will think as I do. I do verily believe I have as good a right to ordain, as to administer the Lord's Supper. But I see abundance of reasons why I should not use that right, unless I was turned out of the Church."[82] This leads Lawson to comment that "King convinces him about a detail; Stillingfleet about the whole question of church government."[83]

John Wesley's testimony seems to support this view. His developed ideas about the doctrine of the Church appear in the Minutes of the fourth Annual Methodist Conference in 1747. The conclusions of that Conference, set out in catechetical form, were that in the New Testament a 'church' signified a single congregation, that there were no scriptural grounds for a national church, that although three orders of ministry are to be found in the New Testament, there is nothing to show that they were determined for all time since this would exclude all foreign Reformed churches—"a consequence of shocking absurdity"—and noted that the first claim to episcopal divine

[81] Letter to the Reverend Mr. Clarke, July 3, 1756, *The Works of John Wesley,* XIII, 211.

[82] Letter to Charles Wesley, June 8, 1780, *ibid.,* XII, 147. This was the theological conviction that provided Wesley with his justification for 'ordaining' preachers for America. (Cf. A. W. Harrison, *The Separation of Methodism from the Church of England* [London: Epworth, 1945], pp. 8ff. *The Journal,* III, 232, n. 2.) This letter to Charles should be compared with another letter in which John castigates his brother for expelling someone from a Methodist society for not attending the parish church: "Your gross bigotry lies here, for putting a man on a level with an adulterer because he differs from you as to church-government." Quoted by Lawson, *op. cit.,* p. 74.

[83] *Ibid.,* p. 70.

right appeared in the middle of Elizabeth's reign. The Minutes continued:

> Q. 12. Must there not be numberless accidental variations in the government of various churches?
>
> A. There must, in the nature of things. As God variously dispenses his gifts of nature, providence and grace, both the offices themselves and the officers in each ought to be varied from time to time.
>
> Q. 13. Why is it that there is no determinate plan of church-government appointed in Scripture?
>
> A. Without doubt because the wisdom of God had a regard to this necessary variety.
>
> Q. 14. Was there any thought of uniformity in the government of all churches until the time of Constantine?
>
> A. It is certain there was not, and would not have been then had men consulted the word of God only.[84]

On the other hand, it should be noted that the ecclesiological issue had already come up at the Conference in 1745; and although at that time Wesley probably had not read King or Bishop Stillingfleet, we can already discern a radical shift from his earlier position.

> Q. 5. Is Episcopal, Presbyterian, or Independent church-government most agreeable to reason?
>
> A. The plain origin of church-government seems to be this. Christ sends forth a preacher of the gospel. Some who hear him repent and believe the gospel. They then desire him to watch over them, to build them up in the faith and to guide their souls in the paths of righteousness. Here then is an independent congregation, subject to no pastor but their own, neither liable to be controlled in things spiritual by any other man or body of men whatsoever. But soon after some from other parts, who are occasionally present while he speaks in the name of him that sent him, beseech him to come over and help them, also. Knowing it to be the will of God, he complies, yet not till he has conferred with the wisest and holiest of his congregation and, with their advice, appointed one who has gifts and grace to watch over the flock till his return.
>
> If it please God to raise another flock in the new place, before he leaves them he does the same thing, appointing one whom God has fitted for the work to watch over these souls also. In like manner, in

[84] Wednesday, June 17, 1747. From the record of John Bennett, in Outler, *op. cit.*, pp. 173f. The extract is also to be found in A. B. Lawson, *John Wesley and the Christian Ministry*, pp. 74f.; and Colin Williams, *John Wesley's Theology Today*, pp. 121f., etc.

> every place where it pleases God to gather a little flock by his Word, he appoints one in his absence to take the oversight of the rest and to assist them of the ability which God giveth. These are deacons or servants of the church, and look on their first pastor as their common father. And all those congregations regard him in the same light and esteem him still as the shepherd of their souls.
>
> These congregations are not strictly independent. They depend on one pastor, though not on each other.
>
> As the congregations increase, and as the deacons grow in years and grace, they need other subordinate deacons or helpers, in respect of whom they may be called "Presbyters," or elders, as their father in the Lord may be called the "Bishop" or Overseer of them all.[85]

We agree that despite the apparent support this passage gives to the Independent position, it was in fact an explanation of how the threefold ministry developed pragmatically from the apostolic mission.[86] However, it is extremely significant for several reasons in the light of Wesley's later views and actions—first, because it suggests that he held an essentially pragmatic attitude to church order perhaps before he had read King or Stillingfleet; secondly, because it parallels the pattern that his own missionary endeavors were to take; and thirdly, because it is clear that his pragmatism is *evangelical* pragmatism—it is a pragmatism controlled by the gospel message and justified by the mission of the Church.

He had moved not from an Anglican position, but from a high church position to a 'broad church' position that was founded on evangelical reality rather than on latitudinarianism.[87] This suggests that Wesley held within his own experience all the essential ingredients for a distinctively ecumenical doctrine of the Church, for he had been wrestling with all the essential channels of authority. He had begun with an Angli-

[85] Cf. the record of this Conference (Saturday, August 3, 1745) in Outler, *op. cit.*, pp. 153ff., and the discussions of the problems raised by it (Colin Williams, *John Wesley's Theology Today* [Nashville: Abingdon, 1960], pp. 218ff.). How is this position to be reconciled to the firm episcopal position expressed in December of that year? (Cf. above, p. 148.) Does Wesley distinguish between his *legal* position as a priest of the Church of England and his pragmatic theory of the way in which that position developed in the life of the early Church?

[86] Colin Williams, *op. cit.*, p. 220.

[87] This seems to be Williams' conclusion, although he makes the comment, "to dispute over the terms, High, Broad, Low is probably unprofitable." *Ibid.*, p. 218. This is because none of these terms really describes the way Wesley tried to hold the differing views of the Church *together*. Cf. pp. 152ff.

can's reverence for the Church's traditional order, and for some years he had rested content in the belief that tradition and Scripture agreed. But his belief in the divine right of the episcopal order was shaken by insights into New Testament faith and practice that came from the heart and the head, and which he could not apparently deny without denying the ground and authority of his own Christian assurance. This did not cause him to reject church tradition, but it forced him to see that it had to be judged in relationship to Scripture and to Christian experience.

Here, then, was the context for a fresh approach to ecclesiology—one that took its origin in the *spirit* of the New Testament Church, and which based its justification on the contemporaneity of the pentecostal society and the imperative call to evangelize.

(1) The Aldersgate experience may not have been the immediate cause of Wesley's change regarding the doctrine of the Church, but I suggest it was an indispensable setting in which the change could occur, or at least in which it had significance. Because of that which he experienced himself—an experience which he had first seen in German Moravians, read about among Puritan New Englanders,[88] and was to witness again and again during the revival among members of every denomination and of no denomination—he could not deny the reality to which the experience witnessed. Nor could he deny that it was closer to the Pentecostal spirit of the New Testament than either traditional churchmanship on the one hand or literal biblicism on the other. This appeal to immediate revelation and to Christian experience had its dangers, and Wesley was well aware of them[89] —which is why he always tried to relate

[88] The *Journal* entry for Monday, 9th October, 1738 (II, 83f.) reads: "I set out for Oxford. In walking I read the truly surprising narrative of the conversions lately wrought in and about the town of Northampton, in New England. Surely 'this is the Lord's doing, and it is marvelous in our eyes.' " The book Wesley had read was Jonathan Edwards' *A Faithful Narrative of the Surprising Work of God in the Conversion of Many Hundreds of Souls in Northampton,* which had been published in London in 1737. We can only guess at the influence this account had upon the newly converted John Wesley, who was soon to witness the effects of revival in Whitefield's field preaching at Bristol.

[89] This is seen in an extremely forthright letter that he wrote to his brother-in-

his own experience to Scripture and to his church's tradition, and sought the advice of brethren in the work—but the final responsibility for action had to be taken by the individual as he heard the call from within to 'go out and preach the gospel.' Only as this pentecostal reality came back would the Church truly become what it should be, for the Church's purpose was fundamentally evangelical. "Your business as well as mine," he reminded his brother Charles, "is to save souls. When we took Priests' orders, we undertook to make it our one business. I think every day lost, which is not (mainly at least) employed in this thing. *Sum totus in illo*."[90] The nature of the Church was ultimately to be governed by the nature of the evangelical task given to God's people: this was its first and basic characteristic.

(2) The experience shared by early Methodists meant that Christian unity was to be understood "not simply in terms of visible continuity, but in terms of the Catholic spirit."[91] The denominational barriers with their exclusive appeal to dogmatic definitions of churchmanship, hitherto insuperable, gave way to the recognition that unity in *spirit* was far closer to the true tradition of Christian faith and the New Testament community than the legalism or literalism on which the dogmatic definitions had rested.

Wesley's acceptance of King's and Stillingfleet's interpretations of New Testament Christianity enabled him to accept ecclesiastical pluralism as a reasonable proposition, but if this

law, Westley Hall, on December 22, 1747: "When you was at Oxford with me, fourteen or fifteen years ago, you was holy and unblamable in all manner of conversation . . . . More than twelve years ago you told me God had revealed it to you that you should marry my youngest sister. I was much surprised, being well assured that you was able to receive our Lord's saying (so you had continually testified) and to be an "eunuch for the kingdom of heaven's sake." But you vehemently affirmed the thing was of God: you was certain it was His will. God had made it plain to you that you must marry, and that she was the very person. You asked and gained her consent, and fixed the circumstances relating thereto.

Hence I date your fall . . . ." *The Journal*, III, 325.

90 "I am wholly in this." Letter to Charles Wesley, April 26, 1772, *The Works of John Wesley*, XII, 139.

91 Colin Williams, *John Wesley's Theology Today*, p. 209. Wesley admitted his help from the earlier English divines, but quite early in his career he had complained that "there was one thing much insisted upon in Scripture—the unity of the Church—which none of them, I thought, clearly explained or strongly inculcated." *The Journal*, I, 419.

had been only an intellectual conclusion it would have made him no more than a rationalistic relativist. The assurance of saving faith gave Wesley a catholic view of the Church that superseded differences in polity and demonstrated unity in the most characteristic gift of the Holy Spirit, the gift of love. He had seen it in Moravians, pietists, and in all those affected by the revival, for under the experienced power of the gospel the ecclesiastical barriers tumbled.

They did not tumble easily for Wesley, but that Christian love triumphed over his prejudices is a witness not only to his honesty but also to the gospel's power. We can hardly overestimate the importance of this feature of pietism in all its forms for the development of modern ecumenism. There may be much more to ecumenism than 'spiritual unity,' but it is obvious that any Christian unity that does not have it at its heart will be worthless. John Wesley did not originate it—he inherited it at Aldersgate Street—but he became its exemplar and its incomparable exponent. His sermon on the Catholic Spirit is a classic:

> I dare not, therefore, presume to impose my mode of worship on any other. I believe it is truly primitive and apostolical. But my belief is no rule for another. I ask not, therefore, of him with whom I would unite in love, "Are you of my church, of my congregation? Do you receive the same form of church government and allow the same church officers with me? Do you join in the same form of prayer wherein I worship God?" I inquire not, "Do you receive the Supper of the Lord in the same posture and manner that I do, nor whether, in the administration of baptism, you agree with me in admitting sureties for the baptized, in the manner of administering it, or the age of those to whom it should be administered?" Nay, I ask not of you (as clear as I am in my own mind) whether you allow baptism and the Lord's Supper at all. Let all these things stand by—we will talk of them, if need be, at a more convenient season. My only question at present is this, 'Is thine heart right, as my heart is with thy heart?'[92]

[92] In Outler, *op. cit.*, pp. 96f. (cf. pp. 91-104). The sermon was preached in September and November 1749, and it should be compared with Philip Dodderidge's sermon, 'Christian Candour and Unanimity stated, illustrated and urged,' which was preached January 12, 1749/50. Together they illustrate the remarkable ecumenical spirit that was beginning to show itself among Protestant evangelicals of all denominations. Cf. *The Miscelaneous Works of Philip Dodderidge, D.D.*, ed. T. Morell (London: William Ball, 1837), pp. 886ff.

(3) John Wesley presses practicality into the service of the gospel. As A. B. Lawson has said, "It seems that Wesley's outlook is always intensely practical, and therefore he is much more concerned with what a minister should do, rather than what he is."[93] That is a very good estimate, if we can assume, as Wesley surely would have insisted, that what a minister does arises first out of what that minister is spiritually. The same would be true of the Church itself: the community of the redeemed cannot be other than a community called by God to proclaim redemption.

For him, mission is the primary mark of the Church,[94] and everything connected with the ordering of the Church and its ministry should serve that primary call. So, despite his prejudices, he adopted Whitefield's method of preaching in the open air, employed lay preachers in the circuits and classes, ignored the legal restriction of parish boundaries, and finally, when he had become convinced that the Scripture permitted him to act, 'ordained' workers for the American mission field, because these practical steps served the gospel more effectively. But Wesley acted with a pragmatism that sprang from the gospel itself, because the nature of the Church and the Church's primary purpose had been brought to a focus and illuminated by his own conversion: whatever Methodism became, John Wesley himself was one of the clearest exponents of what we have called 'evangelical pragmatism.'

The significance of that for our own search for an ecumenical doctrine of the Church may be suggested by A. B. Lawson when he said, "After his evangelical conversion, churchmanship seems to have taken a subordinate place in Wesley's thinking. It did not, as some have supposed, become unimportant. Rather it must be flexible enough to be adapted to changing circumstances and never be in opposition to his evangelistic endeavours."[95] In other words, the Church must be free to adapt itself in its service of the gospel.

93 *Op. cit.*, p. ix.

94 Colin Williams, *op. cit.*, p. 209.

95 *Op. cit.*, p. ix. Cf. Frederick Hunter's comments on the value Wesley placed on 'prudential practices,' in *Wesley and the Coming Comprehensive Church* (London: Epworth, 1968), pp. 49-51. "Whatever we may think of particular Prudential Practices, this widening of the door of common sense was invaluable. It meant that Wesley was free to meet eighteenth-century needs from his wide knowledge of

5

PROS AND CONS

We have already noted that a discussion of Troeltsch's 'third type' in its pure form is not likely to be very profitable, because when the guidance of the Spirit is taken as the sole authority in ecclesiastical matters, the movement tends to slip into sheer individualism.[96] Insofar as this may imply a new Christian involvement in secular society, we may see some striking parallels when we examine the views of some of our contemporaries. On the other hand, since the individual is finally responsible for what he or she accepts as a Christian, no ecclesiology can finally ignore the 'authority' that is granted by God to the individual.[97]

We are left, then, with something like Luther and Wesley's approach to ecclesiology. No longer can we appeal to the absolute and infallible channels of authority claimed in the past, but we have to hold all channels in essential and significant relationship, and recognize that they are true witnesses only as they confirm each other by witnessing to God in Christ.

Does this mean that Luther and Wesley found the perfect ecclesiological formula? Can we simply accept their attempts to combine faithfulness to the Scriptures and the historic tradition with the spiritual insight of pietism and (in Wesley, at least) the practicality of the Enlightenment?

precedents in the Primitive Church, and also by direct common-sense search for the best solutions" (p. 51).

96 Cf. above, pp. 29, 44-46, 122ff.

97 This was clearly seen by Wesley. On Friday, March 25, 1743, he recorded: "I spent some hours in reading an artful book entitled *The Grounds of the Old Religion.* In the first thirty pages the author heaps up scriptures concerning the privileges of the Church. But all this is beating the air till he proves the Romanists to be the Church, that is, the part is the whole. In the second chapter he brings many arguments to show that the Scripture is not the sole rule of faith; at least, not if interpreted by private judgement, because private judgement has no place in matters of religion! Why, at this moment you are appealing to my private judgement; and you cannot possibly avoid it. The foundation of your, as well as my, religion must necessarily rest here. First you (as well as I) must judge for yourself whether you are implicitly to follow the Church or no; and also, which is the true Church; else it is not possible to move one step forward." *The Journal,* III, 72.

Hardly; that would be too large a claim. We would have to consider not only Luther and Wesley, who obviously had their own blind spots, but also Lutheranism and Methodism—not only the insights of the original reformers, but also what the churches allowed themselves to become. The basic problem for the doctrine of the Church is posed by the Church's own history—by the tension of being a faithful witness to a historic tradition that is also *essentially* a living experience. The need for interpretation and re-evaluation is an essential part of our faith as Christians, and the true Church of Jesus Christ will not try to escape it either by becoming freeze-dried in tradition or by floating on the waves of fashion. What the churches have become is a pointer to where they stand in relation to the gospel,[98] an extremely pertinent issue for our present discussion. We have to apply the gospel's own pragmatic principle, "By their fruits you shall know them."

That illustrates the very important place that pragmatism occupies in the New Testament itself. It cannot be brushed aside disdainfully as too 'untheological,'[99] for our Lord himself told us that we were to apply this specific practical test to all would-be apostles and the messages they proclaimed: 'What is being produced?' 'What are its effects?' No amount of theological whitewash can get rid of the essential practicality of this test—the church, the form of ministry, the individual Christian, and the theory of church order that claim to belong

[98] We have had cause to speak a good deal about the 'gospel,' and that word needs some definition. It must be clear that in the mind of the present writer the 'gospel' cannot be equated with the letter of Scripture, a body of dogma, or with a particular ecclesiastical or charismatic interpretation of Christian truth, although all of these are basic resources. We might define the gospel as 'the good news of God in Christ,' or as the 'message of salvation,' or as the proclamation that 'God was in Christ reconciling the world to himself,' and that would be true; but it still needs exegesis. It becomes a parody of the truth if the chosen definition is interpreted in purely static (past) terms: It would be so much easier if we had to deal only with a dead Jesus and his teachings, rather than with a living Christ. The 'gospel' certainly includes the affirmations made above, but it also includes the call to witness to this historic faith within a present and essentially living experience.

[99] As Leslie Cooke suggested, it is perhaps no accident that the first one to call attention to "Non-theological Factors in the Making and Unmaking of Church Union" should have been a distinguished biblical scholar, C. H. Dodd. Cf. *Bread and Laughter,* p. 146. In view of the Anglo-Saxon Freechurch propensity to pragmatism, it may also be no accident that Dodd was an Anglo-Saxon Freechurchman.

to Jesus Christ are all ultimately to be judged by what they produce in his name.[100]

Like all other approaches to the doctrine of the Church this one has its own particular problems.

First, we notice that the point at which the exercise of 'evangelical pragmatism' has appeared to be most uncertain is not in the development of practical policies but in the understanding of the evangelical principle. There have been periods of history when pietism has reduced the gospel to religious 'feelings' associated with the conversion experience. At other times, in reaction to this traffic in the emotions, churches have swung to the other extreme and confined the gospel within their own dogmatic definitions or rationalistic orthodoxies. Methodists and Lutherans have known these tensions.

Even more serious, however, is the temptation to allow pragmatism to become an end in itself. Indeed, the basic criticism we must make of this approach to ecclesiology is its temptation to bypass the gospel standard that should be at its heart: to ask 'Does it produce the fruits of faith in Christ, of life in his spirit?' is not quite the same as simply asking 'Does it work?'

Pragmatism contains three dangers in relation to church order, to which Anglo-Saxon churches in particular have been prone:

First, there is the danger of creating a spurious tradition. Systems of church order that have been worked out pragmatically are just as apt to become self-perpetuating as any other form of church order. In doing so they often assume a false aura of sanctity that sits strangely upon them. Practical structures of power and administration are just as resistant to change once established as those that developed for more theological reasons. Those from the outside, for example,

100 A Scottish Presbyterian of the early nineteenth century, Patrick Mitchell, voiced this when he said: "The superior excellence of any scheme of church polity must, I presume, result from its superior efficacy in promoting the great end of the christian religion, the sanctification of the souls of man; or, at least, from its manifestly unrivalled tendency to promote that important end." *Presbyterian Letters addressed to Bishop Skinner of Aberdeen, on his Vindication of the Primitive Truth and Order* (London: J. Johnson, 1809), p. 17.

ponder upon the fact that a form of Methodist or Lutheran episcopacy may have been excellent in meeting the challenge of the nineteenth-century American frontier or the sixteenth-century political order in Scandinavia, but may be an anachronism in the twentieth century.[101]

Secondly, there is the danger of mistaking the gospel's objectives for our own. Unless the churches can keep the objectives of the gospel in the center of their planning, what right have they to assume that their goals are Christian goals? What guarantee have we that any scheme denominational headquarters has managed to concoct, is really the will of Christ for his Church at this time? We will certainly question whether any program of promotion on denominational rather than ecumenical lines can be true to the Spirit of Jesus Christ. The goals of the gospel are not necessarily those of streamlined efficiency, increased membership, rate of church extension, the money contributed to worthy denominational causes or to causes that somebody at the top regards as worthy. Nor are the aims of the gospel necessarily those of the latest social or political bandwagon.[102] In the New Testament, the practical aims of the gospel are concerned with the 'fruits of the Spirit' (Galatians 5:22ff.); they are concerned with evangelism, with attitudes that may be unpopular and with causes that do not necessarily hit the headlines.

Finally it must be clear that there is always the danger of a 'sellout.' This approach to ecclesiology has its own peculiar danger of apostasy, just as all the others have theirs. Writing of practical politics in secular life, Reinhold Niebuhr observed that "Historical pragmatism exists on the edge of oppor-

[101] This, of course, is by no means limited to the denominations mentioned. Church history has many examples of ecclesiastical institutions or ritual, originally introduced for practical reasons, finally becoming incorporated into a church's theology. If the churches had been prepared to take Dodd's proposal seriously, this is where the research would have been concentrated. Cf. above, n. 99.

[102] Do not mistake me. These things are not necessarily evil, and they may be as good as they are purported to be. But as responsible members of the Church, responsible finally to God and not to the denomination how we use our limited time, talents, and money, we want to know that these things follow *from* the gospel and are not simply someone's 'good idea,' a committee's private ideology, or a denominational executive's decision that we must 'get with it.'

tunism, but it cannot fall into the abyss."[103] Ecclesiastical pragmatism *dares* not fall into the abyss, but has a far harder time avoiding it. Its dilemma is more acute because it is often faced with the hard choice of deciding what simple pragmatism demands and what the pragmatism of the gospel demands; and when that happens it is easy enough to convince oneself that in being ruthless one is simply being 'realistic for the sake of Christ.' Often we have simply 'sold out.'[104]

Furthermore, ecclesiastical pragmatists can fall very easily into opportunism because there often *are* a number of good pious and even theological reasons for doing what they want to do. The gospel is full of paradoxes that have to be held together, but the paradoxes provide a marvelous excuse for invoking one or the other opposing principle when practical politics or popular fashion dictate: it is all too easy to find a biblical text or a theological precedent that 'proves' one is acting from the highest motives.

These are the dangers of an ecclesiology based on pragmatism, even an ecclesiology based on 'evangelical pragmatism.' The approach contains a most important insight into the essential flexibility that the mission requires of all ecclesiastical forms, and points towards an ecclesiology that could speak directly to the twenty-first century; but the problem is to specify the authority to which we can appeal in defining the Evangel in 'evangelical.' Contemporary prophets and modern insights are all very well, but we need a sure resource that will enable us to measure their theories by the gospel—at the theological level we need what Bernard Murchland pointed to

103 *The Irony of American History* (New York: Scribner, 1952), p. 143.

104 E.g., consider a situation where a downtown church seems to have served its usefulness. From a practical point of view it seems as if the denomination should close the church, sell the property, and use the resources to begin in a more promising situation. But it is not quite so simple. What about the few families, the poor, the elderly and the infirm who have depended on this church community for help and spiritual nourishment? If we are called to serve, how do we justify excluding them from our service? On the other hand, another board of trustees might argue—and be in equal spiritual danger—that the church ought to remain downtown to fulfil its 'mission,' when in fact the members were actually more concerned with retaining a stake in rising property values. There is no easy answer. It is extremely difficult to apply the practical test in a Christian way unless there is a firm hold on the meaning of the gospel. And even then, the answer is only along the edge of Christian conscience.

in his criticism of Harvey Cox—"an adequate critical principle."[105]

At the end of this historical survey of approaches to ecclesiology some conclusions stand out:

First, although we have classified the different denominations according to the approach that seems to be most typical in their history, no church exists as a pure example of its 'type' and elements of all three are to be found in each. Roman Catholicism may appear to concentrate more on historical continuity than it does on biblical restorationism, but there were elements of the latter in the Roman Catholic Church long before Vatican II made it acceptable to speak of the Church as the People of God. Similarly there are aspects of Protestantism that powerfully favor historical continuity[106] and the pragmatic principle—although it is often hidden behind theological rationalizations.[107]

Secondly, we have seen that although all ecclesiologies are open to criticism, we have to be particularly critical of those doctrines of the Church that claim exclusivity for their own

[105] Daniel Callahan (ed.), *The Secular City Debate* (New York: Macmillan, 1966), p. 19.

[106] I.e., in their claim to apostolicity through continuity with the apostolic gospel; cf. Daniel Jenkins, *The Nature of Catholicity.*

[107] There has been a persistent trend in Protestantism towards a more pragmatic approach to ecclesiology, which was in part due to the demands of evangelism and in part to the loosening of the strict scriptural foundation. (Cf. the quotation from the Presbyterian Patrick Mitchell, and the note on Baptist ecclesiology, above, pp. 157, n. 100, 106, n. 70.) Protestants have regularly appeared who questioned even their own churches' claims to divine right, and in 1809 Mitchell declared that he would leave "the *jus divinum* to be scrambled for by senseless and arrogant bigots of all denominations, praying heaven to send them, in its own good time, a little more judgment and candour, and a reasonable portion of humility." *Presbyterian Letters,* p. 7. Even as convinced and thoroughgoing a restorationist as the Baptist, Dr. Dana, admitted "Expediency has its place. Principles of Church polity must be adapted to the character and functions of a church if they are to survive and enable a church to perform its characteristic purposes." *A Manual of Ecclesiology,* p. 209. From the Congregational side the same trend is seen in Robert Dale, who in 1884 declared, "The New Testament does not contain any law declaring that a particular scheme of church government is of universal and permanent obligation." *Congregational Principles* (London: C.U.E.W., 11th ed. 1920), p. 4. The New Testament still provided the general basis of ecclesiology for these churches, but it was ceasing to be used as a literal blueprint.

polity or order: the form of the Church can never be of more importance than the spirit of its Lord.

Thirdly, the only adequate doctrine of the Church is an ecumenical doctrine of the Church, and the problem of spiritual authority lies at its heart. Moreover, we suggest that the most promising approach to this issue is one that recognizes that all channels of authority from Jesus Christ witness to the same Spirit and in the name of the same Lord; but it must be an approach that brings these channels of authority also in relationship to the proper exercise of practical reason.

Fourth, we need constant penitence for our ecclesiastical pride in the past. The present century has made fools of us all, and we must see the hand of God in that. For if we have been brought to the point where providentially the arrogance of the past is impossible, we also discover, for the first time since the Reformation, that we may have to undertake the search together.

This basic search must be theological. The old tacit assumption of ecumenism in the 1940s and 50s, that we could solve the problem by taking some episcopacy and modifying it with a little bit of presbyterianism and a dash of congregationalism, will not do. We have to rediscover a truly theological basis for the Church and its ministry. That is the priority; the rest will follow.

PART THREE

CONTEMPORARY SCENE

Chapter VI

PROTESTANT REVOLUTION

1

THE ECUMENICAL REVOLUTION

The scene may be set by an illustration that is frankly nostalgic. Near the end of World War II, I remember ascending Saddleback in the English Lake District. We climbed the mountain in fog, following cairns built by generations of former travelers, and although the mist would occasionally lift it never lifted completely. Then when we had arrived almost at the summit we noticed what appeared to be a small golden spot in the fog off to the side and below us, and as we watched it grew larger and larger until the whole valley was bathed in sunshine. For a moment we caught a glimpse of the magnificence around us and we knew where we were in relation to it all; but within a few minutes the clouds rolled in again and we returned to our base in the fog.

That is not a bad illustration of the impact the ecumenical movement made upon those who were influenced by it during those years, or of our thinking about the Church since the fog returned. For a moment a vision of 'the Great Church'[1] opened up before Protestants, just as I imagine it presented itself to Catholics during Vatican II; but I have the strong

[1] The term belongs to P. T. Forsyth. Cf. *The Church and the Sacraments* (1917; London: Independent Press, repr. 1953), p. xv.

impression that for many the vision has dimmed and has left us all floundering again in obscurity.

But the vision had been there and it was real. No survey of the doctrine of the Church in the mid-twentieth century should ignore the tremendous influence of the ecumenical movement on a whole generation of theologians and churchmen, or of the theological, biblical, and ecclesiastical influences that seemed to come to a focus within it.[2] It was a period of excitement about the Church and its possibilities, when denominations rediscovered the venerable ecclesiologies they had buried beneath eighteenth-century rationalism, nineteenth-century sentiment, and twentieth-century liberalism. Yet it was also a time of wider horizons, when we heard of Episcopalians experimenting with the house church and the parish meeting, and when convinced Free-churchmen claimed they were 'catholic'[3] and thought it no dishonor to be considered 'high church.'[4] Even a redoubtable Baptist scholar thought it no betrayal of his principles to call for an 'Oxford

[2] From the continent of Europe the dominant influence was that of Crisis Theology in general and that of Karl Barth in particular, while in the Anglo-Saxon world the major influence seems to have come from the liturgical and ecclesiastical interests of the front-running Anglican Church. In 1942 the British Congregationalist, Daniel Jenkins, declared, "It is undeniable that much of our present interest in the doctrine of the Church is due to the witness of the Church of England . . . . The Reformed Churches of the Anglo-Saxon world owe a debt of gratitude to the Church of England for her constant witness in recent generations to the reality of the Body of Christ when many of them regarded the Church as little more than a convenient form of religious association, and for her preservation and restoration of much of the rich content of the life and worship of the Great Church throughout the ages when again many of them were busy light-heartedly casting away their heritage through ignorance of its true value." *The Nature of Catholicity,* pp. 8f.

[3] Cf. the Free Church response to the Archbishop of Canterbury's proposals, *The Catholicity of Protestantism,* ed. R. Newton Flew and Rupert E. Davies; Daniel T. Jenkins' *The Nature of Catholicity*; and Nathaniel Micklem's *Congregationalism and the Church Catholic* (London: Independent Press, 1943).

[4] The influence on the Free Churches may be traced in John W. Grant, *Free Churchmanship in England, 1870-1940* (London: Independent Press, n.d.), chapters 7 and 8; R. Tudur Jones, *Congregationalism in England, 1662-1962* (London: Independent Press, 1962); and in the series of Forward Books issued by the same press under the general editorship of John Marsh in the 1940s and 50s. It was reaffirmed for the American branch of the family in Douglas Horton's *Congregationalism: A Study in Church Polity* (London: Independent Press, 1952); and the same emphasis may be seen in Presbyterianism in Geddes MacGregor's *Corpus Christi* (Philadelphia: Westminster, 1958).

Movement' of the Baptist churches,[5] and Congregationalists devoted their decennial international meetings to studying Congregational churchmanship in relation to the ecumenical dimensions of the Church.[6] Protestants not only gained deeper appreciation of their own history and ecclesiologies, but stretched their horizons and had their appetites whetted for a form of the Church that would transcend the current dividedness.

Nor was this simply a synthetic or eclectic approach to the problem of church union, for the way to understanding had been prepared by the objective results of biblical scholarship to which all churches stood in debt. These results came to a confluence in the 'new consensus' of biblical scholars that largely governed the ecumenical thinking of the 1950s and early 60s, and seemed to provide a solid base for 'biblical theology.'[7] The question of authority appeared to be resolved—or, if that were too premature a judgment, we at least saw the direction in which the resolution should be sought.

[5] H. Wheeler Robinson, *The Life and Faith of a Baptist* (London: Kingsgate, 1927), p. 146.

[6] Cf. *Congregational Churchmanship,* a study booklet prepared for the Seventh International Congregational Council at St. Andrews in 1953. One of the major concerns of this Council was to explore the relationship between the traditional center of Congregational ecclesiology—the local congregation—and the wider expressions of the Church in its synodical and ecumenical dimensions. They did not succeed in defining this relationship in any of the formal statements; but one of the most significant aspects of the Council was that that which eluded definition in formal debate was given very concrete and explicit expression in the case of the Telugu Church; cf. "A Letter to the Telugu Church Council," *Proceedings of the Seventh International Congregational Council,* ed. Ralph F. G. Calder (London: Independent; Boston: Pilgrim, 1953), pp. 154-56. This statement, which was the response of the Council to a specific instance, gives clear indication of Congregationalists' understanding both of the nature of spiritual authority in their councils and of their relationship to the ecumenical movement.

[7] Cf. "Guiding Principles for the Interpretation of the Bible, as accepted by the Ecumenical Study Conference at Wadham College, Oxford, 1949," in *Biblical Authority for Today,* ed. Alan Richardson and Wolfgang Schweitzer (London: S.C.M., 1951), pp. 240ff. It is significant that no such consensus has been reached, or even attempted, in the post-Bultmannian era.

The interest and centrality of Bible study to the ecumenical enterprise was stimulated by the World Student Christian Federation and S.C.M.s all over the world, and by Suzanne de Dietrich in a remarkably vivid series of Bible studies and books. See "Ecumenism and the Bible," *The Student World* (Geneva: W.S.C.F., 1956), 49/1, in which the editor, Philippe Maury, commented that his journal had last published an issue on the Bible in 1949, but that the national movements

This was perhaps the most significant factor behind the achievements of the ecumenical movement in the years immediately following World War II—achievements, such as the consummation of the Church of South India in 1947 and the founding of the World Council of Churches in 1948, that were born not out of the negative desire to protect and conserve the churches' diminishing strength but out of the positive vision of their common purpose.[8]

Bishop Lesslie Newbigin's *The Household of God*[9] is an excellent illustration of the contribution the ecumenical theology of that time made to the doctrine of the Church, just as the author himself—a Reformed theologian and bishop in the Church of South India—is an exemplar of its concern and commitment. One of the fundamental insights of the ecumenical movement, and one that we shall not be able to discard without undermining the Church itself, is the essential relationship between the unity of the Church and the Church's mission.[10] But there were further insights into the essential nature of the Church that ecumenical involvement brought to light—a catholicity that exceeded tolerant pluralism in the

reported "that Bible study was having a profound effect on the lives of most of them . . . . Reports coming to Geneva in 1952 indicate that such study is continuing, and the movements are seeking to improve their methods of Bible study so that more and more students may come to recognize the Bible not merely as a great book, magnificent literature, or as a historical record, but to find in it the Word of God for them" (pp. 1f.). This interest and excitement is also illustrated in J. K. S. Reid's *The Authority of Scripture* (London: Methuen, 1957), and William Neil's *The Rediscovery of the Bible* (London: Hodder & Stoughton, 1954).

8 The dramatic decline in the churches' influence during the past few decades could lead to a serious misunderstanding of the ecumenical movement and of the fundamental motivation behind the concern for Christian unity. They could be too easily dismissed as a desire to conserve dwindling resources. The plain fact is that this concern came to a focus in 1910 when the Anglo-Saxon churches were at the peak of their power and prestige; and even at the time the World Council of Churches was founded in 1948 (after church decline in Europe), the movement won the enthusiastic support and leadership of the American churches when they were at the height of their influence, growth, and missionary potential.

9 London: S.C.M., 1953.

10 A fascinating illustration of this insight is seen in that at much the same time when Lesslie Newbigin—the representative missionary bishop of the period—was writing on the unity of the Church in *The Household of God*, the representative statesman of Christian unity, W. A. Visser 't Hooft, was thinking deeply about the Church's mission and purpose; cf. W. A. Visser 't Hooft, *The Pressure of Our Common Calling* (New York: Doubleday, 1959).

name of the Church's organic unity and 'plenitude,' and a conviction that the essential truths of Christian tradition could be established on a firm basis of biblical theology.

Newbigin begins by frankly recognizing that we have entered a new world. He asserts that the breakdown of traditional 'Christendom,' the missionary experience of the Church, and the eruption of the ecumenical issue placed the doctrine of the Church at the center of theological discussion.[11] The heart of his thesis is that there have been three basic answers to the question of what truly constitutes the Church of Jesus Christ: the Church may be understood essentially as 'the congregation of the faithful,' as 'the Body of Christ,' or as 'the community of the Holy Spirit.'

> The first is, briefly, that we are incorporated in Christ by hearing and believing the Gospel. The second is that we are incorporated by sacramental participation in the life of the historically continuous Church. The third is that we are incorporated by receiving and abiding in the Holy Spirit.[12]

So far we might consider Newbigin's views as simply an ecumenical justification of Ernst Troeltsch, but the significance of Newbigin's book is that its base rests not on sociology but on a biblical appeal. For this reason a new element enters the old debate; Newbigin cannot regard these categories of churchmanship as discrete, alternative forms of the Church or, therefore, as mutually exclusive. On the contrary, he shows very clearly the parody of true churchmanship that each of these approaches becomes as soon as it takes that exclusive stance. At the same time he maintains that if they are to be obedient to scriptural truth they must accept each other as complementary, mutually corrective and supportive.

This is a position that goes as far beyond toleration as it does beyond denominations' exclusive claims. It pointed to a doctrine of the Church which would recognize all the valid insights that the traditional positions had preserved, and which must therefore claim inclusiveness—catholicity—to be of its essential nature. It viewed pluralism neither as something to be

11 *Op. cit.*, pp. 11ff.
12 *Ibid.*, p. 30.

wholly deplored nor as the ultimate goal of ecumenism, but as a stage in the churches' pilgrimage towards a form of the Church Catholic in which the variety of God's gifts to his people could be accepted, shared, and held within a unity visible to all men. We must stress again that this approach claimed to be not pragmatic but essentially theological—an appeal to 'biblical theology.' This gave the ecumenism of the period its tremendous stimulus and spiritual *élan*. It was the ultimate basis for the ecumenical documents of that time, from those of the Amsterdam Assembly to the 'Principles of COCU,' and it was the accepted basis for the works of theologians.

The weak point was that the term 'biblical theology' was never clearly defined. It could mean so many different things to different people. Ordinary people could never be quite sure what could or what could not be legitimately proved in the Scriptures, or of the distinction to be drawn between the biblical theologian speaking as critic, historian, pastor, or private Christian; and often it seemed as if a new kind of fundamentalism was being developed in which the appropriate texts of Scripture were used by the ecumenists to justify what they had already decided should be the future shape of the Church. We may readily admit that biblical theologians honestly sought their evidence in the wholeness of the Bible's testimony, but one suspected that at the negotiating table their views were used by ecclesiastical statesmen to support positions reached in a quite different way and for quite different reasons. Was the biblical evidence for each of the three basic ecclesiologies as clear as the ecumenical leaders maintained, or was it being moulded to fit a hidden agenda, a hidden pragmatism? Was it simply providential that scriptural support could be adduced for the three forms of churchmanship to be found in twentieth-century Christianity, or was the scriptural support inferred *because* three distinctive forms of churchmanship had in fact developed?

When the exponents of biblical theology went on to amass similar evidence for a form of credal orthodoxy which, if not precisely Chalcedonian (in deference to Eastern Orthodoxy's rejection of the *filioque*?) certainly reflected the doctrinal positions of the undivided Church,[13] it appeared to the innocently uninitiated or to the unrepentantly skeptical as if 'good theology' now implied a reversion to uncritical proof-texting little removed from the literalism of earlier times.

This is where the credibility gap developed in the ecumenical enterprise; and it was not helped by the Olympian disdain with which the newer critics—particularly Bultmann and his followers—were often treated in official ecumenical circles, or by the continuing appearance of documents without any sensitivity to the hermeneutical problem that loomed large. A new liberalism appeared in the 1960s that questioned the assumptions of Neo-Orthodoxy, and it soon began openly to be stated that "the ecumenical movement has shot its bolt."[14] With theology moving to the miniskirt, the post-war styles began to look faded, and the change in fashion has been sudden.

The reader will misunderstand if he thinks it is being suggested that the doctrine of the Church should or can be unbiblical, or that the newer critics' position was correct because it became fashionable. We are simply pointing out that in its appeal to 'biblical theology' the ecumenical movement failed adequately to define the sense in which the Bible is to be received as an ultimate authority, and thus failed to convince its constituency that it was honestly concerned with truth; for despite the formal acceptance of historical-critical methods by its leaders, they were unable or unwilling to make clear to the churches how these critical methods affected their *theological* use of the Bible. Possibly the doctrinal positions of Nicaean orthodoxy, traditional church order and liturgy, *can* be justified by a theology that is grounded in the Scriptures, but if so, the scriptural position and method of interpretation have to be clear and believable: the issue cannot be decided on *a priori* grounds alone. The issue is that of theological credibility, which is another way of saying that ecumenists no less than other churchmen have to make clear to others that their

13 Cf. Lesslie Newbigin's *Trinitarian Faith and Today's Mission* (Richmond: John Knox, 1964).

14 As I heard stated openly by a theologian in 1968 at a theological commission of one of our major denominations when COCU was being discussed.

allegiance to the Truth in Christ forces them to deal honestly with all truth.

Obviously the problems posed by the 'biblical theology' of the 40s and 50s raises issues that are too large to be explored at this point, but if the movement's failings and rapid decline in theological influence provide us with a cautionary tale, we are also forced to ask if we can discard its concern for a biblically based theology, which was at its heart. Certainly if the Bible is used simply to sugarcoat orthodox doctrines or to justify a body of dogma, we risk the literalist error in a new form; but surely there *is* a sense in which all Christian theology *must* be biblical? There can be no authority for (or within) the Christian Church without the biblical revelation at its center, but we must be able to demonstrate to ourselves and the world principles of biblical interpretation that bring all orthodoxies under the judgment of the God who was revealed in Jesus Christ—to be joyfully accepted and defended when they express the truth that was revealed in him, but to be just as joyfully discarded when they fall short of it or distort it.

2

DECLARATIONS OF INDEPENDENCE

One questions whether American theology was ever very profoundly affected by the neo-orthodox movement, or whether many theologians on this side of the Atlantic felt very comfortable with ecumenical 'biblical theology.'[15] America was still too close in time to its own Fundamentalist-Modernist rift, and still too bitterly divided by its chosen polarity to receive without suspicion what was being said; furthermore, it had been too distant from Hitler's bombs and concentration camps to hear the authentic ring of Barth's tocsin or to comprehend why it had been necessary. In spite of these presumed deficiencies—or possibly because of them—those

[15] Something of this uncertainty was reflected in Sydney Ahlstrom's article, "Neo-Orthodoxy Demythologized," *The Christian Century* (May 22, 1957), pp. 649ff. For my comments on the difference between the situation Ahlstrom described and the European scene, cf. *The Atonement and the Sacraments*, p. 271.

who *were* influenced by biblical theology brought to their understanding a distinctly American perspective and critique. This stance, which was within but not absorbed by ecumenical theology, enabled American theologians briefly to occupy a position in ecclesiology that represented unique possibilities.

When Claude Welch wrote *The Reality of the Church*[16] he had obviously accepted, although not uncritically, the major thrust of Karl Barth's theology;[17] and in the same way he recognized the primary value of the biblical themes and images used in Newbigin's *The Household of God.* His fundamental agreement with the current direction in ecumenical theology was demonstrated in that he criticized the other writers on theological rather than sociological or psychological grounds,[18] and recognized that the traditional ecclesiologies had gone a long way towards becoming perversions of the Church by reason of their obvious rivalry and inadequacy.[19] Although he drew some vitally important insights on the nature of the Church from American society, he recognized that any serious debate on the Church must be fundamentally theological. So he accepted the centrality of the Person of Jesus Christ in determining the pattern of the Church, and he employed biblical concepts, such as the People of God, the call to Servanthood, the eschatological hope, and the metaphor of the Body of Christ, as starting-points for his own discussion of the Church.

His treatment has a significant difference. Whereas in Newbigin, and even in Barth,[20] the emphasis was upon the Church as an essentially divine society, called by God for his special

16 New York: Scribner, 1958.

17 I have written of living theologians in the past tense not because I wish to give them premature obituaries, but because theological fashions have been so rapid and so widespread that one can never be sure that a theologian would wish to acknowledge in 1972 what he wrote in 1960, much less anything written before that date. Welch's respect for Barth is obvious throughout *The Reality of the Church.* His criticism of Barth's approach to ecclesiology is found on pp. 66f., n. 1.

18 *Ibid.,* p. 140, n. 1.

19 *Ibid.,* pp. 30ff. I have some difficulty with his typology in this passage because I think that Troeltsch's is neater and ultimately more comprehensive.

20 In *The Church and the Churches* (London: James Clark, n.d.) Barth strongly emphasized the mandate that the Church receives from Christ and that it is wholly the work of Christ.

purposes, Welch insisted that it is a human society and that its humanness is essential for the purposes to which it is called. From the context of American pluralism, he was conscious of the "paradox or contradiction between what faith asserts about the Church and what is evident to the unprejudiced eye," between what the Church claims about its own nature and the empirical facts of its dividedness and error. Welch made his readers face the twofold ambiguity, for "how can this divided, faltering, sinful company be rightfully called the new creation, the bride cleansed, the community of the justified, the way of salvation, the first-fruits of the new age, the temple of the *Holy* Spirit?" and at the same time but from the opposite perspective, "how can this association of men, conformable apparently to the patterns of a multitude of other human associations, be rightfully described as the people *of God,* the colony of *heaven,* the royal *priesthood, God's* planting, the body *of Christ?*"[21]

Of course, the paradox had been recognized by others;[22] but what makes Welch's contribution particularly important is his insistence that this humanness, with its fallibility, its incompleteness, and even its propensity to sin and perversion, is as much a part of the Church's essential character as its divine call. "One would think it unnecessary," he observed, "to emphasize such an obvious fact about the church as its real humanity. Yet in our new concern with a theology of the church, and especially in reaction to notions of the church as merely a contractual association of like-minded individuals, we may be tempted to deny just this truth."[23] Reading this at the distance of not much more than a decade, one realizes with a shock that in 1958 Claude Welch had found it necessary to insist on the essential *humanness* of the Church.

This is maintained throughout his discussion of the biblical images and metaphors: the Church is 'the People of God,' but this means that they are a people living within the social

21 Cf. Welch, *op. cit.,* pp. 20f.

22 E.g., Emil Brunner, *The Misunderstanding of the Church* (London: Lutterworth, 1952); Daniel T. Jenkins, *The Strangeness of the Church* (New York: Doubleday, 1955); Robert McAfee Brown, *The Significance of the Church* (Philadelphia: Westminster, 1956).

23 Welch, *op. cit.,* p. 44.

process, and he pointed out that the societal images—city, nation, kingdom, commonwealth, race, household, colony, family—are just as numerous in the Scriptures as the more organic—flock, tree, field, building, temple, etc. The image of the People of God must also mean that they are a people which lives in time and which therefore has to come to grips with the institutional forms that exist in history. That the Church is subject to sociological analysis like any other human institution "is not a fact to be deplored, as representing an accidental and rather unfortunate aspect of the church's being. It is of positive import for theology, for it is but a reflection on the nature of the church as a humanly concrete body of responding people."[24] Welch insisted that the polarity between this human character and the Church's dependence upon God are not to be set against each other, but must be "thought into each other," for the two sides of the polarity are centered in the reality of the Incarnation itself.

Welch's doctrine of the Church centered in the Incarnation; that is, for him the essence of the Church's nature is that it is founded on an "indissoluble relation to the very temporal, socio-historical act of God in the person of Jesus Christ."[25] Because God chose to work by means of this 'everyday pottery,' Welch recognized that "the Holy Spirit is not only free to judge and remain transcendent over all human forms and formulations, but free to bind himself to the concrete, to use precisely the fragile vessels, the workaday pots of our historical forms";[26] and because God is prepared to take chances with us "the way is open for corruption and sin in the church."[27] This is the point at which he criticized some aspects of neo-orthodox theology: he criticized Barth because although Barth had recognized the duality of the Church, by making a distinction between the 'real' Church and the 'apparent' Church, "the emphasis is so strongly placed on the identity of the real church with what the Holy Spirit makes out of the empirical community that the latter is no longer a

24 *Ibid.*, p. 61.
25 Cf. *ibid.*, pp. 65-67.
26 *Ibid.*, p. 75.
27 *Ibid.*, p. 80.

real church, but only possibility of church."[28] He also took issue with the Anglican theologian Lionel Thornton for making the identity of the Church and the Incarnation so complete that he seems "ultimately to absorb the church in the incarnation,"[29] and he took Congar and Roman Catholic theology to task because:

> We are not to speak of the church as adapting and conforming itself to the patterns of human society as if the church itself were some entity essentially above this poor history and humanity. On the contrary, the church is that lowly humanity and history to which and in which God condescends to be present in Jesus Christ, calling it to be and by his Spirit working in it the new humanity which is at the same time true humanity.[30]

In each case, it will be seen, Welch was not criticizing Christian 'orthodoxy,' but he was criticizing those 'orthodox' emphases by which the trend at that time was distorting the doctrine of the Church either by deifying the Church or at least by passing over the human, fallible, social aspects of its life and character. Just as docetism was a basic error in respect to the person of Christ, so it could also be an essential error in our thinking about the Church, for the real glory and lordship of Christ "does not lie in his 'majesty,' but in his obedience, i.e., in his humiliation. It lies in his coming not to be ministered unto but to minister."[31]

Whereas others linked the Church to the Incarnation and ended by claiming that the Church is divine, Welch found in that doctrine the fundamental reason for insisting on its essentially human character: Jesus is man in society, and man in relation to God, and thus the humanity of Jesus provides an important clue

> to a more adequate understanding of what truly constitutes humanity. Man is man, not only as part of and over against nature, but man in relation to society and to God. And this being-in-relation is not merely accidental to his being, or simply a reference to the "mean-

[28] *Ibid.*, pp. 66f., n. 1.

[29] *Ibid.*, pp. 78f., n. 5. The reference is to Lionel Thornton's *Revelation and the Modern World.*

[30] *Ibid.*, p. 81. The reference was to M. J. (Yves) Congar's *Divided Christendom.*

[31] *Ibid.*, p. 84. Welch stands firmly with Barth here; cf. p. 85.

> ing" of his selfhood, but constitutive of his *being man*. He exists only in this way.[32]

By bringing this aspect of the Incarnation to bear on his understanding of the Church, Welch brought the basic claim of biblical theology—that the Church finds its essential nature in the person and work of Jesus Christ—into integral relationship with the empirical truth about the churches as experienced within the realities of American pluralism.

The relation between the Church and the Incarnation is, however, that of analogy and not of identity. The Church

> is distinguished from other communities, not because it has a "true" and "perfect" transcendent reality, of which the earthly form is only an imperfect expression, but because the loyalties and signs which are the bonds of its social and temporal existence direct it always to the God who is the source of its being, because its constitutive historical memory is of the event of Jesus Christ, because its common worship is directed to its Lord who calls forth adoration and thankfulness and obedience by his continual presence in grace and love, because its hope is ever in what he has done and will do.[33]

The Church is an eschatological community, but it does not thereby cease to be a human community;[34] and Welch reminded us (following Barth) that it exists in the interim between the first *parousia* of the forty days and the last *parousia* of judgment, and that during this period the struggle is centered within its own life. Then "how," he asks, "are we to understand the eschatology of the church in relation to its ontology, the being of the church in relation to its coming-to-be?" Whatever 'perfection' the Church has belongs wholly to Christ, "and the church has these qualities only as it depends upon and shares in him." It is not to be thought of as a separate self-justifying entity, nor does it even possess its own *esse* as something "delivered over to it from God, but always as being-in-relation to God in Christ through the Spirit."[35]

His fundamental insight into the nature of the Church

[32] *Ibid.*, p. 91.

[33] *Ibid.*, p. 119.

[34] For this reason Welch prefers the image of 'the Bride' as the most appropriate of the biblical images for the Church. This figure emphasizes the Church's dependence on her Lord while also pointing to the eschatological role.

[35] Cf. *ibid.*, pp. 138-141.

comes to a focus in this statement: "Precisely in its existence as a socio-temporal society, it exists by an openness to God. Thus, to say that the church lives by the mercy of God is not a pious sentiment, but a statement about the ontology of the church, which defines its self-existence as inseparable from and determined by its existence in dependence upon God."[36] It is clear that here is no room for relating the Church to the Incarnation without also relating it to the Atonement: "the church," declared Welch, "is always 'for a purpose,' and the final end of its being is always God and his kingdom."[37] By the very nature of its task the Church stands in and with the world, as the object of God's covenant and calling, as the arena in which the struggle ensues, as the recipient of God's judgment and grace, as the community called for that particular mission, and as the community responsive to God's will in the world's behalf.[38]

In his final chapter on "The Community of the Spirit" Welch had some pertinent things to say on the flexibility that the Church needs to meet its task of bringing the Kingdom to this world. He pointed to the centrality of Pentecost in the New Testament and noted that the New Testament does not separate the work of the Spirit from Jesus Christ (cf. John 16:12-15). The work of the Spirit emphasizes God's freedom with respect to all historical forms, a freedom that respects human responsibility and recognizes that it is possible to respond to God's will in many different ways. Although there had been a concentration in history on discerning the external 'marks' of the Church, the real problem "is not one of deciding what minimum of 'marks' is necessary for the existence of the church; it is the task of allowing the Spirit to work more fully in all his ways of presence."[39] The centrality of the Spirit within the New Testament Church meant that the Church's face was set towards the future and to God's purpose in the world, for although the Kingdom is not to be identified with the Church, the Kingdom is present in the Church and is

[36] Cf. *ibid.*, pp. 142f.

[37] *Ibid.*, p. 211.

[38] *Ibid.*, pp. 205ff.

[39] *Ibid.*, p. 246.

proclaimed by the Church. This, he observed, "requires openness to the ways of form and freedom in which the Spirit will move in the future of the church, ways which will manifest continuity with his working in past and present but which may involve transformation and fulfillment of the patterns and forms we now know, as he leads the church toward its final goal."[40]

In my view *The Reality of the Church* has much more significance than that of simply being a good book on the nature of the Church. It might have been the point of departure for a genuinely ecumenical doctrine of the Church that would have been biblically based without being biblically bound, for although Welch operated within the context of biblical theology he attacked the temptation to interpret the biblical images of the Church with a new literalism; and what makes his book particularly insightful is that he did so by appealing to the redemptive incarnation at the heart of the biblical revelation. It is the protest of one who sees that the 'orthodoxy' of the gospel goes beyond legalism or literalism, and it represents the claim that the revelation of God's own nature and redemptive purpose must govern our understanding of the Church.

We must see his emphasis on the essentially human character of the Church in the light of this. It is because of Jesus Christ that the Church is not only human but ontologically human, and she receives her call from God and can fulfil his purpose only because she is human. If there is any sense in which the incarnation of our Lord may be analogous to the Church's ministry in the world, it is as we take the carnality of the Incarnation with absolute seriousness, and only as we see the Church witnessing to Christ's redeeming life and death within the ambiguities of her own place and time.

One detects a similar concern in Langdon Gilkey's book, *How the Church Can Minister to the World Without Losing Itself*. Gilkey also reveals his debt to the biblical theology of the preceding decade, and a good deal of the book is taken up with expounding the biblical concepts popular in the ecumeni-

40 *Ibid.*, p. 248.

cal theology of the period—the Church as the People of God, as the hearers of the Word, and as the Body of Christ. However, *How the Church Can Minister to the World Without Losing Itself* shows too that by the time it appeared the situation was changing. By 1964 we were in a new world where the secularity hinted at in Claude Welch's final chapter was rapidly becoming a commonplace, a world of civil rights and social activism. When Welch had written, the primary danger seemed to come from ecumenists who appeared to be using biblical categories to justify their ecclesiastical goals, but by the time Gilkey's book arrived the thought of Bonhoeffer had popularized 'worldly Christianity'; secularity was becoming fashionable and the churches were bravely attempting responsible involvement in the secular life of man. The new trend may not have reached its zenith, but it speaks a good deal for Langdon Gilkey's honesty that in 1964 he was ready to speak out against its dangers. Indeed, his major concern was with the growing loss of any sense of Transcendence in the Church.[41]

This does not mean that Gilkey rejected the new social involvement of the Church—on the contrary, it was at the center of the gospel. The 'Transcendent' must not be set in opposition to God's immanent presence in this world; "for the life of the congregation cannot in any sense express transcendence of the culture around it unless it is willing to challenge the injustice and sins of the wider community in which it lives."[42] In Protestant churches at least, Gilkey declared, there could be no witness to the Transcendent without response in life to the Word of God in Christ: "the central mediation of the holy in the life of the church comes through the Word, the message of Jesus Christ in lordly claim, in judgment, and in grace."[43] What 'the Word' means to the Church is to be interpreted in no literal or mechanical way.

41 Perhaps the same loss of the Transcendent is at the center of what Edward Farley described in *Requiem for a Lost Piety* (Philadelphia: Westminster, 1966). The difference between Farley and Gilkey, however, would seem to be that whereas the former accepted the loss as natural in the twentieth-century church, the latter did not.

42 *Op. cit.*, p. 71.

43 *Ibid.*, p. 80.

> For the Word that creates and recreates the church is neither a system of doctrine nor of scriptural passages. It is, rather, the living impact of God's revelation in Christ on a community of men: it is the immediate address to a community of God's judgment on their sins; of His forgiveness and love, with which they are received into fellowship again; and of the personal promise of His grace, by which they live in hope.[44]

Beyond this, and at a much deeper level than any merely formal assent to dogma, it must be translated into the active relationships of life, for if "this message is not heard, believed, and enacted, then the main element of holiness in the Protestant church is gone, and it reflects merely the views and ideals of its surrounding society."[45] In line with the growing conviction of the 1960s Gilkey affirmed that there can be no false opposition between that which the Church professes and that which the Church does, between doctrine and ethics.

At the same time, the value of Gilkey's book is that he was ready to affirm with equal conviction that until we are certain that the Kingdom of God has been finally realized we dare not allow the Church to lose its identity and its witness in this world, for although the Church is called to serve the world and work for the Kingdom it is a distinct community that responds to Christ's own word. "It is formed fundamentally by the calling of each one of us by Jesus Christ through his Word, and by His presence in grace and power in the midst of the faithful congregation. The Church is the Body of Christ where His Spirit dwells."[46]

Although each had his own distinctive emphases, Claude Welch and Langdon Gilkey stand on common ground in their approach to ecclesiology. With the advantage of hindsight we can see that this might have been a creative point of departure in the ecumenical understanding of the Church, but the moment was in fact simply a point of balance where the theological concerns of the 1940s and 50s slipped very rapidly into the social activism of the years that followed. This fact represents their significance for the doctrine of the Church: for a brief time all the elements were held in balance without

44 *Ibid.*, pp. 77f.
45 *Ibid.*, p. 80.
46 *Ibid.*, p. 105.

feeling any need to follow a true fashion. Both these writers recognized a solid base in biblical theology but refused to be seduced into neo-literalism, and this enabled them to keep a balance between the Church's relationship to its Lord and the Church's relationship to the world, between the ecumenical imperative to make unity visible and the insights drawn from the secular society and religious pluralism. Nor is 'balance' quite the right word to use, as if these things are to be weighed against each other, for really what we find in these books is the recognition that the apparent paradoxes exist in such dynamic relationship that the one *demands* the other.

At the most fundamental level Welch and Gilkey recognized that the Church's nature is essentially determined by the God who spoke his redemptive Word to man in Jesus Christ, and who in the same Spirit calls the Church into a similar ministry of reconciliation. And when that is understood, the doctrine of the Church has a different dimension; we begin to see something not only of its essential catholicity but also of the universality of its message. For what could be more catholic in its scope or universal in its appeal than the vocation to express "mature manhood, measured by nothing less than the full stature of Christ"?[47]

3

THE SUBURBAN BASTILLE

Humor can be prophetic. Although Stephen Leacock's Plutoria Avenue hardly qualifies as a suburb in the quintessential sense known to our mid-twentieth century, it enjoyed all the most important characteristics—it was self-consciously affluent, it was where the 'best' people lived, and its Mausoleum Club was a more leisured age's equivalent of the country club. In particular, it was served by two churches—St. Asaph's (Episcopal) and St. Osoph's (Presbyterian)—which had advanced in status with the advancing status of their members.

47 Ephesians 4:13 (NEB).

> In one respect the rival churches of Plutoria Avenue had had a similar history. Each of them had moved up by successive stages from the lower and poorer parts of the city. Forty years ago St. Asaph's had been nothing more than a little frame church with a tin spire, away in the west of the slums, and St. Osoph's a square, diminutive building away in the east. But the site of St. Asaph's had been bought by a brewing company, and the trustees, shrewd men of business, themselves rising into wealth, had rebuilt it right in the track of the advancing tide of a real estate boom. The elders of St. Osoph, quiet men, but illumined by an inner light, had followed suit and moved their church right against the side of an expanding distillery. Thus both the churches, as decade followed decade, made their way up the slope of the city . . . .
>
> As the two churches moved, their congregations, or at least all that was best of them—such members as were sharing in the rising fortunes of the city—moved also, and now for some six or seven years the two churches and two congregations had confronted one another among the elm-trees of the avenue opposite the university.[48]

An appropriate ministry was provided for St. Asaph's by the Reverend Mr. Furlong, of whom Leacock says, "there was nothing in the theological system of Mr. Furlong that need have occasioned in any of his congregation a moment's discomfort."[49] St. Osoph's owned a sterner heritage, but no doubt the elders took grim satisfaction that if, in the view of the Reverend Mr. Dumfarthing, their own salvation was extremely questionable, the damnation of everyone else was without doubt. So the churches of Plutoria Avenue dispensed to their congregations the kind of comfort and security that each found most congenial.

In one other way they were a remarkable forecast of the churches in mid-twentieth-century suburbia. They maintained only the most tenuous ties with the rest of the city, and were careful not to become too involved with its problems. So Leacock delicately described the city outside Mr. Furlong's parish:

> Whatever sin there was in the city was shoved sideways into the roaring streets of commerce, where the elevated railway ran, and below that again into the slums. Here there must have been any

48 *Arcadian Adventures with the Idle Rich* (London: John Lane the Bodley Head, 1952 [first published 1914]), pp. 125f.

49 *Ibid.*, p. 128.

> quantity of sin. The rector of St. Asaph's was certain of it. Many of the richer of his parishioners had been down in parties late at night to look at it, and the ladies of his congregation were joined together into all sorts of guilds and societies and bands of endeavour for stamping it out and driving it under or putting it into jail until it surrendered.
>
> But the slums lay outside the rector's parish. He had no right to interfere. They were under the charge of a special mission, or auxiliary, a remnant of the St. Asaph's of the past, placed under the care of a divinity student, at four hundred dollars per annum. His charge included all the slums and three police-courts and two music halls and the city jail. One Sunday afternoon in every three months the rector and several ladies went down and sang hymns for him in his mission-house.[50]

Leacock was prophetic, for his account appeared in 1914; and yet the satire stings as much now as it did then. What his wit saw in North America before World War I, later sociologists have fully documented, for he had placed an ironical finger on the way in which the churches were becoming acclimatized to the affluent culture, and in particular he had the measure of the distinctive forms of churchmanship that would become most at home in suburbia.

Plenty of modern writers on the Church have pointed out that there is a basic paradox between what the Church claims to be and what it actually is. Claude Welch had frankly accepted the 'human' character of the Church and made it a major thrust in his ecclesiology, while Langdon Gilkey had pointed out that neither liberals nor conservatives in America—neither St. Asaph's nor St. Osoph's—had been very successful in withstanding the inroads of materialism: the difference between them "is not that one affirms and capitulates to modern culture while the other rejects it. Rather the difference lies in the way the two deal with the culture they both accept—for they drive the same Chevrolets, go to the same doctors, stare at the same TV sets, run the same businesses, are protected by the same missiles, and are afraid of the same sputniks."[51]

50 *Ibid.*, pp. 132f.

51 *How the Church Can Minister . . .*, p. 47. Langdon Gilkey said that religious liberals tried to reinterpret Christian faith in the light of the new scientific world view, and in doing so "made Christianity into the religious expression of this

Nevertheless, in 1961 James Gustafson could complain with some justice that although a spate of books had been written on the Church, there had been very few which had tried to relate it to social theory.[52] The appearance of his own book with those of Peter Berger and Gibson Winter in the same year indicates that a similar thought had occurred to several people at the same time, and that around the turn of the decade there had been a change in the ecclesiological climate. As the writings of Bonhoeffer became more widely known, theologians began to suspect that they had been far too glib in disparaging 'the secular'—that in many ways 'secular man' was much more truly human and adult than those who used religion as a crutch to lean on or as a funk-hole of escape, and that there is something inherently false about the churches' appeal to men when they were weak and most fearful.[53] Furthermore, as sociologists probed America's postwar 'revival of religion' and noted the ways in which denominations accepted the characteristic mold of American culture and supported its more questionable shibboleths, there were some who wondered whether the Church should be described as paradox or as simple contradiction.

Ecumenical circles first became conscious of this sociological critique with the appearance of *Protestant-Catholic-Jew,*[54] by Will Herberg, a Jewish sociologist of religion who admitted his debt to Protestant thinkers like Reinhold Niebuhr, and who in turn was to have a profound influence on Protestant thought in America. Described as "An Essay in American Religious Sociology," the book was in part an explanation of the paradox of the American nation itself,[55] and in particular of the contrast between the incredible numerical

scientific and humanist culture." Conservatives, on the other hand, solved the problem by maintaining a strict division between the secular and the sacred—they let the prevailing culture "dominate their life six days in the week and allow it no truck with their religion on Sunday." *Ibid.*

[52] James M. Gustafson, *Treasure in Earthen Vessels: The Church as a Human Community* (New York: Harper, 1961), p. 1.

[53] Cf. *Letters and Papers from Prison,* ed. Eberhard Bethge, trans. R. H. Fuller (London: S.C.M., 1957), pp. 121ff.

[54] 1955. My quotations will be from the Anchor Book edition, New York, 1960.

[55] *Op. cit.,* pp. 1f., 72f., 219ff.

growth of the churches after World War II, and the equally incredible materialism of their members; the blatant contradiction in the facts that more Bibles were sold, but fewer were read, or that while the churches were crowded Sunday by Sunday and often during the week, those who attended had only the vaguest knowledge of the faith they were supposed to profess. The phenomenon was all the more striking ecumenically because the eyes of the world were upon America, and her churches were enjoying their religious boom at a time when churches were having a very hard time everywhere else.

Certainly the American people's new international responsibilities stimulated some of this remarkable return to religion, but Will Herberg showed that alongside this, the 'church,' whether represented by Protestant meeting house, Catholic chapel, or Jewish synagogue, was fulfilling a vitally important role in the development of national consciousness. The United States of America is a nation of immigrants. Herberg showed that the churches provided a community-of-transition for the immigrant—a community that was fully accepted in the new nation, but where the immigrant could sustain significant aspects of the traditional culture he had left.[56] This, of course, was particularly true of the ethnic churches: they enabled the transplanted European to hold on to the past while he and his family became adjusted to their adopted country.

A half-century before this Max Weber had suggested that in the anonymity of the American frontier membership in a church had served the important social purpose of guaranteeing a newcomer's credit and financial trustworthiness;[57] now Herberg showed that in the equally anonymous conditions of immigration, the 'churches' served a similar function of guaranteeing the newcomer's trustworthiness as a potential citizen. Religion—it didn't really matter which—was equated with all that was essentially 'American.'

Instead of the single American 'melting pot,' we should

56 *Ibid.*, chapters 1 and 2.

57 "The Protestant Sects and the Spirit of Capitalism," in *From Max Weber*, trans. H. H. Gerth and C. Wright Mills (New York: Oxford, 1946).

rather think of three discrete but equally acceptable melting pots, Protestant, Catholic, and Jewish, which comprised a kind of corporate religious establishment. The major thrust of Herberg's thesis appears when he said:

> Just as sociologically we may describe the emerging social structure of America as one great community divided into three big sub-communities religiously defined, all equally American, so from another angle we might describe Protestantism, Catholicism, and Judaism in America as three great branches or divisions of "American religion."[58]

However, it was the social character of this 'American religion' behind the facade of the churches which really interested Will Herberg and his Protestant followers. "That 'religion,'" declared Herberg bluntly in the 1950s, "is the system familiarly known as the American Way of Life. It is the American Way of Life that supplies American society with an 'overarching sense of unity' amid conflict. It is the American Way of Life about which Americans are admittedly and unashamedly 'intolerant.' It is the American Way of Life that provides the framework in terms of which the crucial values of American existence are couched. By every realistic criterion the American Way of Life is the operative faith of the American people."[59]

Herberg's insights clarified many things that had previously been obscure or accepted without question—the rise of religious pluralism and powerful 'denominations,'[60] the apparent contradictions in the American approach to ecumenism,[61] the

[58] Herberg, *op. cit.*, p. 38.

[59] *Ibid.*, p. 75. Cf. also the following: "Americanness today entails religious identification as Protestant, Catholic, or Jew in a way and to a degree quite unprecedented in our history. To be a Protestant, a Catholic, or a Jew are today the alternative ways of being an American" (p. 258).

[60] These matters began to receive some attention. In addition to other works treated in this section, we might mention Paul Harrison's *Authority and Power in the Free Church Tradition* (Princeton, N.J.: Princeton U.P., 1959). There is also a brief unpublished study that unconsciously brings together the interest in denominational organization, middle-class values, and capitalistic economics: *Investment Policies of Churches in America (Three Case Studies)*, S.T.M. thesis of Francis Symington Gibson, Hartford Seminary Foundation, 1962.

[61] There has been a curious ambivalence in American attitudes to ecumenism. On the one hand it is far broader than in Europe, because, as Herberg says, "Interfaith is . . . the highest expression of religious coexistence and co-operation within the American understanding of religion." *Op. cit.*, p. 259. On the other

churches' identification with capitalistic economy and 'healthy' competition, and their opposition to the 'godlessness' of Communism. It went a long way to explain the post-World War II 'revival of religion,' why—in the midst of more affluence than the world had ever seen—American culture had centered in such middle-class values, and in particular, why there was such concentration of church power in the suburbs to which America's rising middle class had been migrating in droves.

> It will not escape the reader that this account is essentially an idealized description of the middle-class ethos. And, indeed, that is just what it is. The American Way of Life is a middle-class way, just as the American people in their entire outlook and feeling are a middle-class people.[62]
>
> Self-identification in religious terms, almost universal in the America of today, obviously makes for religious belonging in a more directly institutional way. It engenders a sense of adherence to a church or denomination and impels one to institutional affiliation. These tendencies are reinforced by the pressures of other-directed adjustment to peer-group behavior, which today increasingly requires religious identification with some church. Thus a pattern of religious conformism develops, most pronounced, perhaps, among the younger, 'modern-minded' inhabitants of Suburbia, but rapidly spreading out to all sections of the American people.[63]

Herberg also raised a basic theological issue—a point at which he revealed his deep agreement with Karl Barth, Reinhold Niebuhr, and other theologians of the neo-orthodox movement—when he drew a sharp distinction between the biblical Faith and 'religion,' and made the comment that "to a man of biblical faith, religion is not self-validating or self-

hand, the operative words are 'coexistence' and 'co-operation,' for these define the normal *limits* of American ecumenism. Church members are still extremely reluctant to consider organic unity, and it should be remarked that a proposal such as COCU—which came from the leadership—still has to meet the challenge of the parishes. The most common American mood is illustrated in the report of a Baptist minister in Pennsylvania who organized an interdenominational day-care center in his church. *Life* reported that "It is now a happy, roaring success. 'But we don't scare the local people by calling it ecumenical', he says, 'We prefer 'cooperative Christianity.' " *Life,* 70/1 (January 8, 1971), 16B.

62 Herberg, *op. cit.,* pp. 80f. Americans should not feel too bad about being damned as 'middle class,' since it is inevitably the dominant class in any dynamic national economy. Napoleon dismissed the British as 'a nation of shopkeepers.'

63 *Ibid.,* p. 257.

justifying: it has to be tested, critically examined, and evaluated in terms of its authenticity in mediating the will, judgment, and redeeming grace of the God who can be 'met' only in repentance and the abandonment of all claims to human sufficiency."[64] The stage was set; and if those who came after Herberg used the same sociological tools that he used, the primary criticism of the American churches voiced by many critics also centered in essentially the same theological criticism.

One of the writers whose work received the most attention was the Christian sociologist Peter Berger, who published two books in 1961 directed to this theme. In *The Noise of Solemn Assemblies*[65] Berger continued the exposé of the American religious establishment in well-written prose and telling illustrations. He then went on to suggest ways in which Christians might work for a true disestablishment within American society. Not only was religion in general the way in which an individual found acceptance in America,[66] but the denominations themselves—with interesting regional variations—had developed along class lines, so that membership of a particular denomination and parish became a fairly accurate indication of social status.

> At the risk of sounding offensive, we should thus say there are upper-strata individuals who "consume," say, Congregationalism in the same way and for the same reason that they "consume" *filet[s] mignons,* tailored suits, and winter vacations in the Caribbean. All these elements of consumption indicate to the world (and perhaps to themselves as well) that these individuals have attained a position in society where such things belong.[67]

A Christian could only dissociate himself completely from such spurious 'religion' and face the gospel of God's redeeming

64 *Ibid.,* p. 255; cf. pp. 254-56.

65 Garden City, N.Y.: Doubleday, 1961.

66 "The act of joining a religious group manifests publicly the adherence to this value system and to the majority of the nation which embraces it . . . . Religion is something for those who have a stake in and a commitment to society as it now exists." *Ibid.,* p. 89.

67 *Ibid.,* p. 77. Berger draws from others who had worked in the sociology of religion, particularly H. Richard Niebuhr, *The Social Sources of Denominationalism* (New York: Henry Holt, 1929); Liston Pope, *Millhands and Preachers* (New Haven:

love in Jesus Christ. This would demand something akin to new personal conversion,[68] new theological seriousness and social responsibility, and a willingness to experiment in new forms of churchmanship.

At this point it is clear that *The Noise of Solemn Assemblies* has to be set within the context of Berger's broader critique of cultural religion that he published in the same year, *The Precarious Vision.*[69] Although he later drew back from some of the views he expressed in these books, particularly from the neo-orthodox distinction between 'religion' and 'Christian faith,' which he could no longer regard as empirically valid,[70] I am not sure that this recantation seriously affects his fundamental criticism of what the American churches had allowed themselves to become.[71]

In *The Precarious Vision* he probed behind the facade of cultural religion. His major thesis is that all forms of society are precisely that, a facade, tragi-comedy, a 'precarious vision' in which "all of us are balancing our acts like acrobats pre-

Yale, 1942); Kenneth Underwood, *Protestant and Catholic* (Boston: Beacon, 1957).

68 "Again we would be careful not to circumscribe the conditions under which God's grace can enter a human life. However, speaking empirically, we would suppose that conversion to the Christian faith in our situation will likely involve a break through the social-psychological functionality of the religious establishment. Furthermore, we would suppose that this break-through is also likely to be associated with at least a measure of alienation from the 'O.K. world' of the culture. To say the least, it is difficult to imagine how the religiously mature, socially respectable, and psychologically adjusted church member in our situation can come to terms with the naked horror of Calvary or the blazing glory of Easter morning. Both his religion and his culture compel him to sentimentalize, neutralize, assimilate these Christian images." *Ibid.,* p. 118.

69 Garden City, N.Y.: Doubleday, 1961.

70 Peter Berger, *The Sacred Canopy* (Garden City, N.Y.: Doubleday, 1967), Appendix II, pp. 179ff.

71 Although it may be illegitimate to draw a distinction between 'Christian faith' and all other religion in the way many neo-orthodox theologians did, the impact of Berger upon the churches was precisely because they recognized that there *is* a very real distinction between the kind of cultural religion they had become and the ethical imperatives at the center of their own mission and message. It is certainly not legitimate to use the distinction as a means of dissociating Christianity from other religions, or of avoiding the empirical examination of all that makes faith part of human experience, but to accept the distinction *within* any religion is no more than to recognize how faith in actuality falls short of the revelation or insight that called it forth. As far as I can see, on this basis Berger's criticism of the churches is still valid.

cariously standing one on top of the other. One false move and the whole human edifice comes crashing down. Thus society is comedy indeed—but tragedy at the same time, for as the acrobats come crashing down there is real pain and real terror."[72] Within this charade, the traditional function of religion has been to validate "the carnival of masks," to give an illusion of absoluteness to the structure and the social roles we play.[73]

> Religion, then, functions by integrating the actors' values and beliefs in such a way that they are made capable of co-operation. Religion lets the actors believe that their play is ultimately right, and, of course, as a result of this belief the play is facilitated. Or one could put the same thing by saying that religion provides the *imprimatur* for the libretto—or the *fiat spectaculum* for the whole operation.[74]

To this end religion supports the Establishment by co-ordinating the public consensus regarding conduct, norms, and mores, controls the inner conscience by stimulating the sense of guilt, and ultimately endorses coercion and the punishment inflicted by society upon those who transgress its rules. This involves fundamental 'bad faith'; and when churches carry their support of the Establishment to the point of sanctifying executions and blessing the weapons of the military, they become an 'indecency.'[75] His fundamental criticism of the American churches was that they became the validating agent for the American Way of Life, and that they support the 'O.K. world' epitomized by the rising executive who uses the city to make money, but whose life, values, and prejudices are those of middle-class suburbia from which he commutes.[76]

Pressing the distinction between culturally conditioned 'religion' and 'Christian faith,' he urged that whereas "Religion functions in society as a basis of morality, of law and order, of respectability, of a sound and sober way of life,"[77] Christianity cannot allow itself to become the basis for any system

72 *The Precarious Vision,* p. 53.

73 *Ibid.,* p. 21.

74 *Ibid.,* pp. 104f.

75 *Ibid.,* p. 21.

76 *Ibid.,* pp. 174f., 120ff.

77 *Ibid.,* p. 173.

of morality because "before the cross of Jesus Christ *all* systems of morality are relativized and judged," and to be a Christian means a willingness to live out God's love in faith "which makes it possible freely to seek moral solutions to the ever-new problems that face us"; it cannot be a basis for law and order because "there is no social order without violence" and Christ meets violence with the cross; it cannot be the basis for respectability or a sound and sober life because Jesus himself was content to live "among the despised, the rejected, and those living on the sorrowful peripheries of society," and because the gospel does not reassure men about their sound and sober plans but "tears them out of their security, puts them and all that is theirs under judgment, and throws them up against all the metaphysical questions that can be asked and thence into the luminous night of God's desert, a night stabbed with terror but also with pangs of joy."[78] In a passage that would have done credit to Peter Taylor Forsyth he declared that the God of Christian faith is entirely personal and judges all human institutions in the light of his essentially personal relationship with men.[79]

We called Stephen Leacock 'prophetic' in the sense that he spoke to a future situation, but Peter Berger was prophetic in the deeper biblical sense of bringing home to God's people the judgment of the God whom they profess to worship and insisting that they face the meaning of his self-revelation. Berger defined precisely the dilemma in which Christians find themselves in society.

And yet it is a *dilemma*, as perhaps Berger recognizes in his later work. The establishment of human society on the basis of justice, law and order, and even sober respectability is not to be brushed aside as totally irrelevant to the life of man; and insofar as this corporate life needs validation that points beyond individual and sectional self-interests it indicates a fundamental human need. That religions of all kinds have been pressed into this role may itself have a significance that goes far beyond the immediate need for security and may say something about human destiny in terms of its communal

[78] *Ibid.*, p. 176.

[79] *Ibid.*, pp. 193ff.

relationships and responsibilities. On the other hand, Berger reminded Christians how far this admittedly human use of their religion comes short of the reconciliation and at-onement at the center of their own faith, and recalled them to a faith that always stands in protest against any society that tries to contain it within its own cultural box.

Will Herberg's critique of the churches had been pushed further by Peter Berger in his own examination of society and of the part religion played in undergirding its cultural principles and prejudices; but although he recognized the significance of American suburbanites and their cultic practices, his concern with the suburban churches *per se* was incidental. On the other hand, they became the major focus of Gibson Winter in *The Suburban Captivity of the Church.*[80]

Winter put the spotlight on the exodus of Protestants to the suburbs and its consequences. He pointed out that the main branches of Protestantism had become firmly aligned with the aspirations, prejudices, and values of the American middle class,[81] and that within their patterns of churchmanship there were pressures which would keep them this way and make their congregations economically and socially homogeneous. The major 'respectable' denominations had failed to win the poor, the socially depressed and disinherited people in the inner city, and even the accent upon lay evangelism tended to make them more segregated and more class conscious.[82] The 'organization church' with its busy work of committees and 'activities' was well equipped to call forth the energies of the class of person for whom it had been started, although the members might have great difficulty in stating clearly what its purpose was or what was the focal point of their loyalty. Winter saw the continual round of largely irrelevant activity as

80 Garden City, N.Y.: Doubleday, 1961.

81 *Ibid.,* p. 48. This solid identification of Protestantism with middle-class America would make it extremely susceptible to the middle-class values of Americanism. Cf. Herberg, *op. cit.,* pp. 80f.

82 "The lay ministry is a means to recruit like-minded people who will strengthen the social-class nucleus of the congregation. Churches can be strengthened through this process of co-option so long as the environs of the church provide a sufficient pool of people who can fit the pattern of economic integration." *The Suburban Captivity,* p. 72. Cf. also pp. 74, 156.

a Protestant form of "secularized penance" and therefore the perfect vehicle for what Bonhoeffer had called 'cheap grace.'[83] Because of its ingrown clannishness and introversion, the organization church had become "a secularized sect, whose distinctiveness is created by middle-class life, not faith."[84] He commented:

> It is ironical that Protestantism, after rebelling against the institutional character of Roman Catholicism, should emerge in the 1960s with a membership predominantly oriented to organizational activities and concentrated in the middle years—families with growing children, high earning power, and more than average energy. In other words, Protestantism today represents the dominant group in America's productive process.[85]

The middle-class criterion of success is very clearly centered in what a person does and achieves, and the sheer busyness of institutional Protestant churches would obviously attract this kind of person.[86] Winter went on to point out that those who were active in church affairs also tended to be active in community associations;[87] and although this appeared as simply further evidence that the Protestant middle-class American was constitutionally committed to activism for its own sake, in the light of later events the involvement of church people in civil affairs may be open to a more positive interpretation.[88]

The Protestant churches had become concentrated in the suburbs, except for those churches—Ethnic, Black, Sectarian—which were tied to special groupings within the city. Mainline

83 *Ibid.*, p. 97.

84 *Ibid.*, p. 124.

85 *Ibid.*, p. 100.

86 The concern with action probably lies deeper in Protestantism than Winter realized. I argued in *The Atonement and the Sacraments* that Protestant theology was essentially grounded in the *magnalia dei;* and if theology is centered in God's *action,* then it is to be expected that this will be reflected in Protestant churchmanship. Activity simply for the sake of activity is clearly a bastard form, but we must be careful in criticizing this not to imply that action—ethics—can be divorced from faith.

87 *Ibid.*, p. 100.

88 Within a few years some Protestant churches were in the thick of the Civil Rights movement and involved in an incredible number of movements for social reform in American society. Perhaps the irrelevant busyness of church life during

Protestantism was leaving the inner city spiritually destitute; and Winter showed that as the inner city became more and more populated with those most heavily disadvantaged, a crisis in urban leadership was bound to descend upon the cities in which the churches of the exodus would be unrepresented and impotent.[89] The cleavage in society was paralleled by a cleavage among the churches to the detriment of both: "The blue-collar and white-collar schism of the metropolis is thus crystallized in the schism between sectarian churches and the major denominations. This schism, as much a matter of style of life and culture as of economic interest, now cuts through the Negro community and complicates the division between Negro and White communities."[90] He made the prophecy in 1961—which all recent figures on the churches seem to support—that if the trend continued and a real ministry was denied the inner city, "within a score of years, Protestantism will be fatally weakened as a significant religious force in the United States."[91]

To reverse this trend, renewal would be necessary on two fronts—in the Church itself, and in the metropolitan society within which it was called to minister; for the basic failure of the Church was its failure to minister to those in the inner city who needed help. Winter's fundamental concern, as was Peter Berger's, was with Christian ethics, and with the Church as the expression of its own ethic. The question of 'credibility,' which Hans Küng has raised very pointedly to Roman Catholics, was implicit in Gibson Winter's statement that "the organization of faith expresses or denies the Word to the world. When it expresses the Word, it channels ministry into

the 1950s and 60s was as much due to confusion about significant goals as it was an indictment of superficial faith. There is no *necessary* identity between Protestant activism and middle-class irrelevance.

89 Apart from all other considerations, the flight from the city was incredibly shortsighted. If the country will be covered by huge groups of urban clusters, what happens to the suburbs then? Even a wealthy executive can only spend so much time in commuting to and from his suburban haven; for megapolis may arrive long before we have solved the problems (e.g., transportation, pollution, the balance of nature, the need for privacy) that at the moment prevent it from offering an acceptable way of life.

90 *Ibid.*, p. 127.

91 *Ibid.*

mission and servantship."[92] The churches had acted irresponsibly towards the metropolis, and were exhausting their resources in an almost exclusive preoccupation with the private sector of life. For their renewal the denominations would have to turn back the trend of separation between the suburb and the city, and begin to think in terms of a ministry that embraced the needs of urban areas in their totality.[93]

The suburbanization of the churches, however, had not only denuded the city of ministry, but it had impoverished the very congregations that appeared so strong and self-sufficient, for they discovered themselves to be "in captivity to the private interests of middle class enclaves."[94] He suggested that in the last analysis the divisions between the races may yield to solution quicker than the divisions between the classes.[95] "The task of the Church," he declared, "is reconciliation of men with God and with one another in human society. The reconciliation between blue-collar and white-collar, Negro and White, outsider and insider, central city and suburb is the work of the churches." When the churches turn themselves into middle-class social clubs, this ministry of reconciliation "becomes a ministry of division and estrangement."[96] That is, the Church becomes a denial of its own gospel.

With regard to renewal within the metropolis, Winter admitted that although Protestantism had failed in part because of its own structural weaknesses, it had also been the victim of the 'pathology of industrialism'; and the cause of the present situation was that "the doctor was not only infected by the patient, but also spread the infection."[97] The almost exclusive concentration of the Church on the private sector of life had caused an identity crisis in the ministry, for whereas in earlier societies the parson had stood "at the point of intersection

92 *Ibid.*, p. 169.

93 Winter suggested the adoption of the 'sector parish,' in which the parish lines would run from the suburbs into the inner city along the arterial lines of communication. He also suggested the expansion of special ministries to industry, political life, etc. *Ibid.*, pp. 149ff.

94 *Ibid.*, p. 151.

95 *Ibid.*, p. 156.

96 *Ibid.*, pp. 164f.

97 *Ibid.*, p. 164.

between the communal and private lives of the congregation," now he was pushed back entirely into the private sector. The implication was, of course, that if we place ministers at the point where life can again be seen and experienced in its totality, they would lose their frustration. We may agree in part with that, even though we may think the problem of the minister's self-image is rather more complicated.[98]

Recognizing the experimental ministries that were being tried out in various parts of the world, Winter said that the renewal of the Protestant churches would be tested "by the extent of its formative power" to create ministries that could really minister to the whole metropolis, and he said that the general conclusion that came from his work was that "the Church is deformed by the struggle to survive and reformed only as ministry and mission"[99] —an essentially theological conclusion from an essentially sociological study.

We have concentrated on Herberg, Berger, and Winter, not because they were alone in their criticism, but because I

98 *Ibid.*, p. 165. Winter correctly diagnosed the change in ministerial status, but there may be a historical fallacy in his argument. It is true that in former societies the minister stood at the intersection between the public and private experience of his congregation, but he was in that position because he was the interpreter of God's will, to which an individual was finally accountable both in public and in private. The ultimate destiny of the eternal soul was involved, and insofar as the minister was the acknowledged interpreter of God's will he controlled the issues of eternal destiny (just as a doctor may hold the issues of life or death, a lawyer the issues of temporal security or misery, or a psychiatrist the issues of neurosis or adjustment). That is not generally believed today. Therefore, in comparison with other professionals, whose areas of competence and authority have been more clearly established, the minister's area of competence and authority has been pushed further into the private sector of life. The Church certainly occupied the point of intersection in the village life of earlier societies—Winter was right there—but he was wrong if he was suggesting that the point can be occupied again by means of an urban strategy.

The tragedy of the parson's position today is not so much that he has been moved from a central position to the private sector of life, but that he has diminishing authority with which to speak effectively to either; and insofar as the Church avoids answering the question of the authority on which it now bases its claims, there is very little that the parson can say. Only because religion was recognized as giving *ultimate* meaning to life, and hence as governing one's eternal destiny, did the parson occupy that central position in the first place. It is futile to think that position can or should be recaptured in society generally, particularly when many have no clear convictions about the ultimacy of the Church's faith.

99 *Ibid.*, p. 176.

believe their writings represented a turning-point in the way in which the Church was considered.[100] No later writer could afford to ignore the human and sociological aspects of the churches,[101] to which American theologians like Claude Welch and Langdon Gilkey pointed but which, as James Gustafson noted, had been more often brushed aside by their theological colleagues.[102] Many of the later writers, however, did not show the balance that Peter Berger, for example (for all his prophetic intensity), recognized;[103] and they began to concentrate on the human aspects of the Church as if these should be finally and wholly determinative of its character: ecclesiology became dominated by the search for 'relevance,' which Arthur Herzog, himself no overly mild critic of the churches, pointed out should logically cause them to disappear.[104]

100 This is my reason for concentrating on these books rather than on James Gustafson's *Treasure in Earthen Vessels.* Gustafson's book was a plea that the churches should recognize their own sociological structure as a valid element in any sound ecclesiology, but his book is more in line with Claude Welch's balanced position and is more descriptive in its methodology. In a sense the very virtues of the book are the reason I do not deal with it in detail here; it was not the way followed by the later writers.

101 Examples will occur readily to anyone conversant with the mass of material that has appeared since that time. The following books illustrate the point: Pierre Berton's unexpected best-seller, *The Comfortable Pew* (Philadelphia: Lippincott, 1965); Stephen C. Rose (ed.), *Who's Killing the Church?* (Chicago: Chicago Missionary Society, 1966); Arthur Herzog, *The Church Trap* (New York: Macmillan, 1968); Colin W. Williams, *Where in the World?* (New York: National Council of Churches, 1963), and *The Church* (Philadelphia: Westminster, 1968). Even John E. Dittes' *The Church in the Way* (1967), which was in some ways a telling protest against the exclusively sociological emphasis in the recent literature, was no less focussed on the human—in this case, psychological—aspects of the Church.

The influence in denominational and ecumenical circles is illustrated in Herbert T. Neve, *Sources for Change* (Geneva: World Council of Churches, 1968), published for the Commission on Stewardship and Evangelism of the Lutheran World Federation; Grace Ann Goodman, *Rocking the Ark* (New York: Board of National Missions of the United Presbyterian Church in the U.S.A., 1968); *The Church for Others,* ed. Walter J. Hollenweger (Geneva: W.C.C., 1967).

102 *Treasure in Earthen Vessels,* pp. 5f.

103 "A Christian view of our situation can . . . emerge from the tension between theological doctrine and sociological diagnosis. The diagnosis without the doctrine may lead to resignation, which is bad, but the doctrine without the diagnosis almost certainly leads to illusion, which is much worse." *The Noise of Solemn Assemblies,* p. 131.

104 "If organized religion wants to be relevant the way is not to abandon its theology and ideals, as it seems sometimes all too willing to do. Indeed, religion

The sociologists had touched the churches at two sensitive points. They criticized them both as exemplars of their own professed ethical standards, and also for their disregard of the urban crisis that was hitting American society. The two concerns are obviously related.

(1) The ethical issue was the more fundamental. Had sociology criticized the churches merely for their inefficiency or faulty deployment of resources, there might have been cause for alarm but not for guilt. The real trauma was caused because impartial study on scientific principles revealed that the churches in both their policies and structures had become practical denials of the very gospel they preached, and that they had become so identified with the surrounding materialism that secular influences were nearer to the message of Jesus Christ than the communities that professed his name. This insight brought on the agonizing reappraisal in the churches which has caused them to be divided within themselves, and it is interesting to notice that one of the more perceptive and impartial of the Church's critics found that this schizoid tendency centered in anomie or loss of self-identity.[105] We would point out that this is an inevitable consequence of the fact that for many churchmen the traditional authorities had been largely discredited. Sociology has accurately described the symptoms; theology should be ready to clarify the cause.

(2) It is clear that the flight of many Protestant churches from the city to the suburbs provided a striking example of

appears to act like a person whose low self-esteem will make him do almost anything to be popular. But instead of trying to blend with secular culture, religion could separate out, declaring itself distinct from secular man and his thinking.

"Those churches which are obsessed by relevance to the point where there is little or nothing distinctively religious left might well stop calling themselves churches and give themselves another name or disband altogether, since it is quite apparent that much of their ministry and membership do not believe in the official formulations of faith or anything approaching them. At any rate, a ruthless honesty would add to churchly credibility." Herzog, *The Church Trap,* p. 73; but cf. pp. 8f., 20-22, 55f., 61, 97, 131-152, 166, 173f.

105 Herzog comments: "religion in America displays the symptoms of a serious crisis in identity, and it is not too much to say that the churches, though still possessed of large resources and reservoirs of good will, are at the moment holding operations, searching for something to do, something for which to live, some clearer conception of just why they are here and what they are here for." *Ibid.,* p. 13; cf. pp. 18f., 61.

the ethical issue. The suburban and bourgeois character of Protestantism had been implicit in Herberg, more explicit in Berger, and most explicit in Winter. "The separation of residence from place of work," declared Winter, "has given an artificial hothouse character to the middle-class neighborhood. The church is one of the plants that grows profusely in the hothouse atmosphere";[106] but hothouse plants are a notoriously bad survival risk when they become exposed to the cold blasts of the open air. Beyond that, however, the churches had neglected their mission and ministry to the inner city. The churches heard this just at the time when the American public was beginning to be conscious of the word 'megapolis,' and to be told that it would probably be the predominant pattern in its cultural future. This was obviously 'relevant,' and this was the aspect that was taken up and developed in the debate on Harvey Cox's *The Secular City*.

4

SABOTAGE AND THE SECULAR

To write a comprehensive account of ecclesiology in the 1960s one would have to cover practically the whole range of modern theology, [107] and as Bonhoeffer had shown, it would have to start with Karl Barth.[108] In particular it would have to deal with the sharp distinction he drew between 'religion' and the Christian faith, and would then examine the way in which Bonhoeffer developed the seed in Barth from which his own idea of 'religionless Christianity' sprang. From this point we could trace three or four distinct lines of development—first, a direct line to the biblical theologians who dominated

106 Winter, *The Suburban Captivity of the Church,* p. 81. Cf. Don Benedict, "Structures for the New Era" in *Who's Killing the Church?,* pp. 42ff.

107 No systematic theologian can ignore saying something about the doctrine of the Church, but this may have very little effect on the way in which the churches think about themselves. I would hold that the significance of Barth, for example, was not in what he said specifically about the Church, but his Christocentric theology. However, there may be some significance in that the projected *Christliche Dogmatik* ended as the *Kirchliche Dogmatik.*

108 *Letters and Papers from Prison,* p. 123.

the ecumenical movement; then a direct relationship to the new theological concern with the 'secular,' and in the extreme Christocentric emphasis that became 'Christian atheism' and 'death of God' theology;[109] and finally, its influence on the 'theology of mission' and through Hendrik Kraemer upon the Dutch missiologists.[110] These separate trends often clash dramatically, but they also had important points of interaction.

This comprehensive study is obviously beyond the scope and intention of the present work, for we are not concerned *per se* with the ways in which the insights of Barth, Bonhoeffer, or any other theologian have been developed, converted, or perverted, but with the making of a new mood: What has contributed to the present confusion and lack of grip in the Church about its own essential nature when, in many ways, the ecumenical possibilities have been more promising than at any time since the sixteenth century? For the answer to this question we must turn not to the tomes of major theologians, but to those who wrote the paperbacks and captured the headlines.

It is a period when popular theology suddenly hit the headlines. For the churches had no sooner caught their breath from the incredible publicity enjoyed by Bishop J. A. T. Robinson's *Honest to God* in Great Britain,[111] than the furor of the 'death of God' theology in the United States broke upon them, and the unexpected stir caused by Pierre Berton's

[109] In the writings of Thomas Altizer, William Hamilton, and Paul van Buren. The Barthian influence is generally acknowledged in van Buren and also in Gabriel Vahanian, whose thought sometimes runs parallel to the death of God theology but who should not be wholly identified with it.

[110] Hendrik Kraemer's first great work has been *The Christian Message in a Non-Christian World,* which was written for the International Missionary Council conference at Jerusalem in 1928. His influence on the point at issue, and on ecumenical ecclesiology, is seen in the distinction implied in *Religion and the Christian Faith* (London: Lutterworth, 1956), and in shorter but influential works, *A Theology of the Laity* (Philadelphia: Westminster, 1958), and *The Communication of the Christian Faith* (Philadelphia: Westminster, 1956). Kraemer's major concern was with the mission of the Christian Church, but for that reason he could not ignore how it was to be communicated and by whom. The interest was continued in the work of Arend Th. van Leeuwen and J. C. Hoekendijk.

[111] London: S.C.M.; Philadelphia: Westminster, 1963.

Canadian best-seller, *The Comfortable Pew.*[112] There can be no doubt that the public interest in these books was because acknowledged churchmen and theologians seemed to be launching a devastating attack on the most revered tenets of the Church's traditional faith. To this we must add the complete revolution in ecumenical relationships caused by the Second Vatican Council,[113] and Marshall McLuhan's awakening the Western World to the impact of the mass media culture.[114] Even theologians began to recognize that they needed to get their point across: book titles became brief, bright, and brash.

It was a theological climate in which all the most respected religious concepts were open to question. There was an air of apocalypse which reflected the mood of society at large. We were in a world of exploding technology that promised unlimited leisure and made the Protestant ethic of work obsolete,[115] a world of reversed values where unlimited freedom seemed to make more sense than discipline and where the secular became the sacred. We thought of humanity as on the brink of a mutation that would produce the 'new man' as far in advance of the present species as we had been of the ape, and the success of the space programs threw open the cosmos.[116] On the other hand, there was the other aspect of apocalypse—the tensions suffered through the Bay of Pigs and Cuban missile crises, the threat of nuclear holocaust or of suffocation through our own propagation, and insistent whispers of doom no less suicidal and no less certain.[117] Like Milton's 'pendant world,' the human race is poised between

112 Pierre Berton had no official membership in the Church, which made it all the more remarkable that he should have been asked to write his book by an official agency of the Anglican Church in Canada.

113 The Council lasted from October 1962 to December 1965.

114 Marshall McLuhan began to receive public notice in 1966.

115 Cf. Hoekendijk's article, "On the Way to the World of Tomorrow," *Laity,* No. 11 (August 1961), pp. 5ff. (Geneva: W.C.C.).

116 Both these ideas were dramatically brought together in the film, *2001: A Space Odyssey.*

117 Rachel Carson's *Silent Spring* appeared in book form in 1962 (Boston: Houghton Mifflin).

the excruciatingly beautiful possibility of heaven and the excruciatingly horrendous prospect of hell.

Through these years and by these routes Christians began to rediscover God's concern with planet Earth, and to wonder whether they had been too cavalier in their condemnation of the secular. In April 1966 a provocative article appeared in *Christianity and Crisis* entitled "Crisis in the Ecumenical Movement," written by Albert van den Heuvel, the Executive Secretary of the Youth Department of the World Council of Churches.[118] The author pointed to a growing split developing in the movement between those who saw its main purpose in the unity or union of the separated denominations, and those "who regard the ecumenical movement as pertaining to the relation between church and society rather than the relation of the churches among themselves."[119] The former, which comprises most of the ecclesiastical leaders and administrators, he called 'churchly ecumenists,' and he pointed out with some justification that they are increasingly out of touch with their constituency. Their position was based upon the fundamentally false assumptions that church members understand their own tradition and that in the history of denominational division nontheological factors "are less real than the theological ones."[120]

On the other hand,

> For the secular ecumenists the movement has as its first and only objective the renewal of the churches in mission; the unification of

[118] *Christianity and Crisis,* 26/5 (April 4, 1966), 59ff. Other examples of the 'secular' emphasis are to be found in Colin Williams' "Witness in a Secular Age," *Andover Newton Quarterly,* 7/3 (January 1967), 127ff.; William R. Miller, "Is the Church Obsolete? The Crisis of Religion in a Secular Age," *The American Scholar,* 36/2 (Spring 1967), 221ff., and also the volume he edited, *The New Christianity* (New York: Delacorte, 1967).

[119] *Ibid.,* p. 61.

[120] *Ibid.,* p. 60. Insofar as the official position taken by denominational leaders was still based upon the fiction that a denomination holds the ecclesiology on which it was founded, van den Heuvel's criticism is correct. On the other hand, Jeffrey K. Hadden's *The Gathering Storm in the Churches* (1969) and Arthur Herzog's *The Church Trap* (1968) show that the rank and file of the churches are even less happy with their leaders when they jump on the radical and secular bandwagon.

> the historic confessions is a by-product of missionary renewal and, as such, is not very interesting. The ecumenical way leads through (not into) the world; and intermediary stages on that road are not increasing numbers of united churches but joint actions for mission. It is only in concrete dialogue with the world of atheism, other religions, philosophy, science and culture, politics and social questions that theology is united in diversity and that the genuine structures of the Church are to be found.[121]

We admit that the secular ecumenists reached their position largely under the stimulus of the ecumenical movement, and the crisis in that movement touches the doctrine of the Church at its deepest level because it centers in the relation of the Church to its mission, a mission that takes its character from the One who comes to the world in Jesus Christ.

This approach to ecclesiology is illustrated in van den Heuvel's countryman, J. C. Hoekendijk, whose work had been known for some years in ecumenical circles but did not receive much attention in the English-speaking world until *The Church Inside Out,*[122] a selection of his writings, appeared in English in 1966. His debt to Barth and to Kraemer is obvious, and although Harvey Cox later acknowledged his own debt to Hoekendijk,[123] the solid biblical base of the latter's work gives it a significance beyond the excitement caused by the debate about Cox's *The Secular City.*

Hoekendijk started with the assumption, generally admitted by responsible missionary thinkers since the end of World War II, that 'Christendom,' together with all the social, political, and economic imperialisms associated with it, was dead; but he pointed out that all previous doctrines of the Church had either openly or tacitly assumed the benevolent protection of a 'Christian' state. Therefore all previous definitions of the Church, from the Reformers on, had been defective.[124]

121 *Ibid.,* p. 61.

122 J. C. Hoekendijk, *The Church Inside Out,* trans. Isaac C. Rottenberg, ed. L. A. Hoedemaker and Pieter Tijmes (Philadelphia: Westminster, 1966). The book had originally been published in slightly different form as *De Kerk Binnenste Buiten* (Amsterdam: W. Ten Have, 1964).

123 "The extraordinarily fresh thinking of J. C. Hoekendijk underlies much of the present writer's thinking about the church. Unfortunately most of his writing appears in Dutch." *The Secular City* (New York: Macmillan, 1965), p. 148, n. 11.

124 Chapter 1.

The real goal of evangelism is the manifestation of the Messiah, and the establishment of his Kingdom—or, to give that Kingdom its proper quality, his *shalom;* and he comments, "shalom is much more than personal salvation. It is at once peace, integrity, community, harmony and justice."[125] This involves reconciliation at all levels, involvement in a mission that is all-inclusive and truly 'ecumenical,'[126] a reaching out into the issues of war and peace, social ethics, ecumenical relationships, and not simply missionary activity as it was narrowly conceived in the past. This *shalom* has to be proclaimed (*kerygma*), lived (*koinonia*), and demonstrated (*diakonia*). It will be noted that for the methodology of the mission Hoekendijk used the language of the New Testament, but for the purpose and objective—*shalom*—he used the language of the Old Testament, with its concrete emphasis upon the relationship between Israel 'the chosen people' and Israel the nation, and upon shalom as a quality to be enjoyed here and now—a material, tangible kingdom on this earth and in this life.

The traditional approach to the doctrine of the Church had to be turned upside down, particularly the church-centered thinking which had dominated the missionary movement since the Jerusalem conference of 1928.

> Where in this context does the *church* stand. Certainly not at the starting point, nor at the end. The church has no fixed place at all in this context, it happens insofar as it actually proclaims the Kingdom to the world. The church has no other existence than *in actu Christi,* that is, *in actu Apostoli.* Consequently it can never be firmly established but will always remain the paroikia, a temporary settlement which can never become a permanent home . . . .
>
> Whatever else may be said about the church may be of only little relevance. The nature of the church can be sufficiently defined by its function, i.e. its participation in Christ's apostolic ministry. To proclaim the gospel of the Kingdom throughout the oikoumene is the church's *opus proprium,* in fact, it is not her work at all but *ergon Kyriou.*[127]

The Church is nothing of itself, it can demand nothing, and it possesses nothing (not even an ecclesiology). It does not *en-*

125 *Op. cit.,* p. 21.

126 Involving the whole *oikumene*—world-wide.

127 *Ibid.,* p. 42.

gage in mission, but insofar as it is truly the Church, it *becomes* mission.

Using a characterization drawn from Alfred Weber,[128] Hoekendijk declared that we are moving into a totally new society in which the 'Third Man' (the product of classical-Christian culture) is giving place to the 'Fourth Man,' and this demands a totally different approach to evangelism. The Fourth Man belongs to the world of *1984* where revolution will be impossible, and he is therefore essentially a 'rebelling conformist'; realistic to the point of cynicism, he regards all attempts to give meaning or to make sense of life as 'spiritual suicide,' and he plods out his life like Sisyphus in incessant boredom. [129] Hoekendijk regards the advent of this kind of person as an apocalyptic sign, the evidence of a new time beyond the end of our era that is post-Christian,[130] post-ecclesiastical, post-bourgeois, post-personal, and post-religious.

He pointed out that the Bible begins the story of man in a garden and ends it in a city, and just as there was no altar in the garden there would be no temple in the city. [131] In order to meet the challenge of future urban society, the Church would have to be ready to adapt itself to a situation of constant change.[132] The older strategies for evangelism in the city were always defective and are now obsolete, and a new strategy would have to be ready to meet the new mobility of city populations, willing to adapt itself to a constantly changing situation; it would have to be more lay-oriented and prepared to work through small secular groups, less judgmental of those outside its borders and ready to cooperate with all who were prepared to work for common social objectives. The

128 *Ibid.*, pp. 47ff. He cites Alfred Weber's *Kulturgeschichte als Kultursoziologie;* p. 47, n. 1 (cf. p. 196).

129 *Ibid.*, p. 49.

130 He insisted, however, that this can only mean 'post-Christendom.' For him, Christ is the Alpha and Omega, and he made it clear that he would not use the term to imply that we can supersede the cross of Christ. *Ibid.*, p. 51.

131 *Ibid.*, p. 71.

132 There may be inconsistency here. If the future holds the prospect of *1984* and the totalitarianism implied by the existentialist 'Fourth Man,' it is difficult to see society becoming more fluid. However, the supposition of future uncertainty seems to be Hoekendijk's main reason for advocating fluid church forms, and his

Church, therefore, does not *engage in* mission; it *becomes* mission, "the living outreach of God to the world."[133]

This represents but a small part of Hoekendijk's book,[134] but it represents his essential approach to ecclesiology. Indeed, perhaps we have to speak not so much of 'ecclesiology' in his case as of a 'theology of the Church,' for the key to all he says is surely given in that conception of the Church as the outreach of *God* to the world. If the Church is this, then the marks of the Church, its form and character must also point to God himself and his reconciling mission to men. The point of Hoekendijk's confluence with other theologians of the secular was in the extent to which he looked for the dispersion of the Church in society, the willingness of its members to give up formal structures and embrace an existence in diaspora.[135] The reason for this new style of Christian witness is, for Hoekendijk, grounded in the biblical revelation. That is important.

5

CITY OF APOCALYPSE

The expectation of apocalypse seems to pervade the context in which Harvey Cox's book *The Secular City* appeared. It has been pointed out that the insights that we find in that book had been around for some time—as James Gustafson said, they had been 'in the air'—but Cox managed to bring them signifi-

major point must be conceded—we *cannot* predict the immediate future and the need for adaptability arises from that: the Church needs *now* the flexible forms that will enable it to avoid drifting into conformity with societies which (I would point out) are as likely to show the marks of Antichrist as they are of the Kingdom of God. We cannot pre-judge future society; Jacques Ellul, for example, sees the city in very much the same way as Peter Berger sees all society—as the supreme work of man—in stark contrast to the urban utopians. Cf. Jacques Ellul, *The Meaning of the City* (Grand Rapids: Eerdmans, 1971).

133 *Ibid.*, p. 43.

134 He has some extremely perceptive things to say about the "World of Tomorrow" (Part II of the book, especially chapter 10), but I found this part less consistent than the earlier part of the book. For me, he is much more persuasive and cogent—and incidentally, more 'radical'—when he exegetes biblical images than when he is being consciously 'modern.'

135 *Ibid.*, pp. 185ff.

cantly together.[136] There had even been hints as to the primary importance of the metropolis which technology seemed to be developing as its own distinctive social style,[137] although it was pointed out that the city and particularly the plight of the urban ghetto received new attention after the passage of the Civil Rights legislation in 1964 and 1965.[138]

In considering *The Secular City* we enjoy the advantage of being able to read it in the light of the extended debate it stimulated and the response drawn from its author. Cox acknowledged his theological debt to Barth, Bonhoeffer, and Hoekendijk; and one can add that when he wrote the book he was clearly *au courant* with the ecumenical discussion on the Church, with the prevailing trends in biblical theology, and with the sociological critique of the Church that was going on in America: his book reveals the changing currents of that time.

Harvey Cox began by observing that there seems to be a relationship between the rise of urban civilization in the West and the decline of religion, and he suggested that this process of secularization represents man's 'coming of age,' in the sense that idea had been described by Bonhoeffer. Indeed, the process of secularization was not accidental but providential. Later on, in response to the debate that his book caused, he put it very succinctly: "Today I feel more strongly than ever that the secularization should not be viewed as an example of massive and castastrophic backsliding but as a product of the impact of the biblical faith itself on world civilization."[139] The cultural forms that ruled society had first centered in the village, then in the town, and now they found their center in the full expression of computerized, urban technology, the 'technopolis,' which, said Cox, "provides the indispensable social setting for a world of 'no religion at all,' for what we have called the secular style."[140]

136 Cf. Daniel Callahan's editorial comments, *The Secular City Debate* (New York: Macmillan, 1966), p. 1; also Gustafson, *ibid.,* p. 12.

137 Particularly in Gibson Winter's *The New Creation as Metropolis* (New York: Macmillan, 1963).

138 Daniel Callahan in his introduction to *The Secular City Debate,* pp. 1f.

139 *The Secular City Debate,* p. 190.

140 *The Secular City,* p. 2.

This is the point to which history has been propelled, and to which the biblical faith has been pushing it. Cox found evidence in the accounts of creation that man was forced to recognize the disenchantment of nature, in the exodus man had been taught the desacralization of politics, and in the Sinai Covenant he had been given the code that led to the deconsecration of values.[141] This process of secularization was the call to achieve the maturity for which man was created, a maturity that will be able to recognize the old idols for what they are, "for secularization places the responsibility for the forging of human values, like the fashioning of political systems, in man's own hands."[142]

The Church, as conceived by Cox, has the task of bringing man to this secular maturity. Quoting from the Pauline passages where the apostle declares that he has put away childish things, and where he urges his readers to strive towards Christian maturity, Cox observed:

> These images of maturity and responsibility are crucial for our argument here since secularization itself can be viewed as a process of maturing and assuming responsibility. Secularization signifies the removal of religious and metaphysical supports and putting man on his own. It is opening the door of the playpen and turning man loose in an open universe. Consequently it is important to notice that maturation and responsibility symbols are by no means exceptional in the New Testament.[143]

Turning to the shape of the secular city itself, Cox uses two of the basic features of technopolis to illustrate the liberating characteristics of the new society—the telephone switchboard, epitomizing anonymity, and the cloverleaf, as the illustration of mobility. In contrast to the usual homiletical use made of these as sticks with which to beat the callousness of city life, Cox claims that they are liberating qualities that free us from the bondage of our past. The anonymity of the city enables us to be ourselves, preserves our privacy, and gives to us a kind of liberating loneliness in contrast to the stifling intimacy of the

[141] In an odd way what Cox seems to prove here is the necessity of 'religion' for the progress of man.

[142] *Ibid.*, p. 35.

[143] *Ibid.*, p. 119.

small town, while modern mobility frees us from economic or emotional bondage to one small plot of ground: we can pick up our roots and go.[144] He found his biblical support for this in the worship that Israel, the nomad people, gave to Yahweh in contrast to the worship of the Baalim, the gods of the land, and he interpreted Christendom as the attempt "to fashion a sacral civilization to transmute the Christian Gospel into a Baal culture."[145]

In describing the style by which the secular city operates he used John F. Kennedy and Albert Camus as exemplars of its two dominant characteristics—pragmatism and profanity (profane in the sense of nonreligious). Pragmatic technopolitan man is a kind of ascetic who has disciplined himself to accept rational answers. "He approaches problems by isolating them from irrelevant considerations, by bringing to bear the knowledge of different specialists, and by getting ready to grapple with a new series of problems when these have been provisionally solved."[146] Similarly, the characteristic of the profane man is seen in Albert Camus' refusal to accept the traditional ideas about God because he found them irreconcilable with human freedom and justice: he would not be bound by ideas that had no relation to his own experienced reality.

Significantly, Harvey Cox did not begin to expound his view of the Church until he began to discuss the theology of social change. We must admit that the present study would supply a good deal of support for this passage on the Church:

> Our doctrines of the church have come from the frayed-out period of classical Christendom and are infected with the ideology of preservation and permanence. They are almost entirely past-oriented, deriving their authority from one or another classical period, from an alleged resemblance to some earlier form of church

144 It is evident that these features of urban life do grant freedom. It is far less evident that we have reached the maturity that can use that freedom responsibly. E.g., the problem of the aged suggests we have not used our mobility in a very responsible way towards our parents. My major question is not with the potentially liberating character of the secular city, but with the assumption that we have achieved the maturity it demands.

145 *Ibid.*, p. 58.

146 *Ibid.*, p. 63. He also recognized how these qualities could be abused. E.g., pragmatism can degenerate into mere 'operationalism' (p. 67).

> life, or from a theory of historical continuity. But this will no longer do. A church whose life is defined and shaped by what God is *now* doing in the world cannot be imprisoned in such antiquated specifications. It must allow itself to be broken and reshaped continuously by God's continuous action; hence the need for a theology of social change.[147]

On the other hand we should notice that a shift has taken place in that paragraph; what begins by speaking about traditional doctrines of the Church and with some justifiable comments on the way they were historically conditioned, ends by calling for a theology of social change. That really encapsulates Harvey Cox's view of the Church.

In one sense he is a follower of Hoekendijk, since the nature of the Church is wholly determined by its mission; but he goes further than Hoekendijk in suggesting that the mission of the Church is entirely political, aimed at promoting the 'social change' that is, as he admits, simply a euphemism for revolution.[148] He agreed with Hoekendijk and other ecumenical scholars of the period on the primacy of the Kingdom of God motif in the gospels,[149] but his distinctiveness was in tying this completely to the secular style of the technopolis. He conceded that in the New Testament the Kingdom of God is represented as the work of God whereas the secular city is obviously the work of man; but he argues that because the Kingdom of God is the work of the God-Man, Jesus Christ, the theological problem of the Kingdom becomes christological:

147 *Ibid.,* p. 105. While agreeing with his observations about the history of ecclesiology, there are some pertinent questions that I would want to raise on this passage: (a) Can the Church be defined wholly in terms of the changes it manages to bring about in society? (b) Could any body of people live in the constant state of flux that Cox seems to envisage for the Church? (c) Is the Church interested only in what God is doing here and now? How do we judge that it is *God* who is doing these things if we are totally unconcerned with what he did and how he did it in the past? For all the New Testament's emphasis upon the future, is there not also a call for fidelity to the testimony of the past? (d) Do we need a 'theology of social change,' or do we not rather need a deeper biblical *theology,* i.e., a deeper understanding of the God revealed in the Bible?

148 *Ibid.,* p. 107. We should note, however, that the word 'revolution' is a trigger word in more ways than one, and there is need to have it very carefully exegeted before one reacts.

149 This had also been pressed by J. A. T. Robinson in his chapter, "Kingdom, Church and Ministry" in *The Historic Episcopate,* ed. Kenneth M. Carey (Westminster: Dacre, 1954).

> The Kingdom of God, concentrated in the life of Jesus of Nazareth, remains the fullest possible disclosure of the partnership of God and man in history. Our struggle for the shaping of the secular city represents the way we respond faithfully to this reality in our own times.[150]

Although he was careful to emphasize that the Kingdom stands beyond history, whereas the secular city stands within history, he insisted that the Kingdom is in process of being realized, and the New Testament writers certainly envisioned the Kingdom taking place also in this world. Using Amos Wilder's interpretation of the Kingdom in the New Testament as the renunciation of the old and the entry into a new discipleship, he said,

> the Kingdom came in Jesus when God's doing something wholly new *coincided* with man's laying aside previous values and loyalties, and freely entering the new reality. Life in the emerging secular city entails precisely this kind of renunciation. So it does require penitence. In fact, the emergence of the secular city may help us discard our moralistic perversion of repentance and return to a more biblical version.[151]

He concludes this section by stating that the objections to the secular city "as a viable concretization of the ancient symbol of the Kingdom of God" do not stand up to careful examination.

In working towards a revolutionary theology Cox discerned four necessary elements—an idea of why action is needed now, which can act as a catalyst (a catalytic element), an explanation of why people have thus far hesitated to act (an interpretation of catalepsy), a view of how they can be stimulated to action (an idea of catharsis), and an understanding of how the situation can be changed so that they can act (an understanding of catastrophe).[152]

[150] *Ibid.,* p. 112.

[151] *Ibid.,* p. 113. One's reaction to this will largely depend on what content one reads into Cox's Christology.

[152] *Ibid.,* chapter 5. It may be noted that occasionally Cox hedges his bets. Cf. the following: "The summons in no sense requires a thoughtless novelism, a scurrying after the new simply because it is new. It means rather that antiquity is no longer *per se* a mark of authenticity. Old ideas and practices must compete on an equal basis with new ones. What one has accepted must be constantly tested in the light of a world which never stops changing. Thus the past is celebrated and

He was then in a position to examine the Church in more detail. Again we find ourselves in agreement when he declared that "a doctrine of the church is a secondary and derivative aspect of theology which comes *after* a discussion of God's action in calling man to cooperation in the bringing of the Kingdom."[153] Chapter six takes up Hoekendijk's insight about the Church as God's avant-garde in the world. The Church is not an institution but a people, and it is 'where the action is.'

> Phrased in more traditional terms, the forms of church life are dependent on the function, or mission, of the church. They must be designed to facilitate locating and participating in the "mission of God." They must effectuate rather than hinder the congregation's capacity to discover and cooperate in the work of God in the world. This means that the content of the church's ministry is simply the continuation of Jesus' ministry. It cooperates and participates in the ministry of Jesus. But what is the character of Jesus' ministry?[154]

Cox answered that question by reference to our Lord's own statement that he came to proclaim release to the captives, to set at liberty the captives and to proclaim the year of the Lord's favor.[155] This Cox interpreted in wholly political terms, and he then applies what he has said to the mission of the Church.

appreciated, but it can never be allowed to determine the present or the future" (p. 121). Of course, this still leaves the open question how past experience and present imperatives are to be evaluated. Is it pragmatism, and if so, what kind of pragmatism? Is it the view of 'the party' or an intellectual elite? For a Christian, it must be the will of Christ; but this simply pushes the question one stage further back, for how is Christ's will to be known when the authority of the Church has been discredited, the authority of the Scriptures discarded, and when the individual conscience is unreliable? This is the question that needs to be answered.

153 *Ibid.*, p. 125.

154 *Ibid.*, p. 126. My fundamental question to Cox is not what he says here—indeed I believe this is what the Bible says (cf. *The Atonement and the Sacraments*, pp. 386f., and *Ministry*, *passim*)—but the content that he puts into those terms. Was the mission of God in the Incarnation wholly social? Was the ministry of Jesus wholly political? If the gospel is interpreted in purely secular terms, it seems that one half of man's life and responsibility about which the gospel speaks is missing.

155 Luke 4:18f. Jesus was quoting Isaiah 61:1ff. Again one asks, can one explain these images *only* in social terms? Without wishing to detract in the slightest from the social dimension which Cox rightly emphasized, how are we to explain the way in which the New Testament writers added a different dimension? E.g., the interpretation of 'blindness' in John 9, or of 'freedom' in Paul's writings?

> The church is the avant-garde of the new regime, but because the new regime breaks in at different points and in different ways, it is not possible to forecast in advance just what appearance the church will have. It is not even possible to delineate the mission of the church "in the city." Cities differ, and the visage of the church in any given urban environment will differ.[156]

However, the Church has responsibility for kerygma, diakonia and koinonia. Cox gives his own secular thrust to these New Testament terms—kerygma represents 'broadcasting the seizure of power,' diakonia is fulfilled by healing the urban fractures, and koinonia by 'making visible the City of Man.' He reminded us that Jesus was regarded as an exorcist in his day, and in the same way the Church is called to be a cultural exorcist by ridding society of the myths by which men have been oppressed and kept oppressed. He has some pertinent things to say about ecumenism in relation to the Church, maintaining that the real split is no longer between Protestant and Catholic but between traditional and experimental forms of church life.[157]

He illustrated his idea of the Church by some excursions into the meaning of urban exorcism, discussing the change from a work-oriented society to a leisure society,[158] the changes in sexual mores, and the relationship of the Church to the secular university. In relation to the latter he rather hopefully, I think, saw Christian scholars bridging the chasms that open up between departments and disciplines, faculty and administration, power structure and the students, and occasionally having to recommend (more in sorrow than in anger, perhaps) separation from the Church in order to achieve the Church's essential ends.[159]

The last part of the book, which probably received the most

156 *The Secular City,* p. 127.

157 *Ibid.,* pp. 160f.

158 In this section I think Cox laid himself open to David Little's charge of inconsistency for apparently approving secular civil bureaucracies while condemning ecclesiastical bureaucracies; although it should be noted that forms appropriate in civil society may not necessarily be appropriate in the Church. Cf. *ibid.,* pp. 173ff., and *The Secular City Debate,* p. 73.

159 If Christian scholars are noted for this kind of reconciling work in the secular university they are better Christians there than they are in the seminaries! Perhaps we are too busy fighting to decide who will be chief reconciler.

attention, explored what it means to speak about God in a secular way. I believe Claude Welch is probably right that Cox "really means for us to speak of God," and that *The Secular City* stands or falls on this last chapter[160] or, at any rate, on the conception of providence to which it points. But again, everything will depend on whether Harvey Cox and the reader are putting the same biblical content into the terms that are used.

Harvey Cox described *The Secular City* as "a study book, intended to provoke college students to discussion,"[161] and it is perhaps unfair to demand of it the completeness and finality that one would expect of a work designed primarily for academic consumption. More than that, it would be an act of rank stupidity to attempt a comprehensive critique of a book that has probably been subjected to more concentrated criticism than any other book in the decade. Yet because of its widespread influence and also because of the radical view of the Church that it presents, we are forced to raise questions that have been insufficiently stressed by previous critics.

(1) My first question is concerned with the advent of the Kingdom of God, the when and the where.

It is true that Cox is careful to distinguish between the Kingdom and the appearance of the secular city, but we are left with the impression that even if the latter is not to be identified with the Kingdom, it hovers on the brink, for the characteristics of technopolis—the anonymity and mobility that guarantee the privacy and freedom of urban man, the technical methods that increase his happiness and leisure, and the political structures by which his society is governed—are hailed as features of a society that is clearly God's will. One must ask what are the grounds for choosing this present time and its emerging urban culture as the ultimate form that history must take. It has always been the temptation of Christians, particularly those who have thought they lived in an apocalyptic time, to trace signs of the Eschaton within their own generation, and to identify the day and the hour of the

160 *The Secular City Debate,* p. 156.
161 *Ibid.,* p. 85.

One who is 'not yet' but expected. What are the criteria for saying that we have reached this *kairos?*

A similar question might be posed about technopolis as the locus and style of the Kingdom, for if it is true that the biblical view of history ends with the vision of the City of God, the New Jerusalem, the penultimate stage features the destruction of another city, Babylon the Great (Revelation 16:17ff.); and if one is going to be literal there seems no more reason to bank on the one than on the other. Cox's emphasis on the positive contributions urban technology has made to the improvement of human life is instructive and important. We are in his debt for reminding us of them; but it has been pointed out with justification that he made his point by glossing over the less attractive, even diabolic features of urban society with its depersonalizing and dehumanizing tendencies.[162] The city and the technology that supports it are at best ambiguous, capable perhaps of great good but equally capable of great evil; and the society they produce may develop either into a genuinely enlightened community or into the empire of Big Brother. One feels that if pietists make the issue too simple by emphasizing personal commitment and ignoring the social imperatives of the gospel, they rightly point out that good organization and the best legislation may be abused and perverted by bad people.

(2) Does *The Secular City* represent evolutionary progressivism in a more sophisticated form? It is a criticism that has been made before, and we agree that to identify Cox with the earlier exponents of the Social Gospel is too easy if we fail to recognize between them the cautionary figure of Barth.[163] But the question is whether in Cox's thesis the advent of the technological society into which we have erupted cancels out

[162] Cf. the remarks of Murchland, Stackhouse, and Tyson in *The Secular City Debate*, pp. 18f., 33, 52.

[163] Cf. David Little's criticism (*ibid.*, pp. 69ff.) and G. D. Younger's reply (pp. 77ff.). I was surprised that none of the critics in *The Secular City Debate* pointed out that at a much deeper theological level Cox's position reflects the Puritan doctrine of Providence—a view of history in which God is intimately and constantly involved. For me a major significance of his work is that he has tried to provide a doctrine of Providence for the Church—a concept that has been very largely lost. But cf. Welch's comments, pp. 166f.

Barth's solemn warning about the temptation to deify the human.

It matters little whether one conceives of human history in terms of a gradually ascending straight line or a series of dialectical jumps; if at the end we judge it to be an inevitable upward movement so that 'our' secular society is thought of as nearer to the Kingdom of God than 'their' society in the past, then we have to describe it as a form of progressivism, about which Nicholas Berdyaev made some pertinent comments.[164] They are particularly relevant because Cox appears to confine our hopes vigorously to this secular world. Cox's post-Barthian insights are valuable in that they point to an element in biblical history that we may have brushed aside too easily, and a place may have to be found in our theology for the recognition of secular progress. He forces us to look at this again; but, we suggest, in doing so he reduced it to a far too simple issue.

(3) There is the question of what 'maturity' means, and

164 "In the light of progress every human generation, every individual, every epoch of history, are but the means and instrument to this ultimate goal of perfection, this ultimate humanity perfect in that power and happiness which are denied to the present generation. Both from the religious and ethical points of view this positivist conception of progress is inadmissible, because by its very nature it excludes a solution to the tragic torments, conflicts and contradictions of life valid for all mankind, for all those generations who have lived and suffered. For it deliberately asserts that nothing but death and the grave await the vast majority of mankind and the endless succession of human generations throughout the ages, because they have lived in a tortured and imperfect state torn asunder by contradictions. But somewhere on the peaks of historical destiny, on the ruins of preceding generations, there shall appear the fortunate race of men reserved for the bliss and perfection of integral life. All the generations that have gone before are but means to this blessed life, to this blissful generation of the elect as yet unborn. Thus the religion of progress regards all the generations and epochs that have been as devoid of intrinsic value, purpose or significance, as the mere means and instruments to the ultimate goal.

"It is this fundamental moral contradiction that invalidates the doctrine of progress, turning it into a religion of death instead of resurrection and eternal life .... No future perfection can expiate the sufferings of past generations. Such a sacrifice of all human destinies to the messianic consummation of the favoured race can only revolt man's moral and religious conscience." *The Meaning of History* (London: Geoffrey Bles, 1936), pp. 188f.

One may add the comment that it revolts the conscience still more when the favored generation is one's own, or when one remembers the (pathetic?) words of Paul, "If it is for this life only that Christ has given us hope, we are of all men most to be pitied" (I Corinthians 15:19, NEB).

whether Christian maturity and secular maturity can ever be quite the same thing.

Again there is no doubt that Bonhoeffer singled out an element that had been ignored during the generations of self-complacent religiousness in church history. But the quality to which he pointed is by no means limited to our age—Renaissance man had it in great abundance,[165] although the technological dexterity of the twentieth century and the comprehensiveness of man's command over his natural environment give new point to this humanism. There is a sense in which man *has* 'come of age,' and there is a sense in which Bonhoeffer was entirely right to criticize the Church for appealing to men through their worst and weakest fears rather than addressing them as the race to whom God has given the governance of this world. Bonhoeffer was surely right in his observation that adult man rejects the idea of God as Someone to call in when the going gets tough, Someone to lean on. By appealing to man in his guilt-ridden, fear-haunted state of misery, the Church had been psychologically and theologically wrong—psychologically, because it showed no understanding of where twentieth-century man is in thinking about his human destiny, and theologically because it does less than justice to the God of the Bible, who gives human beings responsibility to be themselves and to stand before him on their own two feet.

Is this, then, all there is to maturity? I may be fully responsible for what I do and think and say, but am I wholly responsible for what I *am*? Is the height of maturity the person who puffs on his cigar and boasts he is a 'self-made man'? Is there not another side to maturity in which, while taking full responsibility for my own actions and what I have made of myself, I recognize the constant dependence I have had on other persons, influences, forces that come to me from outside my own being and which have been entirely independent of my control? Surely the economic and social complexity of the

[165] Cf., for example, Pico della Mirandola's "Oration on the Dignity of Man." In his history of Western civilization, Lord Clark observed, "Well it is certainly incorrect to say that we are more graceful than other animals, and we don't feel much like immortal gods at the moment. But in 1400 the Florentines did." *Civilisation* (London: B.B.C. and John Murray, 1969), p. 89.

modern metropolis, and the new awareness we have of our ecological relationship to the rest of nature, point to this interdependence: my life is not wholly of my own making, for even at the most material level, maturity means recognizing that it is made up of qualities, sacrifices, and services from millions in the past and the present whom I will never know, and from the rest of nature to a degree that I shall never fathom—the whole complex of environment and heredity that I can only receive as a gift. For the man of biblical faith this is not fortuitous: the gift has an origin and a purpose, and beyond all that I have received from my contemporaries and from the mute testimony and sacrifices of nature, there is That or Who which Jesus addressed as 'Father.'

What I am really questioning is whether there can be any real maturity without an ultimate sense of gratitude. Cox's view of human maturity seems to omit this essential dimension, and I cannot recognize the result as real maturity. Although we understand the protests of our teenage children that they should be allowed to make their own decisions, make their own mistakes, and learn to stand on their own feet, we do not recognize them as most mature when they are stamping their feet and screaming about it, nor even when they win top prize at the Science Fair and boast about it. We recognize that the loosening of parental ties and the exercise of personal independence are absolutely necessary for the child's growth into maturity, but that is not necessarily achieved when they shout the loudest or hive off to 'do their own thing.' It may come many years later when they understand that what they received is beyond repayment, except by simply saying "Thank you for everything." That surely belongs to the maturity of a race no less than to an individual.

It is in the Bible. We have to hold the apostle's exhortations to become grown men in the faith (e.g., I Corinthians 13:11; Hebrews 5:12), together with our Lord's reminder that we cannot enter the Kingdom of God except as little children;[166] and perhaps in the end these childlike qualities are the pre-

[166] I cannot interpret these passages (Mark 10:13-16; Luke 18:15-17; cf. Matthew 18:1-5; Mark 9:36f.; Luke 9:46f.) except with reference to the *qualities* of childhood—simplicity, trust, gratitude.

requisite for the mature manhood which the apostle said is to be measured "by nothing less than the full stature of Christ."[167]

(4) Several writers have criticized Harvey Cox for the use he makes of the Bible, and not without reason. As George W. Peck remarks, there is a tendency in discarding the *deus ex machina* to call in *scriptura ex machina.*[168] At this distance what appears even more significant is that Cox really tried to undergird his interpretation of the secular city with scriptural evidence, and what he demonstrated was not only the extent to which ecumenical theology at that time was based on the Scriptures, but also the dangers of the neo-literalist position and the quandaries into which ecumenical theology was falling. It comes as something of a shock to realize how close Cox's view of the modern age would be to that of a Second Adventist who appeals literally to II Timothy 3:1-5 and similar apocalyptic passages. They would probably disagree radically on their interpretation of the signs and character of the Kingdom, but in their reading of the signs of the times in this modern age they would not be very far apart. As Peck commented:

> On many occasions Cox's style of interpretation reminded me more strongly than anything else of the spiritualizing of the exegetes of the Middle Ages. But the trouble is that what these men were doing was based upon, and quite in accord with, a doctrine of Scripture which justified their methods. Cox does not have this going for him. His doctrine of Scripture is as difficult to pick up as are his principles of hermeneutics, and I fancy something drastic is going to have to be done about both these matters before we can hope to make the Bible speak adequately and truly to our generation.[169]

I hope that call is loud and clear.

There is the question of Cox's selectivity. In the laudable desire to be relevant are we forced to select only one set of biblical images or truths and to ignore everything in Scripture that does not support it? Is there not in the Bible a paradox that emphasizes both the sacred and the secular, the prophet

167 Ephesians 4:13.

168 *The Secular City Debate,* p. 39; cf. also the criticisms of Stackhouse and Tyson.

169 *Ibid.,* p. 41.

and the priest, the world-affirming and the world-denying, the election of 'the people of God' and the destiny of the world to which they are given, the Church and the Kingdom? Surely we are not doing justice to the biblical revelation if we cite one set of these ideas and discard the other. Furthermore, something of the real genius and creativity of biblical faith is centered in the tension between these apparent opposites, in the fact that both have to be preserved while the Kingdom, in its cosmic temporal sense, is still 'in prospect'; for until the Kingdom in prospect becomes the Kingdom in fact, the people of biblical faith have often found it necessary to use one to redress an over-emphasis on the other. Only those who are absolutely sure that they stand on the brink of the Eschaton can risk the luxury of going hell-bent in one direction. Literally. For up to now they have been wrong.

There are also questions regarding the doctrine of Scripture and the hermeneutic principle which Peck indicated. In what sense is the Bible still the 'Word of God'? What standards of historical and literary scholarship are demanded and what principles of interpretation must be applied? These questions have to be answered before we can decide how much speculative freight any one text or passage can legitimately carry. What we select from biblical history and how we interpret it will affect not only the form of the Church and our understanding of the society in which it is set, but also the very nature and content of our faith and the decisions we make personally and politically.

It is crucial for Christian ethics, social and personal. A situation ethic may point to Christian answers in our ethical dilemma as long as the Christian community and the Christian individual can look somewhere for guidance on what it means to be 'Christian.' Otherwise it means nothing more than 'do as you think best in your own situation,' with all the ambiguity of what one regards as 'best' and of one's personal ability to think accurately or responsibly. Joseph Fletcher seems to allow President Truman's decision to drop the bombs on Hiroshima and Nagasaki as within the boundaries of 'agapeic calculus,' and if I understand that term correctly, it means that that action fell within the Christian possibility of action at that moment. Any pragmatically motivated government might make a similar decision.[170] I am not convinced. However, my reason for disagreement is based not only on personal revulsion, but on ethical insights drawn from Scripture and on theological and critical principles that I bring to the Bible, the Church's tradition, and to my own conscience when I arrive at that conclusion.

I am not asking for a new rule of law, but for theological methods and norms to guide us in actions that go beyond legal 'justice.' One thing is certain, if the choice is between the justice of law and a normlessness that encourages governments to fall below those standards of justice, most people will choose the law as nearer to the ideal 'good.'

(5) On the conception of the Church that is presented in *The Secular City* I find myself in an ambivalent position. On the one hand I find solid biblical support for some of Harvey Cox's positions about the nature of the Church.

The idea of the Church as God's avant-garde is a case in point. I am sure that when this is linked to the idea of ministry in the New Testament, it provides us with the basis for a doctrine of the Church that is not only deeply grounded in biblical truth but also relevant to the demands of this century.[171] Furthermore, the same has to be said from my own perspective about Cox's insistence that the structure of the Church must serve its mission.

On the other hand, this does not mean that the structure of the Church is to be so pragmatic as to be unrelated to the Church's essential theology. In his reply to his critics Cox denied that he rejected all forms of ecclesiastical institution, but he leaves the impression that the institutional structures can be created on purely functional grounds. Of course, he could argue that insofar as they serve the mission the structures *are* related to the Church's essential theology, but is this all that can be said? I would maintain that institutional order, or flexibility, must be clearly incarnational in intent and form, not in any sense that claims divinity for itself, but in the sense that it reveals the actions of God in Christ.[172] This should

170 Cf. *Situation Ethics* (Philadelphia: Westminster, 1966), pp. 98, 167f.

171 It is close to the view I put forward in *Ministry*. Cf. also Anthony T. Hanson, *The Pioneer Ministry* (Philadelphia: Westminster, 1961).

mean that beyond the pragmatism by which the Church may adapt its forms to serve its mission, the forms adopted should themselves witness to the nature of the gospel, or at least not be in flagrant contradiction: I can conceive of an extremely efficient system of ecclesiastical organization for carrying out the Church's mission, but one in which the structures and the way they operated would be a complete denial of what was being said and done in Christ's name.

Fundamentally, however, my criticism of Harvey Cox's view of the Church is not in the pattern of churchmanship he presents, but in the secular limitations he places upon the gospel and its expression. That may change the total character of the Church.[173]

This is related to criticisms that I would offer not only to *The Secular City* itself but also to churches in which the debate about the issues has been hot and heavy. Most people would agree that reconciliation in the Church—between the races, the sexes, the social and economic classes—is the heart of our problem, as the theologians and sociologists about whom we have written in this chapter very clearly saw. But this has revealed an aspect of reconciliation which many are not prepared to face; for before the Church can effectively exercise its prophetic function in contemporary society, reconciliation will have to take place between those who want the Church to be God's avant-garde in society by giving up its institutional forms, and those who feel that the Church should have a recognizable form in order to be God's avant-garde in

172 Of course, if we look ahead to the fulfilment of the Kingdom of God, this incarnational action will also be demonstrated in the willingness of the Church to sink its own identity in the Kingdom. My disagreement with Cox is not on this final objective, but on the assumption that we have reached the point where the Church should give up its own identity, and that secular progress is the standard of measurement.

173 I think this was behind Hendrik Kraemer's comment in his Foreword to van Leeuwen's *Christianity in World History*, trans. H. H. Hoskins (New York: Scribner, 1964), when he wrote: "I for one, therefore, express the wish for a fuller explanation and motivation from Dr. van Leeuwen's pen in the near future of what is *concretely* implied in the whole world. Admirable as that expression is, it is in danger of remaining a seductive slogan" (pp. x-xi). As Kraemer saw well, everything depends on the *content* that is given to those terms.

society; between those who see the need primarily to speak to 'man in his strength,' the mature men of this age who have created the technopolis, and those who see the need primarily as speaking the word of hope and encouragement to 'man in his weakness,' the fearful and immature people who are being unmade by the technopolis;[174] between those who rightly declare that the gospel must be relevant to the age in which it is being proclaimed, and those who with equal justice declare that in the pursuit of relevance we may leave the gospel behind. So one could go on. I am simply pointing out that reconciliation begins here.

There is a further curious feature of the whole debate. Harvey Cox approves urban secularity, and he wants the Church to fulfil its prophetic function in that society kerygmatically by announcing the crisis of the Kingdom, in terms of diakonia by healing the brokenness that still exists, and in terms of koinonia by making visible the City of Man, i.e., by supporting the secularizing process. He conceives this being done in many ways, many of them unstructured and not necessarily visibly connected with the Church as such. The kind of society that would emerge would be necessarily bureaucratic in structure, comprehensive in its planning and governmental responsibility, pragmatic but benevolent.[175] The Church within it would deliberately seek to have less and

[174] 'Future Shock' and the extent to which the population is having to turn to psychiatry is an indication that this is not a minor problem. It was illustrated for me by a psychiatrist at a church meeting in Connecticut after I had given a lecture trying to explain Situation Ethics. During the question period he asked, "Are you saying that the ethicist can offer no principles, no rules, no norms of conduct? Do you realize that my waiting room is full each day of people who come to me precisely because they *cannot* make their own decisions or deal existentially with their own problems? What help do you have for them?" It is a good question.

[175] Harvey Cox was anxious to retain variety of ethnic and other forms of culture in the new society and does not want it to become 'monochrome' (*op. cit.*, p. 85), but it is difficult to see how this could be preserved in the society he envisions. One is reminded of the comment made by the Socialist writer, J. B. Priestley, after the establishment of comprehensive welfare legislation in Britain after 1945, "We are trying to do a wonderful thing in this country of ours,—but somehow not in a wonderful way. There is a grey chilly hollowness inside, when there ought to be gaiety, colour, warmth, vision." (*The Linden Tree.*) In fairness it should be said that Harvey Cox recognized the problem in his later book, *The Feast of Fools* (Cambridge, Mass.: Harvard, 1969).

less identity, would be secular and group-oriented, and would support the civil organism in achieving its secular ends.

What has not been clearly seen is that in such circumstances 'the Church' would for all practical purposes become so identified with the prevailing social and political structure that it would be the new religion of technopolis. We have turned full circle from Peter Berger: instead of the Church being called out from the surrounding culture in order to be prophetic, it is suggested that the Church should immerse itself in the surrounding culture in order to be prophetic; and instead of the Church being chided for not speaking out against the secular establishment, the Church is invited to give its fundamental support to the new secular establishment of technopolis.

In the last analysis I can see little to choose between the support churches gave to the 'American Way of Life,' and the kind of support that Cox's unstructured Christian groups might give to a secular welfare state, except one's own personal political preferences; and although a society concerned for the welfare of the total population is more deserving of Christian support than one which is cruelly competitive, that is by no means the whole story, as those who have lived under other systems can testify.[176] Certainly if the Church becomes totally absorbed by secular society, the ancient tension between the Church and society is very easily resolved, but Christians can agree to this only if they become convinced that absolutely no distinction is to be drawn between secularity and the gospel.

Fundamentally it should be seen that all these issues come to a head in what we believe about the Christian revelation and why we believe that revelation. Until we can reach precision at that point, all discussions about the Church are mere words.

[176] I shall be misrepresented if this is regarded as an attack on any system of government *per se*. It is simply to point out that all systems of government are the work of man and therefore imperfect. Even under the most just and humanitarian political system the Church should not allow itself to become identified ideologically with it, and still less, absorbed by it. To do so is to sell out.

Chapter VII

CATHOLIC REFORM OR ROMAN REBELLION?

1

A QUESTION OF CREDIBILITY

John is an apocalyptic name. When Angelo Roncalli took the title Pope John XXIII there was much in his nature that suggested the humility of the forerunner who came simply to bear witness to the Light,[1] or to the beloved disciple who was so intimately associated with our Lord's days on earth.[2] It may be equally significant that the name John points to the coming of the Kingdom, and is forever associated with the apocalyptic vision of the End.[3] Whether consciously or not, Pope John's unexpected and dramatic decision to call the Second Vatican Council of the Roman Catholic Church[4] recognized that we are on the brink of a new age in the history of humanity. The call to *aggiornamento* had within it the implicit recognition that the Church needed to undertake a

[1] John 1:6ff.; cf. Mark 1:7f.; Matthew 3:11f.; Luke 3:13ff.

[2] Over half the Fourth Gospel is concerned with events during the last few weeks of our Lord's life.

[3] John the Baptist's message centered in the announcement of the Kingdom, and 'St. John the Divine' recorded the Apocalypse.

[4] October 11, 1962-December 8, 1965. We have used the collation of texts from the Council published jointly by the Guild Press, America Press, and Association Press of New York, 1966, *The Documents of Vatican II,* ed. Walter M. Abbott, S.J.

thorough review of its own structures in light of the scientific, sociological and political revolutions of the twentieth century: tremendous events for the human race were afoot, and for the Church time seemed to be running out.

The basic problem was the Christian Church itself, and not least the problem of pluralism. Vatican II provided the first conciliar statement on the doctrine of the Church,[5] for Roman Catholic treatments since the Reformation had been largely dominated by apologetic and polemical considerations. It is true that the doctrine has received more attention during the past century, and Vatican I reflected this interest, but there could hardly be a greater contrast between the spirit of the Council in 1869, and that of the pope and fathers who gathered in the Vatican in 1962. Whereas the earlier Council confronted change like an embattled fortress, John XXIII struck the new keynote when he suggested that the Church should meet error not with anathemas but with compassion; and as an earnest of his desire to establish fraternal relations, he established the Secretariat for the Promotion of Christian Unity and generously invited other churches to send observers.

The change of attitude comes sharply into focus when we compare how the question of 'credibility' was faced by Vatican I and Vatican II. Christians have always believed that the Church is an essential part of its own gospel, that its spiritual style should witness to the truth that it proclaims, and that the Church is the place where faith is not only to be found but also to be exemplified. Karl Rahner puts it concisely when he describes the Church as "not only an object of faith but a motive for faith," and he shows that this was recognized by the First Vatican Council when it declared that "the Church herself is a great and enduring motive of credibility and an irrefutable testimony to her divine mission by her wonderful growth, eminent holiness and inexhaustible fruitfulness in all good, and by her Catholic unity and unshakable stability."[6]

This becomes a contemporary issue in our time because the twentieth century has forced us to have deeper insights into

[5] Noted by Albert Outler, *ibid.*, p. 102.

[6] Quoted by Karl Rahner in *The Dynamic Element in the Church* (New York: Herder and Herder, 1964), p. 68.

the gospel. The very characteristics on which the church of Vatican I based its claims sound more like the arrogant imperialisms of that date than the Man of Nazareth. Even those nations which were greedily establishing empires and claiming the support of Providence for their rapacity, now understand—albeit reluctantly—that to grant freedom and to give up the claims of empire are more worthy of a civilized people. How much more should this be true of the Church.

A huge credibility gap developed over the very triumphalism on which the Victorian Catholic based the claims for his church, for to be the Church of Jesus Christ, the humility of the Man of Sorrows, the unpretentiousness of the Incarnation and the forgiving love of the Crucified must be manifested at the center if the Church is to receive respect. The issue in Roman Catholicism is precisely the same as that which harasses Protestantism in the ecumenical issue—how can the Church become a credible, believable exponent of Jesus Christ?

The problem went deeply to the roots of the Church's own self-understanding. Pope Paul VI, in supporting the initiative taken by his predecessor, very explicitly directed the attention of the Council fathers to the ecclesiological issue in his first encyclical. Catholics had reached an hour "in which the Church should deepen its consciousness of itself," and he reminded them that the very doctrine that is concerned with "the origin of the Church, its own nature, its own mission, its own ultimate destiny,"[7] had never been properly studied and understood. It was "a duty today for the Church to deepen the awareness that she must have of herself, of the treasure of truth of which she is heir and custodian and of her mission in the world." He underlined the need for renewal, the contrast between the Church in its ideal form and the empirical church known to man, and it was therefore necessary to consider again the relationship of the Church to the world in which it is set. Certainly there are urgent problems in the world—international peace, social strife, poverty and want, the demand for political independence—and Pope Paul wanted the Church to

[7] *Ecclesiam Suam,* published in English as *Paths of the Church* (Washington, D.C.: National Catholic Welfare Conference, 1964), p. 5. Cf. pp. 7f. (§ § 15, 18).

be able to speak to these issues; but first the Church should understand its own mission: the agenda may have been written by the world, but for the members of the Church the subject matter must first be the nature of the Church itself.

The new Roman Catholic attitude towards ecumenism has to be seen within this context: it was an extension of the question of the Church's credibility. It is true that the Council was called in the first instance not to deal with ecumenical relationships but to deal with internal problems within the Roman Catholic Church; but the seriousness with which the leaders of that church approached the need for renewal and their genuine desire to bring that church closer to the gospel meant that ecumenism was bound to have an important place in their deliberations. Perhaps the Protestant scholar G. C. Berkouwer is right when he suggests that Catholicism's change of attitude to ecumenism may have been at first no more than an apologetic means of commending Catholic claims to other Christians,[8] but it is clear that if the Catholic leaders were sincere in their objectives it could not remain at that level.

Berkouwer is also right to remind us that there is a Roman Catholic *a priori*—just as historically there has been an Anglican *a priori*, a Presbyterian *a priori*, a Congregational *a priori*, and several others—namely, a doctrinal assumption "that the Roman Catholic Church is the one Church."[9] He very properly asked whether this assumption will ever really permit that church "to open the door to new perspectives for the unity of the Church." But he raised this question before the Council

[8] G. C. Berkouwer, *The Second Vatican Council and the New Catholicism*, trans. Lewis B. Smedes (Grand Rapids: Eerdmans, 1965), p. 14. It should be noted that a movement that begins as simple apologetic may very well end at a deeper level. A good example of this is seen in the deepening insights which Roman Catholic thinkers have had into the place of the laity in the Church. The earlier attempts to give the layman a place in the ordering of the Church arose from their possible contribution to evangelism—the Lay Apostolate, Action Catholique, and the like. But the more seriously this was related to the New Testament mission of the Church, the deeper became the fundamental understanding of the *laos tou theou*, until we reach the significant insights of Yves Congar. Cf. Yves Congar, *Jalons pour une théologie du laïcat*, published in English as *Lay People in the Church* (London: Geoffrey Chapman, 1957), and *Si Vous Êtes Mes Témoins* (*Laity, Church and World* [Baltimore: Helicon, 1959]). See also the works on the subject by Gérard Philips, J. M. Perrin, E. Schillebeeckx, and George H. Tavard.

[9] *The Second Vatican Council and the New Catholicism*, p. 19.

had completed its work, and with the advantage of hindsight we can see that this doctrinal base did not prevent the Church from an entirely new openness towards the rest of Christianity. The *rapprochement* may not have been as complete or as rapid as many would have liked, but it *has* produced a totally new climate of ecumenical relationships.

One could have foreseen that when the desire for churchly credibility is honestly pursued, it is bound to clash head on with all our *a priori* judgments about the Church, and particularly with claims that are exclusive, proud and arrogant. The call for credibility may have been advanced as a means whereby the separated brethren could recognize the authentic marks of the one true Church,[10] but the very attempt to make the Church closer to the nature and spirit of her Lord was bound to introduce the dynamite of the gospel into a situation prepared and ready; and nobody can tell what the end result will be. Vatican II may not have done very much for traditional Roman Catholic claims, and still less for any triumphalist interpretations of those claims, but the honesty and the persistence with which the call for credibility was initiated and pursued, have called forth the love and respect of all Christians who are not too blinded by prejudice to recognize the authentic work of the Spirit.

In evaluation, however, the clash was inevitable; and therefore both the realities behind it—both the traditional *a priori* and the determination to make the Church a more credible servant of Jesus Christ—must be given due weight if we are to recognize what has been going on in Roman Catholicism during the Vatican Council and since.

2

COUNCIL OF RENEWAL

A complete analysis of the emerging ecclesiology of the Roman Catholic Church would be presumptuous, and it would mean considering the documents of Vatican II in their totality. However, although that does not fall within the competence of the present writer, it should be evident that the Dogmatic

10 *Ibid.*, p. 32.

Constitution on the Church (*Lumen gentium*) and the Decree on Ecumenism are primary for our purpose;[11] and the Introduction to the Decree on Ecumenism makes the priorities perfectly clear—ecumenism has to be seen in terms of the Church's understanding of itself.[12]

It is possible to interpret this as if no change were implied in Rome's traditional position.[13] Such Protestant appraisals have not looked deeply enough into the documents, and are—however unwittingly—demanding a different standard from Rome than they would accept of other churches. Surely it is unreasonable to expect any church to change in a trice the basic ecclesiology on which its whole history has been built. The process by which any church moves from a *jure divino* doctrine of the Church to one that recognizes a plurality of ecclesial forms, must inevitably be long and painful, and apart from penitence for past misunderstanding, it will involve the careful separation of sincerely held but erroneous beliefs from that which must be held at all costs.

As we have seen, a change in ecclesiology almost inevitably means that the Church is questioning its relationship to what it has traditionally accepted as ultimate spiritual authority, and to the historic channels by which it believes it has received and guaranteed that apostolic inheritance. A church may be forced to recognize that it has received the treasure of the inheritance in earthen vessels, but it knows that the treasure is there, and the pastoral leaders of the church have a particular responsibility to see that it is preserved intact.[14]

11 The Dogmatic Constitution on the Church, *The Documents of Vatican II,* pp. 9-96; The Decree on Ecumenism, *ibid.,* pp. 341-366.

12 Having noted the growing desire for unity among Christians, it went on to say, "This sacred synod, therefore, gladly notes all these factors. It has already declared its teaching on the Church, and now . . . it wishes to set forth before all Catholics certain helps, pathways, and methods by which they too can respond to this divine summons and grace." *The Documents of Vatican II,* p. 342.

13 E.g., Rudolf Ehrlich, *Rome—Opponent or Partner?* (Philadelphia: Westminster, 1965), pp. 209ff., and especially pp. 216f., 231f. On the other hand, in fairness to this author it should be pointed out that his reservations seem to have been penned before the Council had completed its work. After 450 years of bitterness one cannot altogether blame Protestants for receiving the new trend with some caution.

14 For example, it is pastorally irresponsible for church leaders who have made a theological shift to their own satisfaction to enforce a similar change on church

A church can begin its reform and renewal only from where it is. The churches have transmitted the gospel through certain trusted channels. Events may show—and the issue of credibility is the evidence—that these traditional channels have become recognized as inadequate, or that they have been misunderstood and misapplied; but a church can begin the task of review, revision, and renewal only from the point that it has reached in history. It cannot simply begin *de novo,* because that would be to deny the very means—though imperfect—by which it *has* received the gospel. This appears to be particularly true for Roman Catholicism, which has based its claims on organs that seemed to guarantee historical continuity with the Apostolic Church. From the point of view of one who looks at Rome from the outside, Rome has always appeared to have a peculiarly acute problem in this regard, since it has made less distinction than most churches between the gospel itself and the historic channels by which that gospel has been transmitted; so that to question the channels has often been interpreted as an attack on the gospel itself.

All this is really prefatory. It should remind us that when we consider the nature of Rome's dogmatic inheritance, we have even more cause to acknowledge the miracle of grace that happened during Vatican II. What Protestants and other non-Catholic Christians should look for in the documents of the Council is not for evidence that the Roman Catholic Church has taken a new basis for its doctrine of the Church, but for signs that it has reached new insights into the gospel that will enable it to be more truly itself—not so much *the* Church as the *Church.* It would be as untrue to speak of a change of basis

members whom they have hitherto taught differently. Perhaps this is a major reason for the split between the clergy and the laity in Protestantism, documented in Jeffrey K. Hadden's *The Gathering Storm* (especially chapter 3). Of course, it is expected that church leaders will arrive at new insights, theological, social, and ethical—presumably that is why they become leaders. But the question is whether they can expect the membership to follow them just because they say so, and without giving the people in the pews adequate preparation, or time to test the truth of the new insights. Is it pastorally responsible to say in effect, "For years we have been teaching you so-and-so, and threatened you with hell hereafter if you refused to believe it. Now we think we were wrong, so you must jettison all we taught you up to last year, and believe what we believe now"? One could reasonably expect a sizable credibility gap to develop.

as it would be unreasonable to expect it; but if we discern a change of heart, that is ultimately more important.

Lumen gentium is the central document of the Council, and it illustrates what we have been trying to describe. On the one hand, as one of its distinguished Roman Catholic commentators has observed, although it is "called a Dogmatic Constitution, the most solemn form of conciliar utterance, *Lumen gentium* does not actually define any new dogmas. It sets forth with conciliar authority, the Church's present understanding of its own nature."[15] It provides plenty of ammunition for those who expected or wished Vatican II to be merely a reassertion of Rome's traditional claims.

For example, in the first chapter, which treats of "The Mystery of the Church," there is the usual strong emphasis on the Church as the Body of Christ, and the same concretization of the image in the visible hierarchy of the Roman Catholic Church, that we have learned to expect:

> Christ, the one Mediator, established and ceaselessly sustains here on earth His Holy Church, the community of faith, hope, and charity, as a visible structure. Through her he communicates truth and grace to all. But the society furnished with hierarchical agencies and the Mystical Body of Christ are not to be considered as two realities, nor are the visible assembly and the spiritual community, nor the earthly Church and the Church enriched with heavenly things. Rather they form one interlocked reality which is comprised of a divine and a human element. For this reason by an excellent analogy, this reality is compared to the mystery of the incarnate Word.[16]

Anyone who through preference or prejudice wishes to maintain that Rome stands pat can also point to the emphasis on the primacy of Peter and his successors,[17] on the place the hierarchy occupies in the structure of the Church,[18] on the distinction the document makes between clergy and laity,[19] or on the importance of the Virgin Mary.[20]

[15] *The Documents of Vatican II,* p. 11. The comment belongs to Avery Dulles, S.J.

[16] *Ibid.,* p. 22.

[17] *Ibid.,* p. 23 (§ 8).

[18] *Ibid.,* also chapter 3.

[19] *Ibid.,* and also chapter 4.

[20] *Ibid.,* chapter 8.

On the other hand, they would be overlooking features of *Lumen gentium* that have probably been far more significant for the development of Roman Catholic ecclesiology since the time of the Council. The first of these is that the biblical concept of the People of God is placed before that of the hierarchy. Fr. Avery Dulles may be right in suggesting that for the Roman Catholic Church itself the most significant doctrinal achievement of the document is chapter 3, which deals with the hierarchical structure and develops the principles of collegiality;[21] but for immediate ecumenical relationships and perhaps ultimately for the doctrine of the Church, one cannot underestimate the importance of chapter 2 on the Church as 'The People of God,' or the fact that it stands where it does in the document.

Similarly we might point to the emphasis on the Kingdom of God as the goal of the Church's proclamation, a feature of *Lumen gentium* that is even more significant when read in connection with the Pastoral Constitution on the Church in the Modern World. This does not mean that the Council fathers went overboard in favor of a 'theology of the secular,' but at least the way is open for a proper appreciation of the human advances that have come from men's secular engagement.[22]

This is closely related to a new recognition of laymen in the total witness of the Church. The traditional distinction between clergy and laity is certainly reflected in certain parts of the document, but, on the other hand, we must notice the laity is given a very positive and entirely integral place in the witness of the Church.[23] It is frankly recognized that "a secular quality is proper and special to laymen,"[24] and they

21 *Ibid.*, p. 12.

22 This is seen, for example, in Avery Dulles' appreciation of Dietrich Bonhoeffer, in *The Dimensions of the Church* (Westminster, Md.: Newman, 1967), chapters 4 and 5.

23 Compare the almost total lack of recognition in the *Codex Juris Canonici* (1917). Yves Congar charged that only one canon really dealt with the laity (No. 948), although others mentioned lay people incidentally. Cf. Congar, *Lay People in the Church,* p. xxvii. Msgr. Gérard Philips estimated that 44 canons made some mention of lay people (out of 2,414 canons), and pointed out that *La Dictionnaire de Théologie Catholique* does not deal with the word; Philips, *The Role of the Laity in the Church,* trans. James W. Maudry (Chicago: Fides, 1955), p. 10.

24 *Documents of Vatican II,* p. 57 (§31).

have a special responsibility in bringing justice, charity and peace into human society.[25] Surely no prophet deserved more the belated recognition he was granted than the champion of the Roman Catholic layman, Fr. Yves Congar.

More significant even than this is the attitude of *Lumen gentium* to Jesus Christ. Any document on the Church must start with our Lord, but we notice a complete change from the former triumphalism that centered in the image of Christ as King and Judge and would then progress via the Church as the Body of Christ to assert the perfection, sinlessness, and sovereignty of the Church in this world. In contrast, in *Lumen gentium* we begin with the redemptive ministry of Jesus Christ, "who came to serve and to give his life a ransom for many."[26] The relationship of the Church to the Incarnation is therefore set firmly within the *purpose* for which Christ became man, the redemptive love and compassion that brought him into our life to share our lot; and it is within this framework that the identity of the Church with the Body of Christ must be understood: the accent is no longer exclusively upon the divine claims of the Church, but upon her continuation of our Lord's redemptive ministry (*diakonia,* service).

> The Church, consequently, equipped with the gifts of her Founder and faithfully guarding His precepts of charity, humility, and self-sacrifice, receives the mission to proclaim and to establish among all peoples the kingdom of Christ and of God. She becomes on earth the initial budding forth of that kingdom.[27]

The same emphasis is to be found in the last part of the same chapter in *Lumen gentium.* It recalls the kenotic passage in Philippians 2 where the apostle speaks of Christ emptying himself and 'taking the nature of a slave,' and declares that the Church is called to take the same path in her mission. "Thus, although the Church needs human resources to carry out her mission, she is not set up to seek earthly glory, but to proclaim humility and self-sacrifice, even by her own example."[28] It veers away from the temptation, to which in the eyes of many

25 *Ibid.,* pp. 62f. (§ 36).
26 Mark 10:45; cf. *The Documents of Vatican II,* pp. 15f. (§ 5).
27 *Ibid.,* p. 18.
28 *Ibid.,* p. 23.

Roman Catholic theology had often succumbed, of using its involvement in our Lord's mission as a justification for claiming his sinlessness. Instead it states clearly that

> while Christ, "holy, innocent, undefiled" (Heb. 7:26) knew nothing of sin (2 Cor. 5:21), the Church, embracing sinners in her bosom, is at the same time holy and always in need of being purified, and incessantly pursues the path of penance and renewal.[29]

At the same time we can see that the more faithfully *these* insights were pursued, the more acute becomes the problem of credibility with regard to the empirical church that we know; and it is to the credit of the Council fathers that they did not try to gloss over the issue or hide the paradox.

The Decree on Ecumenism illustrates the same general attitude we have been describing. Again, if one wished to be skeptical, not to say cynical, about Roman Catholic objectives, one might question whether the Council's statement would change very much in the religious situation, since the basic ecclesiology remains what it always has been. It has been pointed out that in speaking of "churches and ecclesial communities" in the West,[30] the distinction between these two classes of Christian experience was left vague,[31] and clearly different grades of authenticity are implied in the principle of the hierarchy of truths:[32] the Eastern Orthodox have a special place of recognition and rate a Decree of their own,[33] and the Anglican communion is also spoken of as occupying 'a special place.'[34] We could note that the primacy of the Petrine succession is carefully stated,[35] and with regard to the unity sought by all Christians the Decree affirms that this unity "dwells in the Catholic Church as something she can never lose, and we hope that it will continue until the end of time."[36] The Roman Catholic *a priori* is there. It declares,

[29] *Ibid.,* p. 24.

[30] *Ibid.,* p. 361 (§ 19).

[31] Cf. Rudolf J. Ehrlich, *Rome—Opponent or Partner?,* p. 233.

[32] *The Documents of Vatican II,* p. 354 (§ 11).

[33] *Ibid.,* pp. 357-361; also the Decree on Eastern Catholic Churches, *ibid.,* pp. 371-388.

[34] *Ibid.,* p. 356 (§ 13).

[35] *Ibid.,* pp. 344, 346 (§ § 2, 3).

[36] *Ibid.,* p. 348 (§ 4).

> our separated brethren, whether considered as individuals or Communities and Churches, are not blessed with that unity which Jesus Christ wished to bestow on all those whom He has regenerated and vivified into one body and newness of life—that unity which the holy Scriptures and the revered tradition of the Church proclaim. For it is through Christ's Catholic Church alone, which is the all-embracing means of salvation, that the fullness of the means of salvation can be obtained.[37]

In summary, the Decree asserts that "the Catholic Church has been endowed with all divinely revealed truth and with all means of grace"[38] —a statement that led one sympathetic Protestant commentator, Samuel McCrea Cavert, to observe that the Decree has not reconçiled "its ecumenical outlook with its assumption that the Roman Catholic Church is the only true Church."[39]

Exactly. Perhaps the major ecumenical significance of this Decree is that although the Roman Catholic Church honestly stated its traditional position, it did not obey the traditional logic of that position;[40] it is prepared to live with two truths that for the moment appear to be irreconcilable. This seems to be frankly recognized at the beginning of the Decree where it says that the Church of Jesus Christ is one and unique, but goes on to say, "yet many Christian communions present themselves to men as the true heritage of Jesus Christ. To be sure, all proclaim themselves to be disciples of the Lord, but their convictions clash and their paths diverge, as though Christ Himself were divided."[41] This is the dilemma. The

37 *Ibid.*, p. 346 (§3).

38 *Ibid.*, p. 348 (§4).

39 *Ibid.*, p. 369.

40 The inflexible logic of the Roman Catholic Church has always attracted a certain kind of mind. It is illustrated by the line of reasoning that Lamennais used in his earlier ultramontane days:

"No pope, no church;
No church, no Christianity;
No Christianity, no religion (at least for any people that has once been Christian):
No religion, no society."

Alec R. Vidler, *Prophecy and Papacy* (New York: Scribner, 1954), p. 112. But although this kind of reasoning attracts the head, it often repels the heart; and the changes of Vatican II suggest that the heart is to be given its proper place in the definition and expression of Christian faith.

41 *Op. cit.*, p. 341 (§ 1).

Roman Catholic Church now seems to recognize that other Christian churches sincerely believe about themselves very much the same as what the Roman Catholic Church has taught about itself; in recognizing the dilemma it neither discards its own firm conviction nor spurns others for maintaining theirs, but holds out the hope that as the spirit of Christ animates our search, we shall find our unity in him. It is the call to join in a pilgrim adventure in faith, rather than the expectation that everyone will return to '*my* house.'

Furthermore, even though Rome believes she already possesses the essential unity, she confesses that this unity is centered in Jesus Christ himself;[42] and the more this is taken seriously by any church, the more imperative and urgent becomes the question of credibility with respect to the way in which we make his sovereignty manifest. So if the dogmatic basis of Roman Catholic ecclesiology is firmly stated, the ecumenical intention of the document is equally clear, not only in that an official document of the Roman Catholic Church for the first time refers to other Christian denominations as 'churches,' or in its generous recognition of Christian service and ecumenical incentive undertaken by the non-Roman churches, but much more significantly in the confession that we all share responsibility for the schisms of the Church:

> St. John has testified: "If we say we have not sinned, we make him a liar, and his word is not in us" (1 Jn. 1:10). This holds good for sins against unity. Thus, in humble prayer, we beg pardon of God and of our separated brethren, just as we forgive those who trespass against us.[43]

We called the ecumenical concern of Vatican II an extension of the problem of credibility. It is a sign of the seriousness with which the Council fathers pursued their intention of making their church a fit vehicle of the gospel; for the issue of Christian unity touches the credibility of the Church at its most sensitive point—the patent example of rival 'churches,' when by the very nature of the gospel they profess they ought to be the exemplars of love and reconciliation. But behind this

42 *Ibid.*, pp. 343f. (§2).
43 *Ibid.*, p. 351 (§7).

new recognition of other Christians, the issue of credibility seems to be conceded at two levels—first, honesty demanded that the obvious fruits of the Spirit to be found outside the Roman communion should be recognized, and secondly, the Church could support its claims only by exhibiting the love and compassion that would manifest its own true patrimony.

Although our comments have been limited to these two basic documents of Vatican II, these are by no means the only statements from that Council that have direct bearing on the development of Roman Catholic ecclesiology. Other documents are hardly less significant—the Dogmatic Constitution on Divine Revelation, the Constitution on the Liturgy, the Pastoral Constitution on the Church in the Modern World, and the Decrees on the Eastern Catholic Churches and on the Church's Missionary Activity—all these have direct and obvious relevance for this subject. To work out the implications of this immense body of material will take many years of study and deep insight, for the whole of Vatican II appears to have been devoted to the doctrine of the Church, and the full implications will become clear only through the exegesis of the Church's ongoing life.

Fr. Edward Schillebeeckx said it would be a great mistake to ignore the Council because it is 'only pastoral,' and one can only agree when he says that the pastoral character of the Council's work "is nothing but a new dogmatic sensitivity."[44] Indeed, it seems that the documents of Vatican II will prove what one has suspected for a long time about all theology—that good theology comes only from those whose concerns are essentially pastoral.

3

ROMAN CANDLES

It has been said that Vatican II caused a sigh of relief to go up from the Christian world, but the relief was also heard from the depths of the Roman Catholic Church itself. It seemed as

44 E. Schillebeeckx, O.P., *Vatican II: The Achievement,* trans. H. J. J. Vaughn (London: Sheed and Ward, 1966), p. 15.

if we were witnessing the luxurious freedom of a statuesque and venerated star who had finally decided to discard her girdle and be herself. Certainly the fabulous symmetry suffered, but for the first time we caught glimpses of a lovable personality with which it was suddenly much easier to live.

But the image is only partly useful. Was the new openness to be interpreted as a venerable institution simply relaxing into a more natural pose, or was this the original beauty of the Church revealing her perennial youth? To those Roman Catholics who had agonized through the Council in the hope of a new approach it was undoubtedly the latter. In 1964 *Concilium* began to explore the implications of the Council's work for the church's emerging ecclesiology, and its editorial lists read like a roster of Roman Catholic ecumenical pioneers – to cite but a few, Yves Congar, Karl Rahner, Gustave Thils, and Maurice Villain from the older generation, Hans Küng, George Tavard, Gregory Baum, and Avery Dulles from the younger men. This publication was supplemented by a spate of books, series, and periodicals from Catholic presses which pushed the exploration further and extended the dialogue that had already begun between Catholics and Protestants.[45]

However, one cannot get rid of a girdle without losing the impression of symmetry. It very soon became apparent that the variety of opinions among Roman Catholic theologians was no less extensive and hardly less explosive than that to be found among Protestants. A complete survey of Roman Catholic thought since Vatican II would be impossible, not only because of its extent but also because it will take years to explore the implications of the Council. The writers we consider in this section simply indicate something of the ecclesiological debate within Catholicism in North America.

The Dimensions of the Church by the American Jesuit, Avery Dulles,[46] probably represents the right wing of the

45 E.g., a series called "Theological Soundings," under the general editorship of Edward Schillebeeckx, came out of Nijmegen, the Netherlands; Herder and Herder's "Quaestiones Disputatae" produced the work of Karl Rahner; cf. also *The Ecumenist; Unitas; The Journal of Ecumenical Studies;* etc.

46 Westminster, Md.: Newman, 1967. Since the purpose of this section is primarily descriptive rather than critical, most of my own comment will be relegated to the notes.

left—that is, a relatively orthodox approach among those who received the new winds of the Council with enthusiasm—and it was written a year after the Council's work had ended. It starts with the recognition that the Dogmatic Constitution on the Church is at the center of the Council's work, but it recognized that all the documents of the Council were intimately related to the emerging ecclesiology. The author confessed that he wrote the book because Catholics felt their need "for new ways of envisaging the Church as a whole,"[47] and it is therefore essentially a book with a pastoral intent—written to explain to the membership of the church what the Council had accomplished and the implications of its work for their thinking about the Church.

It recognized that Catholicism had become increasingly isolated in the modern world, and the Second Vatican Council had sought to break through this isolation and bring the church back into the center of human affairs. "To achieve this goal," Fr. Dulles said, "there was no need to forge a new idea of the Church; it was enough to recover the true idea of the Church as established by its divine Founder."[48] Protestants will at once recognize a restorationist climate with which they are familiar: what is said here could be accepted by any Disciple or Baptist.

Dulles rejected the closed (i.e., exclusive) view of the church and society put forward in the seventeenth century by Cardinal Bellarmine. This view had defined the Church in terms of its unity and its visibility, and therefore it omitted "what makes the Church the Church, namely, the communion of minds and hearts through sharing in the same divine life."[49] He went on to explore the new dimensions of the Church in terms of three separate but complementary spatial concepts: first, the 'height' (perfection) and the 'depth' (sin) of the Church; then the 'breadth,' for Vatican II had refused "to identify the Church of Christ exclusively with Roman Catholicism"[50] but had recognized that the Church's mission is

47 *Ibid.*, p. vii.
48 *Ibid.*, p. 1.
49 *Ibid.*, p. 5.
50 *Ibid.*, p. 10.

directed to the universe and that the lines between the Church and the world could no longer be precisely drawn. Finally, he considered the 'length,' pointing out that the Church's history is not to be limited simply to the time between Pentecost and the Parousia, but embraces the history of the People of God from the beginning and extends through the total pilgrimage of the human race until it is fulfilled. Within this framework Dulles concentrated particularly on what the Council implied with regard to the Church's 'breadth,' that is, the Roman Catholic Church vis-à-vis the issues of ecumenism, mission, and the secular.

On ecumenism Dulles observed that the first tentative modification of the earlier exclusivism occurred in 1863 when Pius IX cautiously offered the possibility that some outside the Roman Catholic Church might be saved because of 'invincible ignorance,'[51] and he traced the modest extensions of this principle. The Decree on Ecumenism appeared to suggest that Protestant denominations and churches are to be graded according to their preservation of the Catholic values,[52] but he agreed with Gregory Baum that it would be contrary to the Council's intention to suggest that these churches are to be evaluated only in institutional terms. Against the complaint that the Decree presupposed Catholic ecclesiology he commented, "If the charge means that the Catholic Church should disguise or surrender its claim to have preserved the essential fulness of the patrimony conferred by Christ on his Church, the charge is unreasonable. According to Catholic faith, Christ himself has guaranteed that this heritage would never be lost."[53]

With regard to the Church's mission, he approved J. C.

51 *Ibid.*, p. 24.

52 *Ibid.*, pp. 30ff.

53 *Ibid.*, p. 40. The charge *is* unreasonable. But there is a lot of unfinished business for Catholic theology. The desire for credibility demands that ultimately the doctrine of the Church will have to be brought into more obvious relationship to the Catholic Church's new ecumenical spirit and goals. For if Catholicism has been putting its priorities in the wrong place, and if, in certain aspects at least, the evangelical succession of faith has had to take a different route in order to be preserved, it can no longer be claimed that the heritage has been preserved inviolate in one Christian confession.

Hoekendijk's statement that the Church in her totality becomes God's outreach into the world.[54] *Lumen gentium* recognized that the Church's goal is the Kingdom of God; the Church had to involve itself in mission and witness because that is an expression of its own inner nature.[55] In order to do this it would have to become representative of the world's ethnic and cultural variety, and missionaries engage in the mission whenever they work for universal brotherhood. He emphasized the break with earlier and more questionable missionary methods by underscoring the significance of the Declaration on Religious Liberty: "if missionary activity is viewed as Christian witness, it is quite evident that the truth of the gospel cannot be imposed by force or threats."[56]

This prepared the way for the consideration of Christian secularity. Dulles admitted that Protestantism has a certain secular bias that is not found in traditional Catholicism, and that "a certain Christian secularity has an undoubted appeal to the contemporary Western mind."[57] But he reminded his readers of the emphasis on the Kingdom of God in *Lumen gentium,* and suggested that the Council fathers had tried to balance "a supernaturalism that would press the initiative of God at the expense of the proper activity of man, and a naturalism which would look upon the kingdom of heaven as a merely human achievement."[58] He admitted that the church did not have a very good record in respect to its influence on society, but claimed that Church and world must exist in fruitful polar tension, for "the world will lose its way unless guided and sustained by the Church. But the Church will become ineffective unless it listens to the world."[59]

We would add that, in spite of the monastic tradition and the 'other-worldly' emphases in Catholic history, the main

54 *Ibid.,* p. 45; cf. *The Church Inside Out,* p. 43.

55 *The Dimensions of the Church,* p. 52.

56 *Ibid.,* p. 64; for the Declaration on Religious Liberty see *The Documents of Vatican II,* pp. 675-696.

57 *Op. cit.,* p. 72.

58 *Ibid.,* pp. 75f.

59 *Ibid.,* pp. 84f. This is probably true enough, but is this to be a real dialogue, or simply an agreement to 'live and let live' that will keep some status for the Church?

thrust of that history had been in terms of Troeltsch's 'church-type,' which clearly relates the Kingdom of God to human society; 'Christendom' had had that goal.[60] Perhaps because of this ambivalence in Roman Catholic history, no aspect of recent Protestant theology has exercised more fascination for Catholic theologians than its rehabilitation of the secular.[61] Fr. Dulles shares this interest and in his last chapter introduces his readers to the life and thought of Dietrich Bonhoeffer. In a very sensitive treatment, he shows the relationship between secular man's legitimate aspirations and the demand for 'credibility' which has acted like a scourge of grace in the hearts of contemporary Catholic scholars. He observes of Dietrich Bonhoeffer, "he longed for an open, penitent, self-effacing Church, and many sincere Christians today share that longing."[62]

Such then is Avery Dulles' little book. It is an honest attempt to bring together the elements that bear upon ecclesiology in the documents of Vatican II, and it especially tries to interpret the new dimensions of the Church in a way that respects traditional ecclesiology and sees them as a development out of the Roman Catholic's own history rather than as a denial of that past.

No one of Gregory Baum's writings tries to do exactly what Avery Dulles tried to do in *The Dimensions of the Church,* but there is a sense in which all his many writings through articles and books have at their center the desire to put Catholic faith

60 The two objective types of churchmanship—church-type and sect-type—appear to be complementary. This receives unconscious testimony from their own history. Catholicism, supreme example of the church-type since Constantine, is known today for its monastic, celibate, and essentially 'puritan' ethics, whereas Protestantism (including the spiritual ancestors of the Puritans), which began as pure sect-type, is in the forefront of the movement for secularity. Without making any value judgments on this, it suggests that they have both recognized a dual emphasis in the gospel, and have unconsciously been trying to provide for it.

61 The very first issue of *Concilium,* ed. Edward Schillebeeckx, was on *The Church and Mankind* (1964); and although it was not specifically on the secular, it was not long before the subject received special attention: cf. *Spirituality in Church and World* (No. 9); *Spirituality in the Secular City* (No. 19); *Sacralization and Secularization* (No. 47); *Secularization and Spirituality* (No. 49). The problem was implicit also in many of the other subjects treated.

62 *Op. cit.,* p. 110.

on a more acceptable basis and to work out a more ecumenically viable apologetic.[63] At this point of our survey I introduce one aspect of the Roman Catholic reappraisal that Gregory Baum has put in particularly sharp and simple terms—the fundamental authority on which the Church's claims are based. For his own church Baum posed the question, does the claim of the Catholic Church to be the one true Church still make sense? Baum held that it cannot be sustained on the traditional bases:

> In the first place the traditional apologetical arguments in favor of the Catholic Church's uniqueness are generally no longer regarded as valid. We cannot offer a strict historical proof that the Catholic Church is in essential continuity with the Church of the New Testament. As Catholics we affirm this continuity because we believe that the developments that took place in the Church and her ministry were guided by the Spirit who preserves the Church in the original apostolic gifts; but few historians today would suggest that this continuing self-identity of the Church can be demonstrated historically. When, for instance, we look at the profound change that occurred in the early Church when the monarchical episcopate replaced other forms of apostolic ministry, we realize that we cannot 'prove' that throughout this change the Church remained identical with herself . . . .
>
> We also have lost the taste for the apologetical argument that appealed to the unity, catholicity, holiness and apostolicity of the Catholic Church. In traditional apologetics, we tried to prove that the Catholic community exhibits more unity and universality, more holiness and greater fidelity to the apostolic heritage, than do other Christian Churches . . . . Today we have great hesitations in proposing such an argument . . . . Remembering the four marks of the Church, we discover in how many ways we are *not* united, *not* universal, *not* holy and *not* faithful to the original gift. The four marks proclaim the redemptive action of Christ and denounce the extent of our failures. They are both gifts we receive, and tasks summoning us. This twofold character of the four marks prevents the contemporary theologians from using them in an apologetical argument.[64]

63 E.g., in his many editorial contributions to *The Ecumenist* (first published by the Paulist Press in 1962 in collaboration with St. Michael's College of the University of Toronto, Canada, where Gregory Baum teaches), and in *Ecumenical Theology Today* (1964), which he edited and which contains a great deal of material from *The Ecumenist,* and *The Credibility of the Church Today* (1968).

64 *Faith and Doctrine* (New York: Newman, 1969), pp. 92f.

Fr. Baum fully understood that something more convincing than the subjective belief of Roman Catholics will have to be produced if Catholic claims to uniqueness are to have any substance. He also recognized that the ultimate authority on which our churchly claims are based is central to ecclesiology; and he tried to provide for this in his consideration of 'The Church as a hermeneutical Principle,' i.e., as an ongoing vehicle of interpretation through which the essential scriptural gospel could be made real in any age.[65] He suggested that two characteristics make the Roman Catholic Church unique—first, that of all the churches it alone can "formulate a doctrinal consensus that is accepted as normative by all its members,"[66] and secondly, that it is the only church "which is able to reformulate the Christian Gospel as the Good News for the contemporary world"[67] because not only can it reach an accepted consensus but it also recognizes the creative presence of the Spirit that can free it from obsolete and static formularies. Tradition is not simply a matter of handing on the past, but it happens in the present.[68]

One may seriously question how conclusive these arguments

65 *Ibid.,* pp. 91-133.

66 *Ibid.,* p. 96.

67 *Ibid.,* p. 97. Cf. also his *The Credibility of the Church Today* (New York: Herder and Herder, 1968).

68 *Ibid.,* p. 97. It is clear, however, that there is a very distinct difference between Catholic and Protestant approaches to the ecumenical question, to which Rosemary Ruether has directed our attention. She pointed out that although Catholic ecumenists sound as if they want to meet others half way, their theological base really imposes a thesis of 'return' upon them: "In principle, Catholics assume that they already know the end result of ecumenical dialogue, whereas Protestant ecumenism started out with the acknowledgement that they did not know this end result." *The Church Against Itself* (New York: Herder and Herder, 1967), p. 125. Cf. also Lukas Vischer's perceptive article, "Roman Catholic Understanding of Ecumenism and the World Council of Churches," *The Ecumenist,* 4/3 (March-April, 1966), 37-44. It may be that these two positions are actually incompatible this side of the Resurrection. They certainly leave us with some stubborn questions that have to be faced if the institutions of Protestantism and Catholicism decide to move beyond ecumenical bonhomie. Is Catholicism's insistence on *its own* (not necessarily, please note, the Church's) rightness the unshakable loyalty of faith, or a residue of pride? Is Protestantism's unwillingness to accept these claims the unshakable loyalty of faith, or a residue of pride? The odd thing that the churches do not seem to have seen is that in this argument the only way to prove your point is to forego forever the Luciferian luxury of making claims based on it.

are,[69] but there are important things to notice if we are better to understand the significance of the ecumenical revolution of our time. First, we notice Fr. Baum's unwillingness to base his arguments for Rome's catholicity and uniqueness on the traditional historical foundation on which those claims had been made; but secondly, we note his recognition that if the Church claims to be 'the Church,' it must have an authority which will make its claims credible. Thirdly, we notice that in defining an authority that intends to hold Scripture and tradition together, he places the ultimate responsibility on the Church as the vehicle of the Spirit which can define the development of its own doctrine:

> The Catholic Church is convinced that the Word of God, addressing her now, enables her to hand on the original Gospel in a creative process—not simply repeating past doctrinal formulations but also re-interpreting them in the light of her present experience of the Gospel. Because of her collegiality (pope and bishops) and her affirmation of a divine tradition, the Catholic Church is open to the future.[70]

It is precisely this concept of a closed, self-authenticating development that the radical lay theologian Rosemary Radford Ruether protests against in *The Church Against Itself.* If Avery Dulles looks for reform and renewal, she looks for the Church to be re-formed and made over; if Gregory Baum looks for the revivification of the Church through the Spirit's mov-

[69] First, we may question how authoritative any consensus can be or should be if (a) it excludes others who have faith in Jesus Christ, and (b) the exclusion was based upon principles that are no longer regarded as valid. The positions adopted at Vatican II, and Gregory Baum's own distrust of the traditional arguments, I suggest, undercut his line of reasoning.

The continuing presence of the Holy Spirit in the reformation of doctrine is not the exclusive possession of the Roman Catholic Church; in the reinterpretation of Scripture the Protestant churches have not been laggards. These arguments, I suggest, do not substantiate the claim to uniqueness. The only thing that is unique to the Roman Catholic Church is the claim to inerrancy enshrined in its own institutions, and at this point the argument becomes circuitous if not circular. Protestants remember what the Roman Catholic historian Lord Acton said of Papal infallibility, that 'power tends to corrupt, and absolute power corrupts absolutely'; and although the experience with John XXIII showed that not even this dictum could be turned into an absolute principle, the rest of church history causes us to treat it with respect. Fundamentally the concept of a church's indefectibility has to be reconciled with the fate of Israel (cf. I Corinthians 10:1-13).

[70] *Faith and Doctrine,* pp. 97f.

ing institutional offices in collegiality, she expects renewal to come to the Church only as it is prepared to question all its traditional forms. Against those who tried to reconcile the new spirit with these forms she argued that the apostolic understanding of fulness was itself totally incompatible with the idea of divinely instituted offices.[71]

The keynote of her book is struck in the foreword by Gabriel Vahanian when he says that just as the temple in the apostolic age was destroyed, so must the contemporary Church be destroyed, that *aggiornamento* is not enough, and that the new Church of Jesus Christ would arise out of Christian involvement in the social and political imperatives of our time. Although Rosemary Ruether has membership in the Roman Catholic Church, it is claimed that her position is neither Catholic nor Protestant; and the relationship of her book to Vatican II would be tenuous indeed were it not for her claim that it had been written to test the degree of openness really intended by the Council: "we make bold to test this spirit to see what it is, where it is from, and whether it is equal to the freedom for faith."[72]

The Church Against Itself is a book that the reader will either love or hate, bemoan with regret or hail with joy, regard as virtual treachery or as obviously prophetic; or one may, like the present writer, feel several of these emotions at the same time. Perhaps part of the illogicality of one's reactions is because Mrs. Ruether does not follow the sequential logic usually found in books of theology but thinks of her enquiry more as lines of investigation radiating from a central focus, like spokes from the axle of a wheel.

She admits that this focus cannot be defined, although she believes we can come to understand it better by moving out in various directions and viewing it from various angles.[73] Nevertheless, not only is it impossible to define the focus but there is also a general lack of clarity about where one should look for the building bricks of a definition. This puts us in a fundamental quandary about Mrs. Ruether's basic position. If

71 *The Church Against Itself,* p. 126.

72 *Ibid.,* p. 6; cf. also p. 9.

73 *Ibid.,* p. 1.

we accept her strictures against the ecclesiologies she criticizes, she can present us with no good grounds (i.e., undeniably *Christian* grounds) for accepting her own approach to this subject. On the other hand, her criticisms should be heard. We cannot hope to deal with the book adequately here, but we can deal only with those issues that affect her major thrust.

She first launches a devastating criticism of institutionalism in the Church because she maintains that "the church has become its own chief theological problem." The basic problem is not the sin of the Church or sins in the Church, but it centers in that the Church has misappropriated its own relationship to God and man. That is, the Church has misunderstood and misused its own fundamental theology about itself, and thus has become an institutionalized denial of its own gospel: "Now we find truth suppressed in the name of truth, freedom suppressed in the name of those spiritual principles which originally guaranteed the new birth in freedom: indeed, disobedience to the very gospel in whose name the church demands obedience to itself."[74] Furthermore, she makes it clear that insofar as ecumenism is conceived as improving the relationship between institutional 'churches,' the criticism extends to that movement, and that her own work must be regarded as post-ecumenical.[75]

The situation calls for radical *metanoia,* and acceptance of the theo-anthropological structure of the gospel gives us the ability to sift the Word from the words once we have

[74] *Ibid.,* p. 4.

[75] *Ibid.,* pp. 7f. She is just in her criticism of the institutional churches. A mistaken view of ecumenical relations, acted upon in terms of churches' claims, can bring institutions very close to Antichrist. On the other hand, she may fall into the absolutist trap of those from whom she dissents when she assumes that there is *nothing* in the present structures that can carry the gospel and be worth preserving. The issue is not to dispense with all structures (which is to deny incarnation), but how to hold them Christianly—which means to hold them in relation to their *service* of the gospel. Mrs. Ruether may recognize this at the end of her book; cf. pp. 156ff., 190ff.

Although she calls her book 'post-ecumenical,' she bitterly castigates the dividedness of the churches, which produces "the terrible paradox of the very instrument for the proclamation of man's freedom from the law of death, itself most deeply entrenched in the law of death" (p. 10). In this sense 'post-ecumenical' means a position that *assumes* the fundamental insight of the ecumenical movement; it does not try to evade it.

undergone "the conversion of the whole self in faith through grace."[76] Because the gospel is both grace and judgment, the justification of the Church cannot be cast in terms of continuity, for

> the judgement which it lays upon the historical church reveals not simple continuity, but an ambiguity fraught with elements of radical discontinuity between the gospel and the church. It is for this reason that continuity with the gospel demands a mode of speaking the 'new' in the church which is dialectical as well as developmental. Indeed, the very continuity of the Church with the gospel itself demands a relationship which is less that of 'restatement' than of a call for repentance and conversion. That is, the call for the conversion of the church is itself the mode by which the church keeps its continuity with the gospel.[77]

This radical demand that the Church must be ready to accept *dis*continuity with its own past in order to be true to the gospel in the present and the future is the heart of Rosemary Ruether's thesis. She believes that at this time it demands the acceptance of the 'theo-anthropological structure' of the gospel: "ecclesiology must start by affirming the coherence of the church's existence with man's existence."[78]

She found testimony to this discontinuity in her examination of the Catholic, Reformed, and Radical approaches to the doctrine of the Church at the time of the Reformation,[79] and in her distinction between the Jesus of history and the Christ

76 *Ibid.,* p. 5. I find her less than clear at this point. She maintains that her position "is not a normless polemic against the institutional church as such," but her own principle for interpreting the gospel may not differ very materially from that of Harnack and other liberal Protestants whom she later criticizes (cf. pp. 92f.).

The concept of 'conversion' enables her to define spiritual authority in terms of a conjunction between 'Word and Spirit,' and this, perhaps, prevents her from slipping into the gnosticism implicit in most liberal positions; but one is often left questioning whether conversion to the 'theo-anthropological' meaning of the gospel is principally a spiritual experience or an intellectual insight.

77 *Ibid.,* pp. 10f.

78 *Ibid.,* p. 12.

79 *Ibid.,* chapter 2. The survey has many good insights, but the categorization into 'Catholic,' 'Reformed,' and 'Radical' is somewhat too simple. The center of this problem of the Church was in the concept of ultimate authority for doctrine, and the line between 'Reformed' and 'Radical' branches of the Church ran through the *center* of the Anabaptist movement (i.e., between those who turned to the Scriptures and those who appealed to an immediate revelation of the Spirit).

of faith in the apostolic era. The delay of the Parousia resulted in "the historifying of the church and the deeschatologizing of the faith," and thus in the struggle between the eschatological Kingdom and the historical Church one has had to take sides and pay the price;[80] but she suggested that there may be a way of reconciling the two positions along Bultmannian lines:

> By demythologizing (and this means de-historifying) the drama of the turn of the aeons, we can encounter it as an ever renewable dialectic which does not exclude but rather continuously reconstitutes the historical existence of the church . . . .
>
> This means that the church can exist in history only by not clinging to what it has become, but by letting itself go. Therein lies the paradox of "tradition," for tradition is really tradition—that is, true continuity with the gospel—only when tradition is free to be discontinuous with itself. This paradox can be expressed in the old formula that the church must be in the world but not of it. This formula, however, has been so misunderstood that we might have to reformulate it in some new language, such as "the church must be in history, but not of it."[81]

Here is the central theme which she traces in the history of the Church. Her plea is, of course, that a similar cataclysmic break is needed by the emergence of the new world that began with the Renaissance, was accelerated by the Reformation, and became full-fledged in the scientific and social revolutions of the past two centuries. The seriousness of her point is that she would call for radical change in the Church, not because the Church needs reform, but because only by taking a radically different shape can the Church be true to its own gospel. This is very much in line with the Reformation's claim that the

[80] "If one opts for the ecstatic state of eschatological expectation, then the community has no durability, but is swept to the end of history, only to be disastrously thrown back to the other side of the dialectic and overtaken by history itself with all too terrifying rapidity . . . . Or else, in accepting the church qua institution, one discovers a structure which can handle history, but only by expelling the Spirit." *Ibid.,* p. 59.

[81] *Ibid.,* pp. 61f. However, she is not very clear in saying how the continuity and discontinuity of the Church are to be related. "Is there any possibility," she asks, "of an inner kernel of continuity which can move across any two or three of these chasms of discontinuity? Insofar as this author has an answer to this question, it lies in a stress on the radically historical character of all theological and even credal systems relative to their contemporary world view, and the radically apophatic character of that continuous inner essence of Christianity itself" (pp. 91f.). I am not very sure where this gets us.

Church is *ecclesia semper reformanda,* a principle that the churches of the Reformation have found to be rather too radical for comfort.

Rosemary Ruether suggested that all forms such as the Scriptures, episcopal succession, apostolic office, and *regula fidei* have been institutional means whereby the Church has coped with living in the temporal dimension; and the present problem is caused by their having been employed to pass on 'the faith once delivered to the saints,' although those same saints did not make any such provision because they expected to be caught up in the End. This anachronism has produced a succession of anachronisms,[82] and therefore "the institutional office can put itself back into a positive relationship with the Spirit when it understands that it is *not* instituted by Christ, but was instituted by history."[83]

She insisted that church unity is certainly not institutional unification, although she conceded that the kind of Christian unity experienced on some campuses in 'free-floating' communities will need to recognize some structure if it is to survive.[84] The Church is both koinonia and diakonia, and these qualities are inseparable because "koinonia manifests

[82] Agreed. But is this all there is to church history? Surely faith insists that mixed in with our human rationalizations there was more, and that it preserved something that came essentially from Christ, for otherwise how could the Church have retained any capacity to repent? If we are to do justice to the Church in history we not only have to explain the human steps by which it reached its present position, but also must leave room for that which has enabled it to be the vehicle of grace to the millions of ordinary Christians who live out their lives in faith and love. Otherwise, all talk of the 'Spirit' is mere nonsense. Certainly what has been handed on to us is ambivalent, and we must recognize that ambivalence: it makes us continue to try to sift the gold of the gospel from the dross of human sin and imperfection. The inheritance was not *all* human imperfection, otherwise there would be no further call for us to exercise faith. If the Spirit of grace and judgment is a present reality in the Church, it must have been preserved for us in some way and in some measure.

[83] *Ibid.,* p. 138.

[84] *Ibid.* Also see the following: "The institution in all its ambiguity and finitude is, nevertheless, the support around the community of faith. A post-ecumenical Christianity that would be gathered only by its own discernment of spirits has not fully understood what it means to be a community of faith. It must ask itself this question: what kind of community can subsist around the experience of the absence of God? If the Church is not simply to dissolve around this experience, it must be sensitive to the dark nights of the community's soul as well" (p. 156). Perhaps there is another question it should ask: does the Church of Jesus Christ

itself in diakonia, and diakonia recreates koinonia."[85] Indeed, the only mark of the New Testament Church about which she is reticent and somewhat vague is the kerygma.[86] It is clear that she has a good deal in common with radical Protestant theology and with its theology of the secular, although she has some perceptive criticisms of *The Secular City* and issues a sharp warning against Christians becoming too easily converted "to 'waves of the future' which rapidly turn into new prisons."[87] Any Christian who has appropriated the spirit of the Reformation must agree with her when she says that Christian living demands a willingness to live "by faith alone, without vain boasting of works."[88]

In her final chapter she turns again to the crucial problem of our ultimate spiritual authority as Christians. "The inner or divine Word," she says, "finds its primary communication in the living personal relation of man to God"; and that may be readily agreed. But how can we be sure that this 'inner' word is truly the Word from God, and not our moral rationalizations, or our political preferences, or an ephemeral wave of emotion? How are we to distinguish between the true Word that belongs to Christ and the seditious arguments of the demagogue, the faithless reasons of the religious establishment, or the subtle persuasions of the inner devil? She admits that she has no final answer to this, but claims that her position does not mean 'normless subjectivism' because "the interplay of objective norms, the 'cloud of witnesses,' are good, reliable, and trustworthy norms, and most of the time they can serve to judge the spirits"; but in the final analysis they are "not absolute, either individually or collectively."[89] Where Gregory Baum

consist only of those with whom I feel intellectually and theologically cozy? What about fellowship with those simple souls whose faith might make God more of a present reality?

85 *Ibid.,* p. 179.

86 She says of the new Christian, like his Lord, that "his life is kerygma" (*ibid.,* p. 214), and that is true. But in order to be kerygma and not merely whim or whimsy it has to manifest in clear and unmistakable ways its relationship to and its foundation in that original kerygma.

87 *Ibid.,* pp. 211, 215.

88 *Ibid.,* p. 215.

89 *Ibid.,* p. 227.

relies ultimately on the collegiality of the Church, Rosemary Ruether rests finally on the Spirit within.

What is valuable in Rosemary Ruether's position is not that she provides us with a solution, but that she honestly faces the dilemma and shows us that the crisis in ecclesiology centers in the uncertainty of the modern Christian about the authority on which ecclesiology is to be based. She points to the immense contrast between our contemporary position and that of our reforming forebears:

> Unlike the sixteenth century Reformers, today's reformers no longer know where to stand to lift the world. They no longer feel the assurance that Luther and Calvin felt of having one certain place in the tradition on which one could take a stand, which was itself infallible and without error, and from the security of which one could apply a critique to subsequent tradition. These places of sure ground have eroded from under our feet, leaving us no certain area of positive norms by which to judge tradition through tradition . . . . Thus Catholicism and Protestantism are together in this more complete cultural crisis which undermines the Protestant infallibility just as surely as the Catholic infallibility.[90]

This is honestly said, and our own study supports it. Yet she can still speak of a renewed Church that allows the Spirit to change it and bring judgment on its cultural and social failure, causing it to rely upon God's gracious act alone and to stand penitently before him, for "to be itself the church must constantly repent of itself, so that it can ever again find itself as God's good creation."[91]

That is clearly an expression of faith, but that faith itself needs to be explained. The problem of authority (and of any doctrine of the Church that is tied up with it) runs between Rosemary Ruether's devastatingly frank *exposé* of discontinuity in the Church's history and her faith that the Church *can* respond in penitence and that the Spirit *is* able to lead Christians towards God's will. This is the area that has to be illuminated and clarified, for if we are to say anything to the world in the name of Jesus Christ we have to discover what it is in the Church's history—its kerygma, and even perhaps in the shapes it has taken—that has enabled God's call to be

90 *Ibid.,* p. 230.
91 *Ibid.,* p. 237.

transmitted through the centuries to us. To search for this is not to seek for new grounds for arrogance, nor even to seek a position that feels more secure, but it is to look for the very basis for the Church's mission—the content that encourages lives to become kerygma.

4

TWENTIETH-CENTURY REFORMER?

What will be the significance to the Roman Catholic Church of Hans Küng's amazingly candid and comprehensive studies in ecclesiology? With the somewhat mysterious turn of recent events,[92] it may be too early to judge; but his work may very well have a deep and lasting influence on Protestants.

Küng's theological mentors were Karl Barth, the Protestant, and Karl Rahner, the Jesuit; and if the influence of Barth is seen in his biblical and kerygmatic theology, the influence of Rahner is seen in his passionate desire to see his church, the Roman Catholic Church, made credible before men. For Karl Rahner recognized the essentially charismatic nature of the Church,[93] and the sovereign freedom of the Spirit to go where he willed. Thus Rahner could not limit the Spirit's gifts to the official ministry in the Church, or to special groups within the Church, or even to the formal boundaries of the Church itself. Furthermore, although Rahner claimed that the charismatic element of the Church is present in almost a primary sense within the hierarchical structure of the Church, he is anxious to maintain balance:

[92] In 1968 Küng was invited by the Holy Office to defend his views in Rome, but declined because there were no specific charges; but after the publication of his latest book, *Unfehlbar? Eine Anfrage [Infallible? An Inquiry]* (1970), he has been engaged in "an intense but friendly exchange of information" with the German Conference of Catholic Bishops; cf. *Newsweek* (Jan. 25, 1971), pp. 57f.

[93] Karl Rahner, *The Dynamic Element in the Church [Quaestiones Disputatae]* (New York: Herder and Herder, 1964). Rahner's views on the Church may also be traced in the following books: *The Church and the Sacraments [Quaestiones Disputatae]* (New York: Herder and Herder, 1963); Vol. II of his *Theological Investigations, Man in the Church* (London: Darton, Longman & Todd, 1963); and his chapter in *Obedience and the Church,* by Rahner, *et al.* (Washington: Corpus Books, 1968).

> Ecclesiastical authority must always realize that a subject's study of obedience, and the fact that such authority has competence to determine what its competence is, neither makes the subordinate devoid of rights as against authority, nor guarantees that every action of authority in the individual case is correct and the one willed by God.[94]

Those who exercise ecclesiastical authority should remind themselves constantly that "it is not they alone who rule the Church,"[95] and even more important that the spirit in which government is exercised must be that of love, for "ultimately only one thing can give unity in the Church on the human level: the love which allows another to be different, even when you do not understand him."[96]

If this is so, the question of the Church's credibility is raised very sharply. It was taken up in Küng, and it has been pointed out that Küng's great contribution in contemporary Catholicism has been to bring this issue into the forefront of Roman Catholic thinking about the Church.[97]

The point was put very simply in *Strukturen der Kirche,*[98] a book that was addressed particularly to the Roman Catholic situation, which Küng regarded as prolegomena for his more systematic construction of an ecumenical ecclesiology in *Die Kirche.* Here is the issue:

> "That the world may believe" (Jn. 17:21) depends entirely upon whether the Church presents her unity, holiness, catholicity, and apostolicity *credibly* in accordance with the Lord's Prayer. Credible here does not mean without any shadows; this is impossible in the Church composed of human beings and of sinners. Credible does mean, however, that the light must be so bright and strong that darkness appears as something secondary, unessential, not as the authentic nature but as the dark immateriality of the luminous essence of the Church during this time of pilgrimage.[99]

[94] *The Dynamic Element in the Church,* p. 71.

[95] *Ibid.,* p. 69.

[96] *Ibid.,* p. 74.

[97] Rosemary Ruether, *The Church Against Itself,* p. 182, note 1.

[98] *The Structures of the Church,* trans. Salvator Attanasio (New York: Nelson, 1963).

[99] *Ibid.,* p. 29.

The Church has to be made credible in its claim to oneness, its claim to catholicity, its claim to holiness; and he commented, if it became credible in all these respects, who would doubt its apostolicity? [100]

This was the major obstacle that prevented Protestants and others from recognizing the spiritual primacy of the Petrine office; therefore the Catholic Church should see that the office was made a more credible representative of the gospel before men,[101] and "this involves nothing more than the *service character* of every ecclesiastical office, which, however, the Petrine office must make concretely visible in the most *outstanding way*."[102] This line of thinking was bound to encroach on the extremely sensitive area of papal infallibility. Küng held that the bearers of the teaching office in the Church have a function that is derived from Christ and his word, but then forthrightly declared that "officeholder over and over again must hear, receive, and learn the word of God in the human utterance of Scripture, and he must always subject himself to it and regulate himself accordingly."[103]

Sentiments such as these may have caused certain people in Rome to desire opportunity for further discourse with Professor Küng, but what these insights might do to the shape of

100 *Ibid.*, p. 69. Without denying Küng's demand for credibility, however, note well that there can be a danger that the old triumphalism which has been pushed out the front door may creep in at the back. The spiritual pride of a church that offered its own profession of humility, service, and compassion as the *proof* of its own claims would be even more damning than that of a church that rested its claims on its universality, structural unity, and historical connection with the apostles. We should desire the gifts of the gospel for their own sake, and not as proof of that which should be obvious to all.

How far the Church reveals its Lord is ultimately something that can be recognized by God alone. Our job is not to spend time studying our own spiritual midriffs, but to follow Christ and leave the recognition of Christ's triumph in the Church to God. That surely was the way of Christ himself.

101 *Ibid.*, pp. 225ff. Küng may have been over-sanguine at this point. Apart from Protestant prejudice, which is always formidable, it is not only the question of making this office credible, but of explaining how it became otherwise. When such vast claims have been made of an office as *necessary* for the true existence of the Church, how was it possible for this to become an obstacle for the gospel, and what steps would have to be taken to prevent it from happening again?

102 *Ibid.*, p. 245. Küng's italics.

103 *Ibid.*, p. 363.

the Church he indicated in a moving passage from which no Protestant could dissent:

> It has become clear that the Church, the great community of all the faithful, is the ecumenical council of all believers, which God himself has gathered in Christ and under Christ. Here there is only one Christ; all others are brothers. Even the pope is not the ruler of the Church but her servant, the servant of all. He cannot be pope unless he is first of all and ever anew again, with all others, a humble believing Christian man.[104]

But although the nature of the papacy and the spirit of the pope raise the issue of the Church's credibility in its most obvious form, it extends into every part of the Church's life, past and present: it springs from the growing conviction that the Church cannot claim to be custodian of the Truth unless it is also prepared to face with candor any truth, wherever it happens to be found.[105] As Hans Küng wrote in his later work:

> Nothing is to be gained from concealing the fact . . . that a frightening gulf separates the Church of today from the original constitution of the Church . . . the Church of the present must face up to the history of its origins in the matter of Church constitution as well. In order to ensure continuity it must take note of the gulf that separates it from its origins, without fuss but perhaps a little ashamed. In order to ensure its continued existence, it must constantly confront the challenge of its origins, and ask itself, in the light of its early history, and in the light of the better future it hopes for, what aspects of its present constitution are justified, and what are not.[106]

He added the comment, "A Church which is founded not on itself but on its Lord and his message need not fear these questions."

In *The Church* Hans Küng offers the ground plan of an

[104] *Ibid.*, p. 312.

[105] E.g., with regard to the use made of the false decretals; *ibid.*, pp. 324ff.

[106] *The Church*, trans. Ray and Rosaleen Ockenden (London: Burns & Oates, 1967), pp. 413, 417. I have only one quibble to make against this, and that is his somewhat too mild suggestion that it should be 'perhaps a little ashamed.' Of course, he may be using irony, but I submit we need more than 'a little shame' for making Christ a lie, and hounding thousands of Christians to horrible deaths for daring to oppose our views in the name of the gospel. Unless all churches—Protestant and Catholic—will undertake a deep and lasting *metanoia* that goes further than 'feeling a little ashamed,' mother church will abort her own renewal.

ecumenical conception of the Church drawn from biblical theology.[107] In the preface to the English edition he states this theological perspective:

> Though there is much talk nowadays about the Church in the secular world, there is not a corresponding awareness of what the Church is. One can only know what the Church should be now if one also knows what the Church was originally. This means knowing what the Church of today should be in the light of the Gospel.[108]

The author may be revealing that he was sensitive to the charge that his book neglected the relationship of the Church to the world,[109] but I prefer to think that he is offering a timely reminder about a priority that modern Protestants in general, and modern Anglo-Saxon Protestants in particular, are always tempted to ignore: the shape of the Church cannot be understood apart from the nature of the gospel. There is no more point in seeking modernity for its own sake than there is in resting on tradition for its own sake, but the renewal of the Church is to be sought by first "looking to its own origins, to the events that gave it life."[110]

What challenges Protestants in *The Church* is that Küng accepts so many of the basic premises that up to now they have regarded as peculiarly their own; and this is true not only for venerable and respected Reformation doctrines such as justification by faith and the priesthood of all believers, but also the implications with respect to the nature of the Church itself. He refused to divinize the Church, recognizing that it "is the pilgrim community of believers, not of those who already see and know," and that it "must ever and again wander through the desert, through the darkness of sin and error."[111]

Much more fundamentally, he solidly bases both his criticism of the institutional church and his positive development of ecclesiology on New Testament exegesis—indeed, this scrip-

107 When it first appeared it was in a series of *Oekumenische Forschungen.*

108 *The Church,* p. ix.

109 This charge was made by François Biot, and it is cited by Yves Congar in his review of Küng's book, "*L'Eglise* de Hans Küng," *Revue des Sciences Philosophiques et Théologiques* (Paris), 53/4 (Oct. 1969), 704 and note.

110 *The Church,* p. xi.

111 *Ibid.*

tural base led Yves Congar to charge him with holding a kind of 'sola scriptura' theology that did not give proper recognition to the Church's tradition.[112] Congar reminded him that Catholic theology, and in particular the Dogmatic Constitution on Divine Revelation (*Dei Verbum*), declares that Tradition, the Scriptures, and the Magisterium are so related that one cannot be held without the others.[113]

At the same time, although Küng respects the work of liberal Protestant scholars, he does not fall into that pattern. Against the liberal tendency to excise from the canon anything that conflicts with what is regarded as the authentic 'gospel,' Küng insisted that a Catholic hermeneutic demands that the New Testament be considered as a whole.[114] Nor is he a literalist, for in developing an adequate doctrine of the Church, a simple reversion into New Testament restorationism is not enough:[115] the texts have to be explicated by means of careful and honest exegesis that takes full account of the scriptural context, New Testament scholarship, and of the situation to which the Church is addressing itself.

Fundamentally his approach is theological and christological. God's saving act in Christ is the origin of the Church, "but it is more than the starting-point or the first phase of its history, it is something which at any given time determines the whole history of the Church and defines its essential nature."[116] In other words, the nature of the Church is basically governed by the nature of God's purpose revealed in Jesus Christ: this is where the call to credibility is centered, and this is where any genuinely ecumenical or catholic view of the Church must look in order to find its form.[117]

112 "*L'Eglise* de Hans Küng," p. 697.

113 *Ibid.*, p. 698; cf. p. 700.

114 *The Church*, p. 180; cf. p. 16.

115 *Ibid.*, p. 6.

116 *Ibid.*, p. 14.

117 This means that despite similarities with Rahner—particularly the emphasis on the charismatic element in the Church—or with Rosemary Ruether in the recognition of discontinuity in the Church's history (cf. what he says about the change from Luke to Acts, from the preaching of Jesus to the Christ who is preached, p. 88), he concedes far less to the traditional structure of the Church than the one, and far less to 'secularity' than the other.

The major insight that comes through the five parts of *The Church* is the dialectical ambiguity within which the Church fulfils its mission. We are close to Claude Welch's insistence on the human and the divine in the nature of the Church, if not to Luther's basic Christian paradox.[118] So in the first two sections Küng considers the Church both as it is, essentially grounded in historical forms, and as it is in relation to the coming reign of God, an essentially eschatological community. History is essential for its existence and there is no ecclesiology in any Platonic or ontological sense, but the Church exists to serve the Kingdom which was the goal of Jesus' message; and yet, because our Lord's message did center in the proclamation of the Kingdom of God, Küng refused to build his ecclesiology exclusively either on an eschatology of the future or on a realized eschatology of the present:[119] beyond the work of the Church in present society there is the kerygma that centers in the resurrection.[120]

The dialectic can be seen in other forms, e.g., in the balance between the third and fourth parts of his book. In the third part he developed his constructive view of the Church under the three fundamental biblical concepts—the Church as the People of God, as the Creation of the Spirit, and as the Body of Christ—while in the fourth part he explored the dimensions of the Church through the four catholic (traditional) marks of the Church—its oneness, its catholicity, its holiness, and its apostolicity. One must notice the balance that he maintained between the foundation in the biblical revelation, and the Church's appropriation and development of that foundation in a living tradition. He refused to ignore either or to base his ecclesiology exclusively on either. In the same way in the fifth and final part of the book he discusses the Offices of the Church under two basic concepts—the priesthood of all believers, and ecclesiastical office as Ministry. The implication in Küng is not that we have to maintain the two sides of the paradox because we have no way of resolving it, but that these

118 In his *Treatise on Christian Liberty:* "A Christian is a perfectly free lord of all, subject to none; A Christian is a perfectly dutiful servant to all, subject to all."

119 *The Church,* p. 56.

120 *Ibid.,* p. 78.

insights must be maintained because they are equally important if we are to have a biblical view of the Church. Congar may have had his reservations about some of Küng's views and methodology, but he was surely right to perceive that Küng had indeed taken 'a great step towards' the kind of 'ecclésiologie totale' for which Congar had called earlier.[121]

The dialectic is not only to be discerned in the actual structure of the book, but throughout the discussion of each subject he treats. This gives him a perspective that leads into some very fruitful insights: for example, that the Church is truly the people of *God,* truly the creation of the Spirit, but also capable of sin and in need of constant repentance:

> . . . the Church is the people of God, which, following the Old Testament people of God, is always a people of sinners, constantly in need of forgiveness. The Church journies through the darkness of failures and wrong turnings, constantly in need of God's grace and mercy. Constantly exposed to temptation, it has every cause for its constant attitude of humility and metanoia. The phrase "*ecclesia semper reformanda*" is not just a slogan for times of special difficulty, but God's everyday demand to his people as it journies, the repeated demand for greater faithfulness towards him . . . . Only by accepting the distinction [between the Holy Spirit and the Church] can we truly face up to the all too human aspect of the Church, its failures and shortcomings, its sins and guilt, in a proper liberating way. A Church which identifies itself with the Holy Spirit cannot say the *Confiteor.*[122]

Nor can a Church that identifies itself with the Incarnation, for "a Church which is identical with Christ stops listening, and merely teaches; or rather, it only needs to listen to its own teaching to know what God says."[123] He recognized that the 'perfection' which the Church has is given to it by God, and that "this Church without spot or wrinkle will only be a complete and revealed reality at the end of time."[124]

121 "*L'Eglise* de Hans Küng," p. 706. His call for a 'total ecclesiology' came in the introduction of his best-known work, *Jalons pour une théologie du laïcat* (cf. the English edition, *Lay People in the Church* [London: Chapman, 1957], p. xxviii).

122 *The Church,* pp. 131, 174; cf. also p. 284.

123 *Ibid.,* p. 240; cf. pp. 238-241.

124 *Ibid.,* p. 327. I never expected to hear a Roman Catholic theologian offer this insight. A year or two before 1960 I wrote the following:

. . . if the purpose of our Lord's Incarnation were wholly redemptive and if his

Similarly we might dilate on his insistence on the New Testament as both history and kerygma, upon the insights he offers regarding the relation of Israel to the Church, or upon the essential relationship between the apostolic mission of the whole Church and the function of those who exercise pastoral office as *service:*[125] so he says of the pope, "the Petrine ministry can be correctly and biblically described as a primacy of service, a pastoral primacy: *primatus servitii, primatus ministerialis, primatus pastoralis.*"[126]

Those who have followed the last few footnotes may assume that I applaud Hans Küng's book because it happens to voice insights into the gospel that I happen to share. It is, of course, always pleasant to find one's own ideas independently supported by a Catholic scholar of Hans Küng's eminence, but that would be a superficial way of judging my intention or Küng's book. When Catholic and Protestant scholars can honestly seek a basis for the doctrine of the Church that will be biblically based without being literalistically bound, and find themselves pointing in the same direction, that is surely a matter of more than merely casual interest to the Church.

Yves Congar criticized Küng for having leaned so far in the Protestant direction and for not having taken sufficient account of concerns that would be voiced on this issue by Orthodox and Anglicans.[127] But that is to miss the point. If I read Küng correctly, he did not set out in the first instance to lean as far as he could in the Protestant direction, and he would probably be still less interested in developing the eclectic type of ecumenism that has to find a place for things that everyone wishes to preserve. He set out to discover a truer

perfection and glory were in some sense hidden until the revelation of that supreme purpose at the Resurrection, should we not expect the same to be true to the Church if she is in any sense an extension of his incarnation? . . . To claim a part in his Incarnation or glory *as a right,* far from being a manifestation and proof of the Church's purity and holiness, might become nothing less than the sin of Lucifer. The Church is part of his life, incarnate and glorified, but how it is so and why it should be so is a hidden mystery of grace that can be revealed by God alone and probably will not be revealed until the Resurrection of all things. (*The Atonement and the Sacraments,* p. 286; cf. pp. 282-87.)

125 One of my major concerns in *Ministry* was to show that these two forms of ministry are integrally related, and cannot properly be separated.

126 *The Church,* p. 477.

127 "*L'Eglise* de Hans Küng," p. 696.

pattern for the Church of Jesus Christ, and to do this he had to decide first on the basic authorities and their relationship to Jesus Christ. If he started with the New Testament it was not because it *is* the Source, but because it is the record of that Source; if he recognized the living tradition, it was not because it was tradition, but because it pointed to that Source.

We must, however, end this section by asking the question with which we began: What will be the significance of Hans Küng's ecclesiology for the Roman Catholic Church?

We do not know, although there are some unhappy parallels with another period of history. In 1518 John Staupitz, the man who inspired Martin Luther to pursue his biblical studies, was ordered to remonstrate with the Reformer; and in January 1971 Karl Rahner, the Jesuit theologian to whom Küng had dedicated *Structures of the Church,* joined in the public criticism of Küng for the views on papal infallibility expressed in his book on that subject, and said that if the author had really denied this doctrine "one can only carry on a discussion with Küng as one would with a liberal Protestant." [128]

We cannot answer the question we posed. The debate is on, and the answer will be given only by our commitment to the Truth, the commitment of our Catholic friends, and most particularly by the commitment of our brother, the bishop of Rome.[129]

5

ON WHICH ROCK?

We must carry this just one step further, because there are vital relationships between the issue of credibility and the basic problem of Authority. Hans Küng pointed to one aspect of this when he said that "Authority in the community is derived not from the holding of a certain rank, not from a special tradition, not from old age or long membership of the community but from the performance of a ministry in the Spirit,"[130] or when he spoke of John XXIII's "evangelical

128 From the *Newsweek* report (Jan. 25, 1971), p. 57.

129 John 15:13-15; Matthew 23:8.

130 *The Church,* p. 401.

renunciation of spiritual power" and said that no man can undertake that kind of renunciation of power without having "grasped something of the message of Jesus and of the Sermon on the Mount in particular."[131] In other words, the credibility of the Church has a direct relationship to the *way* authority is exercised and manifested in the Church: what the Church does and the way it does it demonstrate to everyone what manner of Spirit rules the Church.

This subject has been put under the microscope by the Jesuit, John McKenzie, of Notre Dame University. His book *Authority in the Church*[132] is directed primarily to the credibility gap in the Roman Catholic Church on this very issue, throwing into the sharpest contrast the nature of authority exercised in the New Testament Church and authority as it is exercised in the Church today.

McKenzie says that it is natural to think of ecclesiastical authority as a type or species of authority in general; but this is contrary to the New Testament, where authority in the Church is unique. He then examines authority in the New Testament in detail, pointing out at the outset that there can never be any successor to Jesus Christ as head of the Church because (a) our Lord has never left his Church, and (b) "it is the whole Church in all its members which continues and extends the life and mission of Jesus Christ."[133]

He then looks at the style, the distinctive characteristic of our Lord's ministry, and finds it in diakonia—but he hastens to remind his readers that this means something far more menial than 'service.' It means to serve as a lackey.[134] This kind of service inspired by Jesus' kind of love governs the nature of authority that is used in the Church of the New Testament. The New Testament does not present us with a church that is formless, but it shows us churches in which the structural forms serve this kind of authority and are therefore expected to function in a radically different way from the authorities in the secular world. The sayings of Jesus in Matthew 23 show

131 *Ibid.*, p. 472.

132 New York: Sheed and Ward, 1966.

133 *Op. cit.*, p. 22.

134 *Ibid.*, p. 23.

that the structures of the Church were parallel neither to those of the secular state nor to those of Judaism; and McKenzie makes the dry comment that if Jesus had wished to describe the government of his community in more moderate terms than 'child,' 'lackey,' 'slave,' there were plenty of alternative options in Aramaic and Greek.

Jesus left no specific instructions about church government, except that the Church was *not* to be governed in anything like the way in which secular authorities exercised their power: he left clear instructions on how the Church was *not* to be governed.

> The conclusion to be drawn, if this interpretation is correct, is not that Jesus left no instructions on how the Church should be governed, but that he commissioned the Church to find new forms and structure for an entirely new idea of human association—a community of love. In an organization capable of indefinite expansion in time and space, it is more vital that it have unity of spirit, achieved by the indwelling personal Spirit, than that it have rigid forms incapable of adaptation to cultural changes and the movement of history. The Church could not fulfil its commission unless Jesus also endowed it with the resources to find new forms. He did endow it with these resources in the ideal of *diakonia* in love, a new and revolutionary form of authority which Christians could see in their own personal life and mission.[135]

Authority in the Church has to be seen in the light of the Church's mission. Peter was given a special place among the Twelve (although McKenzie points out that there is no full expression in the New Testament of the way in which the Petrine office was later developed), but Peter's commission was given in response to his confession of *faith*.[136] Simon Peter's leadership therefore goes far beyond jurisdictional power, for he was to be the shepherd of the flock, in the same sense that our Lord was the Good Shepherd, the one who would protect the flock without thought for himself. The authority was essentially pastoral.

The same was true for Paul. McKenzie notes that when Paul issued his sentence of excommunication it was "medicinal, not vindictive; his purpose was the salvation of the spirit of the

135 *Ibid.*, pp. 32f.

136 *Ibid.*, p. 40.

offender."[137] Furthermore, in his letters we notice the frequent reappearance of *diakonia, diakonos* to describe the work of an apostle. The Church is the community which is governed by the Spirit and in which the charismata are exercised by every member according to his gift. The supreme gift is love.

> Authority exercised through any other species of power is not Church authority. That authority is one of the works of the Spirit demands that authority be respected as such; that other works of the Church are also works of the Spirit demands that the bearers of authority respect the other works as such . . . . The base of power of authority is the love which those in authority exhibit; for the mission of the Church is the work of the love of Jesus Christ for men.[138]

McKenzie noted that even in the later New Testament writings there is a surprising absence of exhortations urging the faithful to be obedient to their leaders, and he also suggests it is significant that the early Church did not carry over from Judaism the specific titles—hiereus (priest), rabbi—that were associated with particular forms of sacerdotal or rabbinic authority.

Throughout his study Fr. McKenzie shows that he is a firm believer in the principle of the development of doctrine,[139] and it is clear that he did not undertake his New Testament study simply to restore the New Testament forms. Therefore in his reflection upon the New Testament evidence he asks how we are to apply these insights in a situation as far removed from the circumstances of New Testament times as our own. What seems clear from the New Testament is that "a

137 *Ibid.,* p. 52; cf. p. 54.

138 *Ibid.,* pp. 60f.; cf. 67. Again I confess my earlier skepticism, for I had never expected to see this gospel principle so explicitly recognized by a Roman Catholic writer. In *Ministry* I included a passage on this theme (pp. 177-190): "The Church *is* given authority by Jesus Christ. We must assert that just as firmly as any medieval pope, but we must also go on to emphasize that Jesus Christ *is* the Authority—his nature determines the nature of the authority entrusted to his Church, his character determines its character, his Spirit defines its spirit. To exercise the authority of Christ in a way that is entirely contrary to the Spirit revealed in the Jesus of the Gospels, is to relinquish the very authority that the Church claims . . . . We must therefore establish this ecclesiological axiom, that *the authority given by Jesus Christ to his Church is his authority only as it is exercised in accordance with his revealed Spirit*" (p. 181).

139 Cf. *Authority in the Church,* p. 38.

new type of authority emerges to suit a new type of community," and hence, "if we are to apprehend the reality of this authority, we shall have to find words other than those we are accustomed to associate with authority."[140] The exercise of authority through power can compel no one to be a Christian, but authority in the Christian sense can proclaim the truth and persuade others by the quality of its own living: "Proclamation by action is true leadership, and this is the only kind of leadership recommended in the New Testament."[141]

He admitted that if this were introduced into the Roman Catholic Church forthwith it would produce administrative chaos; that is not his aim, but rather a movement towards the "transformation of the idea and use of authority."[142] The Dogmatic Constitution on the Church pointed in this direction by emphasizing pastoral rather than juridical functions of bishops,[143] and McKenzie seems to be very close to Peter Berger's distinction between the impersonal (secular) and personal (Christian) way of dealing with people when he insists that the New Testament Church laid down for itself the principle of government by men rather than government by law.[144]

The only restraint that the New Testament puts upon freedom is love,[145] and in line with his concept of the Church with its developing structures, he asks if it might not be possible for the Church to move in a more democratic direction so that it could reflect the spirit of the New Testament a little better. "Structurally," he said, "there is no way to correct abuses of authority except rebellion, and no one thinks rebellion is a good way to do things."[146] He summarized his basic purpose as seeking to show that according to the New

140 *Ibid.*, p. 91. We must seriously ask whether our Catholic and Episcopal brethren would be prepared to put the word 'bishop' in this category, if the gospel content could be maintained?

141 *Ibid.*, p. 93. This is also close to Rosemary Ruether's insight of life as kerygma.

142 *Ibid.*

143 *Ibid.*, pp. 99f.

144 *Ibid.*, p. 115; cf. above, pp. 190ff.

145 *Ibid.*, p. 167.

146 *Ibid.*, p. 169.

Testament the authority that is to be employed in the Church must be fundamentally different from authority as it is exercised in the secular realm,[147] because the mystery of the Church is the union of love between all who constitute its membership, officers and people.

> The Church rises above her humanity when both officers and members cherish the divine element in her, which is the surpassing love diffused by the Spirit. When authority and members are united in this love, human error and human malice cannot have their full consequences. How this is accomplished is the mystery of the Church. Authority and obedience are not enough.[148]

However, this simply raises in another form the deeper problem of authority, the quest for the ultimate authority on which all faith and churchmanship is based. Küng, McKenzie, and others simply illustrate that an increasing number of Roman Catholics face a similar problem to that which haunts Protestants. The old simplistic view of authority is no longer credible.

It is significant that in this dilemma Catholic scholars have turned primarily to the New Testament, but it is evident that in doing so they do not approach it as biblicists but in order to come closer to Jesus Christ and to the spirit of the Church that arose from his life, death, and resurrection. Christ is the rock on which the Church is founded, the rock that other builders rejected, a stumbling stone for many and a rock of offense.[149] If scholars like Küng and McKenzie go first to the New Testament, it is not because they identify it with 'the Word,' but because it contains the record (the words, if you will) of that eternal Word; if they recognize the continuation of a living tradition in the Church, they accept it not because it is tradition but insofar as its 'livingness' witnesses to the same Spirit that Jesus manifested while he was here on earth; if they understand the responsibility of the individual Christian to appropriate this Truth for himself,[150] they also understand

147 *Ibid.,* p. 176.

148 *Ibid.,* p. 183.

149 Cf. I Peter 2:1-8.

150 Cf. what McKenzie says about the prophet, *Authority in the Church,* chapter 12. Also we may reflect on Küng's comment that even if his supporters in

that this is not a matter of individual will but of willingness to follow that same Spirit. And besides this, in the honest use of all scholarly aids in dealing with Scripture and history, they recognize the crucial but humble place that God has given human reason in the search for truth.

Ultimately the issue is ethical. At the center we have to face the moral imperative of Jesus Christ himself: Hans Küng insists that above all other characteristics that the Christian Church may have, it must be *Christ*-ian;[151] that our Lord's proclamation of the Kingdom means the victory of his *life* in the world;[152] but he insists that what the Church needs is not a new moral code or ethical program but an ethical decision for God which begins and continues in repentance.[153] With similar earnestness John McKenzie castigates the 'Organization Church' for its failure to follow Christ in the basic moral issues raised by our society.[154] In one sense it has been at the center of the Church's message from the beginning. It was expressed succinctly by Heinrich Suso, the medieval German mystic, when he observed, "let not him ask what is highest in doctrine who yet stands on what is lowest in a good life."[155]

The ethical issue goes even deeper. Does Jesus Christ ask anyone to accept a lie in his name? To dismiss the contemporary questioning of traditional authority, Protestant or Catholic, as if it were due entirely to the faithlessness of twentieth-century Christians would be a far too facile way of explaining the malaise in the Church. Probably the twentieth century has had its share of Christians who have lost their faith, but for them there is little problem, for they will simply drop out. We are talking about those who have not lost faith in Christ, who are committed to the Church as the community of

the Church withdraw their support, "I am ready to go it alone." Shades of Worms? Cf. *Newsweek* (Jan. 25, 1971), p. 58.

151 *The Church,* p. 39.

152 *Ibid.,* pp. 45f.

153 *Ibid.,* pp. 52ff.

154 *Authority in the Church,* pp. 101ff.

155 From Suso's *Das Büchlein der ewigen Weisheit* (1335), quoted in John Baillie, *The Idea of Revelation in Recent Thought* (New York: Columbia, 1956), p. 145.

his people, but for whom the clear-cut, exclusive answers of their churches have lost credibility.

It may be somewhat venturesome for anyone standing outside the Roman Catholic Church to make any generalizations about it, but it is suggested that the writers in this chapter indicate that there is a crisis of Authority within that church similar to that which exists in Protestantism. Other evidence might be cited, such as the drift from the ministry and the priesthood,[156] although in that other factors are likely to be operative. We cannot say which way the issue will go—Charles Davis thinks that Catholicism "will shy away from the sharp change which is called for and will prefer rather to become a sect turned in on itself," while others, such as Gregory Baum, are far more optimistic.[157] One thing, however, seems fairly sure: the time has passed when such problems could be tackled by the churches unilaterally. We need each other.

156 On the Protestant side one might point to the studies undertaken by the United Church of Christ (Gerald Jud, *et al., Ex-Pastors—Why Men Leave the Ministry* [Philadelphia: Pilgrim Press, 1970]), and by the Episcopal Church (David R. Covell, Jr., *et al., Satisfaction and Dissatisfaction Among Parish Priests: A Preliminary Discussion* [New York: published for the Coordinating Research Committee of the Executive Council of the Episcopal Church, June 1970]). For Catholicism there are studies in progress, but cf. Eugene J. Schallert, S.J. and Jacqueline M. Kelley, "Some Factors Associated with Voluntary Withdrawal from the Catholic Priesthood," *Lumen Vitae,* 25/3 (Sept. 1970); and the report of John Koval of Notre Dame in *Newsweek* (Jan. 25, 1971), p. 58.

157 Cf. the review by Gregory Baum of Charles Davis' book, *A Question of Conscience,* in *Frontier* (London), 1/11 (Spring 1968), 64.

PART FOUR

FUTURE PROSPECT

Chapter VIII

THE NATURE OF THE CHURCH

1

GOD OF THE BIBLE

"The Problem of God is more important than the problem of the Church," declares Hans Küng, "but the latter often stands in the way of the former."[1] Why should the credibility (or integrity) of the Church have any direct relationship to belief in God? Why is it, with full recognition that the Church is composed of sinful erring human beings, people still have a right to expect an authenticity and inner consistency from this community which they would demand from no other? That question gets to the heart of the ecclesiological problem.

It is clearly related to a basic thesis of this book, that the authorities by which the doctrines of the Church have previously been judged are almost wholly discredited. But this thesis carries with it the conviction that insofar as these 'secular' criticisms are offered the name of an honesty that strips faith from its myths and prejudices, they force Christians to take the gospel *more* seriously and to ask what is worthy of Jesus Christ.

Thus we question the view of the Church built on historical continuity not only because more is claimed for apostolic

[1] *The Church,* p. xiii.

succession than the evidence warrants, but because it has not guaranteed the 'fruits of the Spirit' which are the distinctive marks of the Church of Jesus Christ. If 'secular man' turns away from the Church at this point, his expectations are centered *in* the gospel. When he reads accounts of how the representatives of valid succession employed fire and sword against their opponents, or witnesses today their neglect of the dispossessed while assuming all the trappings of wealth and power, he is right *in the name of Christ* to question what is claimed for the 'apostolic' succession.[2]

We question biblical restorationism not only because it was built on inaccurate assumptions about the Bible, but also because the acrimony with which the worship and polity of the New Testament Church were debated has been a blatant denial of the love that is the Church's most distinctive quality, and the competition into which we have fallen visibly contradicts the unity that is intended to be one of its most obvious characteristics. When an African animist, an Asian Buddhist, or an Arab Moslem sees the rivalry of Christian churches, suffers the warfare of so-called Christian nations, and witnesses their arrogant affluence in the face of other peoples' misery, he is right *in the name of Christ* to question what is claimed by churches that profess to have restored the New Testament ideal.

Spiritual pragmatism has to be questioned, not primarily because it puts a premium on the practical, but because it so often loses touch with its spiritual source in Christ and makes pragmatism an ultimate authority divorced from the gospel. When a black city laborer, or a poor white in a depressed rural area sees denominations pulling up their roots from the places where they could exercise a sacrificial ministry and settling

[2] In his description of Vatican II, Edward Schillebeeckx recalls that occasionally the General Secretary of the Council would address the members as 'patres ornatissimi,' the Latin equivalent of 'Most honoured Fathers.' A Brazilian archbishop, Henrique Golland of Botucatu, used this to make the point of the Church's credibility extremely clear. "That is what the people also call us, though in a different sense," he protested, "when they see us bishops walking through the streets polished and arrayed from head to toe." He requested that they might appear in simple black cassocks. Schillebeeckx, *Vatican II: The Real Achievement,* p. 21.

themselves in well-endowed suburbs, or when they hear an emphasis almost to the point of obsession with the physical plant and material prosperity of the church, then the critics are right to question the churches because they do so *in the name of Christ.*

If the criticism were on any other basis we could afford to ignore it, but when the secular world challenges the Church for virtual apostasy, we have to listen. Moreover, these criticisms may be pointing to something basic about the nature of the Church which could help us in our search for that surer ground on which the Church is based. Hitherto a church might justify itself in terms of its own favorite brand of legitimacy, but now the world will no longer allow the dust of ages to be thrown in its eyes: it looks to the center, and criticizes the Church for being a flagrant contradiction of its own gospel, for denying in action and in form what it has proclaimed about *God.*

The purpose of the Church is the fulfilment of God's will towards the world. Some years ago H. Richard Niebuhr defined the Church's goal as "the increase among men of the love of God and neighbour,"[3] but those words need to be given full value if they are not to be made the excuse for vague sentimentality or a rather bloodless moralism. They were based on Jesus' summary of the law, and if we are to give "the increase among men of the love of God and neighbour" its context, we must reflect on the one who was behind that summary. That presents the proper dimension to Niebuhr's definition—the kerygmatic aspect of the Church's work, what God has done that makes "love of God and neighbour" possible. Jesus Christ himself stands behind the definition of the Church's goal, and his life, death, and resurrection puts content into what the love of God and neighbor means.

As the Church works for the fulfilment of God's will towards men it also reveals his nature, not because it has any claims on his divinity, but because it is called to a ministry in the name and spirit of Jesus Christ: to the degree that it fulfils that ministry it cannot help revealing by its own actions how God treats humanity. The world turns a cool eye on our liberal

[3] *The Purpose of the Church and Its Ministry* (New York: Harper, 1956), p. 31; cf. pp. 27-39.

enthusiasms and our casual, condescending charities, and it muses on the fact that the Church is supposed to be promoting among men the love of *God* and neighbor. Presumably this is not a one-way street and the reason God expects us to respond is because he has first loved us. Indeed, the Church has been declaiming for a long time that in Jesus Christ this love became incarnate and poured itself out in man's behalf even to the point of the cross. Is that the God you worship? Then, show me.

The doctrine of the Church must be biblically based but not biblically bound, and the search can end only at one place—in biblical *theology;* but because this term is open to misinterpretation, it needs to be carefully defined. By 'biblical theology' I mean what the Bible has to say about God, his purpose in creation, his essential nature as it is revealed in the covenant and in relationship to Israel, and supremely as it is revealed in Jesus Christ.

The doctrine of the Church must be based on 'biblical theology' understood in this sense, not on historical legalism nor on biblical literalism nor even on 'biblical theology' as it was used to defend the orthodox *a priori;* for we are seeking a basis for the Church and its ministry firmly centered in the biblical revelation but not bound by the limitations of the biblical writers, their world view, or the perspectives of any later period. Instead of mining in the Scriptures for textual rocks to throw at the Roman Catholics and Episcopalians, with an occasional side-heave at any other denomination that happens to raise our ire, we all must ask what the Bible has to say about God and his relationships to his people, and how this affects their mission in the world and the nature of the community they should be. The old arguments as to whether presbyterianism, episcopacy, or congregationalism can be proved out of Scripture will not do, any more than it will do to appeal legalistically to the apostolic blue blood of one ecclesiastical family tree over another: the very bases on which our forefathers ground out their polemic are not only questionable in the name of historical truth, but they are also invalidated by the Christian ethic, which first demands the honest acceptance of all truth and then the recognition that a claim to possess the

Spirit must show evidence of the Spirit. And what is that but an appeal to the righteous nature of the God of the Bible?

Another ecumenical dimension makes its appearance, the relationship between church and synagogue. Long before Vatican II had made it official from the Catholic side, it was clear that the ancient antipathies between Christian and Jew were an offense before God. It is also clear that in the history of Western Christendom the Jew has often been far more sinned against than sinning.

Behind all our professions of worship there is the God of the Bible, whose nature and will were proclaimed and revealed by the whole succession of Hebrew prophets in which succession Jesus stood. As we understand that testimony better, we realize that such a God does not rescind his promises, that the Jewish people was a prophetic people before the Church arose, and that it continues to be a prophetic people within the world. Even in our own century Jewry became a community of suffering largely through the indifference of 'Christian' nations. Furthermore, an uncomfortable feeling has been growing among Christians that if the modern Jew rejects the claims of Jesus as Messiah, it may be due to the churches' virtual denial of his gospel.

The American experience described by Will Herberg, which brought Protestant, Catholic, and Jew together in one place, showed the members of these faiths that they could live together constructively and with mutual respect. It ought also to show them that insofar as they are all trying to proclaim the God of the Bible in terms of a living community, their destinies belong together. For Christians, the person and life of Jesus Christ must be the final 'hermeneutical principle' in exegeting the essential nature of that God—as Pascal argued in the *Pensées,* the Old Testament prophecies do not so much prove the divinity of Christ, as Christ proves the genuineness of the prophecies—but Jesus is also set firmly within the history of God's dealings with the Jewish people. This brings Christians into an inevitable relationship with that ancient people of God: the bitter hatred of the past might have been justified, if we had not both claimed to be the people of *such* a God.

We are not proposing that we should unite. Union is out of our hands as far as Jewish-Christian relations are concerned. It is obviously nonsense to speak and act as if no vital differences of faith remained between us (even if the nation of Israel did not complicate relationships at a very different level), and one feels that the Christian who implies that the differences can be disregarded really insults Judaism by assuming that the Jew knows and cares as little about his Jewish faith as many Christians do about their own. Perhaps one cannot go further than to maintain an openness for dialogue on the deeper issues, to encourage the closest relations possible within the framework of our convictions, and to come together for common action in society to achieve a more righteous social order. For the rest let us continue to 'rival' each other in expressing the nature and the will of the God we worship, and let our communities of faith proclaim whose people we are.

If the way of service is the true task of the Church in this world, it is the vocation of all God's true people. Whether the Jews will ever recognize Jesus of Nazareth as Messiah in the way Christians have wished to see him acknowledged is perhaps immaterial; but if the Jewish people reveal and proclaim their own corporate servanthood for humanity, and in doing so reveal the nature of the God who brought them out of Egypt and communicated his will through the prophets, they will recognize the Messiah in a more fundamental way than any formal recognition of the man Jesus. And the Christ whom Christians recognize in Jesus would probably not ask for more.

We have been using the word 'theology' in a precise sense. 'Theology' is often employed loosely to cover any discussion of doctrine, and hence it becomes the area of debate within which particular orthodoxies advance their claims. We are suggesting that theology is concerned much more fundamentally with the nature of God, and with his actions in creation and redemption. As Christians we believe that the nature of God was uniquely revealed in relation to a people chosen to be his emissaries within the world, and supremely in the person of Jesus Christ.

That is why any theology of Church and ministry must go

back to the biblical revelation and find its center in the relationships that our Lord expressed towards God and men. In trying to determine the character and shape of the Church in any age, we are concerned with a people which is in pilgrimage towards becoming the true people of *such* a God. A true doctrine of the Church will not imply that this people has already reached perfection—that has been the constant temptation of every ecclesiology—but it will recognize first, that its call is to witness to the God it worships, and secondly, that the pilgrimage (i.e., the context of its struggle, its finitude and imperfection) represents the *given* conditions of that calling: it is the proof that it is called of God to this end in this world, its confession that it shares the lot of human frailty with all men.

What is the nature of the God that we serve? That is the basic question which sends us to the biblical evidence. In asking questions concerned with ecclesiology we should go to the Bible not so much to discover what institutions were set up by the People of God in former ages, but to see how those institutions illumine the relationships between God and his people. The Covenant is a case in point. The Puritans made it the very basis of their theology, and because God's covenants with Israel were at the center of biblical religion, they religiously established the National Covenants of Scottish Presbyterianism and the church covenants of Congregationalism. As institutions, however, their covenants may well be irrelevant and out of date. What *is* important about the covenant in the Bible is what it tells us about God and his dealings with men—his willingness to choose them for his purposes, his acknowledgment of their capacity to respond, his faithfulness, his intention to enter into a living relationship with them, and finally, in the vision of the New Covenant (Jeremiah 31:31-33) God's desire that this relationship should not be interpreted in terms of law, but written in the hearts of his people. This is not an institution to be copied but a relationship to be entered and enjoyed.

Something similar may be said about the institutions of the New Testament. Almost every book on the Church since 1950 has emphasized that the Church must carry the three distinctive marks of New Testament Christianity—the kerygma (the proclaimed gospel), koinonia (the distinctive fellowship), the diakonia (the vocation of service); and let it be admitted that it is impossible to conceive of a true church in which they would not be at the center. Furthermore, it is true that in dealing with the Apostolic Church, its missionary proclamation, its shared fellowship, and its mutual service, we are not dealing with specific institutions but with characteristics of the New Testament community.

On the other hand, one feels that many writers have been using these characteristics of the Church in the New Testament as if they were institutions, that we should make them characteristics of the Church today *because* they were there in the Church of the New Testament—a sort of demythologized restorationism. But in order to find out the true nature of the Church—not simply the Church of the New Testament but the Church of any age and all ages—the first question to ask is, "What do these characteristics of the New Testament community tell us about God and about his relationships with his people?" The reason why a kerygmatic church is needed today is not because this best reproduces the Church of the New Testament, but because unless God's redeeming love for man was offered to us in Jesus Christ, we have no gospel to offer anyone. All that the Church says and does and should be has its source in this Good News and takes its character—imperfectly, perhaps, and in a struggling, pilgrim way—from what God said and did for mankind in Jesus Christ.

The same is true of koinonia. If we are getting down to the fundamental basis of the Church, all the mutual love and sharing that koinonia represented in the early Church belongs to the true nature of the Church in any age, not because it belonged to the New Testament community, but because it belongs in the first place to God himself. As E. Clinton Gardner has pointed out in *The Church as a Prophetic Community*, the New Testament writers see that this belongs to the very relationships within the Trinity, between the Father and the Son, and unites God in the Spirit with the Church: "the fellowship that the believers have with God is primary; their fellowship with one another is derivative."[4] But it should also

4 *The Church as a Prophetic Community* (Philadelphia: Westminster, 1967), pp. 150f.

be seen that this is where fundamental ecclesiology begins, in the nature of the God we worship, whose nature and purpose were revealed in Jesus Christ.

The issue is seen most clearly in respect to diakonia. There seems to be general recognition that service, of the kind that Jesus showed throughout his ministry, belongs essentially to the ministry of the whole church; but here too, that quality of service, the complete giving up of the self that Jesus showed to men, points to a quality within God himself: "My Father has not ceased his work till now, and I am working too" (John 5:17, NEB), and the character of that work is diakonia.

An ecclesiology that is understood in this way will try to show what is the nature of the people *of God,* those who are the people of *such a God.* It will be less concerned with proof-texts about how the church organized itself in the time of Paul or Peter, less concerned with certificates of ecclesiastical heredity, than with trying to manifest the Spirit and his gifts, and to set up the temporary structures (tabernacles, tents) of life, witness, and worship that most truly reflect the one who in Jesus Christ calls mankind to join him.

2

A THEOLOGY OF THE CHURCH

We are speaking about a 'theology of the Church.' That is, we are suggesting that the doctrine of the Church must be related *essentially* to God's revelation of himself, and all other foundations for ecclesiology are secondary; the basis is theological in that fundamental sense of being directly related to the nature of God himself.[5] Obviously the dimensions of this are far greater than we could adequately explore in this book.

[5] A good example of how theology may correct ecclesiology is seen in the Allocution of Pius IX in 1854. Berkouwer has pointed out that Rome's attitude to its own professed exclusivity has been equivocal. (*The Second Vatican Council and the New Catholicism,* pp. 190f.) On one side it seemed clear that outside the Roman Catholic Church there could be no salvation, but by the pronouncement of Pius IX this was modified to recognize that God does not condemn those who live and die in ignorance of the truth. This was a *theological* qualification, i.e., the dogmatic position was modified because of what the Church believed about *the nature of God himself:* the Church could not conceive of the God and Father of

What follows simply sketches some of the distinguishing features of a new landscape.

(1) By beginning with the biblical revelation of God we obviously put the question of credibility on a different plane. At the end of his book, in what he calls a 'Sermon from a Secularist,' Arthur Herzog observes, "Whether religion is regarded as tradition or revelation the churches will be forced to show that they bear witness to a meaningful faith, as demonstrated by their own actions and lives. There is always the smallest chance that the churches—in some fashion undefined—are right, but the proof is up to them."[6] Proof of 'rightness' or 'wrongness' may be somewhat irrelevant—it cannot be the motive for the Church's work, since the Church's task is to bear testimony to the revelation of God in Jesus Christ, and the rest of the world must make up its own mind about the truth of that testimony. And yet Herzog is right in pointing out that the ultimate testimony to faith is in ethics—what the Church does and in the kind of life her members manifest, individually and corporately.

Look at this from the perspective of what the Bible tells us about God: he is a God whose claim to recognition is centered not in metaphysical arguments or mystical experience but in what he *does*. This is his own self-disclosure, the proof and the justification of his purpose and character. There are so many ways in which one may be justly critical of churches, but let us commend the emphasis of a recent Statement of Faith which begins, "We believe in God, the Eternal Spirit, Father of our Lord Jesus Christ and our Father, and *to his deeds we testify.*"[7] This is true to the God who called Israel to be his people not primarily because he is territorial god over a certain plot of land, but because he is a God with a certain 'nature' and who reveals that nature to them in the way he acts towards his people. Their ultimate reliance was not in any objectified form—"Thou shalt not make unto thee any graven

our Lord Jesus Christ condemning men for an ignorance that they genuinely cannot help.

6 *The Church Trap,* p. 177.

7 The Statement of Faith of the United Church of Christ, approved at its Second General Synod at Oberlin, 1959 (italics mine).

image"—but in the character revealed by God's 'mighty acts' for their redemption. They recognized him as the Creator and sustainer of all men, but he revealed this character supremely in the loving-kindness and mercy shown to Israel through its history. At its height, Hebrew faith had the insight that if Israel worships such a God, Israel itself should be a servant people that reflects his purpose.

This is even more dramatically represented in the New Testament—God in Jesus Christ becoming incarnate among men in a situation of obscurity and ordinariness; God in Christ willing to work side by side with men and listening to them in the daily experiences of Nazareth; God in Christ allowing his life to bear testimony to the truth of his words; God in Christ making no claims but giving, in human terms, the evidence that he was fulfilling the meaning of the law, and that he represented the Father's will for men; God in Christ showing the disciples what it meant to serve the brethren, the people of Israel and all mankind; God in Christ pouring out his life in death that he might reveal the love of the Father. "From first to last," said Paul, reflecting on the gospel, "this has been the work of God. He had reconciled us men to himself through Christ, and he has enlisted us in the service of reconciliation. What I mean is, that God was in Christ reconciling the world to himself, no longer holding men's misdeeds against them, and that he has entrusted us with the message of reconciliation" (II Corinthians 5:18f., NEB).

In these words we see the essential but simple relationship between theology, Christology, and ecclesiology: that which Christ came to proclaim about the nature of the Father, the Church is called to proclaim in word and action. The Church is to make Christ corporate, to interpret what this gospel must mean in terms of a living community before the Kingdom can become real among men. Somewhere Dietrich Bonhoeffer expressed this essential idea when he wrote, "The Church is not a religious community of worshippers of Christ, but it is Christ himself who has taken form among men."

Yet it should be clear that far from being an occasion for pride or arrogance in the Church, this direct relationship between the Church and what it proclaims about God and Jesus Christ is the measure of its imperfection, the occasion of its penitence and confession before him. The simplicity and the magnitude of the Church's task manifest the enormity of the pretensions with which churches have tried to establish their claims: that task, which obviously can be accomplished only by grace and by the help of God, has so often been represented as a special claim to honor, something that can be achieved by the Church's own innate virtue.

We have all applied the biblical images of the Body and Bride of Christ to our own church in the wrong way. Some reflection on the history of Israel should have taught us differently;[8] but because within the context of the New Testament these are figures of obedience and 'perfection,' we have often claimed them in a way that is flat idolatry, failing to recognize that both the 'Body' and the 'Bride' reflect the perfection of *Christ:* the 'Body' is perfect only as it manifests itself as the active agent of its Head, and the 'Bride' only as she demonstrates complete union with her Lord. Moreover, I question whether any expressions of the Church, whether 'gathered' and covenanted or institutionalized and geographic, can make such claims about themselves without negating their claim to be the true Church; for if there is anything we know about the claim to divinity it is that it is not to be grasped at:

> Let your bearing towards one another arise out of your life in Christ Jesus. For the divine nature was his from the first; yet he did not think to snatch equality with God, but made himself nothing, assuming the nature of a slave. Bearing the human likeness, revealed in human shape, he humbled himself, and in obedience accepted even death—death on a cross. *Therefore* (*dio kai*) God raised him to the heights and bestowed on him the name above all names, that at the name of Jesus every knee should bow—in heaven, on earth, and in the depths—and every tongue confess "Jesus Christ is Lord, to the glory of God the Father."[9]

This describes the pattern of divine glory and how it is to be won, and this is what the Church is called to manifest before men. We have all been so wrong.

What we seem to have manifested before men is the one sure way of invalidating our claim to be the Church of Jesus Christ,

[8] Compare the figure of the bride in Hosea, or Paul's comments on Israel's failure in I Corinthians 10:1-13.

[9] Philippians 2:5-11. The same point was emphasized in *Ministry*, p. 117.

the one certain way of revealing our claims to be false. The Catholic branches have flaunted their 'perfection' through the impeccability of historical succession and the correct ordering of their clerical hierarchy, while Protestant churches, particularly those of the Reformed or 'gathered' type, have claimed 'perfection' through their fidelity to the New Testament pattern, their emphasis on church discipline and insistence that the members should be 'visible saints.' The one aberration led to institutional churches that sought to impress by magnificence and were ready to persecute where they were opposed, while the other manifested the subtle pride of ostracizing and divisive communities. Both offered to the world the evidence of Antichrist, because both *claimed* a perfection that can never be claimed, but which can only be demonstrated in the unselfconscious acts of the Spirit, which delights to serve and which points always away from itself to our Lord, just as Jesus pointed away from himself to God and the Holy Spirit points to Jesus.[10] Our churches have been so bemused by their rival claims that they have not seen, what has been patently obvious to the world, that when they are most exclusive and arrogant they are farthest away from the Church of Jesus Christ.

(2) It means that we have to put the Incarnation at the center of our faith not only as it is professed but also as it is practiced.

The meaning of the Servant Songs in Isaiah should be explored by Christian and Jewish biblical scholars, and in particular we would like to know how far the character of the Suffering Servant in Isaiah 53 was drawn from insights that the Hebrew religion had into Yahweh's own essential character. Why does this figure of the Servant of Yahweh appear at the highest point of the Hebrew faith, why should this figure of service and suffering be thought of as the servant *of Yahweh,* and why should that ministry be offered to Israel vicariously in Yahweh's name?

To fulfil the Church's mission, argument and declamation are not enough. Martin Buber, the Jewish philosopher, described how on one occasion in the Ruhr valley he managed to convince a tough, skeptical worker that rational theism was

[10] John 16:13f.; cf. 7:18.

more reasonable than agnosticism. Then Buber was struck aghast at what he had done, because he realized he had simply sold the worker the idea of 'God' as an intellectual proposition, and done nothing to bring him face to face with the personal reality. "On the next day," said Buber, "I had to depart. I could not remain, as now I ought to do; I could not enter into the factory where the man worked, become his comrade, live with him, win his trust through real life-relationship, help him to walk with me the way of the creature who accepts the creation."[11] That kind of identity with people is at the heart of biblical faith, and Buber came to realize that the only way to bring the erstwhile skeptic face to face with the personal God of faith is by accepting the servanthood of identity within this man's life and by his side.

For the Christian, of course, the Incarnation is at the very center of the gospel. This event, we hold, tells us something central about the nature of God and his relationship to man. When the gospel writer appropriated the prophecy of Isaiah about the young woman giving birth to a child whose name would be Immanuel—'God is with us' (Matthew 1:22f.; Isaiah 7:14f.)—and applied it directly to the birth of Jesus, he was offering insight not so much into Isaiah's earlier prophecy as into the nature of the God who had spoken through the pages of the Old Testament but who was now speaking his final word, making his ultimate self-revelation, in the person of Jesus of Nazareth. This is the God whom Israel worshipped, the One who in love and mercy gives up the seat of celestial power in order to become totally identified with the human condition and human destiny. What we see in Jesus Christ is God entering into the human factory where man lives and works, living with him and winning "his trust through real life-relationship." That is the first step to 'atonement'—God becoming 'at one' with man, so that man may learn how to become at one with himself and his neighbor. There is real point in the insight that the Church *must* be in some sense a continuation of that Incarnation.

However, churches appropriated this insight in the wrong way. It was used to claim the presence of divine perfection

11 *The Eclipse of God* (1952; New York: Harper Torchbook, 1957), pp. 5f.

residing in our all too human frailty, forgetting that such divinity belongs not to the Church but to its Lord, and that to claim it is to prove that you do not have it. It is not to be claimed, but in unself-conscious identification with mankind it may be revealed. There may even be a sense in which this divine nature within its chosen instruments shows itself only to those to whom it is addressed. Jesus never seems to have made any claims for himself but claimed only that he was doing the will of his Father; and when he wanted to know the impact of his ministry, he asked his disciples: "Who do men say that I am? Who do you say that I am?" The call is to humility and faith in the exercise of our ministry, and this becomes hopelessly invalidated when we use it to justify a special status in the sight of God. It becomes ludicrous when we use it to justify a special status before men.

This might have been avoided if the churches had remembered that the Incarnation is never to be separated from its redemptive purpose that is manifested in action—or perhaps, more accurately, in the quality of life revealed in action.[12] The quality of our Lord's life was demonstrated in the actions of redemptive and reconciling love, and the quality of that life manifested the divine presence among us. If there is any sense in which the Church continues his work, we have to start from that, beginning with the actions of love and mercy. Instead of arguing that because we have the presence, *therefore* what we do must be redemptive, the churches have to reverse the order and begin with the actions of redemptive and reconciling love, and leave God to manifest himself among them as he will. The ethic of compassionate love, far from being an extra that springs from sound doctrine and good churchmanship, is at the center of the Church's ministry, mission, and doctrine, because it reveals the essential nature of God in Christ.

(3) The high churchmen who believed that the Church has a God-given character were right, but there is a sense in which, with all their human arrogance, they set their sights too low. They thought the primary character of the Church was determined and guaranteed by a series of divinely ordained laws, a carefully preserved succession of officers. Instead of such legal

[12] Cf. *The Atonement and the Sacraments,* pp. 85f.

forms, God gave the Church himself in the gift of the Spirit. Pentecost is primary,[13] and all other 'marks of the Church' must inevitably be judged by the fruits of the Spirit. Once that is recognized, the Church may make mistakes of judgment and change its forms but it will not lose its basic integrity, for the life of the Spirit will be primary and all other things secondary.

Certainly the Church of Jesus Christ should be one, holy, catholic, and apostolic; but we must not give these marks precedence over the Holy Spirit, who is the source of the marks and whom they are supposed to exemplify. Certainly the Church is where the word is sincerely preached and the sacraments truly administered, but we must not think that the institutions of preaching and the sacraments can guarantee the presence of the Spirit in a church that simply receives them as forms. When the primary characteristics of the Spirit are ignored, the 'marks of the Church' can often be used as rival slogans turning churches into a denial of the Church's essential nature. Church history has had many periods when the oneness, holiness, or apostolicity of the Church have been so emphasized that they have contradicted that which makes the Church truly catholic. A church shows itself to be authentically the Church only when it acts in a truly catholic way, i.e., when it shows itself representatively or corporately to belong to the Church Universal.[14]

13 One good thing to be said about New Testament restorationism is that it has within it the seeds of its own destruction. Sooner or later, if the literalist is honest with his biblical material, he has to come face to face with Pentecost, and hence has to find a place for the prophetic and charismatic elements of the New Testament Church. True, this is often an embarrassment to a sect that has determined to its own satisfaction the exact pattern of the New Testament community. It may hold the revolutionary spirit within the boundaries of an exact order by developing a 'tradition' of its own, but this can never be done completely; and therein lies the restorationist's salvation.

14 The imperative to make the Church visibly one can obviously prevent the Church from becoming truly catholic, in the sense that we are often tempted to strive for partial unities rather than universal unity.

This is particularly seen in the modern drive to achieve the unity of the Church along geographical, national lines, and to ignore that the Church should be universal and international. Certainly each national culture has something distinctive to offer in forms of worship, insights, style of Christian life and commitment, but not at the expense of the more basic unity that must be made visible across national and

Let me illustrate how a 'mark' of the Church can be used to hinder or to promote catholicity, by reference to one of the most revered principles of the Congregational tradition (through which I received the gospel)—the autonomy of the local church (congregation, parish). Within Congregationalism the local covenanted fellowship or 'gathered church' was regarded, in accordance with Dominical (Matthew 18:15-20) and Pauline authority, to be a microcosm or local outcropping of the Church Universal. It was spiritually autonomous, and the local church members were held to exercise the authority of the Holy Spirit in the discipline of a mutual ministry.[15]

However, this is obviously not true if the local congregation uses its autonomy to justify an exclusive claim to truth, to sanctify unwillingness to join in common witness with neighbor congregations, or to avoid fellowship with the wider Christian community. It was recognition of this which led some of the Congregational forefathers in both England and America to modify and even to deny the strict independency of Separatism.

On the other hand, in a situation where the churches are proscribed or persecuted, and where no possibility of wider fellowship exists, a local congregation may truly become the representative of the Church catholic. When local churches have been prevented by the state or by distance from taking counsel with their sister congregations, then they become the guardians of the faith of the whole Church in that place.[16]

Schism enters the situation of the Church when a principle that should be secondary is regarded as primary, something to

cultural boundaries, or in such a way that it causes us to ignore our brethren in other lands and cultures.

15 We refer here to Congregational ecclesiology in its earlier, ideal form. There are sound historical reasons for thinking that in the early nineteenth century the principle of 'local autonomy' exchanged its original spiritual content and became explained and defended in terms of the contemporary political Liberalism and post-Jeffersonian democracy.

16 There are numerous examples of this in history, from the English Independent churches that maintained the Trinitarian faith through the persecutions of the Restoration period, to the evangelical outreach of the Disciples and Baptists in the isolation of the American frontier. One could also point to the principle of *sobornost* and autocephalous churches that sustained faith for Eastern Orthodoxy through long years of persecution.

be defended at all costs, and when the love and fellowship that could be extended to other Christian communities is denied.

This is not to prejudge the question how the wider fellowship of the Christian churches should be expressed organizationally, or whether the principle of local autonomy is a 'good thing' or not—if that claim has produced schism on one side, the claims of those who would have enforced 'fellowship' have led to equally regrettable results on the other—but it is simply to illustrate that when a secondary principle is made primary it tends to destroy the Church's essential character, the character of the God-given Spirit.

(4) The same truth may be faced with regard to church 'renewal,' about which churches sometimes speak as if we could plug in to it, as to some spiritual power supply. Do the churches want renewal in order to be effective as Christ wants them to be effective, or in order to be 'successful' religious institutions? These alternatives are not necessarily incompatible; on the other hand, who can assume that the church that is truly effective in the Christian sense will show any more visible sign of success than the churches in present-day Europe or Asia? There were times—for example, on the day he entered Jerusalem—when Jesus appeared briefly to have caught the imagination of the populace; but later events showed that it was because the real meaning of his message had been misunderstood. There is nothing in the gospel that promises the Church consistent popularity, and a good deal to make us ponder about its motives and methods when it becomes fashionable.

The renewal of the Church starts with its own essential theology, what it believes about God. During the 1950s and early 60s there was a good deal of talk about 'renewal' in progressive church circles, and it is no accident that the ecumenical movement provided many of the examples. American churchmen became curiously fascinated by the Evangelical Academies, Industrial Missions, 'house churches,' new insights into the Laity issue, and even by the temporary popularity enjoyed by Bible study[17] —experiments which, let us readily

[17] E.g., in the popular and very insightful works on Bible Study by Suzanne de Dietrich.

admit, did reveal the work of the Spirit within the context of European Christianity at that time. But what are we to say of those who hurried across the Atlantic to pick up the material for a quick vacation book on 'the signs of renewal'?[18] Were they looking for genuine signs of renewal, signs of a renewed integrity in the Church, or for examples of successful gimmickry? They might have looked nearer home, to the self-criticism of the Church that was beginning in the works of Peter Berger and Gibson Winter. That is where renewal must begin, not in techniques but in painful and critical heart-searching.

This is deeply embedded in the gospel itself, the same Good News that the Church is called to proclaim and exemplify, for fundamentally the gospel declares that we have nothing of our own of which we can be proud before the world, and nothing to offer except God in Jesus Christ. The churches' temptation has always been to put their trust in things that are at best peripheral and at worst self-deceiving, such as their identity with a particular culture, or in the expertise of their priests and ministers, or in the supportive role they play to economic or political imperialism. All the Church really has is Jesus Christ and the proclamation of God's love that comes to us in him. Renewal starts with the judgment that his Spirit brings upon men, and that judgment starts at the household of God. This should help us take courage from the self-criticism of the 60s, although it is certainly nothing to boast about, for even this comes from God, wholly from God.

(5) If the Church has the biblical revelation of God at its center, its essential task cannot be other than to proclaim this God in word, deed, and presence. It is not a structureless

[18] Forgive this personal reference, but the occasion of it is firmly fixed in my memory. We arrived in this country in 1958 after spending four years on the staff of the Ecumenical Institute at Bossey, Switzerland, which was at the very center of these movements in the Church. Those working in the ecumenical movement knew that not only was publicity the last thing desired by the pioneers who had taken these initiatives, but premature publicity could easily ruin what they were trying to do. I will say nothing of the self-advertising culprits on the prowl whom one met in the normal course of working in this ecumenical *milieu,* but on arriving in the U.S.A. I was approached several times for information by hopeful authors who brazenly admitted that they intended to skip round Europe for a summer and produce a book on the experiments and evidences of renewal in the European churches.

society of spiritual individualists, for the form it adopts is integral to its proclamation and should point to the nature of this God both in its institutions and in the way they operate: what the Church *is* is just as much a part of its total witness as what it proclaims from the pulpit or manifests in social service. Far from being able to bypass ecclesiology as irrelevant, everything connected with the Church witnesses to the God it worships. Churches in the past have witnessed to gods of changeless omnipotence and omniscience, of strict justice, of power and prestige, of wealth and respectability, of self-advertisement and material success; for the way in which they were organized and the manner in which they achieved their ends told the world much more about the God they truly worshipped than what was said in their official dogmas or pious devotions.

Renewal begins with allowing God to be the center of the Church's life and witness, and our task is to see that the structures of the Church explicitly reflect his nature and his purpose. Their form should declare his unchangeable purpose of Love and Judgment, of mercy and redemption; it should manifest his readiness to invite men into his service, and the freedom of his Spirit in using human resources and the opportunities of history to proclaim and demonstrate his Word of grace. Unity is obviously at the center of the Church's work because unity is essential to the nature of God himself and reconciliation is central to his purpose in Jesus Christ. Visible unity is not an optional extra, because it belongs to the very *esse* of the God whom the Church proclaims in word, deed, and presence.[19]

[19] Those who reject ecumenism are in an inescapable dilemma. They must either define the Church entirely in their own terms and reject all who do not fit their definition—which very clearly says something about the God they worship—or they will be tacitly witnessing that they do not believe unity belongs to the nature of God himself. My quarrel with such people is not so much for their rigidity or narrowness—in some ways it has an honesty that I do not find among many liberal churchmen—but for their unwillingness to face the essential unity of the God of the Bible.

On the other hand, of course, one can hold no brief for the casual acceptance of competitive denominationalism ("Worship in the church of your choice") which appears to be the general attitude of most American churchmen to this subject. It proclaims to the world that every man worships his own god, that you may pick

(6) To take such a theology of the Church seriously would radically affect the way in which we approach the practical questions of church reunion. As we try to find the patterns of churchmanship that can say the things that are essential, it would be strange if we did not recognize features characteristic of the Church in past generations, for our forefathers were not men without faith nor were they without genuine insights into the meaning of their faith.

When the Consultation on Church Union, for example, speaks of a church that should be truly evangelical, truly catholic, and truly reformed, we recognize features of the Church's life and witness without which the true Church would be unthinkable. However, we suggest there is a great difference between a plan of union that accepts evangelical, catholic, and reformed aspects of the Church because the participating denominations consider one or more of these features as belonging to their own tradition, and a plan of union which, after serious study of the kind of Christian community required to serve God in our day, decides that it must be evangelical, catholic, and reformed. For one thing, those who participate in the latter kind of search will not have preconceived ideas about which are the particular evangelical, catholic, and reformed elements that must at all costs be preserved. Perhaps the threefold ministry of bishops, priests, and deacons *is* one of the catholic elements that ought to be preserved in the Church, possibly a preaching ministry does sufficiently represent the evangelical emphasis, and the principle of *ecclesia semper reformanda* may satisfy the Reformed; but there is a great difference between saying that these things reflect essential aspects of the nature and purpose of God, and maintaining them because certain denominations have made them part of their historic platform.

Of course, church traditions have often represented genuine insights into the gospel, and this is why they must be treated with respect; but if this is true, and if churches are convinced that their ecclesiastical forms have been an essential expression

your gods in the market to suit the tastes of your race, affluence, and social class, and that the only thing which unites this concept of deity is its common Americanness.

of God's nature and his redemptive incarnation among men, then, I suggest, they have nothing to fear from laying them freely on the table. It is only when we have doubts about the theological basis of our revered traditions that we are tempted to preserve them by using them as bargaining counters.

However, we must pause to make one thing clear. The Church is not God; but the Church does exist to point to God and to his nature, to push forward prophetically God's experiment of becoming 'at one' with man and of inviting humanity to share in his own creative and redemptive purpose.

That shows the enormity of the Church's task, and the reason it has always been tempted to preen itself before the rest of mankind and claim a kind of divinity. A truer understanding of its mission would have sent it in a very different direction—far from being any excuse for hybris, the nature of its task should have been the very measure of its contrition before God and of humility before the world; for in spite of the gift of the Holy Spirit, the Church has often sold her birthright, 'gone a-whoring after strange gods and murdered the prophets.' She has rarely understood her mission or the true nature of the God she professed with her lips, otherwise she would have known that pride in any form, and particularly the claim to divinity, is the one sure proof that the divine nature is not present. God is too great to make claims like that, and the Church's pretentious claims to special status in the past were clear evidence that she had not grown up and was nowhere near 'the measure of the stature of the fulness of Christ' to which she had been called. That maturity could be revealed only in servanthood.

3

THE CHURCH'S MINISTRY AND MISSION

We have maintained that the ministry and mission of the Church are centered in what it believes about God: what the Church does, how it does it, and the content of its message are finally determined by the nature of the God it worships. More specifically for Christians, mission centers in the redemptive incarnation of Jesus Christ, who "is the image of the invisible God" (Colossians 1:15). Christ's ministry demonstrates not only the lengths to which God goes for the redemption of man, but also that this redemption, this 'at-onement,' is to be sought only by the deepest and most intimate involvement in human life. The Incarnation forbids any false separation of the secular and the sacred,[20] or any thought of trying to win man by proclaiming salvation from a position outside the human experience.

In denying the pretensions of those who claim too much by identifying the Church with the Incarnation, the proper response is to insist on *true* incarnation. The Church has to be, in Bonhoeffer's phrase, "Christ himself who has taken form among men," but this demands incarnation that asks nothing other than the opportunity to reveal love and compassion (*cum patior*—'to suffer *with*'), and which enters fully and redemptively into the human predicament. All claims, particularly claims that cannot be backed by the quality of life and action, are not only inappropriate, they are a contradiction of the gospel.

A. Diakonia—servanthood

This is seen when we reflect upon our Lord's ministry as *diakonia*—servanthood. We remember John McKenzie's insight that diakonia in the New Testament was the service rendered by a *diakonos, doulos,* a slave. Leadership in the Kingdom of God is given to the one who was prepared to fulfil most perfectly this servant role—a role that deliberately gave up celestial splendor, to empty itself and take the form of a servant; it meant being prepared to wash the disciples' feet, to live without earthly home, and to be ready to embrace even the cross. There is no other pattern for the Church. Insofar as it is not prepared to accept that pattern it is not the Church of Jesus Christ; but insofar as it does, whatever its more formal theological shortcomings, it cannot be anything but the Church of Jesus Christ.

20 This does not mean that we should ignore proper distinctions between the secular and the sacred in the life of men. Cf. *Ministry,* pp. 107f., 146ff., 236ff.

Perhaps, even in those periods when it has been most dazzled by material power, the Church has always known this deep within its own consciousness. No age has been without its martyrs and saints, its anonymous men and women of conscience and its self-sacrificing missionaries; ancient conventions from the communal memory live on, 'servus servorum dei,' foot-washing on Maundy Thursday, ashes on Ash Wednesday; but perhaps one of the most illuminative images from its apostolic past is the word 'ministry' itself, *diakonia*—the only word adequate to describe the total service of the Church, yet which does double duty in specifying the lowest rank in the clerical hierarchy.

Diakonia describes both the content of the Church's ministry and the way in which it is to be performed. It is offered without any strings and without thought of return; it is patient and is not jealous of others; it is not boastful, conceited, or boorish; it is selfless, is not easily offended, and does not hold grudges; it takes no pleasure in other people's failures, and is devoted to the truth; it can face all things, and "there is no limit to its faith, its hope and its endurance."[21] That is diakonia as it was revealed to us in Jesus Christ, and the apostle called it 'love.'

However, the language of faith can so easily be devalued that it has constantly to be redefined. The misuse of the word 'love' is an example, and even the New Testament form *agape* could be on its way to becoming a cliché in the circles where casual theology is fashionable. 'Servanthood' is also such a term, and this kind of service has some connotations in the New Testament that are never likely to be popular: "*Diakonos* means a lackey, a menial . . . . In the original force of the word, the *diakonos* is a person whose function is not determined by his own will; he is entirely at the disposal of others. Jesus not only washes the feet of others, he puts his life at their disposal."[22]

With this concept behind it, it would be all too easy to think of this servanthood as implying not only service but servility, not merely that which is menial in function but that

[21] I Corinthians 13, somewhat following the NEB.

[22] John McKenzie, *Authority in the Church*, pp. 23f.

which is menial in attitude. Yet this would totally contradict what we see in Jesus himself. The New Testament does not call the Church to be servile, or suggest that Christians should masochistically enjoy subjugation as an end in itself. I was never very impressed by Ignatius of Antioch chasing martyrdom for its own sake, and no one would suggest that the Church should simply accept its call passively, as something to be endured: the New Testament puts no more premium on the doormat than it does on the jellyfish.

To discover the content of what this ministry means we have to return constantly to the ministry of Jesus himself, and to men like Peter and Paul whom he inspired.

(1) The *diakonos* in the gospel serves not because he is *diakonos* to the people to whom he has been sent, but because he is *diakonos* to God who has sent him. I once used the illustration of "a doctor or a farmer who has been sent to a primitive country as part of an international aid program. He may give years of devoted service at considerable self-sacrifice to the people who need his help, but in the final issue he does so because his primary allegiance is to the United Nations or to the agency that has sent him."[23] That was said of the minister in relation to his congregation, but it must first be said of the Church in relationship to the world: just as our Lord served us first because he was obedient to the Father's will, so the Church serves the world because of its obedience to Jesus Christ. As John McKenzie warns us, the concept of *diakonos* will only go so far as a metaphor in the Church: "It breaks down in the kind of service that the *diakonos* renders and in the identity of the person to whose command he is submitted. The service of Jesus is not determined by the arbitrary will of those whom he serves as a slave, but by the will of the Father

[23] *Ministry,* p. 119. The problems experienced in such programs after World War II should make us realize, however, that this illustration must be applied to the Church with reserve. What of the person who 'serves' an underdeveloped country by woodenly doing his duty but nothing more, or who admits, "I do what I was sent to do, but I hate the sight of the place and its people"? Obviously this will not do as an illustration of what the Church is called to be. To be *diakonos* to Christ means first of all to have the Holy Spirit of love which was in Jesus.

that the *diakonos* should serve them by the complete surrender of himself."[24]

(2) Willingness to be *diakonos* in the Christian sense is a decision of strength and not of weakness. The servant figure of Christ in the Gospels is the figure of one who knows that he has the power to control events, but who voluntarily allows events to work their will upon him. What happened to Jesus was the result of his own choice. So when he became aware that events in his life were moving to their climax we read that "he set his face resolutely towards Jerusalem" (Luke 9:51), and it has been pointed out that there may be conscious echoes in this of the Servant Songs in Isaiah.[25] Throughout the life of Jesus what he does in submission he does of his own volition: he voluntarily submitted to his parents and returned with them to Nazareth (Luke 2:41-52); but when the time came to obey a higher allegiance, he made that choice (4:1-13) and began his ministry. The same can be seen through the Passion narratives: he voluntarily decided to go to Jerusalem, and chose his own time (John 11:1-15); he voluntarily allowed himself to be taken (cf. Matthew 26:53-54), voluntarily maintained his silence before Pilate and submitted to sentence.[26] Even in the garden when his own human desires and the will of his Father appear to have been in tension, one feels that the

24 *Op. cit.*, p. 24.

25 Cf. "The Lord God has given me
the tongue of a teacher
and skill to console the weary
with a word in the morning;
he sharpened my hearing
that I might listen like one who is taught.
The Lord opened my ears
and I did not disobey or turn back in defiance.
I offered my back to the lash,
and let my beard be plucked from my chin,
I did not hide my face from spitting and insult;
but the Lord stands by to help me;
therefore no insult can wound me.
I have set my face like a flint,
for I know that I shall not be put to shame,
because the one who will clear my name is at my side." (Isaiah 50: 4-7, NEB; italics mine).

26 Mark 15:1-5; Matthew 27:11-14; cf. Luke 23:1-4; John 18:33-38.

final choice was his own.[27] We have the impression of one who is in charge but who allows events to take the course they will take.

(3) This was not an act of passive acceptance, but one of initiative and leadership. Paul had that insight when he saw that the very act of the Incarnation itself was one of divine initiative—Christ *made* himself nothing and assumed the nature of a slave (Philippians 2:5-8); and the apostle adjures the Church to "Let this mind be in you, which was also in Christ Jesus" (KJV). It is only as we see the ministry of the Church centered in the ministry of our Lord himself that we can properly speak of the Church as a prophetic community (E. Clinton Gardner), or of a pioneer ministry (A. T. Hanson), or regard the Church as God's *avant-garde* (J. C. Hoekendijk and Harvey Cox).[28] If the Church is to understand its servanthood correctly it must see that it is grounded in the divine initiative: we are back at its essential theology.

B. The Church's ministry

However, the Church has one distinctive element in relation to ministry that is its own. That is its corporateness, for in the Church the meaning of our Lord's ministry is translated into terms of an ongoing, living community. The Church is therefore an essential link between our Lord's ministry and the realization of the Kingdom, for the Kingdom of God cannot be realized until it can be demonstrated that what Jesus brought to men can produce this kind of new community: the *koinonia* of the New Testament Church is the love of Jesus Christ expressed in community.

This is the unique significance of the Church. Throughout church history we seem to have veered between emphasis on the corporateness of the Church and an emphasis on the election of its members. The one tended to deify the Church's unity but lost the commitment of the individual, whereas the other maintained individual commitment at the expense of the Church's corporate unity. The significance of the Church is

[27] Mark 14:32-42; Matthew 26:36-56; Luke 22:36-46; John 18:1-11.

[28] Cf. *Ministry,* especially chapter 3, "The Messianic Ministry."

that it is called to be both holy and united, and the guarantee of this catholicity is in the evident possession of the Spirit. That Spirit, as John McKenzie and others have shown, has a totally different quality and manifests a wholly different kind of authority from anything comparable in this world: it is love.

The vocation of the Church *is* to become 'Christ in community,' but as we have tried to show, when a community represents itself as having already achieved the perfection to which it is called, it actually reveals how imperfectly it has understood its own gospel.[29] The Church is *en route* to the Kingdom. Paul understood it when he acknowledged that the Christian life is a striving towards the goal of perfection in Christ rather than a claim of having achieved it. "It is not to be thought," he confessed, "that I have already achieved all this. I have not yet reached perfection, but I press on, hoping to take hold of that for which once Christ took hold of me. My friends, I do not reckon myself to have got hold of it yet. All I can say is this: forgetting what is behind me, and reaching out for that which lies ahead, I press towards the goal to win the prize which is God's call to the life above in Christ Jesus" (Philippians 3:12ff., NEB).

On the other hand, the Church is not simply an aggregate of Christians, however committed or however holy. It is a *community* which has been called into covenant with God, and in which the members find themselves in covenant with one another. To quote the erratic genius of Separatism, Robert Browne, "The Church planted or gathered, is a company or number of Christians or believers, which by a willing covenant made with their God are under the government of God and Christ, and keep his laws in one holy communion."[30] The literalism of the Separatists' restorationism often led them into a defective view of catholicity that limited the visible Church to the local congregation, but they were surely right to insist that the Church should be corporate and visible and that its task is to express the covenant in a living community. Their

29 Cf. *The Atonement and the Sacraments,* pp. 282-87; *Ministry*, pp. 79ff.

30 *A Booke which sheweth the life and manners of all true Christians* (1582), section 25 (*The Writings of Robert Harrison and Robert Browne,* ed. Peel and Carlson), p. 253.

mistake was very similar to that which has often been made by 'Catholic' branches of the Church, the assumption that because Christ is perfect the Church can claim perfection. Whereas the Catholic based his claim on the institutional legality of his church, the Separatist based his claims upon fidelity to the New Testament model and excluded all who did not conform to predetermined ethical standards. The attempt often resulted in terrible schisms born of even more horrendous pharisaism.[31] Both branches of the Church, however, forgot that the Church receives its 'perfection' as a gift from its Lord, that here on earth it can only 'press towards the goal,' and that the indispensable proof of its vocation is love. Without that, neither charisma, nor faith, nor even martyrdom is worth anything.

The point was brought home to me some years ago by a little book in which the writer reminded his readers that our Lord's original band of disciples contained within it almost all the elements that make for human friction.[32] Reading between the lines of the Gospels we can see tensions between forceful personalities such as Peter, and retiring personalities such as his brother Andrew; between working-class men who were employees (Peter and Andrew) and the sons of their employer (the sons of Zebedee); between the representative of Greek culture, Philip, and the simple faith of a Hebrew "in whom there is no guile," Nathaniel; between Matthew, who was prepared to collaborate with the Romans, and a patriotic revolutionary like Simon the Zealot; between the implicit faith of John and the realistic doubt of Thomas; and, if "James the son of Alphaeus and Judas the son of James" are the father and son combination they suggest, between youth and age.

The miracle of the Church is not only that these men were brought together by their common commitment to Jesus Christ, but that after he left this earth, they stayed together. Through the years of his ministry Jesus was able to make them into a community. "And," the writer went on to comment, "Jesus did it by helping them to see that the thing that matters

[31] Cf. Browne's account of the schism at Middelburgh, *A True and Short Declaration*, etc., *op. cit.*, pp. 396-429.

[32] F. C. Bryan, *Concerning the Way* (London: S.C.M., 1946), pp. 38-42.

is not an individual's predilections and point of view, but God's purpose for him and for mankind—God's will. He gave them a vision of a world order as it would be if men accepted God's rule over their hearts and lives."[33] This was the primary miracle that made Pentecost possible; but if the Church was to point to the Kingdom, the unity of this little group was essential, a unity grounded in love: the meaning of our Lord's ministry had to be demonstrated in the living community.

This distinctive corporateness of the Church's ministry has yet to be manifested in two areas of human experience if the Church is to witness to the truth of God in Jesus Christ.

(1) First, it cannot be made real to the world until it is clear for all to recognize it in the Church itself. This is the inescapable implication of John 17:21-23. Within the fellowship of the Church, minister and people exercise a mutual ministry towards each other. If it is true that the Church needs the witness, encouragement, and pastoral care of its ministers, it is equally true that the minister can be sustained only by the witness of the Church, the encouragement of his fellow members, and the pastoral care of the whole fellowship in which he is placed.[34] Let us freely admit that this has become an almost entirely neglected aspect of what was formerly a basic Reformation insight, and the reason is clearly that in rejecting a sacerdotal approach to ministry we have put 'the professional' in the place of the priest. We are far from suggesting that we can immediately discard a professional form of ministry, but this should not be maintained at the expense of the corporate, mutual ministry of the whole fellowship. In the next chapter I suggest ways in which this mutual ministry may perhaps be reclaimed, but it is sufficient at this point to note its importance, and to note that until it is reclaimed and practiced the Church will never quite be able to close its credibility gap: there is something utterly false about accepting Christian commitment and paying someone else to fulfil it, and this falseness seems obvious to almost everyone but those who are involved in it.

33 *Ibid.*, pp. 156f.

34 *Ministry*, pp. 156f.

The ministry of the Church is the ministry of the whole Church to every member. Of *course* there will be differences of function in the exercise of that ministry, but it is of primary importance that every member should consciously have a ministry to fulfil and should understand his or her own part in the corporate ministry of the whole body. In matters of the Spirit every member has a responsibility to every other member; and as this is worked out in the life of a congregation, synod, diocese, denomination, or in ecumenical expression of the Church, the unity of the members in mutual love and service should be so obvious that the lineaments of the Lord's Body can be discerned. This principle of mutual ministry has its finest expression in Paul's letter to Corinth:

> There are varieties of gifts, but the same Spirit. There are varieties of service, but the same Lord. There are many forms of work, but all of them, in all men, are the work of the same God. In each of us the Spirit is manifested in one particular way, for some useful purpose. One man, through the Spirit, has the gift of wise speech, while another, by the power of the same Spirit, can put the deepest knowledge into words. Another, by the same Spirit, is granted faith; another, by the one Spirit, gifts of healing, and another miraculous powers; another has the gift of prophecy, and another ability to distinguish true spirits from false; yet another has the gift of ecstatic utterance of different kinds, and another the ability to interpret it. But all these gifts are the work of one and the same Spirit, distributing them separately to each individual at will . . . .
>
> Now you are Christ's body, and each of you a limb or organ of it. Within our community God has appointed, in the first place apostles, in the second place prophets, thirdly teachers; then miracle-workers . . . . Are all apostles? all prophets? all teachers? Do all work miracles? Have all gifts of healing? Do all speak in tongues of ecstacy? Can all interpret them? The higher gifts are those you should aim at.
>
> And now I will show you the best way of all.[35]

And he did. He followed this with the great chapter on love in I Corinthians 13. This is what mutual ministry should mean within the context of the Church, and the highest gift of the Spirit is love.

This obviously contains an ecumenical imperative. I have deliberately not applied the passage in I Corinthians 12 to relationships between the denominations, for I can see no

35 I Corinthians 12:4-11, 27-31, NEB.

justification for forcing the apostle's words to fit a situation that he would have considered inconceivable; but the implications are there if you wish to make the connection. We are living in a fool's paradise when we talk glibly of the Church's ministry to the world while churches are as yet unprepared to minister (i.e., to become a *diakonos*) to each other. If this means that we must bring about a more visible and organic form of unity before this can be done, then so be it: let us not hypocritically use faithfulness to Christ as an excuse for hindering his Kingdom.

(2) The Church's ministry is directed to the world. The Church is not an end in itself, and the ministry that is exercised to the members within its own borders is important only because without it the Church cannot present a proper koinonia to the world. It is to be God's *avant-garde,* a prophetic *community.* Within its corporate life and service the Church is called to proclaim the Kingdom of God by word, deed, and presence, as a people 'on the move'; and within the Christian community there should be the ever living testimony to the victory that God has already accomplished in Jesus Christ, and to his continuing victories in the Holy Spirit as we press on towards the full hope of the Kingdom.[36]

The Church is to be a people on the move, not claiming that it is the Kingdom of God but showing that the Kingdom is possible. It has to reveal to the world that Christ can take form in the human *community,* in the living relationships that can reconcile the sexes and bring unity between people of different races, nations, classes, and cultures. The Church is called to demonstrate that there are no human barriers that need alienate a man from God, from himself, or from others. Mankind has to be shown that it can be one people of God, capable of discovering unity in its diversity, capable of serving the great end of creation and of expressing the love and compassion of God to the whole cosmos. We can speak about the cosmic Christ only if we see that our Lord's ministry and mission is directly related to man's destiny in creation, and the Church has the indispensable task of showing that his mission can be

36 *Ministry,* p. 57.

realized *corporately* in the whole human race. This is what it is about: this is its mission.

C. Ministry and mission

There can be no separation between the ministry of the Church and its mission. Hoekendijk was right in saying that the Church has no reason for existence apart from its mission, but we could say with equal truth that it has no other reason for existence than its ministry. Ministry and mission may place the emphases in slightly different places, but both involve not only what the Church proclaims but also how it acts and what it is.

Bonhoeffer showed that the Church's mission involves acceptance of the secular, but it is acceptance of secularity in a particular way. The secularity that the Church endorses is not that which is centered in hybris or in temporal power, but that which treats the creation with humility and compassion. The secular life of man has to be redeemed not in order to become something else, but to be freed of its greed, its selfishness, and its pride. Only so can it become the vehicle of grace to the rest of the created order. Shall man be encouraged to take his hydrogen bombs into the rest of the universe, or permitted to exploit the ecology of distant planets as he has exploited his own? Are we to treat other races as yet unknown with the rapacity and cruelty that we have inflicted on our own kind? How can we regard any contribution of man as ultimately significant for the rest of creation until his own nature has been redeemed?[37]

The redemption of mankind is the goal of the Church's mission, and its ministry is the method by which it engages in it. Paul speaks of it as a ministry of reconciliation, and reconciliation is the basic need of man at every level of his life—reconciliation first of all with God (which involves reconciliation with man's own destiny as a mortal human being), reconciliation with himself (i.e., with the conflicting drives within his own personality), and reconciliation with his neighbor next door, in the next block, across racial lines, in the ghetto

[37] Cf. Romans 8:19-23.

and across ideological and national boundaries. Wherever he looks, reconciliation is his most urgent need, and the lack of it offers the most ominous threat to the continuance of his race. This same reconciliation the Church exists to proclaim in word, deed, and presence. "From first to last," says the apostle, "this has been the work of God. He has reconciled us men to himself through Christ, and he has enlisted us in this service of reconciliation. What I mean is, that God was in Christ reconciling the world to himself, no longer holding men's misdeeds against them, and that he has entrusted us with the message of reconciliation. We come therefore as Christ's ambassadors. It is as if God were appealing to you through us: in Christ's name, we implore you, be reconciled to God!" (II Corinthians 5:18ff.).

"It is as if God were appealing to you through us." It is indeed. We are back at the essential theology at the heart of our doctrine of the Church.

4

THE CHURCH IN THE WORLD (I)

It is with this essential theology that we should begin any consideration of the Church in relation to the world. It is clear that in the New Testament there is a certain ambiguity about that relationship—the world ultimately inherits the gospel, and yet the members of the Church are warned not to become conformed to its standards (Romans 12:2); and although they are in the world they are regarded as hated strangers (John 17:11-19). But there is no ambiguity about the way in which God regards the world: "God loved the world so much," we read, "that he gave his only Son, that everyone who has faith in him may not die but have eternal life. It was not to judge the world that God sent his Son into the world, but that through him the world might be saved" (John 3:16f., NEB). The disciples were to pray that the Kingdom should come on earth, as it is in heaven; and although Jesus went unrecognized in this world, he is still the Light of the World; the Kingdom was not of the world in a way Pilate could understand, and yet while Jesus was on earth the Kingdom was at hand and among men. The world is the object of God's love, the reason for his redemptive incarnation in Jesus Christ and his plan of salvation.

Furthermore, this redemption is an event in which all of God is involved. God holds within 'his' own being a community of love and service, and all parts or aspects of the Godhead are involved in 'redeeming' mankind: the 'Father' predetermines the plan (Acts 2:32), the 'Son' voluntarily undertakes the Incarnation and the work of redemption (Philippians 2:5-11), and the 'Spirit' continues that work in the Church (John 15:27; 16:7-11; Romans 8:26ff.).

These passages are cited not as proofs of an orthodoxy. We are not concerned with defending Nicaean or Chalcedonian theories of the Trinity, except insofar as they give us insight into the essential nature of the One who speaks to us through the biblical revelation. The New Testament writers are hinting at an Immensity of love and service beyond the wildest dreams of man. They proclaim a divine love and compassion that elects the human race into fellowship with itself and into service for the rest of creation, and are saying that this fellowship and service are really not two different things but two parts of a single whole because they arise within the very nature of God himself. The 'glory' and the 'lordship' about which the gospel speaks are never symbols of status to be flaunted and exploited before others, but they are manifested as they were in Jesus through obedience to the Father's will and so that this creation may become what it was intended to be.

The objective is *shalom,* the concrete, Old Testament term that Hoekendijk reminds us carried within it far more than individual salvation, and which is to be realized in "peace, integrity, community, harmony and justice."[38] It is a state which embraces the whole *oikumene* (the whole inhabited world), and it is obviously and essentially societal, a *community* that reaches out to the whole of God's creation within which all things may reach their own fullest self-

[38] Above, p. 205.

realization. This self-realization is not simply individual, an aggregation or an agglomerate of individuals: it has fundamentally to be experienced and fulfilled in community, a society. If there is any essential characteristic in the image of the 'Kingdom,' it is that. Edward Hicks, the American primitive painter, was obviously more influenced by the Quakers than by any sophisticated biblical exegesis when he painted his interpretation of the messianic Kingdom, "The Peaceable Kingdom" (cf. Isaiah 11:1-9); and in his various versions of the painting the animals are apt to change places and appear in a somewhat individual and startled relationship to each other.[39] One significant element, however, remains constant—the picture of William Penn and his followers concluding a covenant with the Indians; and surely the Quakers had a true insight into the messianic Kingdom when they saw that it is the task of the redeemed community to bring about the reconciliation of man to man, the advent of a new kind of civil society, which would be the center of a new relationship to all creation.

In the Bible the central figure is Christ, 'the New Adam' (the New Man), who by achieving the redemption and reconciliation of man with God, puts man back into the center of God's purpose for the creation, "for as through the disobedience of one man many were made sinners, so through the obedience of the one man many will be made righteous."[40] Our goal, says the apostle, is to strive towards "mature manhood measured by nothing less than the full stature of Christ";[41] and if the members of the Church are called into being as the New Creation, it is with the realization that what they represent has almost unthinkable promise for the rest of God's created order, for "the created universe awaits with eager expectation for God's sons to be revealed."[42] And the

[39] This element of separateness is a distinct feature of other primitives, as one can see by comparing "The Peaceable Kingdom" with Henry Rousseau's "The Dream."

[40] Romans 5:19, NEB. Cf. Romans 5:12-19; I Corinthians 15:22, 45.

[41] Ephesians 4:13, NEB.

[42] Romans 8:19, NEB. Cf. Romans 8:19-21; II Corinthians 5:17; Galatians 6:15.

servant form is at the center because servanthood within the Kingdom is the destiny of a redeemed humanity.

One should begin to see the significance of the Church in the progression between the revelation of Christ, the New Adam, and the realization of the Kingdom and the New Humanity. Any future discussion of the Church must begin with what Christians affirm about God: it is the revelation of God in Christ that finally determines what the Church should be and what its purpose is in this world. This implies a deeper, more spiritually discerning and therefore less arrogant understanding of the Church's own relationship to the Incarnation, and a readiness to become redemptively involved in the whole life of man; it implies that the mission engages the whole Church, involving every member not only as he or she fulfils an individual commitment but also corporately; it means the recognition of the Church's pioneer character, a readiness to become part of the divine initiative in pointing to the Kingdom. We cannot offer detailed expositions, but only suggestions for future exploration; and without attempting to offer a prospectus for theology over the next decade, let us examine three areas of human experience where the theological understanding of the Church may offer light.

A. What it means to be man

Alexander Pope's aphorism, "The proper study of mankind is man," may be used either as justification for the most flagrant hybris or as the starting-point for a theology of grace. Man may be the proper study of mankind, but only if men realize that their lot is cast *within* (i.e., as a part of) creation.

Man has never had much difficulty in placing himself at the center of the cosmic order, but he has had much more difficulty in understanding that if he is there, he has been placed there for a purpose. The former Marxist, D. R. Davies, said that the fundamental sin of Western civilization has been "the enthronement of man at the centre of life, being and thought":[43] it is not being in the center that makes it sin, but

[43] D. R. Davies, *The Sin of Our Age* (New York: Macmillan, 1947), p. 23.

it is the assumption that we have this position by right, and that we can use it as we will. The Church is certainly in no position to feel morally superior on this matter, since it has often fallen into the same error. But it is now forced to recognize the error; and as it enters more fully into the meaning of what it means to live by grace, the Church might become the exemplar of what mankind is called to be in relation to the rest of God's creation.

Part of the paradox of being man in modern society is in finding a proper relationship between the capacities of the individual and the demands of the society in which he is set. In spite of the gloomy forecast that contemporary pressures seem to be forcing the Church into flat uniformity,[44] there has been ecumenical recognition that to achieve the 'fulness' of the Church we have to achieve unity in diversity. Collectivism may increase the pressures that try to crush individual initiative and variety in the name of efficiency, speed of action, mass control, and the like; but as life becomes more drab, there is evidence that the rioting young are not the only ones to protest.[45] With full recognition of all that could push us into enslavement, nothing dictates that Orwell's *1984* and Huxley's *Brave New World* are inevitable. But when collective forms are established and maintained by coercion and fear, and when power is concentrated in fewer and fewer hands, there is considerable threat to the survival of truly human values.

Paul would say at this point, "and now I will show you the best way." The Church has the opportunity to present an alternative as soon as it is prepared to put its own gospel into practice. The Church is called to demonstrate to men the kind of society that the Kingdom of God holds in prospect for the whole human race, a society of mutual service in which members contribute what they alone can contribute to the common good, and in which there is increasing mutual trust.

The nature of spiritual authority which we have persistently

[44] Robert Ardrey, *The Social Contract* (New York: Atheneum, 1970), pp. 409f.

[45] Cf. J. R. L. Anderson, *The Ulysses Factor* (London: Hodder & Stoughton, 1970).

emphasized,[46] and which was underlined by John McKenzie, focusses not only on the organs by which a church is governed, but just as significantly in the spirit that is seen in its leaders; and that was a point at which not only hierarchical churches could be faulted. John Robinson reminded the Separatist exiles at Amsterdam in 1624 of the time when "some of place amongst you would pattern the government of the church now, by the government of the Elders in Israel, which is in truth to transform a service into a lordship."[47] True ministry is service, and the Church can make that explicit.

It would be impossible to achieve this in secular society at this moment—that is my major objection to those who seem to think that the Kingdom has already fully arrived and that the Church can simply dissolve itself in the surrounding culture—but that is precisely why the Church has to take itself and its gospel with more seriousness; for it is its task to demonstrate that what is humanly impossible for the world *is* possible within the community of faith. The church forecasts the Kingdom, but if this is to become real, we have to take a long hard look at our ecclesiastical structures and the motivation for their actions: "You know that in the world the recognized rulers lord it over their subjects. That is not the way with you; among you whoever wants to be great shall be your servant, and whoever wants to be first must be the willing slave of all" (Mark 10:42, NEB).

B. What it means to be man-in-community

This raises the question of the nature of the human community, its inner relationships and tensions. I am impressed with the evidence that societal arrangements have been a crucial factor in the survival and development of the higher animal forms, and most strikingly of all in the story of the human race.[48] What seems equally clear is that it is in the area

46 *Ministry,* pp. 177-190, and throughout a good deal of this present work.

47 The reference was to the unhappy ministry of Francis Johnson. Robinson's letter appears in W. H. Burgess, *John Robinson,* pp. 293-97, and the quotation is on p. 295.

48 E.g., in Ardrey's *The Social Contract.*

of human relationships that the next advance has to take place if the human race is to survive its own inner contradictions and fulfil its promise.[49]

If the Church is pointing to the Kingdom it should show that a community which claims to be redemptive must first know itself to have been redeemed (i.e., therefore under obligation, the recipient of grace). Within the gospel the Church has insights about how the individual can become reconciled to his own destiny (or to That-which-called-him-into-being), and how he can become reconciled to the limitations of his mortal personality; but the point at which reconciliation becomes most obvious to others and most urgent in our human predicament is in achieving reconciliation between man and his neighbor, between conflicting interests, ideological groups, cultural communities, nations. As long as the ecumenical dilemma remains unresolved, the Church's credibility suffers at this crucial point: until the Church puts its own house in order at this level, there is not much reason for the world to listen very attentively when it declaims about reconciliation in any other sphere.

However, the ecumenical issue could be crucial for a more positive reason. *How* the churches approach their own search for a more visible unity, their motives for the search, what they are attempting to achieve, and the spirit that is manifested as they live with their dividedness could say more about the gospel they proclaim than any number of Whitsun pronouncements from Rome or Geneva. The Church was founded to be Christ-in-community, and this is the one thing which our Lord left his Church to contribute to the gospel: it was to be a reconciled community exercising a ministry of reconciliation.

What does reconciliation mean, particularly in a revolutionary society? It is obviously not to be confused with compromise. What does it mean to be a reconciling community in the middle of the urban crisis, in the frustrations and hatreds of the ghetto, or amid the crushing poverty and cruel injustice of some South American para-military dictatorship? There is no universal answer, but reconciliation of the kind that we see

[49] Cf. *ibid.*, pp. 181f.

in Jesus Christ does not compromise with evil. How can it, if the ultimate objective is the 'at-onement' of man with God? But in hating sin Christ does not hate the sinner. Reconciliation surely means that however deep the schisms in society, however bitter and polarized the struggle against injustice becomes, the Christian Church can never treat other people as less than persons, as if God had no further interest in them. Perhaps we do better when we remember that reconciliation and redemption belong together, and that to be reconciled to God means ultimately being bought out of enslavement to greed, selfish aloofness, and cruel apathy.

One emphasizes the ecumenical question without in the least suggesting that the Church can or should remove itself from social issues. The two belong together, for if the Church is to show that 'Christ' can be interpreted in community terms, then salvation involves not merely God's plan for the individual but God's plan for societies. To demonstrate the reality of the Church as a community is the first step in its social witness, and this may very well be the issue on which our fate as a race hinges.

The amateur anthropologist Robert Ardrey suggests that the small hunting band of nine to eleven members in primitive society seems to survive in the normal size of a team in our sports, juries, army squads as the ideal size of a working group, and he adds the piquant comment of a friend that in selecting twelve apostles Jesus may have selected one too many![50] Perhaps so; but then again, perhaps not. If one is going to speculate on such minutiae a Christian might suggest that in choosing one more than the 'natural' group of men, our Lord indicated that this is what the new breakthrough in human relationships implied—pushing the boundaries of that viable working group, with its close-knit, intimate relationships, just a little bit further. And that there was a Judas may indicate just how new, how revolutionary, and how humanly difficult that is. Perhaps this is the next great step mankind is invited to make, and which could mean either an expanding future, or if we fail, ultimate extinction.

[50] *Ibid.*, p. 368.

C. *What it means to be a servant community*

Only recently the frightening growth of the ecological problem has forced the human race to realize that it bears responsibility to the rest of creation. The problems of expanding power and mushrooming technology, problems that have become urgent in this half of the twentieth century, are forcing us to recognize that the basic issues are ethical, and at the most fundamental level involve our relationship to each other.

Yet the Church should have been demonstrating to the world that the servant form is the essential characteristic of the Kingdom of God, and is in fact God's call to humanity itself. That the Church has failed to do this is its own indictment, and ought to restrain Christians from boasting. It also calls for an honest and thoroughgoing examination of our ecclesiastical structures to see how far they serve none but themselves. Do not mistake me, I am not suggesting that the agencies of the Church can be or should be forthwith turned into social service agencies, for some of them do have the responsibility of expressing the Church's love and compassion to those in need within its own borders: it has always been easier for church people to work up righteous indignation about righting the wrongs of society before they pay a working wage to their own janitors.[51] No, I am suggesting that whether the ecclesiastical agency has a responsibility for the church's own missions and charities or for direct social service, it should demonstrate its *service:* it should not simply serve itself.

However, what does it mean for the Church to be a pioneer, servant community to the rest of creation? If that is not simply theological hogwash, or worse, a rather sickening form of the old arrogance, what does it *mean*?

We can answer only by posing a series of issues that the Church itself should explore. It must ask what the apostle meant by his declaration that "the universe itself is to be freed from the shackles of mortality and enter upon the liberty and

[51] The point was well made by a great British church administrator, Howard Stanley, when he was trying to raise the stipends of ministers to something above the poverty level. He said that the churches had "loved mercy before they had done justice."

the splendour of the children of God," and by his statement that while it awaits this manifestation the whole universe "groans in all its parts as if in the pangs of childbirth";[52] or what the apostle meant when he declared of Christ that "his is the primacy over all created things . . . the whole universe has been created through him and for him. And he exists before everything, and all things are held together in him. He is, moreover, the head of the body, the Church."[53] Is this simply Paul getting carried away in extravagant hyperbole?

Well, it could be that, and it would probably be better to forget it if we are tempted to treat such passages as a series of literal propositions about God, Jesus Christ, and the world. On the other hand, if the apostle really has insight into the nature of the God who spoke to his world in Jesus Christ, then surely we see a writer who was struggling to express the inexpressible about the wonder of the gospel and what it means for the destiny of this universe. If that is true, then the Church might begin to think seriously about the responsibility of the 'sons of God' for this world and listen to the silent agony of things around us. It would mean acting as a pioneer and servant community not only in its treatment of those areas in ecology that threaten the future of man (and are therefore fashionable), but also in those areas that would disturb his comfort and convenience—for example, the mute sacrifice of the animal world to our seasonal gluttonies:

. . . get along little dogies!
It's your misfortune and none of my own . . . .

A deeper sense of its servant mission could determine the direction in which the human race should point, and enable the Church to be more a pioneer and less a camp follower.

Here are other suggestions about its implications, in order to get the discussion started.

(1) Theology as a servant science.

It was natural under the old triumphalism for theology to claim that it was 'queen of the sciences'; and at a time when it

52 Romans 8:21f., NEB.
53 Colossians 1:15ff., NEB.

was possible for a Western scholar to have read almost all that was available and worth reading, the claims of a theological *Summa* could be impressive and convincing. But it was a false claim, and the incredible expansion of knowledge in our own time simply underscores its pretentiousness.

Today no discipline has any monopoly of truth, and the serious scholar finds it less and less possible to master even all that is appearing in the field of his own specialty. This is a serious problem for all scholarship, because the specialization on which scholarship rests inevitably prevents us from taking the kind of overview that tries to see and to interpret human knowledge comprehensively.

In this situation theology seems to have been content to become a field of specialization among others, to develop its own concepts and terminology very much in the same way as any other discipline on the campus, and if it cannot inherit what it regards as its ancient birthright, at any rate to settle for its share of the academic mess of pottage.

Yet there is a sense in which theology could become a truly servant discipline—a discipline which, without giving up the rigor of its own inner commitment, would be prepared to forego the luxuries of specialization in order to serve the other disciplines by listening. Specialists of all kinds find it more and more difficult to communicate to each other at any level much more advanced than 'Please pass the mustard' in the cafeteria, and there is a need for those who are simply prepared to listen to the many voices, and without imposing preconceived patterns, to act as catalysts.[54] Theology might make a more significant contribution to the intellectual scene that is emerging if it were less like the lawyer in the Gospels "seeking to justify himself," and more ready to be a disciple.

(2) Pioneer leadership in areas of human need.

This means a readiness to experiment in the problem areas of human need without expecting any return, either materially, apologetically, or in terms of a more agreeable public image. The need itself should be the incentive.

54 This may seem to be an unrealistic suggestion, but it happens in consultations between theologians and members of other disciplines at the Ecumenical Institute at Bossey. Whenever theologians are prepared to *listen* to the sciences, and

Oddly enough, the Church has, almost despite itself, occupied this role in history. Some years ago I was part of a group experiencing the casual, haphazard alchemy that produces scholarship in an Oxford Common Room after dinner. We had been discussing the sociology of religion, how charismatic groups arose, became routinized in society, and ended by becoming increasingly separated from their original charisma. Then with a shock we realized that we had also been describing a pattern common to many diverse interests in the university itself: a need had been seen by the churches and a ministry created to meet it. As the need gained general recognition, a more systematic (secular) approach to the problem would develop, and, as it was studied, a new academic discipline would be born. Routinization meant secularization, but the origin had been charismatic. An Oxford sociologist admitted wryly that his own department had originated in the social concern of churchmen and others at the beginning of this century who had started work among the poor of the city. Direct social action had demonstrated the need to study the conditions systematically, and this in turn led to the establishment of a university department. We needed little reflection to remind ourselves that schools, hospitals, social services, and the universities themselves had had a similar history, and that even the sciences were not totally removed from the pattern.

The incident is cited, not because it gives the churches anything to crow about—the churches have often opposed reform, and they have always fought tenaciously to maintain control of the institutions they established—but because it indicates a principle in this role of servant leadership that the churches have been all too reluctant to recognize. To that we now turn.

(3) The readiness to withdraw.

Bonhoeffer pointed to this when he saw that we were moving towards "a time of no religion at all," and yet he could also speak of God who is "the 'beyond' in the midst of our

not simply to dogmatize on the basis of a credal or confessional bias, they can serve as catalysts in helping disciplines to understand each other. Cf. "Theology and the Technological Revolution," *Hartford Quarterly,* 4/4 (Summer 1964), 36ff.

life," who is content to remain unheralded and unrecognized[55] —a God, in fact, who is continually 'emptying himself,' giving out his own nature to creation.

The Fourth Evangelist seems to have discerned a divine sensitivity, a reticence and mutual reciprocity in the Godhead that is always ready to give glory rather than to take it, a readiness to withdraw from the place of credit. So God the Father glorifies the Son and is glorified in him, while Jesus declares that he seeks not his own glory (John 8:50). The Spirit of truth, which is to be sent to the disciples, comes from the Father and bears witness to Christ (15:26): he does not glorify himself but he glorifies our Lord, and when he speaks he speaks not on his own authority but testifies to the works and teaching of Christ and makes them known to the Church (16:13-15). In the same way we notice that after his resurrection our Lord removes even the physical recognition of himself from his disciples, as if it were a necessary step before they could receive his Spirit and become a community of witness: it is as if that which is most Godlike in God causes him to retire.[56]

The same principle seems to be at the heart of all true ministry. A distinguished teacher of missionaries once remarked that he trained his students for the time when they would have worked themselves out of a job,[57] and the Church works towards the time when the Kingdom will arrive and the Church will be unnecessary. Harvey Cox is true to the Bible when he points out that in the Holy City of the Apocalypse there is no temple because the glory of Christ himself pervades the whole society. The Church belongs to the period 'between the times,' the period of history between our Lord's earthly

[55] *Letters and Papers from Prison,* pp. 121ff.

[56] We must be careful. This does not imply the triumph of unregenerate humanism, or that God commits hara-kiri. The God who is 'beyond' retires from the periphery to reappear at the center of life. To put it into the images of our traditional faith—God the Father glorifies the Son as he recognizes and acknowledges the divinity in the man, Jesus; after the resurrection, Jesus removes himself from visible worship, so that the divine Spirit may be manifested in the faith of the Church. And the extension of this is that the Church of Jesus Christ should be prepared to withdraw as it sees Christ's Spirit of love and compassion entering the world. But not before that.

[57] Malcolm Pitt of the Hartford Seminary Foundation.

life and the advent of his Kingdom in its fulness; but it belongs to its *essential* character that it should be ready to withdraw as it sees the Kingdom appear. The Church exists to bring in the Kingdom, and its withdrawal from areas where it pioneered in the name of justice and compassion should be seen not as a defeat but as a success.

Let us illustrate this. At the time of this writing there was a public announcement that a church orphanage in Pennsylvania which had been started by a denomination in 1867 would have to discontinue its work with children. The church could no longer pay the standard of salaries, provide the working conditions, or operate the facilities now made mandatory by the state for comparable institutions. In addition the need had been almost entirely taken over by the civil authorities. The church therefore proposed to use its facilities entirely as a home for the aging, an area of social concern where there is a growing need and one that is still largely ignored by secular society. This, although it was hardly recognized as a matter for rejoicing by the church, was an example of success: it had pioneered the orphanage when it had been necessary, withdrawn when the state made its greater resources available, and then looked for another area in which it could be the prophetic community.

Of course, sometimes the Church has to be 'persuaded' to withdraw because it can no longer provide the service standards that civil society regards as necessary.[58] If we do not approve the churches' reluctance to relinquish control, we do not necessarily applaud the methods used by secular authorities to take over services that were initiated by the Church. On the other hand, when a church stubbornly refuses withdrawal in an area where it can no longer do adequately what needs to be done, it is still judging success by principles that are foreign to its own essential nature: the Church is the servant community which points to the Kingdom.

[58] It is clear that secular authorities have the resources to do a much better job than the churches in many areas pioneered by the churches, e.g., education and medicine.

Chapter IX

THE SHAPE OF THE CHURCH

1

THE CHURCH IN THE WORLD (II)

We were at breakfast during a conference, and a former college president was describing his experience as a guest preacher at a college where there was still compulsory chapel. "The chapel was full," he exclaimed. "Full! And as I began to go up the steps of the great central pulpit, I began to feel like God." He paused to let us savor the full effect. "I reached the top and gazed magnanimously over the congregation. Then I noticed a student in the front pew reading a newspaper! He paid not the slightest attention to me, and nothing I did or said could get his attention. And," added the speaker sadly, "my godlike feeling rapidly oozed away." We laughed, and there was another burst of laughter when someone at the table observed, "Now you know how God must feel."

Yes, indeed. He is probably too busy studying the newspaper to pay much attention to our antics or to our confident pronouncements in his name. It is this nagging possibility that dictates the form of this final chapter. In dealing with the relationship of the shape of the Church to its theological base, several possibilities are open to us. We could take up Troeltsch's three forms of the Church and discuss the specific contributions that each might make to the future configuration of the Church; or we might try to relate these forms to the central issue of the 'authority' on which they are based; or we might take a specific proposal, such as the Consultation on Church Union's *A Plan of Union,* and show how these issues have been met or not met.

However, we have an uncomfortable suspicion that God may be too busy reading the newspaper, and the only news that has ultimate relevance to the events of the newspaper is the Good News about nature and the purpose of God towards men. What are the appropriate structures for the community that serves such a God? Certainly the insights of Ernst Troeltsch are relevant, the significance of the historic channels of authority needs to be recognized, and since *A Plan of Union* is the boldest attempt to date in meeting the ecumenical *impasse,* it is well worth consideration; but all these approaches are symptomatic or descriptive, and to that extent secondary. The center from which we start must be the revealed nature of God himself and his purpose in the world.

A. *"Paradoxes of the revealed word"*

We can never fully comprehend God. As Cardinal Willebrands recognized, there are paradoxes at the center of the gospel that affect ecclesiology and church procedures, for of Vatican II he observed, "I have seen how formulae can appear to be compromises when, in fact, they are only expressing facets of the tensions or paradoxes of the revealed word itself, tensions," he added wisely, "which must not be eliminated but lived out in a pilgrim church."[1]

One of these paradoxes seems to be fundamental because it appears within the revelation of God's own nature.

(1) Our Scriptures begin with the statement "In the beginning God created the heavens and earth." Nowhere is there any attempt to define the term 'God,' because not only is the term ultimately indefinable, but it is assumed that those who read the Scriptures will read into the concept of 'God' their

[1] In an address to the Consultation on Church Union in 1969. *Consultation on Church Union—A Catholic Perspective* (Washington, D.C.: USCC Publications, 1970), p. 14.

own experience of God's actions and that of Israel's corporate experience. The Bible assumes that behind the word 'God' there stands a supreme being who is One and unchangeable, whose nature is disclosed by his actions and particularly through his relationship to the Chosen People. From the earliest period of Israel's history God's nature is contrasted with man's nature:

God is not man, that he should lie,
or a son of man, that he should repent.
Has he said, and will he not do it?
Or has he spoken, and will he not fulfil it?[2]

In his relationships with Israel the guarantee of his covenant with Israel is his *chesed,* his 'steadfast love,'[3] which appears in the context not only of love, concern, and compassion, but also of consistent faithfulness:

I will recount the steadfast love of the Lord,
the praises of the Lord,
according to all the Lord has granted us,
and the great goodness to the house of Israel
which he has granted to them according to his mercy,
according to the abundance of his steadfast love.[4]

Behind the testimony of the Bible there is the constancy and unchangeableness of God himself, for God would not be God if men could not rely upon his word, or if his purpose was capricious. To the people of Israel this constancy was indicated in their corporate confession that they worshipped 'the God of Abraham, Isaac and Jacob,' but through the shared experience of the people under God, Israel was able to testify to the God who was known through his deeds of mercy, righteousness, judgment and redemption. When the psalmist exclaimed "My God, my God!" this was the Being who was addressed, and although he might cry out that God had appeared to forsake him, yet it was with the confession

In thee our fathers put their trust;
they trusted, and thou didst rescue them.

[2] Numbers 23:19, RSV; cf. I Samuel 15:29.

[3] As *chesed* is translated in the RSV; the NEB uses 'unfailing love.'

[4] Isaiah 63:7, RSV; cf. also the whole context of Psalm 89.

Unto thee they cried and were delivered;
in thee they trusted and were not put to shame.[5]

Job exclaimed, "God himself has put me in the wrong, he has drawn his net around me" (Job 19:6); yet he set his complaint within the confidence,

But in my heart I know that my vindicator lives
and that he will rise last to speak in court;
and I shall discern my witness standing by my side
and see my defending counsel, even God himself. . . .[6]

This God, JHWH, whose absolute name and nature can never be absolutely fathomed by mortals, is known to the people of the Old Testament by an unchangeable purpose expressed in his deeds, and this is the God who the New Testament writers declare has now given his unique revelation of himself in Jesus Christ: The Word was with God, and what God was, the Word was, declares the writer of the Fourth Gospel; and this Word became flesh and dwelt among us, "and we saw his glory, such glory as befits the Father's only Son, full of grace and truth" (John 1:14). Behind the testimony of the Church there is the eternal consistency of God and his purpose as it is revealed to us in the Bible.

Obviously, if what we believe about God affects the Church and the form it takes before men, then this consistency should be explicit. Any straining for relevance that obscures this or contradicts it for the sake of topicality or to agree with the trend will be utterly irrelevant to the Church's main task, for it will undercut the Church's ability to say anything in God's name. Without that the Church has no reason for existing.

Moreover, this changelessness of God's purpose will be reflected not simply in the kerygma, the content of the gospel, but also within the actual form of the community that witnesses to that gospel in the world. To this extent there is a fundamentally theological reason behind the traditional structures of the ancient churches: they witness to something that

[5] Psalm 22:4f., NEB.

[6] Job 19:25f. The Hebrew is very obscure, but the translators are agreed that the writer moves from bitter complaint to firm confidence in God. I have chosen the NEB translation because it appears to be the most consistent.

belongs to the *esse* of God himself, and which will be reflected in his people.

However, we have to be careful. The ecclesiological question we have to ask is not which structures have demonstrated the most permanence and changelessness through history, but which structures have most consistently reflected God's unchanging *nature* and his eternal purpose of redemptive love. The permanence of a church form may be significant, but it is certainly not primary if it does not express something more than the permanence: it should also show that in Jesus Christ God's unchanging nature has revealed itself to be compassionate and redemptive love.

(2) The paradox is thrown into sharp relief when we see the changelessness of God's nature and purpose in relation to his essential freedom. The God of Israel is not to be cast in the form of an idol, because his form is known ultimately only to himself and he is not to be reduced to such a static representation of his nature. The God who spoke his final Word to man in the (free) man, Jesus Christ, had in previous ages spoken in a variety of ways through the prophets, and speaks now to the Church in his Spirit, who is like the wind which blows where it wills (cf. Hebrews 1:1f.; John 3:7f.).

In obedience to that Spirit the early Church found itself recognizing a great variety of gifts and structures. Under the leadership of the apostles we find that 'the Seven' were appointed (Acts 6:1-6), but we also read of prophets, evangelists, teachers, pastors, miracle workers, pastoral helpers, charismatics, bishops (overseers), deacons,[7] and even what seems to have been a separate order of widows.[8] I cannot accept Fr. George Tavard's statement (against Hans Küng) that it "is irrelevant today" that Paul adopted a somewhat freer order in the gentile churches than was practiced in Jerusalem, for although we no longer search the New Testament to discover a blueprint of the one true and permanent ecclesiastical form, the way in which the Church after Pentecost sought obedience to its christological center and mission is by no means irrele-

[7] Ephesians 4:11; I Corinthians 12:28; Acts 13:1; 21:8; Philippians 1:1.

[8] I Timothy 5:3ff.

vant to any age: the details of the New Testament Church's organization may not be normative for all time, but the faithfulness with which it interpreted the gospel for its own age ought to be.

It is clear from such passages as I Corinthians 12 that the Church experienced a great variety of gifts in the Spirit, and the unity of the Body was not something that inhibited or limited the variety but enhanced it. True, the form witnessed to the Church's essential unity through the mutual service and unanimity in action of all its parts, but that vanity by itself was of little account. Paul was not likening the Church to *any* body: it is not the image of the *body* that is important, but that the Church is called to be the Body *of Christ.* The form of that particular Body had to bear the unmistakable imprint of his character, and reveal through its own actions the unmistakable gifts of his Spirit. The variety of spiritual gifts testifies to the fulness (*pleroma*) of Christ.

The problem in ecclesiology is how these two essential principles are to be brought together and held together in such a way that they enhance each other. This is the basic paradox we meet whenever we try to relate that which is essential in the Church's historical continuity with the needs of its ministry and mission. It is, I suggest, a mistake to see one of these as essentially theological and the other as simply human and pragmatic,[9] since they both have their genesis in the revealed nature of God.

All existing churches have failed to resolve, or even to recognize fully this paradox. The Catholic branches of the Church, in common with all other churches that believe their church order is established on 'divine right,' have concentrated upon the eternal and immutable character of God's truth; and this is often impressively reflected in their traditional structures. We may also agree with Catholic critics that modern Protestant ecclesiology accepts pluralism too casually, without the willingness to 'try the spirits' which serious churchmanship demands, and that American ecumenism too easily assumes that its problems can be solved by clever ecclesiastical carpen-

9 As Fr. George Tavard seems to suggest in *Consultation on Church Union—A Catholic Perspective,* pp. 28ff.

try. We can agree with Fr. Tavard that this is not enough, that it starts in the wrong place, and that the ecumenical dilemma is less likely to be resolved by designing new structures than by "recognizing in faith the God-given structure of the Church."[10]

On the other hand, without defending COCU's method, we must say in ecumenical honesty that there are many serious Christians who cannot absolutely recognize that God-given structure in Catholicism—not because it lacks attractiveness, or even a testimony to God's permanent purpose, but because we fear it is attractive and permanent in the wrong way. Its forms seem to have been based on an assumption and practice of power that conflict with what we understand of the gospel. They lack Christian credibility, and especially so when they make claims for themselves that contrast markedly with the humility of the Incarnation.

We are not suggesting that Protestant denominations are any more credible. Indeed, the distance that many Protestants are prepared to go in a 'Catholic' direction is, I suggest, a genuine admission of our own shortcomings, and not always to be dismissed as ecumenical expediency; but at the point where structures conflict with the revealed nature of God, we can go no further. We recognize that church tradition under the guidance of the Holy Spirit produced the biblical record and has testified to the events that gave birth both to the Church and its message; but when any tradition—either by what it proclaims by word, or by what it affirms through structures—modifies the view of God that we have received in Jesus Christ,

10 *Ibid.*, p. 30. His protest against COCU's putting practical organization before the Church's essential theology was voiced in similar terms—but with almost opposite intent—by the Congregationalist, Malcolm K. Burton, against the way the United Church of Christ came into being. "The union of the Congregational Christian Churches with the Evangelical and Reformed Church (to form the United Church of Christ) has been hailed as remarkable because it is the first union [in the U.S.A.] across denominational lines, involving churches of basically different structure. Far more remarkable is the fact that the union was accomplished without ever telling the constituents of either denomination what they were getting into or what the final organization was really supposed to be." Malcolm K. Burton, *How Church Union Came* (Pontiac, Mich.: The Committee for the Continuation of Congregational Christian Churches of the United States, Inc., 1966), p. 1. This protest was obviously inspired by the strict Congregational concern for its polity.

we have to say that it has strayed. And it appears to us that *all* existing forms of the Church lie under that charge.

A Plan of Union may be legitimately criticized at many points. It *is* a human document, the carpentry often shows through the veneer, it has obviously been influenced by issues that had become politically fashionable, and it has by no means solved the relationship between that which should be permanent and that which must be flexible in the form of the Church of Christ Uniting. But it has one thing that is a *sine qua non* for the Church, the humility to recognize that it is not perfect, that it needs the mutual ministry of all its members to move nearer to what the Church should be, and that perfection cannot be claimed until the *Una Sancta* is revealed by Christ.

Everyone who seeks unity in a form beyond mere sentiment must be convinced that authentic and visible symbols of continuity with Christ belong to the Church—perhaps Apostolic Succession in several forms—but one is equally convinced that the Church must never again be allowed to assume forms of power that are foreign to its own essential nature. It is the coercive character of power and the way it is exercised that is at issue. If such authority is justified by the forms of apostolic succession, then the onus of proof is upon those who assert that the specific forms are necessary. There is an obvious credibility gap at this point between the Church and the world, between church leaders and church members, and between particular confessions and other Christian churches; and we ask how this is possible if the very structures were divinely ordained to prevent this from happening. We know that no solution in history will be perfect, and that even under the guidance of the Holy Spirit the Church has to wrestle with its human failings; but we search for what Cardinal Willebrands described as a "healthy dialectic between unity and legitimate plurality."[11] Only as the Church resolutely turns away from the 'lordship' claimed in the past will it have the freedom needed to interpret the everlasting gospel; and when that happens there will be no need to prove its apostolicity.

There is more than pious exhortation behind that last sen-

[11] *Ibid.*, p. 16.

tence. It involves theological principle of crucial importance not only to future credibility but also to the Church's ministry and mission. Ecclesiastical institutions have a habit of confirming their own authority by methods not very different from other political societies, and when this ecclesiastical authority is backed by material power they are able very effectively to block any future change in the Church, good or bad. The Church becomes ossified, and that which is claimed as an essential channel of the Holy Spirit becomes an effective agent of fossilization.

If institutional forms themselves are regarded as the indispensable link with the apostolic tradition, the power to enforce control in the Church often creates a wider credibility gap between the Church's professed gospel and its testimony in the community. One of the most urgent and difficult problems facing the union of the churches is the necessity of building into the structures of the Church the means whereby the Holy Spirit can initiate new forms of ministry, adapt old forms to changing conditions, and above all permit the kind of ongoing critical review of itself that will make future reform possible without schism.[12]

As we have seen, the problem goes back to a basic 'paradox of the revealed word,' and perhaps we ought to look not so much for a permanent solution as for a continuing creative tension. Two things, however, are quite clear—first, that the answer is certainly not to be resolved as in the past by opting either for one or the other side of the paradox; and secondly, that coercive power, however it is camouflaged as ecclesiastical authority, contradicts the gospel. Perhaps only when those who exercise authority in the Church relinquish their exercise of power and make their appeal genuinely to the persuasion of the Spirit, will we be able to hold the elements of continuing historical succession and the freedom of the Spirit in a more Christian leadership.

[12] A useful piece of historical research would be to discover which denominations have been most successful in resisting (or avoiding) major schisms, and the theological and practical reasons for their success in meeting specific situations.

B. "A servant church, truly catholic, truly evangelical, truly reformed"

A significant shift in emphasis between the two sides of this paradox can be illustrated through the meetings of the Consultation on Church Union, and it is clear that the shift was due to a growing awareness of the theological signifcance of the world in relationship to God.[13] The proposals shift from a dominant emphasis on the permanent, historic and given structures of the Church, to recognition of the charismatic, experimental and plural forms in which ministry can be expressed.

The first step came (as Troeltsch realized) with the recognition that there is a 'third type' of churchmanship which turns first to 'the Spirit' as its ultimate authority, which finds its justification neither primarily in historic tradition nor in its appeal to a scriptural pattern but in evangelical outreach. In his San Francisco sermon of December 1960, Eugene Carson Blake had proposed that a united church would have to be both reformed and catholic; and although he included within Protestant tradition all that we understand by the term 'evangelical,'[14] the sermon reflected the basic, twofold approach to the doctrine of the Church that had prevailed at Amsterdam in 1948.[15]

The shift began during the Washington meeting of 1962, and the closing statement of that meeting speaks of the

13 We cannot dismiss *all* the post-World War II interest in the secular as theological 'bandwagoning' or charge COCU with having entirely sold out to 'relevance and topicality' (cf. Tavard, *op. cit.,* p. 42). Bonhoeffer had no bandwagon on which to jump. Although we recognize that American Protestantism is vulnerable to theological fads, the issue Bonhoeffer had raised is real.

14 George L. Hunt and Paul A. Crow, Jr. (eds.), *Where We Are in Church Union* (New York: Association, 1965), p. 48. Blake contrasted Catholic attitudes to the Church and the sacraments with "protestant or evangelical practices and understandings" (p. 49), and pointed out that the principle of *sola scriptura* prevents any bridge between "catholic and evangelical" (p. 70). The identification of Protestant and Evangelical also appeared in an early paper by Lewis Mudge, "The Church Reformed and Evangelical," in *ibid.,* pp. 54ff.

15 A document discussed at the Amsterdam Assembly in 1948 specified the division of the churches as between Catholic and Protestant. Douglas Horton, then Minister and Secretary of the Congregational Christian Churches in the U.S.A., protested that there is a third ordering of the Church, one that takes its authority from the guidance of the Spirit and could be described as 'evangelical.'

churches having met together to explore "the possibility of the formation of a church truly catholic, truly reformed, and truly evangelical."[16] By the time of the Lexington meeting in 1965 this objective had been slightly modified to "unity in a servant church truly catholic, truly evangelical, truly reformed." This was adopted because the principle of *semper reformanda* should apply to both the catholic and evangelical aspects of the Church.[17] The new formulations also recognized the servant character of the Church's role in the world.

By the time we reach the *Principles of Church Union,* published later in 1966, a further development can be discerned. Even the references to the three types of the Church, catholic, evangelical, and reformed, are beginning to be downplayed. True, the Foreword speaks of "the power of the Holy Spirit which enlivens us and chastens us as we seek a united church, truly catholic, truly evangelical, truly reformed";[18] but the phrase had disappeared from the text of the "Principles" and most of its important appendices. It may be argued that it was implicit within the proposals put forward, and particularly in the statement of basic principles put forward in the preamble. That is true, but it seems that the representatives themselves were beginning to question whether the Church's mission in the world could be wholly described in these traditional categories. The terms no longer represented clear-cut ecclesiastical divisions.

The change of mood is made explicit in the "Open Letter to the Churches," in which there is a new note of realism and contemporaneity:

> We are impressed with the ways in which the same tendencies and movements increasingly pervade all our churches. "Evangelical" and "catholic" refer to attitudes, institutions, customs, standards found to some degree in all; "reformed" speaks of a will to seek God's judgment which every church rightly claims. While our structures differ, the currents of American tradition and life sweep through them all.[19]

16 *COCU—The Reports of the Four Meetings* (Cincinnati: Forward Movement Publications, 1966), p. 18.

17 *Ibid.,* p. 67, note.

18 By the chairman of that time, David G. Colwell, *Principles of Church Union* (Cincinnati: Forward Movement Publications, 1966), p. 3.

19 *Ibid.,* p. 62.

It is a significant passage. It recognized that churches could no longer be characterized (or caricatured) as in the past, and that they had increasingly adopted the positive elements to be found in other churches; but it was also a hint that we might have moved beyond the stage when we could think of splicing the Church together, or even of simply putting together ecclesiastical elements that were traditionally regarded as catholic, reformed, or evangelical. The "Open Letter" seemed to recognize that a radical change had occurred in the situation of the Church which called for a new openness, that union itself would not achieve renewal, and that the gospel itself could be 'a sword.'[20]

This "Open Letter" was very soon moved from its position as an appendix to the beginning of the next communication from the Consultation, and in this way it reinforced the new stance.[21] The concept of a church truly catholic, truly evangelical, and truly reformed was not ignored; but one senses that the members of the Consultation no longer found this an adequate formulation in which to describe what the Church should be, and that these historic emphases must be held within a more dynamic view of the Church directed towards the future.

Obviously one may argue how far the Consultation on Church Union achieved its objective in *A Plan of Union.*[22] Roman Catholic critics have every right to question whether it provides a viable basis in terms of their own church's doctrine, and to question whether it is "concerned more about trying to anticipate future developments than about determining on what basis these developments may take place."[23] Any attempt to project the direction this issue may take in the future is ultimately self-defeating, because we can too easily compound the difficulties; it would be a fundamental denial of the

20 *Ibid.,* p. 60.

21 *Consultation on Church Union, 1967* (Cincinnati: Forward Movement Publications, 1967), pp. 9ff.

22 *A Plan of Union for the Church of Christ Uniting* (Princeton, N.J.: COCU, 1970).

23 Fr. Tavard was repeating what he had said previously about the *Principles of Church Union. COCU—A Catholic Perspective,* p. 35.

faith basis that has hitherto given the ecumenical movement its incentive.[24]

On the other hand, if the shift we have indicated was real, the members of the Consultation were surely right to recognize that traditional answers alone simply did not meet the issue. If the terms catholic, evangelical, and reformed are only complementary emphases which when added together produce church reunion, then the matter could be decided simply by scissors and paste. But this would leave untouched the radical re-structuring that seems to be demanded of the Church today, the need to question in the name of the gospel values hitherto held sacred, and to promote a renewal that will affect the Church in all its parts. Certainly there must be in the Church of any age elements that represent "the providential continuity of God's unbroken care for his children," that recall them constantly to their true center in Jesus Christ, and that allow the Holy Spirit to speak his unpredictable word of hope and judgment "out of the sluggish stream of history"; but these things are not necessarily tied to the forms which *we* think guarantee them, however revered and even however effective in the past Catholics, Protestants, and Free Churchmen have found them.

We have been searching for the Authority behind the 'authorities' to which we have appealed in the past—an Authority that not only confirms their common witness to the truth but also shows how their testimonies are related as we try to give

24 An interesting illustration of the way in which attempts to predict trends in the ecumenical stock market can go astray was pointed out to me by my colleague, Ford Lewis Battles. In the 1960s, the liturgical committees of two Protestant denominations seem to have acted in concert to prepare the faithful for doctrinal *rapprochement* with the Eastern Orthodox by publishing the Nicene Creed without the *filioque* clause. As far as I can tell, this radical shift from the Western tradition was introduced without public discussion of the doctrinal issue. Meanwhile, Vatican II was opening ecumenical possibilities with the Roman Catholic Church in which this could very well be an embarrassment. Cf. *The Lord's Day Service with Explanatory Notes* (Philadelphia/Boston: United Church of Christ Press, 1964), p. 11. In the Foreword the authors state that this work had been begun in 1960 in close relationship to the Joint Committee on Worship of the Presbyterian churches (Cumberland Presbyterian, Presbyterian Church in the U.S., and the United Presbyterian Church in the U.S.A.) which produced the *Book of Common Worship; Provisional Services* (Philadelphia: Westminster, 1966), in which (p. 25) there is an identical version of the Creed.

the Church a form that can continue God's mission to the world. There is no fixed point at which the Church can rest content except in God's revealed nature and his purpose of redemptive love towards men. Only if we recognize the eternal consistency of God himself and his faithful relationship to his own creation will we be able to be faithful to his purpose and have the faith to launch out into the new forms that God demands of the redemptive community. The world may write the agenda but it does not initiate it: if contemplation of our secular world has brought us to this point, God may well be using it to put his own handwriting on the wall.

2

THE CHURCH AND ITS MINISTERS

This tension between the permanent testimony to the divine nature and flexibility towards the forms in which that testimony may be expressed comes to a particular focus in the discussion that surrounds the ordained Ministry. One has only to think of the lengthy debates in the past between the 'apostolic succession' and the 'Ministry of the Word,' or of the no less animated debates today between 'special ministries' and the Ministry in its traditional form, to realize that for every kind of ecclesiology there is a related form of ordained Ministry.

There is a reason for this, as I tried to show in *Ministry*. If ministers are given to a church (Ephesians 4) to remind the churches through the nature and quality of their own service of the church's corporate service to the world, there is a direct relationship between the concept of Ministry and the concept of the Church. In light of a biblical theology that holds together the particular call and the universal mission of the Church, both the Church and its Ministry have their genesis in the ministry of Jesus Christ, the one true Minister and the one true representative of God's people. Starting from this view of their essential relationship, in ordination the Minister represents to the Church the nature of its own essential and corporate ministry to the world: a Minister in relation to his congregation represents that which the congregation is called to be to the world. To speak in other terms, as if the Minister could possess powers essentially different from those of his fellow members, or to describe his office in terms of prestige rather than of service, or so to emphasize his being 'set apart' that he is regarded as more 'holy' than other Christians, is not only to misunderstand the gospel but to misrepresent it. This is where the discussion between Protestants on the one hand and Catholics and Orthodox on the other has to be continued in depth.

The ecumenical discussion must be most open and honest with regard to the future form of the Ministry, for if the Ministry is given to the Church to be an exemplar of what the Church is to be among men, then the form it takes will be crucial for the Church's own witness. It also reflects the fundamental paradox of the Church itself, for there is a sense in which both the Church and its ordained Ministry are entirely unessential, and a further sense in which they are both absolutely necessary.

(1) In one sense the Ministry is dispensable. Christ himself is the one Minister the Church needs, and if the Church were a perfect community of his followers, it would not need further help. In the most immediate sense the Church as the Body of Christ draws its inspiration, direction, and pattern from its Head; and its mission is given to it in the redemption and reconciliation that he wrought between God and man. The Ministry stands in a similar position in relationship to the Church as the Church itself does in relation to the world and the Kingdom of God: it belongs to this period 'between the times,' and it serves so that it may be no longer needed.

(2) On the other hand, in this interim between Pentecost and the advent of the Kingdom of God both the Church and its Ministry are needed, and the Ministry is necessary because the Church is necessary. Its leadership reminds the Christian community in concrete situations and immediate relationships what its own corporate mission should be, and its points to the significance of 'election' in the ministry of the one true Minister, Jesus Christ. When the apostle in Ephesians speaks of the different forms of Ministry as given "to equip God's people for work in his service" and "for the building up of the body of

Christ,"[25] it is clear that he is speaking about a spiritual leadership in the Church that is not imposed on the members or to be confused with secular forms of leadership, but is to be received as a gift from God. It is also clear that this Ministry is fulfilled not simply as it is declaimed from a pulpit or celebrated before an altar, but in a *quality* that is exemplified in the relationships of the living Christian community. This essential quality is indicated by its name—Ministry, diakonia (= service)—and this is its reason for existence: in the focus of a Minister's call and his dedication in that local community, it declares the nature of the Church's corporate ministry within the wider community of the world.

A. Ministry and leadership

Ministry involves leadership, and it is clear that in the early Church this leadership was regarded as a charism, a gift of the Spirit.

This is a place where the Church might help human society to understand itself and its own needs, because it is increasingly clear that our society is undergoing a crisis in leadership. It concerns not only the power structures by which leadership is supported and exercised—the way it is chosen and the well-publicized mediocrity that is often selected—but it concerns most fundamentally the kind of person who is prepared to exercise leadership in our world.[26] There is an inherent futility in trying to exercise leadership with the falsely egalitarian presuppositions behind modern 'consensus government,' and this was amusingly portrayed in a *Saturday Review* cartoon: Napoleon before his last battle was receiving a report from an aide, who says, "Sir, a public opinion poll shows that 17 per cent of the public believe you should fight the Duke of

[25] Ephesians 4:12; cf. the discussion of this in *Ministry,* pp. 29ff.

[26] Studies of the drives that lead men to seek political power would be instructive. Do they arise from an innate sense of superior worth, or from inner insecurity? Without subscribing to any political overtones in Robert Ardrey's *The Social Contract,* I believe he was right to point out the fallacy in Rousseau's belief that we are "born equal." However unpalatable, we have to recognize that we are born with very different and sometimes very unusual gifts; and there appears to be overwhelming scientific evidence that the 'Alpha,' the natural leader, has been necessary for the survival of the race. *The Social Contract,* especially chapter 4.

Wellington at Nivelles; 29 per cent believe you should fight him at Wavre; and 54 per cent believe you should fight him at Waterloo."[27]

Representative democracy has to come to terms with this issue and decide how it can enable its own leaders to exercise the very gifts of leadership for which they were presumably chosen; for leadership does not function according to the standards of mass opinion, and there seems to be less and less opportunity in the structure of modern societies for leadership to be recognized and endorsed by the community as a gift.[28] In any sizable American city, the political party that hopes to govern will choose its slate from those who first represent sectional interests—redneck, white, black, Puerto Rican, Italian, Irish, mid-European, and the rest. Individuals are likely to win their place on the slate because they are representative or even typical, and not because they demonstrate any aptitude for government. Yet representative government which ignores such aptitude cannot avoid mediocrity, and even disastrous inefficiency.

Of course, charismatic leadership of itself, control of the group by an aggressive male (or female) 'Alpha,' can be extremely dangerous, and our forms of representative government usually prevent power from being captured by the extremist demagogue, the flashy genius with a gift in public relations, or the ruthless genius with the gift of manipulating other people's self-interests for his own ends. But although we

27 *Saturday Review* (March 13, 1971), p. 101.

28 We may employ an example from the ecumenical field, since there is a striking contrast between the earlier charismatic leadership and the new representative bureaucracies of the movement, and no organization is more consciously representative than the World Council of Churches. During my service at the Ecumenical Institute we began to look for a staff member who, in addition to theological training, would have professional competence in science or industrial technology. That would not be an easy assignment, but it was not impossible until we were told that the appointee should also represent the 'Catholic' branches of the Church, and that it would also be desirable to meet the claims of the Third World and Women. If all these considerations had been observed we would have found ourselves looking for an African or Asian woman in Anglican or Orthodox orders with an advanced degree in science or technology! No one was asking the more fundamentally important questions—whether she/he (a) could teach, (b) had anything creative to say, or (c) could work harmoniously with a confessionally mixed group of colleagues in a small community.

concede that human society is still often ruthlessly competitive, is that the way the future points? Although the ambitious 'Alpha' in a competitive state of nature may suffice, in a society where the inadequacy of the societal forms themselves may be a threat to survival and where the issues are so much more complex, his kind of charisma is always ambiguous and usually dangerous. When man is threatened by adverse conditions in nature or by attack from other species, one form of leadership may be necessary; but when the most ominous threat to survival arises from man's own nature, something very different is needed. Are we moving towards a form of human community in which *Ich dien* (I serve) is not merely an ideal expressed on a princely banner, but the recognized basis of all civil leadership? That is what the Kingdom of God implies.

The Church could make the nature of this leadership clear, and in periods of great charismatic activity it has made it clear. Our problem in church history is that such periods are inevitably followed by periods of 'routinization' when the institutional churches are more likely to follow the secular trend than offer any distinctive example. This is why the Church's Ministry needs to be constantly judged in the light of the One from whom all ministry springs. It is a particular kind of leadership that the Church recognizes, as John McKenzie pointed out, a leadership that reveals itself not in the acquisition of power but in demonstration of the fruits of the Spirit, love, joy, peace, patience, kindness, goodness, fidelity, gentleness and self-control—qualities, the apostle observes, which do not need any laws to hold them in check (Galatians 5:22). McKenzie put it very well when he said, "Paul was simply unconcerned about his position, or his dignity, or his power over other men; he was a *diakonos*."[29] Such leadership has its own integrity in terms of the gospel, but without it the Kingdom of God would not be the *Kingdom* of God.

It is obvious that we are not yet ready for this kind of leadership in secular society on any side of the political and ideological curtains. However, this is precisely the point where the ordained Ministry in the Church is called to be, in A. T.

29 *Authority of the Church,* p. 95.

Hanson's phrase, a 'pioneer Ministry,' and where the Church itself has to be, in E. Clinton Gardner's phrase, 'a prophetic community.' If Christians are serious when they claim that the Church should be giving moral and spiritual leadership to secular society, let us be clear what the Kingship of Christ means for this world, and what kind of leadership the Christian community should be demonstrating. We may be able to retain the historic forms of Ministry in the Church, but only if we see that they are to be servants of the Spirit but in no way take his place.

B. Ministry is service

The leadership of the Ministry is a leadership of service. One testimony to our new appreciation of the place of this world in God's love is that the discussion on ministerial orders seems to be coming to its focus not in the question of the episcopate but in the nature of the diaconate.[30] There seems to be growing recognition that the 'deacon' occupies a significant but curiously imprecise place in the structure of the Church—a paradox reflected in church history. In a large part of restorationist Protestantism the deacon is a layman who shares some sacramental functions but fulfils his main task as a representative of the lay members, while in Catholic branches of the Church the deacon is the lowest rung in the clerical hierarchy. In the New Testament the emphasis was upon his responsibility to administer the charitable resources of the Christian community, while in our day we recognize that this needs to be extended in ministries that express the Church's compassion for the world's need. As I observed in another context, a study of orders in the Church might very well discover that the role and purpose of the diaconate could be "the point on which the whole meaning of ministry turns."[31]

For isn't it somewhat singular that diakonia, the word that describes the messianic ministry of the whole Church, should specifically be drawn from the work of the *diakonos*, the

[30] Cf. Richard T. Nolan (ed.), *The Diaconate Now* (Washington/Cleveland: Corpus Books, 1967).

[31] Cf. *ibid.*, p. 49.

lowest office on the clerical totem pole? Surely it is significant that the messianic ministry of the Church receives its most explicit expression not in overseership (*episcope*), even when this is carefully defined in pastoral terms, or in the idea of priesthood (whether understood in terms of New Testament *presbyteros,* Jewish *hiereus,* or the *sacerdos* of other religions), but in terms of the *diakonos,* the lowest of the low who has been kept low even by the Church. The last shall be first, and the first last.

There are hopeful signs that this insight is becoming increasingly accepted within the churches today. It is implicit within the writings of Hans Küng and John McKenzie, and much of the thinking and writing behind Vatican II. One also sees it in *A Plan of Union,* although the most immediate impression that the casual reader may get is that those who framed the *Plan* used a pattern of pragmatic (Methodist?) hierarchy and fixed it very firmly in power structures of the Church of Christ Uniting. But happily there is a paradox in *A Plan of Union,* and significantly the ambivalence is seen between the concept of diakonia, which very properly governs the concept of the Church's total and corporate ministry in the world, and the place that the 'deacon' should occupy in the life and witness of the Church.

The *Plan* makes it clear that the Church exists for mission and that this is centered in the parish.[32] There is to be no essential, qualitative difference between the lay members of the Church and their ordained ministers, for "all share in the commission and authority of the whole church under Christ the servant . . . . The ministry of the church is one. The ministries of the ordained and the unordained are aspects of this one ministry. Lay persons and ordained share the same basic vocation to become free and responsible members of the new human community."[33] The people of God are one people, engaged in one corporate ministry; and that ministry is essentially that of "Christ the servant": diakonia describes the messianic ministry.

There is, however, honest uncertainty in the *Plan* about the

[32] *Op. cit.,* ch. VIII, pp. 46ff.

[33] *Ibid.,* VII.2,4, p. 38.

place which deacons should occupy within the life of the Church. It is admitted that the matter has not been resolved, and it is suggested that the office "is to be kept as flexible as possible during the period immediately following unification"[34] until clearer definition can emerge. At the same time "some strong directions have emerged": it is clear that the diaconate should represent "a distinctive vocation for mission as well as for the maintenance of the church,"[35] for an ordained deacon's work in the world "symbolizes the universal imperative and may serve to further equip the whole people of God for it."[36] It is recognized that the deacon has a limited but real place in the sacramental life of the church, and that in this sense deacons "exemplify the interdependence of worship and service as well as the encounter between the gospel and the needs of the world."[37] In one important respect the members of the Consultation were fully prepared to break with an ecclesiastical tradition that has been growing over a millennium or more, for "the diaconate will not be treated as the initial stage in the preparation of presbyters."[38]

Although hesitation is not normally to be commended in church documents, perhaps it is to be welcomed here, for one has the impression that the writers were genuinely feeling their way to something new that would better express a very old truth. It is almost as if they were having second thoughts, voicing a deep underlying question—that while they had been concentrating on the traditional structure (forms which would admittedly open the possibility of conversation with the older branches of Catholicism), their own essential theology and biblical base may have been driving them in a different direction, to a different concept of where the Church's ministry should be located. This is expressed in what deserves to become a classic statement of the Church's messianic ministry:

> The church is called to be a servant community, serving as the world's deacon in new and untried ways. It is to put on the servant

[34] *Ibid.*, VII.81, p. 53.

[35] *Ibid.*, VII.82, p. 53.

[36] *Ibid.*

[37] *Ibid.*, VII.83, p. 54.

[38] *Ibid.*, VII.84, p. 54.

> role of Christ, giving up its temporal securities in obedience to his call. It may find it necessary to leave behind old and familiar ways of serving and make daring experiments toward learning what it means to live the life of Christ in the newly emerging patterns of human communities. Such experiments in servanthood may require the surrender of traditional institutional forms. But the purpose of the church's witness is not to protect its own life but to testify to and manifest the Lordship of Christ.[39]

This would be the ministry of a genuinely prophetic community, and the Church's Ministers would be the pioneers who would lead the people of God into that vocation. Such a Church and such a Ministry would have integrity.

C. The paid professionals

However, this will remain pious humbug unless the Church and its Ministers can dissociate themselves from the hypocritical mess into which society has got itself, and in which we are all enmeshed.

Reflect on the facts behind the alienation of young people. As Marshall McLuhan pointed out, modern young people represent the first generation that has grown up under the direct influence of the mass media. Today's young person early trusted and admired the cleverly imaged radio and TV personalities, and accepted their blandishments; but gradually he realized the rank hypocrisy involved in paid testimonies. Such disenchantment bred a healthy distrust of media-made public images in general; yet he could see that it is to these people—the actor, baseball star, or late-night talk show host who recklessly endorses products he has never tried—that society gives its admiration by offering them its most obvious material rewards.

It is against the basic assumptions of a society that accepts blatant hypocrisy without protest that the young, 'well-brought up,' postwar generation has revolted, often, we admit, without realizing the extent to which it falls into stereotypes that are just as false. So they perpetrate senseless violence, or try to escape into communes, or skip the country. As one

39 *Ibid.*, III.7, pp. 16f.

young American exile declared, "I'm 22 years old and I'm tired. I don't believe in God and I don't believe that America is the golden center of the universe. You can get away with not believing in one of these, but not both."[40]

"I don't believe in God. . . ." I can understand that. It is not only the threat of nuclear war, the bitterness of Vietnam, the callousness of affluence unmoved by poverty, or realization that the pursuit of profit has polluted our environment; but much more subtle and eroding to faith is the recognition that ideas, like merchandise, are judged not by the evidence of their truth or untruth but by the attractiveness of their packaging, the persistence of their promoters, and the artistry of their professional salesmen. A church, no less than a theatre or a tavern, will stand more chance of success and popularity if it has a pleasing decor, good musical entertainment, and air-conditioning. Naturally, you will not go to a church if you are out of sympathy with its basic positions, any more than you will go to a cinema to see a film you dislike or to drink in a tavern if you prefer lemonade; but all other things being equal or nearly equal, the church with the best program and facilities is more likely to be well attended than the ones that do not have them.

And the professional salesman? He is the man who interests us, and he is there—three feet above contradiction and uttering noble sentiments with deep sincerity. Of course he does. Like the man who is paid to persuade you to buy Geritol, he is paid to do it. A generation that has been bombarded with spurious sincerity from its earliest years is not going to make much distinction between the professionalism employed to promote the gospel and the professionalism employed to promote anything else. Why should it? It has been forced to the conclusion that if you are paid to sell, you sell, using all your professional competence to put the idea across, whether the idea happens to be that you would walk a mile for a Camel or that God was in Christ reconciling the world to himself. To most of the citizenry in the Western world, it makes not the slightest difference that the man in the pulpit may believe what he is

40 As reported to Thomas Thompson; cf. "Crete: A Stop in the New Odyssey," *Life*, 65/3 (July 19, 1968), 21.

saying with very deep intensity, or that he could have entered a higher paying profession if he did not have that conviction. It makes no difference because the young listener is not conscious of it. All he is conscious of is that the Minister is paid for promoting the Church and its message; and in our society paid professionalism presupposes two things—first, that you are doing it because you are paid, and secondly, if you are paid to do this you will use all your professional skill and competence to sell the product, whether you actually believe in it or not.

Those who have had most insight into the nature of the Church's mission have always recognized the danger when money and the Ministry are mixed. We have the apostolic testimony from Paul's example, if not in his own words: "we did not accept board and lodging from anyone without paying for it; we toiled and drudged, we worked for a living night and day, rather than be a burden to any of you—not because we have not the right to maintenance, but to set an example for you to imitate."[41]

Or we might take examples from church history. Under the leadership of George Fox the early Quaker movement was a genuine period of evangelical outreach in the history of the Protestant churches. Fox was sensitive to precisely the point:

> In the afternoon I went to another steeple-house about three miles off, where preached a great high priest, called a doctor, one of them whom Justice Hotham would have sent for to speak with me. I went to the steeple-house, and sat down until the priest had done. The words that he took for his text were these, "Ho, every one that thirsteth, come ye to the waters, come ye, buy and eat, yea come, buy wine and milk without money and without price." Then I was moved of the Lord to say to him, "Come down, thou deceiver; dost thou bid people come freely, and take the water of life freely, and yet thou takest three hundred pounds a-year of them, for preaching the Scriptures to them! Mayest thou not blush for shame! Did the prophet Isaiah and Christ do so, who spake the words and gave them forth freely? Did not Christ say to His ministers, whom He sent to preach, 'Freely ye have received, freely give'?"[42]

41 II Thessalonians 3:8f.

42 *The Journal of George Fox*, ed. Norman Penney (London: J. M. Dent, 1924), p. 42.

John Wesley's preachers were not to "grow rich by the gospel,"[43] and in describing his ideal of the presbyter-bishop in the New Testament Church, Wesley says, "All that is gained (above food and raiment) by administering in holy things is *filthy gain* indeed; far more filthy than what is honestly gained by making kennels, or emptying common sewers."[44]

It is true that George Fox did not do so badly out of his preaching even though he accepted no salary, and Wesley's provisions clearly represent a step towards a paid, professional caste of preachers; but that is not the point. Both evangelists recognized the danger of allowing the proclamation of the gospel to depend upon money, and attacked the idea of "priests that preach about the love of God, and hold out a collecting box at the same time."[45]

The churches and their Ministers are caught in the vise of a society they helped create. I do not regret that the Reformation moved away from the priestly form of the Ministry, because it enabled Ministers to become closer to secular life, to wrestle with the problems which harass the people to whom they minister, to live as men among men. But in developing a *professional* concept to take the place of the priestly role, Protestant churches really announced that they were willing to settle for their own little segment of society, rather than to stand before men as a prophetic community with a pioneer Ministry that would point society towards the Kingdom of God. Only in its distinctiveness could the Church fulfil its proper mission. If one is tempted to welcome uncritically everything secular, remember that it is this same secular society that has made our churches what they are, that bought their support and silence in the face of its hybris and greed.[46]

43 From the Bennett Ms, Conference of 1744, quoted in A. B. Lawson, *John Wesley and the Christian Ministry,* p. 33.

44 Wesley's comment on I Timothy 3:8, in his *Notes on the New Testament.*

45 A twentieth-century comment, put into the mouth of Christ in the 1970 BBC television program, *The Son of Man.*

46 The process of 'routinization,' by which a charismatic group adapts itself to society, is merely a process of secularization: it was secularization that produced 'Christendom.' The advocates of 'secular Christianity' are strangely reluctant to acknowledge this, or to explain why a process that has done as much to stifle the

Professionalism itself is not to be blamed; and insofar as it is inescapable as the churches are at present organized, it is obviously better that Ministers should be trained to be competent rather than incompetent professionals: professionalism has its positive aspects.[47] Our problem arises because we have allowed the pastoral office to become incarcerated within professionalism, so that instead of pioneering within society, it takes its stance, standards, and status from the other professions in our culture. Renewal may well depend on our ability to break this inhibiting pattern, particularly at two critical points.

(1) First, we should put evangelism back where it belongs. Evangelism is the responsibility of the total membership of the Church; and if willingness to proclaim the gospel is an integral aspect of a Christian's confession of faith, there can be no justification for professional evangelists. There is obviously a profound sense in which evangelism has to be undertaken as corporate witness; but even in terms of individual witness, we have to reach back to the *spirit* (not try to reproduce the situation) of the book of Acts, when every member considered himself (or herself) a witness, and when circumstances even as unpromising as persecution could be used as the occasion for the proclamation of the Good News as far as Christians could carry it.[48] We have to move away from the idea of the Church as a static religious society to which we subscribe in order to be provided with uplift, entertainment, and consolation while here on earth and either stock options in heaven or a reliable insurance policy against whatever may lie elsewhere. We are in the Church because we are committed to its gospel. All of us; totally.

(2) Secondly, and just as urgently, I suggest we must move towards forms of churchmanship that will make a salaried Ministry obsolete, and which would enable the Church to show what all ministry is supposed to be—*service*, freely given to all, and without material rewards.

biblical witness as to advance the Kingdom should suddenly become 'good' in our time. It would perhaps be more realistic to recognize that all movements within history are mixed blessings at best.

47 Cf. *Ministry*, pp. 207ff.

48 Acts 8:1-4; cf. *Ministry*, pp. 103ff.

Because theological students are conscious of the credibility gap that surrounds the clerical profession, many decline ordination and look for vocations in which they can serve the Church's mission by involving themselves in the problems of society. I admire their motives, but I fear they see only half the problem—they would do better to be ordained, but not paid. There is still a great deal to be said for ordination, especially for the Christian who is called to serve the Church in a world where the Church is likely to be less and less socially acceptable as it makes itself and the gospel more and more credible; it needs courage to be publicly identified with unfashionable faith. On the other hand, there is no justification for putting a price on the gospel we proclaim or the service we perform in Christ's name.

Is this unrealistic? In the present state of the churches it probably is, but let the old men dream dreams and perhaps the young men will begin to see visions. Suppose we start with the assumptions (1) that the Church's ministry and mission is something in which we are all engaged, (2) that the Church will continue to need well-prepared Ministers for its leadership, (3) but that these leaders will still not depend on their work as Ministers to support themselves and their families. What sort of pattern would the Church take?

(1) Obviously, if the Ministry is to be well trained, the support of theological education would have to be in the hands of the churches, whether of the denomination or of its area synods or dioceses; but this would be no problem if local congregations could release some of the funds now used for paying their Ministers. Presumably the churches would select the men it wanted for its Ministry and invite them to take the training.[49]

49 The effect on the (free) theological education that would be offered cannot be fully explored here. One aspect, however, seems clear—seminaries would be forced to maintain a fundamental and integral relationship to their supporting churches, and at the same time would be forced into close relationship to other centers of higher education. They would have to relate their assimilation of new thought from the universities to the life of the parishes. They might therefore offer genuine leadership to the churches without the threat of alienation that seems to afflict them whenever their connection with the parish becomes too tenuous.

(2) Seminary training might have to be spread over a somewhat longer period, but there would be less danger of becoming introverted and exclusively theological, because side by side with this training an ordinand would be also preparing himself (or herself) for a career in a secular field—possibly based on his college degree. Education, the social services, even medicine (e.g., group practices) or manual trades might provide the kind of career that could be combined with spiritual leadership of a parish.

(3) On being appointed (elected) to a congregation or team Ministry, the ordinand would also seek appropriate secular employment in the area, and while he was seeking such employment the congregation would use a parish contingency fund to support him and his family. The same fund could be used if it became necessary for him to change positions, or in case of hardship caused by the Minister's secular unemployment.

(4) The Minister would give his services to the parish like any other member of the congregation. He would work for the Church in his own free time, and receive no remuneration for his service except expenses.

(5) Because the clerical leadership of the congregation could give only limited time to parish affairs, the whole parish would have to be organized for *mutual* ministry and mission. The Minister's service to the Church would of necessity concentrate upon priorities. Instead of waiting for the Minister to visit the sick, or to make pastoral calls, "Because that is what we pay him for, anyway," the members of the parish would share the responsibilities of the parish and they would be organized to care for each other and to meet needs wherever they occurred. A new avocation would open out for retired members, while of necessity the local parish would have to undertake serious programs in lay training. The skills and competence of the whole membership would be called into play, and where these were not available parishes would be grouped to sustain each other.

(6) The finances of the local parish would have a wholly different focus. True, more money would be needed for training programs and theological education, and locally for the

ministerial contingency fund; but otherwise the funds of the parish would be entirely directed to its local mission and to the corporate mission of the Church in the world. This would be the main thrust of the work in the parish, the goal of its activity and the measure of its success. The parish would almost inevitably become caught up in serious consideration of the social and spiritual needs of its own locality; and once the burden of paying full-time professionals is removed, even comparatively weak congregations would have the resources that would enable them to move towards their ministry in society.

This is not a blueprint, but an example. Somehow or other the Church has to escape from the box (coffin?) in which we have allowed society to put it; and if it is to get out, the first one who needs to be liberated is the Minister, for he is the one whose vocation should be reminding the Church of the kind of Ministry it is called to fulfil. At the moment we are caught in the professional trap. As Peggy Wat recognized, because Ministers refuse to involve themselves in the programs they try to sell to their parishioners, because they preach standards that they do not accept for themselves, and because too often they fail to show "the meaning of unreserved, compassionate love,"[50] they are the principal thing that is wrong with the Church: they represent the point at which the Church's integrity can be most clearly called into question. It is not because many of them "grow rich by the gospel"—on the contrary, insofar as they are true professionals in the modern age they are not paid half enough—but it is in their having to be paid at all. That which should be free has a price set upon it. Secular society, which depends more and more on the fraud of the well-advertised lie, the calculated exploitation of vice and vanity, and which worships accumulated dollars, has won the bemused acquiescence of the churches and their clergy in exchange for a piece—a very small piece—of the action.

Ministry is service, free and unstinted. There is a very good illustration of what it should mean, and it is still to be found in many homes. Do you know someone in your home who almost unconsciously serves all the members of the family? It

50 In *Who's Killing the Church?*, p. 20.

may be someone who works all day to send the children through college, and then comes home to do the housework or the garden; someone who listened to the teenage problems that seemed so important then, who always seemed to know how to deal with a cut or a bruise and who spent endless hours caring for anyone who was sick; someone who stays up late to see that you are in safely, or meets you after a journey, who irons your clothes ready for the next day, and gets up very early to see that you don't go off to your first job without a good breakfast. Have you known someone like that? That is ministry.

Can you buy it? What status does that person have? How irrelevant those questions are!

3

STRUCTURE AND THE SPIRIT

A. The secular context

Our study seems to be telling us that there is a divinely given character to the Church, but no divinely given structure, except as it reflects that essential character. We no longer have any excuse or stomach for what one Roman Catholic aptly described as "the taut climate of one-upmanship between churches."[51] There is no blueprint for church order, and perhaps that is just as well, for we do not know which way the world will go or the pattern that the Church will need to continue its ministry. We may be just as rash in assuming that the shape of the future will be the urban megapolis as previous generations were in assuming that society was cast forever in the conditions of the rural village or small town. All the pressures pushing us towards urban technology and a computerized society seem also to be pushing us to the point of crisis in the city. The plight of our cities, the belated recognition of nature's balance and our relation to it, and the discovery that we need privacy, opportunity to experience

[51] As quoted by Ardis Whitman, "The Revolt of the Young Priests," *McCall's* (July 1969), p. 102.

variety and renewal—all these insights into the complexity of the human condition are forcing us to place a question mark against the urban image that the planners and futurologists were projecting only a few years ago. We wonder whether anything human could survive in such a depersonalized and computerized technopolis.

We do not know the answer to that; but we do know that the Church's witness can be only in terms of that which is distinctively human: her witness within the emerging culture has to be set against all that dehumanizes, all that tries to press man into a single mold, or reduces him (or her) into a mere cypher within a huge sociological equation. Those who saw the secular city as the predetermined pattern of the new world may be right; perhaps we *are* destined for the freedom (and irresponsibility?) offered by the anonymity of the city, and the freedom (and rootlessness?) offered by our mechanical mobility, although we cannot help noticing that the new freedoms are often more than offset by the controls, taxation, and legal restrictions imposed by the centralized government that technopolis demands. We have experienced our new technical freedom along the edge of an interim period where two cultures met, and we have no right to assume that it will survive when the final culture of technocracy is reached. In any case, the personal freedom that urban anonymity seems to offer now will turn to ashes if it means that instead of being known by name to persons our dossiers are known by number to a computer; and our theoretical mobility will not amount to much if new economic pressures mean that the work force is deployed whenever and wherever a computer disposes it.

If populations are permitted to expand indefinitely, the development of huge urban concentrations, technologically organized and centrally governed, seems to be inevitable; and in that situation the Church will have to assume the structures that proclaim what is distinctively human—mutual service, compassion for the individual caught in the system, and the relationship of at-onement not only in society at large but also at the personal, neighborly level. In the anonymous mass of individuals in a large city, all listening to the same radio programs and watching the same television shows in thousands of identical (and often barricaded) apartments, there is a good deal of similarity to the anonymous thousands who stood side by side but alone in the medieval cathedrals, watching the priest in a distant chancel as he performed the sacred mysteries. It is not surprising to read that the signs of our times "strongly suggest that the church is entering into a new medieval period in which the task centers around the injection of this Word into the processes of history."[52] Perhaps. But if this is to be the pattern of the future, we hope that the Church does not fall into the same or worse ecclesiastical errors than the church in the past, and particularly the error of so identifying itself with the prevailing culture that it no longer witnesses to that which is truly human.

However, the trend may be arrested or changed. If the growth of population is contained, if the warning from our ecological danger is heeded, and if large areas of the earth at present uninhabitable are made available for cultivation and habitation or both, then a very different pattern will emerge in which the size of the urban complex will be deliberately limited and in which it will be supported by smaller satellite communities. Indeed, it is difficult to see any future for our race if the urban sprawl is allowed to grow unchecked. But the point we are making is that the Church must be free to meet all the options, free to develop a wide variety of forms. It cannot tie itself to any one view of what future society will be.

We cannot rule out the likelihood that as secular society assumes increasing responsibility for social services, many traditional functions carried on under church aegis will disappear, and that many of the material resources of the churches will dry up. There are signs that as centralization increases in civil government, sheer economics will force the churches to decentralize their own work and allow more freedom to local parishes, synods, dioceses. Churches may look to a diminishing constituency, for as faith is seen more as a matter of personal decision than as a social convention or an insurance policy against fear, there will be many who will withdraw their

52 Phillip Mayfield, "A Revolutionary Model for the Church," *Newsletter of the Ecumenical Institute,* 3/1, n.d. (Chicago: Church Federation of Greater Chicago), p. 4.

support.[53] The churches of Europe have already experienced the dilemma of trying to meet increasing demands on their service from dwindling resources in money and personnel.

If the churches simply repeat the mistake of trying to maintain all they have been doing, then this is a bleak prospect; but if the changing situation forces them to slough off activities that have become a luxury, if it causes them to take the unity issue seriously and to do cooperatively what they cannot and should not do alone, if it makes them concentrate on priorities, then we have cause enough for optimism.

B. The testimony of church order

All this argues for maximum flexibility in developing new church structures. The temptation to use traditional forms as an excuse for refusing to launch out in faith is seen to be what it is, a temptation that springs from distrust of the Spirit's guidance in our time.

On the other hand, it is an even greater error to think that this allows Christians to discard the testimony of the past and organize simply according to their own whim or the secular fashion. American churches have to be particularly on guard against their tendency to jump on the popular bandwagon, and they have been especially susceptible to the national ideal of capitalizing *now* and making the fast buck. It makes no difference that the 'capital' we have in mind is spiritual and moral rather than financial; but when the churches might have been putting moral capital into the race issue, they were busy guarding their investment in the standards of WASP culture; when they might have been sinking ethical substance into the protest against warfare they were busy pulling in returns from the national crusade against Communism, and when they might have demonstrated the ethics of love by their investment in the cities they were amassing capital from shrewd wagers in suburbia. The moral should be obvious.

[53] The trend can be seen in the large numbers who are now withdrawing their church tax support in Western Germany. Since religion is no longer regarded as a necessity, the exodus has begun; and the first area where the pinch is felt is the economic.

The significance of Ernst Troeltsch's three types of churchmanship is that he was able to show that each had appeared in response to the gospel and had incorporated distinct but essential insights into the nature of the Church, its ministry and mission. To the extent that is true, we had better listen to the testimony of the past.

(1) In the first place, there ought to be enough in the pastoral responsibility we bear to other people to pull us back from a reckless iconoclasm. The traditional position represents where the members of our churches are, and if they are there, it is where we have left them. It is arrogant and irresponsible when theologians and church leaders who have neglected their teaching ministry expect the rest of the Church's membership straightway to do a *volte-face* simply because the pundits have changed their views.[54] Writing of the American situation, Arthur Herzog makes the dry comment, "Savants and seers may cry from the mountaintops that our times are post-Christian and post religious, but the news has hardly become part of that curious bundle of customs, traditions and myths known as the American way. If this is a morning-after ideology, America has a sizable religious hangover."[55] We do not expect the theologian to dissemble his true beliefs or stifle the prophetic word he must declare to the Church, but we do ask him to show the members how his ideas are grounded *in the gospel* and arise from it; we do ask him to be willing to enter into dialogue with the constituency rather than declaiming from an academic hilltop, to show a willingness to help the members prepare for the new forms in which the truth may appear; and above all we ask him to show patience and compassion.

(2) More fundamentally, there is the nature of the truth itself. P. T. Forsyth reminds us in one of his books that if the issues of Christian faith could be put to the vote we would have to deal with the overwhelming testimony of the past. We recognize that truth cannot be decided by a show of hands, and yet we find ourselves asking if everything the martyrs died for could have been illusion. We grant that they were tied to the ideas of their time as we are tied to ours, that they were

[54] Cf. above, p. 231, n. 14.

[55] *The Church Trap*, p. 171.

often prejudiced, and at best they understood only a part of the truth of Christ. But what was it *in essence* that made them prepared to live and die in the name of Jesus Christ? What is it in the testimony that has been handed on from them which we recognize as essential 'gospel,' eternal truth that is 'good news' in any age? Why are we constrained to be identified as 'Christians'? And what of the channels by which their testimony has reached us? We may not be able to accord them the exclusive rights they claimed, but does this mean that they were not used by the Spirit, that they are worthless?

(a) In the first place, whatever channel of spiritual authority a church has used to establish its own doctrine of the Church, each has declared God's grace in Jesus Christ and his continuing Spirit within the Church. They have all borne testimony to that which God has done on man's behalf, that there is a gospel to be proclaimed and that it centers in redemptive incarnation.

(b) The emphasis on historical continuity, for example, has issued clear testimony that God is concerned with human history and that it is the arena in which salvation is brought to us. It has declared that salvation is to be found within the community of God's people, that the community is linked by certain distinctive marks with the events of our Lord's life, and that the form which this community has taken reflects the omnipotent power and unchanging truth of God himself. Remind yourself at this point not so much of the errors into which their exclusive claims led the churches, but ask to what, at its best, the concept of apostolic succession and the traditional forms of church order have been testifying. Surely they have declared that God's purpose towards man is constant and is transmitted to every age the same; that although we may change and our outward conditions alter, God does not change in his purpose of redemption, nor does he leave us without the means to receive his forgiveness and salvation. To this the hierarchical and sacramental forms of the Church have borne constant witness.

(c) In the same way those who have tried to restore the New Testament pattern of the Church have testified that God's salvation is grounded in certain historical events concerning Jesus of Nazareth, and that the Church's faith comes to us from the recorded testimony of the Apostolic Church. They also have declared God's unchanging redemptive purpose towards mankind, but they have emphasized the response of faith to the kerygma rather than response within the sacramental system. They too have held that the form of the Church is itself a testimony to God's unchanging purpose, but have seen it as a community brought into being by response to God's covenant of grace. The continual reappearance of restorationism in church history should remind the Church of the historic events in which it had its source, and of the way in which those who were nearest to those events sought to express their faith within a community of faith.

(d) Theoretically, biblical restorationists should be the most rockribbed traditionalists, because they constantly direct the Church back to an unchanging written record. The churches based on historical continuity stress tradition, but at least they offer the possibility of slow evolution through the members of the hierarchy and through the decisions of the Councils. On the other hand, restorationists return to the same fixed pattern of the New Testament Church, and this would make their view of the Church entirely static if it were not for one element within the New Testament Church itself. One cannot return to the New Testament Church without facing the reality of Pentecost.[56] In returning to its own primary source restorationism has constantly had to face the reality of the Holy Spirit as the constant challenger of dead forms and the constant innovator in the mission. Perhaps this is the reason Protestantism has continually veered between the Bible and the Spirit as its ultimate authority for the doctrine of the Church.

(e) However, as we have seen, within this paradox the emphasis on the Spirit contains its own peculiar polarity between those who have appealed to the Spirit primarily in terms of a charismatic experiènce and those who have sought the Spirit's will in essentially practical means to serve the Church's mission. At its best, 'evangelical pragmatism' has

[56] Cf. above, p. 290, n. 13.

witnessed to the priority of the mission, and declares that the Spirit leads the Church into the most effective ways of conducting the Church's evangelical task.

History forces us to ask which elements in the church structure have constituted and will continue to constitute an essential testimony to God's eternal nature and purpose. Are there institutional forms that belong to the *esse* of the Church and without which the Church cannot truly exist, or is that to which they testify something which ultimately cannot be reduced to a single structural form? We seem to be caught in a dilemma—on the one hand, the form of the Church must testify to God's eternal nature and his everlasting purpose; but on the other hand, no institution without the manifest presence of the Spirit can truly represent the Body of Christ; and all institutions, like the human body itself, have a tendency to develop hardening of the arteries. It seems that no institution can guarantee the possession of the Spirit, and yet there is an inner necessity within the Church's life which determines that if it is to survive in history (be incarnate) it must be given a bodily form.

We would see the problem in clearer perspective if we were less taken up with specific institutions, with their ambiguous history and emotive terminology, and were able to concentrate upon that which the Church is seeking to express within them. For example, we would be closer to our biblical theology and to the spirit of the early Church if we were to concentrate not so much on specific ministerial orders, which in the name of the 'tradition' often veto any proposal that they should adapt or reform themselves ecclesiastically or even sartorially, and could concentrate on recognizing the presence and function of Ministry within the Church. By 'Ministry' I mean the function of gospel leadership that may indeed be put into an institutional form, but which the Church recognizes less in terms of profession, status, or *Amt* than by the quality of its prophetic witness and pastoral care that points to Jesus Christ. In this context we might ask ourselves whether the route by which that gospel leadership has come to that particular church points us to Christ who is the source of all Ministry, or merely to the times in which he lived. If it points to our Lord himself, then to deny it is to come very near the most dangerous of all sins.[57]

Certainly as we look for a more ecumenical form of the Church, Christians will need to translate this Ministry into specific forms in which the traditional orders may well have a place, but we dare not any longer mistake the form for the substance. Again, our study seems to be telling us that the Church itself must walk by faith, that the Church's tradition, the Bible, and the Spirit that speaks in personal faith are all given to us for our guidance and support each other by testifying to the same Christ; but it is also telling us that the nature of the divine involvement that brought Jesus Christ to us determines that each of these witnessing channels of the Spirit should be housed in a body of weak flesh: we dare not deify any of them. Only that which the Spirit expresses as it points to our Lord witnesses without ambiguity to the eternal nature and purpose of God.

In this respect it was exciting to participate at an ecumenical study Consultation, which included Catholics, Protestants, and Orthodox, in which it was suggested that we should understand the traditional threefold Ministry—episcopate, priesthood or presbyteriate, and diaconate—not so much in terms of their survival as distinct orders, as in terms of their continuing testimony in gospel functions, i.e., as *episcope,* that which priesthood and eldership imply, and diakonia.[58] This is essentially the recognition that the spiritual succession, that which the institutional form *points to,* is more important than the form itself. It was exciting to take part in this discussion not only because it seems to offer a way through the hoary old impasse of apostolic succession,[59] but much more fundamentally because it would lead all sides of the dispute into entirely new dimensions of Ministry. Catholics of all kinds

[57] Mark 3:28f.

[58] At a Consultation on Ordination called by the Faith and Order Department of the World Council of Churches and held at Cartigny, Switzerland, September 28-October 3, 1970.

[59] It should be noted that this insight appears to have been recognized but rejected by Anglican representatives in the conversations between the Church of England and the Free Churches after World War II. Nathaniel Micklem, *The Box and the Puppets* (London: Geoffrey Bles, 1957), p. 138.

would be led into new freedom with respect to both their own Ministries and the recognition of other Ministries, while Protestants might begin to recognize the spiritual and evangelical qualities in Ministry to which the Catholic tradition has been witnessing.

This approach might prevent the Church in the future from becoming incarcerated within its own institutional forms. Institutional forms are important—as Lord Clark observed, "one doesn't need to be young to dislike institutions, but the dreary fact remains, that even in the darkest ages, it was institutions that made civilization work."[60] None worked more consistently or more positively to that end than the institution of the Church itself, because as long as the Incarnation remains at the center of the gospel, the Church has to take visible form and make her presence known within human society as a human society.

The basic problem in the reunion of the churches is to discover structural forms whereby the Church of the future can testify to that which is unchanging in its gospel, but in such a way that the structures will promote and not impede the subsequent changes in form that will be necessary. Our concern is that the gospel shall be the same in each succeeding age, and effectively proclaimed within the changing circumstances of human life; but Rosemary Ruether's point has to be well taken—this may demand radical breaks with the traditional institutional forms of the past to *preserve* the constancy of the gospel.[61] To remain unchanged in a changed society where even our traditional terminology has become distorted may be the surest way of perverting the everlasting gospel and the surest way to apostasy. Agatha Christie described this danger in precisely the right terms when she put into one of her characters the comment, "If we seek to keep the past alive, we end, I think, by *distorting* it."[62]

We ask the Consultation on Church Union, no less than the

60 *Civilisation,* p. 346.

61 Cf. above, p. 250. Our question to Rosemary Ruether is not on this point, but on how she would define this gospel that has to be preserved through the changes, and the authority that she would recognize as the basis for her definition.

62 *Holiday for Murder* (1938; New York: Bantam Books, 1969), p. 16.

churches that remain apart from it, what provisions have been made for the Church to be able to modify its own structures when they are no longer a testimony to the Spirit? For if the Church is a testimony to its own gospel, we cannot allow its form to obstruct its essential proclamation. Any churchly body that refuses to become flesh among men has mislaid the heart of its own Good News, but it is equally true that any church that cannot change its form without undergoing either the disruptions of revolution or the excommunications of schism may be stifling the freedom of the Spirit which is the *esse* of the Church.

4

THE PIONEER PEOPLE

We are faced with paradoxes that are consequences of the central paradox of the Christian faith, the incredible proclamation that God was in Christ reconciling the world to himself. The Church is not Jesus Christ, but it is called into being to become Christ in terms of human community; it is not to be so confused with the uniqueness of its Lord that we think of it as a divine extension of his human body, and yet it is incorporated into the work of Christ and is called into his redemptive mission; it is fully in the world as he was fully in the world. From our human perspective it can never be wholly distinguished from the time and place of its work and sojourn, and yet it is distinct from the world and belongs to the 'not yet'; the Church is not the Kingdom and exists only for as long as it takes for the Kingdom to be realized, and yet the Kingdom is within it.[63]

What then *is* the Church? Biblical theology as we have understood it tells us that we cannot begin to answer that question without concerning ourselves about the situation of man; for man finds himself very much at the crossroads in his journey.

In the state of nature, where his enemies were the elements or other species, purely physical and mental skills were needed

[63] Cf. Claude Welch, *The Reality of the Church,* chapters V and VI.

in order to survive. Man seems to have surmounted every evolutionary hurdle in its turn, when he stood upon his hind legs, when he developed the capacity to use weapons and tools, and when he developed a brain that was able to reflect and to organize socially. But a price has been paid for his career of enlightened self-interest, and it has been paid within the nature of man himself. Now he is beginning to realize that what he has made of himself is the immediate problem. As one modern writer recognizes, the danger is perhaps not so much from the development of a new 'technological man,' but from our having the immense technological powers with a hand-me-down human nature.

> Modern man is far from slaying the beast within; why assume that the man of the future will be a completely new creature? What if the new man combines the animal irrationality of primitive man with the calculated greed and power-lust of industrial man, while possessing the virtually Godlike powers granted him by technology? This would be the ultimate horror.[64]

It is as if the Providence that permitted that earlier ascendancy is telling us that the last and most difficult hurdle is to surmount what we have made of ourselves. Up to now our obvious enemies have been external, but the last enemy reveals itself as the selfish, vicious spirit within: Lucifer has a human face.

This, declares the Christian gospel, is where the crucial victory has to take place, and this is the step that has to be taken. If man can surmount the ultimate problem that he has created within his own nature, then an unimagined vista of happiness and fulfilment through service will open up for him; but if humanity fails the end will be suicide either in a bang or a whimper.

The Church points to this by showing the essentially communal nature of the Kingdom of God. However, biblical theology does not present us with any blueprint of the shape that this community should take, but it offers simply a series of pictures that revolve around the nature of God and his purpose for men. In particular, it centers in at-onement, reconciliation,

64 Victor C. Ferkiss, *Technological Man: The Myth and the Reality* (New York: Braziller, 1969), p. 25.

essentially human relationships—the relation of man to God, of man to his own nature and destiny, and of man to his neighbor: the Church participates in the work of Christ by making reconciliation visible.

A. The representatively human

Because the Church's testimony centers in Jesus Christ, the New Adam, it reminds man of his own destiny to be *imago dei.* In earlier periods of history the Minister of a parish was known as the 'parson' (= *persona,* the person), i.e., the representative person before God. There is something right about that idea, for perhaps 'representative man' is one of the best images to describe what ministry should be. On the other hand, we confuse the issue by presenting a public image that denies anything our contemporaries would recognize as manhood—a combination of milquetoast and self-conscious dignity that completely contradicts the manhood we see in Jesus: it is a hybrid of curious shape and essentially worldly proportions. To present the manhood of Christ to the world, to stimulate and prepare God's people for what this should mean in terms of human community, is no milk-and-water affair.[65]

Do not think it strange that we describe the Church by talking about its parsons. We cannot separate the renewal of the Church from the renewal of its Ministry, for at the very center of its own life and worship the Church needs constantly to be reminded of the nature and quality of its corporate service, to be reminded in word and action that its testimony in the world is to the servanthood of Jesus Christ. Why else would the early Church have regarded the ministry as a gift? "And these were his gifts; some to be apostles, some prophets, some evangelists, some pastors and teachers, to equip God's people for work in his service, to the building up of the body of Christ. So we all at last attain to the unity inherent in our faith and our knowledge of the Son of God—to mature manhood, measured by nothing less than the full stature of Christ."[66] The apostle said it there.

65 This may be behind the new image. Cf. Lail E. Bartlett, *The Vanishing Parson* (Boston: Beacon, 1971).

66 Ephesians 4:11-13.

B. The Royal Pioneer Corps

A. T. Hanson has shown us that the leadership of the church in the New Testament was a pioneer ministry. We should extend this to think of the Church as the pioneer community to bring in the Kingdom just as the leaders of the Church should be pioneers in pointing the Church to its true Ministry. There *is* a hierarchical concept embedded in the Church, but it is a hierarchy of servanthood that has nothing to do with status, position, or power—indeed, when status is claimed on those grounds it invalidates the very claims of those who make them.[67]

Durinng World War II there was a special body of men in the British Army known as the Pioneer Corps. They did a good deal of the pulling and hauling, the ground clearing and the road building for the rest of the troops. Among their ranks were many who could not be employed in any other capacity, some because they did not have the ability and others because they were not citizens of the country they were serving—Jews from Hitler's Third Reich, refugees from little countries that had been overrun, people who had been made stateless by the cruel irony of war. They worked as servants and laborers, and yet they were also the pioneers who helped make it possible for the allied armies to advance. I am not sure that they ever won the dignity and honor of becoming the 'Royal' Pioneer Corps; but there would have been a piquant aptness if they had, for what they did illustrates the meaning of Ministry. This is what it means to be the pioneer servant of the world, the royal priesthood to which the Church is called.

C. The servant community

The only royal quality that is appropriate to the Church is that which derives from the Kingship of Christ, and this is the service that is motivated by love.[68] The Church is a servant community that learns the nature of its service from its Lord,

[67] Cf. *Ministry,* p. 124.

[68] Cf. *Ministry,* p. 213; also pp. 95-100, especially 99f.; pp. 145f.

and it is hopefully pointed in that direction by the Ministry within its midst.

However, there is one aspect of the Church's ministry that no Minister, no individual, not even our Lord himself could accomplish alone. This is to interpret what it means to be man *in human community.*[69] Christ, the New Adam, is what mankind is intended to be; we may talk about *imago dei* as the destiny of man and that is true to the biblical revelation, but it conjures up the picture of man standing godlike in his individual beauty and perfection, like Michelangelo's 'David' in the square at Florence, while all the lesser beings scurry around him. Christ is not man in that sense; he is man corporate, man that shows not simply the superior individual qualities with which our race has been endowed, but man that is truly *imago dei,* man 'at one' with himself as a race, a reconciled community.

The most telling charge that the world could bring against the Church is not that it has failed to proclaim salvation for the individual, or even that it has failed to demonstrate it, but that it has persistently refused to do that unique thing which only the Church could do—to proclaim and exemplify what it means to be a redeemed and reconciled community, to reveal Christ-in-Community as the servant king of his Kingdom. True, there have been periods in church history when we have seen the shape of it shining through in particular congregations and even in the Church at large, but it has soon faded. Either by means of blandishments or browbeating the world has brought the Church to heel, and the community that should have been

[69] T. W. Manson showed that the messianic concepts used by the Gospel writers were essentially corporate. For example, the Son of Man idea is, like the Servant of Yahweh, "an ideal figure and stands for the manifestation of God on earth in a people wholly devoted to their heavenly King." So the mission of Jesus "is to create the Son of Man, the Kingdom of the saints of the Most High, to realize in Israel the ideal contained in the term .... Finally, when it becomes apparent that not even the disciples are ready to rise to the demands of the ideal, he stands alone, embodying in his own person the perfect human response to the regal claims of God." *The Teaching of Jesus* (Cambridge: C.U.P., 1931, 1943), pp. 227f. In a later treatment of the concept he saw in it "the 'oscillation' between the individual and the corporate," i.e., between 'the Elect one' and 'the Elect ones,' and that it concentrated in the human willingness to be the "Servant of the Lord." Cf. "The Son of Man in Daniel, Enoch and the Gospels," *Bulletin of the John Rylands Library,* 32 (1949-50), 171-193.

pointing to the Kingdom of God has either opted for acceptance and status within the kingdoms of this world, or turned its back and tried to keep the Kingdom of God for itself.

D. The reconciling community

The Church consists of those who have been reconciled, made 'at one' with God through Jesus Christ, and who know themselves to have been 'redeemed,' i.e., to have been bought out of slavery into the freedom of a new life. But it is of the essence of this Good News that it cannot be kept as a private possession; we receive its assurance that we may pass it on, and if the Church may take comfort in being a people that has been reconciled, it has the proclamation of reconciliation to others at the center of its ministry.

That is the measure of its failure and that is the heart of its ecumenical incentive. The visible union of the Church of itself means very little, or we might have expected the medieval church to have brought in the Kingdom of God—it must be inspired and dominated by Christian love or it will be worthless in the sight of God and useless in the sight of men. But if visible union is not enough, it does at least testify to the unity of God; and that is more than can be said for our casual pluralism, which shows that Christians have lost any real understanding of the significance and dimensions of reconciliation within the Church's own ministry and as the demonstration of its own true nature. How can a community so unthinkingly divided within itself lead the world into the unity of the Kingdom of God?

The churches must face the indictment against them. We often sing Edmund Hamilton Sears' Christmas hymn, "It Came Upon the Midnight Clear"; and in most recent American hymnals I notice that verse four (a rather sentimental approach to the Social Gospel) is chosen in preference to verse three, which is much more realistic:

Yet with the woes of sin and strife
The world has suffered long;
Beneath the angel-strain have rolled
Two thousand years of wrong;

And man at war with man hears not
The love-song that they bring:
O hush the noise, ye men of strife,
And hear the angels sing.

That puts the matter straighter, because implicitly the indictment for the "two thousand years of wrong" must be primarily against the Church. The problem of humanity is that it is unreconciled and unreconciling, and until this problem is met there can be no Kingdom of God, however much we may speak poetically about 'the circling years' bringing in 'the age of gold'; but what are we to say of the community which for almost two thousand years carried the responsibility of demonstrating what reconciliation ought to mean in human society? What are we to say of the callous lovelessness with which it maintained its visible unity in earlier centuries, or the cruel bitterness with which it resolved its differences when that unity could no longer be sustained, or the complacent indifference with which we now justify the anti-structures of our dividedness? What are we to say of this failure of the pioneer community? Do the churches have any credibility, any visible integrity, until that issue of reconciliation is squarely met?

E. A community of grace

Perhaps the Church retains integrity at one point, for within the several communions we recognize that the Church is a community of grace. Because it knows itself to have been the recipient of unmerited grace, the Church declares that the next great step for man is ethical and spiritual and centered in grace.

(1) There has been a growing recognition among thinking people that "humanity is on the threshold of self-transfiguration, of attaining new powers over itself and its environment that can alter its nature as fundamentally as walking upright or the use of tools."[70] We have suggested that this mutation must occur within man's own nature, but there is some un-

[70] Victor C. Ferkiss, *Technological Man,* pp. 17f.

certainty as to how it is to be achieved. At first sight it would seem to be simply a matter of intelligence—of using intelligently our new scientific knowledge and technical skills to produce a 'better' kind of person. The new genetics offers the possibility that in the not-too-distant future 'we'[71] will be able to program into the genes of the race all the desirable traits man lacks at the moment and consequently program out all the traits deemed undesirable. Theoretically, it would be possible to program 'Christ' into future generations.[72]

But would this be 'Christ'—a scientific *parousia?* An essential part of what Christians have worshipped in Jesus Christ is not that Jesus was good, or even that he was better than anyone else, but that he was what he was *by his own volition.* It seems that the Church at this point must declare that there are no shortcuts to the New Man, that we may genetically be able to produce a new being that has many of the qualities of humanity and is in many ways a more agreeable specimen to live with, but if it does not have the capacity to make its own choices, it will not be 'man.' The Church has to declare that if humanity is to achieve the kind of goodness that is worth preserving, it can do so only by taking responsibility for its own moral choices, because the ethical quality of manhood is *in the choice itself.* As one young woman declared, "you have to be free to be Christian in a true sense,"[73] and this is only another way of saying prophetically, "you have to be free (to make responsible moral choices) to be human in a true sense."

(2) The Church also has to declare that man will reach this ethical stature not by way of hybris, but by humility and the recognition that he has been constantly the recipient of grace.

Christian faith witnesses to a paradox about man. On the one hand, the Church points to the goal of "mature manhood

[71] The question who 'we' will be is, of course, one of the toughest political questions to be solved in the immediate future.

[72] It is interesting to note that the Church itself almost envisioned that kind of programming in dealing with the genealogy of Jesus Christ. When its theologians developed the doctrine of the Virgin Birth, and more specifically, the Immaculate Conception, they very effectively removed Jesus Christ from our human race by giving him a divine Father and a sinless mother—the heresy of Docetism! It implies that whatever else he was, Jesus was not "very God, and very *man.*" The evangelical testimony, however, is that there is no gospel unless he was truly man.

[73] Cf. *Life,* 68/10 (March 20, 1970), 27.

that is to be measured by nothing less than the stature of Jesus Christ"; but at the same time it testifies that the way to this maturity is by the way of humility and gratitude. Man has received grace from the beginning: he did not call himself into being, and only by a miracle of grace is he sustained; we share a certain creativity with God, but we share dependence with the rest of God's creation. At least the Church recognizes the miracle of that dependence—the fortunate accidents that allowed this mother Earth to spawn us, the mute service of minerals and matter and the daily sacrifices of the plant and animal world by which we live. We are responsible for none of these things: they are the gifts of an unmeasurable grace towards our race. Wherefore, "we bless Thee for our creation, preservation, and all the blessings of this life."

The Church testifies that before mankind can take its next great leap into a new kind of human nature, it has to allow its arrogance to dissolve in gratitude.

These things shall be; a loftier race
Than e'er the world hath known shall rise,[74]

but only if in planting human lordship (service) in the cosmos we do so as those who are grateful and who will treat the gifts of God's creation with the reverence that comes from a grateful heart. For only the one who is grateful can understand the meaning of grace, and only the man or community that knows it has been the recipient of grace will show the meaning of gratitude.

That is where the Kingdom of God begins, and this is where the new humanity appears. We exist within the Church not to make people more religious or more pious, but we exist to help men and women become real men and women "measured by nothing less than the full stature of Christ," and to show what that should mean in terms of human community. But the first step is penitence and gratitude.

F. A community of faith

It is a community of faith and trust. It is not a community that simply puts its trust in faith itself, but has faith in the God who is revealed to us in the man, Jesus Christ.

74 J. Addington Symonds from his poem "A Vista."

This points to a paradox in the gospel about which Christians today seem to be somewhat confused. Bonhoeffer had a true insight into the gospel and into our twentieth century when he spoke of man having 'come of age,' of men having reached adulthood when they had no longer to depend on the idea of a supernatural God or on a divinely ordained church on which to thrust their unresolved fears and perplexities. Man can stand on his own two feet, and can look his own fate straight in the eye.

We recognize that the Church has often appealed to men in their weakness rather than in their strength, and that there is a firm note in the gospel that calls men out of spiritual babyhood to accept their dignity as men. Paul in particular urges the membership of the churches to move out of their spiritual infancy and become adults, to put away their playthings and become men.[75] On the other hand, there is our Lord's own testimony that unless a person is prepared to accept the Kingdom of God like a little child, he cannot hope to enter it.[76]

It is faith, I suggest, that holds together the two sides of this paradox. On one side, we know that all the old religious crutches, the intellectual *reasons* for belief in God (or regarding him as a high probability) have been taken from us: the arguments for traditional theism no longer seem very relevant or cogent. Jesus once told a story of a man who had reached a position of affluence and who looked around at his possessions and observed to his friends, "Let us eat, drink, and be merry, for tomorrow we die"; and Jesus said that this man was a fool because that very night his soul would be taken from him. *Was* he a fool? If Jesus was mistaken about God, then the 'fool' was sensible, for at least he was wringing one last evening's entertainment out of life. Paul put the matter very bluntly when he said, "If in this life only we have hope in Christ, then we are of all men the most to be pitied." The hedonist who told himself to eat, drink, and be merry could be speaking for twentieth-century man. Everyone is shouting it, from the

[75] I Corinthians 3:1-3; 13:11-13; Hebrews 5:12-14.

[76] Mark 10:13-16; cf. Matthew 18:1-4; Luke 18:15-17.

public entertainers to the politicians to the advertisers: "You owe it to yourself."

That is precisely the adult risk we take. Christians face the issue that if their faith is illusion, they are the fools of history. What is demanded from them in the gospel is not acceptance of a series of intellectual proofs for the existence of Ultimate Reality, but response to the One who makes himself known to us in a person. We are told the story of a slave rabble rotting in Egypt, and how they were asked to trust a God against all the appearances, and how in trusting him they were expected to follow his ethical standards; we are told how they came to believe that he had saved them against all odds, and how a personal covenant was established with him; we are told how this covenant was established in their obedience to his ethical standards, and how some (a remnant) obeyed although most of the people were faithless and did not trust his promises. At the end we are told the story of Jesus, and how his life of faith was rewarded by a cross, and how he experienced the doubt of having been forsaken. We are never promised that it will be intellectually easy to trust God, or that it will ever lead anywhere worthwhile except through crucifixion and even the cry of dereliction. As Bonhoeffer recognized while he was in Death Row, we are not asked whether we *can* believe, but whether we *will* believe.

As a little child. What father or mother would be satisfied to be loved and trusted by their child only because it was the most reasonable thing to do, or because it was expected of him? We wish to be loved for what we *are,* for what others have found us to be. There is a game I have seen parents play with their children in which a little chap of three or four climbs onto a table or a chair and then launches off the edge with shrieks of delight, knowing all the time that he will be caught by his father or his mother. Complete and absolute trust.[77] Why? Because everything the child knows about his parents tells him that he can have this kind of confidence. Just like Israel—"You have seen what I did to the Egyptians, and

[77] There is also, of course, a sick joke based on this which ends, "That will teach you not to trust anyone!" If that is adult humor, it seems a long way from the maturity of the Kingdom of God.

how I bore you on eagles' wings and brought you to myself" (Exodus 19:4). Certainly one can produce arguments for theism that sound impressive enough in a classroom, as Martin Buber discovered; but I do not think the kind of God revealed to us in Jesus Christ would want us to trust them. I think he wants us to be men enough to trust him, as a little child trusts those he loves.

The Church is a community of people who trust God like that, for God expects of the community what he expects of the individual. As Abraham obeyed God's call by leaving his former home and family, and set out not knowing where he was to go, he was always "looking forward to the city with firm foundations, whose architect and builder is God" (Hebrews 11:8-10). The Church is called to trust God in its adventure and to trust him alone in the same way. And it is worth remembering that this kind of trust, and the relationship on which it is based, is an essential step that must be taken if the relationship that was broken at the Fall is to be restored.

* * * * * * * *

That curiously driven but, in many ways, typical saint of the twentieth century, D. R. Davies, wrote an autobiography entitled, *In Search of Myself;*[78] and during the course of writing the present work[79] I was reminded of a visit Davies made to my college while I was a student. For any with eyes to see and ears to hear, his story provides a graphic parable of the Church, and particularly the Church of this century.

David Richard Davies was born into the desperate but respectable poverty of a Welsh Nonconformist home in a coal-mining area. He worked in the mines and was involved in the Great General Strike of 1926, and then under the influence of the social emphases of that time, entered the Ministry. Serving in the industrial north of England he found himself caught up more and more in the vortex of political concern for the economically disenfranchised and the politically under-

[78] London: Geoffrey Bles, 1961.

[79] While reading Leslie E. Cooke's *Bread and Laughter* (pp. 161f.) in which he recalls the salient points in Davies' career.

privileged. His gospel became a wholly political gospel. He left the Ministry, became a Marxist, and took part in the Spanish Civil War. Then he returned to Britain, tried journalism, but proved unsuccessful. There came a day when he found himself without money, without home, without ideals, and without faith. He decided to commit suicide, and waded into the ocean until he was almost swept away; but suddenly with horror he realized what he was doing, and struggled back. This was the moment that began a long climb back to faith, to the reaffirmation of his vocation as a Christian Minister, and a first step towards his own form of radical orthodoxy that ended for him in the Anglican Communion.

We would draw no parallels and make no prophecies about the ultimate destination of the twentieth-century churches, but the course of their pilgrimage has some suggestive similarities. In his autobiography Davies declared that the point of utter despair is the place where we may begin to have hope and where faith can be born anew, and he declared that this is the place to which our world must come. Davies and Bonhoeffer must not be set in opposition to each other, for the Church should have something to say to man both in his strength and in his weakness. The prophet Ezekiel discovered that, for only as we are prepared to drop our pretensions and humble ourselves before God do we hear him say, "Man, stand up and let me talk with you" (Ezekiel 2:1, NEB). The way to the Kingdom includes human dignity, but it does not recognize human hybris.

But first the Church. The Church too has been in search of itself—but not merely to discover a new or even a more authentic image before men; it seeks to find its true *Self,* that which is the essence of its own true character. The story of D. R. Davies is a protest against the hypocrisy of Christians who are not really concerned about the needs of other people, who are not prepared to take seriously or to become involved in—really involved in—the desperate injustice of the world around us. Sound theology can never de divorced from social and ethical involvement in the world we are called to serve; and if one has any doubts on that score it is only necessary to reflect on the social testimony and political activity of men like Karl Barth, Peter Taylor Forsyth, Dietrich Bonhoeffer, William Temple, Reinhold Niebuhr, or for that matter, the Reformers and Puritans who were fairly active in the politics of their own centuries. The community of God's people is not to become an island to itself, but to be God's people incarnate in society.

However, this is only half the story. When Langdon Gilkey entitled his book *How the Church Can Minister to the World Without Losing Itself,* he was recognizing a real danger, for the Church does lose itself, threatens itself with spiritual suicide, when it forgets that true involvement in the world is incarnation and not absorption or assimilation. The community that is called to become totally involved in society is still distinct and unique, for as long as it has a prophetic word to say. The Church finds its true Self always beckoning it forward to a point that always stands before it in history, to the Christ who revealed God to us in human terms, to the same Christ who must now become corporate before the Kingdom will appear among men. The Church's doctrine about its Self is centered in its theology, what it knows of God's own nature.

Peter Taylor Forsyth said it at the beginning of this century. He never developed a doctrine of the Church, although he had promised his readers that he would one day produce a 'theory of the Church.' Then he went on to observe, "it is more than a theory we need, more than a theory of social revolution. It is a theology, both as a source and as an expression of the corporate consciousness of the Church."[80]

It *is* a theology that we need, a radical orthodoxy that is not simply orthodox because it is too lazy to think any differently from the way it has always thought, but because it is trying to understand the Word uttered by the God of the biblical revelation; a radical orthodoxy that is not radical simply to prove that it is 'with it' and going with the trend, but because it is trying to follow the Christ who walked with the poor, the hungry, the outcast and the sinner; a radical orthodoxy that will recapture the meaning of redemptive incarnation.

I would give Forsyth's statement a slightly different thrust,

80 *The Church and the Sacraments* (1917; London: Independent Press, 1953), p. 32.

of which I think he would have approved if he had been living to cry in the wilderness of our day as he lived to cry in that of his own. When we speak about the heart of our doctrine of the Church, we are speaking about theology not so much "as a source and as an expression of the corporate consciousness of the Church," as we are about *the Source,* of which both our theology and the corporate consciousness of the Church should be the expression.

We have nothing to talk about but God in Jesus Christ and his purpose among men. The Church has no other task but to continue the mission to man that was begun in Jesus Christ, and it can have no other character but that Holy Spirit who was manifested in the One who came to reconcile men to God, to their destiny, and to each other. Here is the 'Self' of the Church towards which it must always strive, but which it can never claim it has reached; Jesus put it into human terms for man, and now the Church is called to put it into communal terms for men. It is time we got on with the job; the universe is waiting.

Maranatha. Even so, come, Lord Jesus.

INDEX OF NAMES

INDEX OF SUBJECTS

INDEX OF SCRIPTURE TEXTS

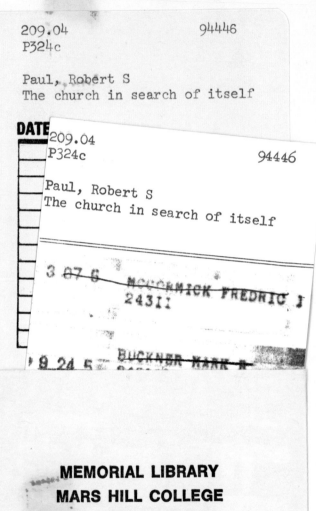